Privacy at Risk

Privacy at Risk

The New Government Surveillance and the Fourth Amendment

CHRISTOPHER SLOBOGIN

THE UNIVERSITY OF CHICAGO PRESS CHICAGO AND LONDON

CHRISTOPHER SLOBOGIN holds the Stephen C. O'Connell chair at the University of Florida Fredric G. Levin College of Law. For much of this project he was the Edwin A. Heafey, Jr. Visiting Professor of Law at Stanford Law School.

The University of Chicago Press, Chicago 60637
The University of Chicago Press, Ltd., London

Printed in the United States of America

16 15 14 13 12 11 10 09 08 07   1 2 3 4 5

ISBN-13: 978-0-226-76283-8 (cloth)
ISBN-10: 0-226-76283-1 (cloth)

Library of Congress cataloging-in-Publication Data

Slobogin, Christopher, 1951–
Privacy at risk : the new government surveillance and the Fourth Amendment / Christopher Slobogin.
p. cm.
Includes bibliographical references and index.
ISBN-13: 978-0-226-76283-8 (cloth : alk. paper)
ISBN-10: 0-226-76283-1 (cloth : alk. paper)
1. United States. Constitution. 4th Amendment 2. Electronic surveillance—Law and legislation—United States. 3. Data protection—Law and legislation—United States. 4. Privacy, Right of—United States. I. Title.
KF45584TH .S58 2008
342.7308'58—dc22 2007021070

⊗ The paper used in this publication meets the minimum requirements of the American National Standard for Information Sciences—Permanence of Paper for Printed Library Materials, ANSI Z39.48-1992.

TO CHARLES H. WHITEBREAD,

The best mentor possible

AND

JERRY ISRAEL,

The eternal skeptic

Contents

Preface

This book is about an insidious assault on our freedom and the failure of the law to respond to it. The assault comes from government monitoring of our communications, actions, and transactions. The failure results from the inability or unwillingness of courts and legislatures to recognize how pervasive and routine this government surveillance has become. To ensure that this powerful tool is not abused, this book argues that something equally powerful—the Constitution, and in particular the Fourth Amendment to the Constitution—must stand guard.

All of us are familiar with electronic surveillance—wiretapping, bugging, and the like—because it has been with us for almost a century. This book focuses instead on a significant new development in the government's surveillance efforts: the use of sophisticated technology to observe our daily activities (physical surveillance) and to peruse records of those activities (transaction surveillance). Our wanderings, our work, and our play can now be monitored not only through binoculars and other types of telescopic lenses but also with night scopes, tracking mechanisms, satellite cameras, and devices that detect heat and images through walls. Transactional information, even that which is financial and medical in nature, is often readily accessible via snoopware, commercial data brokers, and ordinary Internet searches. While some of these technologically enhanced investigative techniques have been around for several decades, most have been developed more recently, and law enforcement use of these techniques (old and new) has increased geometrically in the wake of September 11, 2001.

I pair physical surveillance and transaction surveillance by the government for three reasons. First, as just noted, both rely heavily on technology. Of course, physical surveillance can be carried out with the naked eye, and transactional information can be obtained by poring through papers in a file cabinet. But both types of surveillance today depend substantially on high-tech instruments and complex computer programs, many of which vastly enhance government's capacity to spy on us.

Physical and transaction surveillance also belong together because both can be conducted from afar. The classic law enforcement search requires an entry of some sort, such as a detective barging into a house or police officers rummaging through the contents of a car. Physical and transaction surveillance, in contrast, can occur from across the street, from across town, or even from outer space; more commonly, once the proper technology is in place, government agents can pursue both types of surveillance without ever leaving their offices. Thus, the government can investigate a place or an event without being there.

Of course, electronic surveillance, or what this book calls "communications surveillance," also relies on technology and does not require physical intrusion. There is, however, a third sense in which physical and transaction surveillance are similar that distinguishes them from communications surveillance. Wiretapping, bugging, and other forms of communications surveillance are clearly regulated by the Constitution, more specifically the Fourth Amendment's prohibition on unreasonable searches and seizures. In contrast, many types of physical and transaction surveillance are not formally recognized as searches that implicate the Fourth Amendment. As a result, much of this surveillance, although a search in effect, is not seriously regulated by law.

This book is meant to prod legislatures and courts into more meaningful constraints on physical and transaction surveillance. While these types of surveillance may be different from both classic searches and from communications surveillance in the senses described above, in their current minimally regulated state they do real harm to individual interests and ultimately to society and government itself. That state of affairs must change.

* * *

For their feedback and support, I would like to thank Tom Clancy (director of the National Center for Justice and the Rule of Law at the University of Mississippi Lamar Law Center), David Fontana, Jerold Israel, Wayne LaFave, Lyrissa Lidsky, William Stuntz, Scott Sundby, Peter Swire, Andrew Taslitz, and George Thomas. I would also like to acknowledge the contributions of participants in conferences and workshops at the law schools of DePaul, Florida, Florida State, Frankfurt (Germany), Harvard, Hastings, Minnesota, Mississippi, Monash (Australia), Ohio State, Stanford, and St. John's, and the dozen members of the American Bar Association's Task Force on Law Enforcement and Technology. Finally, I want to thank Benjamin Diamond and Ryan Cobbs for their research assistance. Portions of the following articles appear in substantially reworked form in this book: Technologically-Assisted Physical Surveillance: The American Bar Association's Tentative Draft Standards, 10 *Harvard Journal of Law & Technology* 383 (1997); The World without a Fourth Amendment, 39 *UCLA Law Review* 1 (1991); Let's Not Bury *Terry:* A Call for Rejuvenation of the Proportionality Principle, 72 *St. John's Law Review* 1053 (1998); Peeping Techno-Toms and the Fourth Amendment: Seeing through *Kyllo*'s Rules Governing Technological Surveillance, 86 *Minnesota Law Review* 1393 (2002); Public Privacy: Camera Surveillance of Public Places and the Right to Anonymity, 72 *Mississippi Law Journal* 213 (2002); Subpoenas and Privacy, 54 *DePaul Law Review* 805 (2005); Transaction Surveillance by the Government, 75 *Mississippi Law Journal* 139 (2005).

The reader should be aware that the endnotes often contain useful explanatory information. It is also worth keeping in mind that both the technology and the law described in this book will likely have gone through a metamorphosis since these pages were drafted. The pace of change in this area is dramatic. Nonetheless, I believe the principles developed herein will stand the test of time.

Stanford, California
March 5, 2007

PART I

Surveillance and the Fourth Amendment

CHAPTER ONE

Introduction: Surveillance Techniques and the Law

The term "surveillance," as used in this book, refers to government efforts to gather information about people from a distance, usually covertly and without entry into private spaces. Surveillance can be divided into three types. Communications surveillance is the real-time interception of communications. Physical surveillance is the real-time observation of physical activities. Transaction surveillance involves accessing *recorded* information about communications, activities, and other transactions.

Governments have long relied on all three types of spying. What is new about today's surveillance is the ease with which it can be conducted; over the past several decades, technological advances have vastly expanded the government's monitoring ability. Wiretapping and bugging have been joined by space-age eavesdropping and computer-hacking techniques that make interception of oral and written communications infinitely easier than in J. Edgar Hoover's day. Observation of physical activities, once reliant on naked eye observation and simple devices like binoculars, can now be carried out with night scopes and thermal imagers, sophisticated telescopic and magnification devices, tracking tools and "see-through" detection technology. Records of transactions with hospitals, banks, stores, schools, and other institutions, until the 1980s usually found only in file cabinets, are now much more readily obtained with the advent of computers and the Internet.

A second difference between the surveillance of yesteryear and today is the strength of the government's resolve to use it. Especially since September 11, 2001, the United States government has been obsessed, as perhaps it should be, with ferreting out national security threats, and modern surveillance techniques—ranging from data mining to global positioning systems—have played a major role in this pursuit. But the new surveillance has also increasingly been aimed at ordinary criminals, including those who represent only a trivial threat to public safety. And more than occasionally it has also visited significant intrusion on large numbers of law-abiding citizens—sometimes inadvertently, sometimes not.

Sophisticated surveillance technology and a powerful government eager to take advantage of it make a dangerous combination—a recipe for continuous mass surveillance. While surveillance can be a valuable law enforcement tool, it also poses a significant threat to our legitimate freedoms—to express what we believe, to do what we want to do, to be the type of person we really are. In short, it can diminish our privacy and autonomy.

Accordingly, I argue in this book, government use of communications, physical, and transaction surveillance should be closely watched and subject to meaningful regulation. Furthermore, because surveillance can so drastically alter the relationship between the government and its citizens, the primary source of that regulation, at least in this country, should be constitutional rather than legislative, to ensure that the applicable principles are not subject to the whims of a majority panicked by events of the day. While a number of provisions in the U.S. Constitution are plausible candidates for this role, the constitutional language that most directly speaks to the concerns raised by surveillance is found in the Fourth Amendment, which guarantees our right to be "secure" in our "persons, houses, papers and effects" from improper government searches and seizures. More specifically, because all three types of surveillance involve looking for something, they appear to trigger the Fourth Amendment's protections mandating that government "searches" be reasonable and that warrants authorizing such searches be based on probable cause and describe with particularity the place to be searched and items to be seized.

Unfortunately, the U.S. Supreme Court has never come close to construing the term "search" in the Fourth Amendment as broadly as a layperson would. Rather, for various reasons, it has significantly constricted the scope of the Fourth Amendment. As a result, many types of communications, physical, and transaction surveillance are not considered searches—that is, they are not recognized as constitutionally relevant events. Of course, federal and state legislatures can try to fill this legal void. But as subsequent chapters make clear, legislatures too have ignored or only minimally regulated most types of surveillance.

The one important exception to this judicial and legislative nonchalance is the federal statute usually referred to as Title III, found in Chapter 18 of the United States Code,[1] which is an outgrowth of Supreme Court decisions holding that phone tapping and bugging *do* implicate the Fourth Amendment. Congress's original version of Title III, enacted in 1968, required that interceptions of phone communications be authorized by a warrant based on probable cause. In 1986, Congress passed the Electronic Communications Privacy Act, which, among other things, extended this warrant requirement to the interception of many types of communications made via computer and other electronic technology.[2]

Other types of surveillance, however, are much less heavily regulated. For instance, the Constitution, as construed by our courts, places no restrictions on surveillance meant to ascertain the parties to (rather than the content of) a communication, likewise imposes no constraints on transaction surveillance of records held by third parties, and limits physical surveillance only when conducted with sophisticated technology and aimed at the home. While legislatures have been somewhat more willing to regulate these government investigative techniques, none have mandated the type of warrant and probable cause requirements Title III imposes on surveillance designed to intercept the content of communications.

This book focuses on physical and transaction surveillance, discussing communications surveillance only for comparison purposes. Outside the national security context,[3] the key issues associated with communications surveillance have been resolved in Title III and related case law. The same cannot be said for physical and transaction surveillance. Even though their effects are much more pervasive than communications surveillance and can be just as invasive, these exercises of government power have been relatively neglected, not just by courts and legislatures but by commentators as well. Both types of surveillance deserve much more attention.

The principal thesis of this book is that, given their insult to privacy, autonomy, and anonymity, physical and transaction surveillance techniques must be regulated more extensively than they currently are. This chapter sets the stage for this argument. Sections 1 and 2 provide a more detailed description of physical and transaction surveillance techniques. Section 3 offers an overview of the law governing use of these techniques. Section 4 describes the organization of the rest of the book.

I. Physical Surveillance Technology

It is the year 2008. The Chicago police know that a large and violent drug ring is operating out of Slumville, a downtown section of the city. The gang manufactures drugs, sells them on the streets, and distributes them to other locations in Chicago and outlying areas. Wary of electronic surveillance, the group never uses phones or pagers but instead conducts all its transactions face to face. The city is fed up with having an illegal drug factory in its midst.

The new chief of police wants to mount an aggressive effort to close down the gang's operation, but she does not have the officers she needs to carry out an extensive campaign. Even if she did, she doubts whether traditional foot and car patrols could safely put a stop to the gang's activities. The department has recently spent a considerable sum of money on investigative technology. The chief decides that using the new gadgets to identify and assemble evidence against the kingpins and soldiers of the operation would be the perfect way to prove the worth of the investment.

The attack on the gang proceeds on several fronts. Telephone poles at every intersection of Slumville are conspicuously outfitted with bullet-resistant video cameras, equipped with wide-angle lenses, zoom and night vision capabilities, and twenty-four-hour recording capacity. Miniature video cameras with pinhole apertures are covertly installed in a number of Slumville buildings thought to house gang members. At night, police periodically fly over the area in helicopters, armed with night scopes that have a magnification power of 500 and thermal-imaging devices that detect heat waves emanating from buildings that might indicate the presence of a drug processing laboratory.

Any car that leaves or enters the area is tracked using the Global Positioning System (GPS) or, if the vehicle's transponder has been disabled and a beeper can be surreptitiously planted, through beeper signals. To the extent gang cell phone numbers are known, wireless telephones networks are used to locate functioning cell phones and thus the location of their owners. At various streets leading into Slumville, checkpoints are established. At each one, the department installs devices that produce silhouettes of objects concealed by clothing or car exteriors. Similar handheld devices are used by foot and car patrols to scan passersby. As a final measure, the city contracts with the federal government to have photographs of Slumville taken whenever a satellite is within range; these pictures can be enhanced to highlight suspicious activity.

All this technology exists today, albeit in differing stages of development. Some of it (for example, video cameras) has been available to the police in some form for decades. Other technologies (for instance, sensitive "see-through" technology, GPS, and satellite photography) have only recently begun to find their way into the law enforcement arsenal, partly as the result of the "peace dividend" associated with the end of the Cold War. Although none of this technology is routinely used by the average police department at present, its prevalence is increasing as it becomes less expensive and better known. Cameras, night scopes, beepers, and thermal imagers are staple investigative tools of many large departments and even some smaller ones.

Following the lead of the American Bar Association's Standards on Technologically-Assisted Physical Surveillance,[4] the various technologies alluded to above can be divided into five categories: cameras, tracking devices, telescopic devices, illumination devices, and detection devices (i.e., devices capable of detecting concealed items). These functional groupings describe the spectrum of physical surveillance technologies that exist as well as those that are likely to be developed in the foreseeable future.

Camera technology has been available for some time, but the past three decades have seen dramatic advances in the field. With the advent of wide-angle and pinhole lenses, night vision equipment, and super-magnification capability, video surveillance allows viewing of home interiors, workplaces, and public thoroughfares at all times. Cameras can be placed in picture frames, briefcases, pens, suit lapels, and teddy bears, permitting covert observation in virtually any circumstance.[5] As chapter 4 describes in detail, cameras also can be used overtly and conspicuously to observe private establishments and public places. Furthermore, any surveillance by camera can be recorded—creating a permanent record of activities within the camera's range—as well as digitally transported to squad cars and anywhere else a computer exists.

Tracking devices also come in many forms. The simplest and one of the oldest is the beeper, which emits a signal that can be traced and can be placed in virtually any moveable object, ranging from purses to cars.[6] Other tracking devices under development or already in use include the Global Positioning System, which uses satellites to determine the location, within a dozen feet, of an item containing a GPS device;[7] bistatic sensor devices, which passively pick up various types of emissions (e.g., from a cellular phone or a light source) or utilize an active sonar-like capability;[8] and radio frequency identification technology that rely on signals from chips embedded in credit cards and other objects such as passports to identify people from up to 750 feet away.[9] Intelligent Transportation Systems (sometimes called Intelligent Vehicle Highway Systems) involve fitting every vehicle in a given transportation network with a radio unit that transmits to a base station. While used principally as a means of controlling traffic patterns, these systems can also provide a way of tracking vehicles' current or previous locations.[10]

Unlike modern video surveillance and tracking systems, some types of telescopic and illumination devices—binoculars and telescopes, flashlights and spotlights—have been available for well over a century. Today, however, new technology provides would-be viewers with significantly greater ability to overcome obstacles created by distance and darkness. For some time now, compact night vision equipment using infrared technology has enabled covert observation of virtually any nighttime activity,[11] while mapmaking and satellite cameras have been able to focus on objects only a few feet across from thousands of feet above.[12] Moreover, illumination and telescopic capabilities can be combined in one instrument, as with the well-known Star-Tron binoculars.[13]

Detection systems include a wide range of devices using x-ray, heat sensing, holographic radar, and other technologies. Simple metal detectors are being augmented with handheld devices that can discern the shape and size of items underneath a person's clothing or even behind walls; some of these devices may also reveal anatomical details. One such tool, developed by Millitech Corporation, registers radiation emitted from the body and objects concealed on it.[14] Because these waves readily pass through clothing, and because the body is a good emitter while dense, inanimate objects tend to be bad emitters, inanimate objects show up as outlines against the body. A device developed by Raytheon aims a low-intensity electromagnetic pulse at the subject and measures the time decay of each object radiated, which differs depending on the object.[15] The device then compares the time decay of each object with known "signatures" of items like guns; no image is produced. A third example, from the Idaho National Engineering Laboratory, measures the fluctuations in the earth's magnetic field caused by ferromagnetic material, like the metal in a gun.[16] Other mechanisms have been developed for detecting hidden explosives and biological weapons[17] and for discerning heat differentials from a building (which might signal the use of klieg lights or furnaces connected with the growth or manufacture of contraband).[18]

Each of these technologies provides law enforcement with a powerful surveillance tool. Together, they permit government to monitor almost all of our activities, inside and outside the home. But their reach does not begin to approach the surveillance capability that is provided by the technology designed to access *records* of our activities and transactions.

II. Transaction Surveillance Technology

Like physical surveillance, transaction surveillance comes in many forms. This book will divide it into two general types: target driven and event driven. Using these two categorizations, the following discussion fleshes out the specific ways transaction surveillance can assist law enforcement in investigating street crime.

Target-Driven Transaction Surveillance

Assume that Jones, a federal agent, is suspicious of you for some vague reason—perhaps you often pay for your airplane tickets with cash, or you have been observed with accessories you shouldn't be able to afford, or you are a young Arab male who attends the local mosque on a daily basis. Under these circumstances, Jones clearly does not have sufficient suspicion for an arrest. But Jones feels he would be neglecting his obligation as a law enforcement official if he did not investigate you a bit further; to him, you are a target. So how does he find out more about you?

Jones could confront you directly, either on the street or through a grand jury. But neither approach is likely to net him much information, and both will tip you off that he's checking you out. Ditto with respect to going to your acquaintances and neighbors; they are not always forthcoming and they might let you know Jones has been nosing around. Jones could try the undercover agent approach—there might be rich payoffs if he or one of his informants can weasel their way into your good graces. But success at that endeavor is rare, and expending so much effort on someone who is merely suspicious would likely be a waste of time. Jones could surreptitiously follow you around for a while, using physical surveillance technology or good old-fashioned tailing techniques, but that tactic might not produce much if you make most of your contacts through technological means—phones and e-mail—rather than physical travel. Of course, Jones could tap your phone and intercept your e-mail, but that requires a warrant based on probable cause, which he does not have.

Thankfully for Jones, there are much more efficient ways he can covertly acquire information about you, many of which he can carry out without leaving his desk and most of which, as later parts of this book describe, require little or no legal authorization. The easiest way to get useful data is to contact one of the many companies, usually called commercial data brokers, that use computers and the Internet to dig up "dirt" from public and not-so-public records.[19] One such company is SeisInt, a concern owned by LexisNexis that operates a program known as Accurint (for accurate intelligence). According to its advertising, Accurint can, in mere seconds, "search[ ] more than 20 billion records . . . dating back 30 years and more," armed with no more than a name, address, phone number, or social security number.[20] Through this process, the company says, it can obtain information about a wide array of transactions, including bankruptcies and corporate filings; criminal conviction and criminal and civil court data (including marriage and divorce information); driver's license and motor vehicle records; firearms, hunting, fishing, and professional licenses and permits; Internet domain names; property deeds and assessments; and voter registration.[21] For some states, the information held in "public records" by government bureaucracies and available via computer is immensely broader: medical records, social security numbers, victims' names, credit card and account numbers, psychiatric evaluation reports, jurors' names, tax returns, payroll information, and family profiles.[22] For a time, all of this was made even more easily accessible to state law enforcement officials with the establishment of MATRIX (the Multi-State Anti-Terrorist Information Exchange), a consortium funded in part by the federal government that allowed police to use Accurint for investigative purposes;[23] today, however, the scope of MATRIX is much reduced.

The FBI and other federal agencies rely on commercial data brokers that operate programs at least as powerful as MATRIX. ChoicePoint is perhaps the best known of these companies.[24] Under its contract with the federal government, ChoicePoint can provide Jones, as a federal agent, with "credit headers" (information at the top of a credit report that includes name, address, previous address, phone number, social security number, and employer); pre-employment screening information (including financial reports, a felony check, and verification of education records, employment references, motor vehicle records, and professional credentials); asset location services; information about neighbors and family members; licenses (driver's, pilot's, and professional); business information compiled by state bureaucracies; and bookings and arrests, liens, judgments, and bankruptcies.[25] If you think Jones wouldn't bother running such a check, think again; even in the years *before* 9/11, ChoicePoint and similar services ran between 14,000 and 40,000 searches per month for the United States Marshals Service alone.[26]

The drawback to the type of information Jones can get from commercial data brokers is that it is pretty general. He may want to know more about what you do on a daily basis. Fortunately for him, there are a number of services that can help him out. For instance, advances in data warehousing and data exchange technology in the financial sector allow very easy access to a virtual cornucopia of transaction-related information that can reveal, among other things, "what products or services you buy; what charities, political causes, or religious organizations you contribute to; . . . where, with whom, and when you travel; how you spend your leisure time; . . . whether you have unusual or dangerous hobbies; and even whether you participate in certain felonious activities."[27] If Jones jumps through some pro forma legal hoops (detailed later in this book), he can also obtain from your phone company records of all the phone numbers you dial and receive calls from, and from your Internet service provider (ISP) every Web site address you have visited (so-called clickstream data) and every e-mail address you have contacted.[28]

The latter information can be particularly revealing to the extent you transact your business over the Internet. Some ISPs, like America Online, have stopped maintaining clickstream data, precisely so it won't have to answer such law enforcement requests.[29] No worries. All Jones has to do is invest in something called snoopware. Bearing names like BackOrifice, Spyagent, and WinWhatWhere,[30] snoopware is to be distinguished from adware and spyware. The latter software tells the buyer of the program how to contact people who visit the buyer's Web site. Snoopware, in contrast, allows its buyer to track the target well beyond a single website; it accumulates the addresses of *all* the Internet locations the target visits, as well as the recipients of the target's e-mails. The FBI developed a similar program—once dubbed Carnivore, then called DCS-1000, and now discarded in favor of privately developed programs—that filtered all e-mails that pass through a particular server.[31] Although some transaction snoopware requires access to the server or computer to install, other types, called Trojan Horses, can electronically worm their way onto the system disguised as something useful.[32]

In short, even if you conduct all your business and social affairs at home via phone calls, e-mail, and Web browsing, Jones can easily construct what Anthony Miller has called "a complete mosaic" of your characteristics.[33] And he can do all this without your having a clue he's doing it. Jones could also surreptitiously obtain an even wider array of transactional information—on matters ranging from medical treatment to financial decisions—with very little effort, especially if he can link his investigation with national security interests. But further discussion of that possibility, as well as of the huge amount of transactional information that the federal government can obtain if it is willing to proceed overtly, will have to await explanation of the current legal regime in chapter 7.

Event-Driven Transaction Surveillance

Now consider an entirely different type of scenario, one in which the government has no suspicion of or even interest in a specific individual, but rather possesses information about a particular crime that has been or will be committed. Government efforts to obtain transactional data in this situation is not target driven but event driven. Say, for instance, that the police know that a sniper-killer wears a particular type of shoe (thanks to mudprints near a sniper site), that he owns a particular type of sweater (because of threads found at another site), and that he reads Elmore Leonard novels (because of allusions to those books made in his communications to the police). Law enforcement understandably might want to peruse the purchase records of local shoe, clothing, and book stores as part of their investigation. Once police obtain the credit card numbers of those who bought, say, the type of sweater found at the murder scene, they can trace other purchases made with the same card, to see if the relevant type of shoe or book was bought by any of the same people. Of course, if there is a match on one or more of the three items, the surveillance may then turn into a target-driven investigation.

Or suppose that a CIA informant reports that he believes Al Qaeda is considering blowing up a major shopping mall, using skydivers jumping from rental planes.[34] The FBI might want to requisition the records of all companies near major metropolitan areas that teach ski-diving and that rent airplanes, as well as the "cookie" logs (records of cyberspace visitors) of all websites that provide information about manufacturing explosives, to see if there are any intersections between these three categories of data, in particular involving men with Arab-sounding names. If there are then, again, further target-driven surveillance investigation might take place.

Although the first type of event-driven surveillance is backward looking and the second is forward looking, both law enforcement efforts are a form of "data mining" or "profiling," that is, an attempt to look through transaction information to find patterns of behavior that permit police to zero in on possible suspects.[35] If the information sought is not digitized—which is likely with respect to records kept by skydiving companies, for instance—then law enforcement may have to rely on good old-fashioned human snooping. In this day and age, however, a significant amount of data mining can be carried out using technology. For example, the Defense Department's Total Information Awareness program, before being scaled back by Congress, was able to use software developed by private companies "to sift through virtual mountains of data of everyday transactions, such as credit card purchases, e-mail and travel itineraries, in an attempt to discover patterns predictive of terrorist activity."[36] Whether it relies on computers or humans, event-driven data mining, like transaction surveillance of particular individuals, can easily be conducted unbeknownst to those whose records are surveilled.

III. Surveillance and the Constitution

Technology has made both physical surveillance and transaction surveillance extremely potent law enforcement tools. The information about people's whereabouts, activities, and transactions that can be gleaned from physical and transaction surveillance may often vastly exceed the evidence produced by eavesdropping on or hacking into a person's communications. But as far as the government is concerned, the real beauty of most physical surveillance and virtually all transaction surveillance is that, compared to communications surveillance, legal regulation is minimal. Later chapters in this book will describe in detail the relevant law, both constitutional and statutory. Here only a sketch of constitutional jurisprudence governing these virtual searches will be provided.

Constitutional analysis of government surveillance has to begin with *Katz v. United States*,[37] the most important judicial decision on the scope of the Fourth Amendment. Charlie Katz was indicted for "transmitting wagering information by telephone," based on conversations federal agents overheard using a bugging device attached to the phone booth where he made the calls. Katz moved to suppress the conversations because the agents had not obtained a warrant authorizing the bug. Before the

Supreme Court, the government proffered two reasons why the Fourth Amendment's warrant and probable cause requirements did not apply to the electronic eavesdropping in Katz's case. First, the Fourth Amendment prohibits only unreasonable searches of "houses, persons, papers and effects," and a phone booth does not fit into any of these categories. Second, relying on Supreme Court precedent that had for some time linked the definition of "search" to trespass doctrine in property law,[38] the government argued that a Fourth Amendment search occurs only when the government physically penetrates a protected area, which was not the case in *Katz* because the bugging device was attached to the outside of the booth.

The *Katz* majority acknowledged the language of the Fourth Amendment and the fact that earlier cases had tied the Fourth Amendment to property concepts. But it ultimately ignored both semantics and precedent. In an opinion by Justice Potter Stewart, the Court reasoned that the Fourth Amendment "protects people, not places," and that "what [a person] seeks to preserve as private, even in an area accessible to the public, may be constitutionally protected."[39] A person "who occupies [a phone booth], shuts the door behind him, and pays the toll that permits him to place a call is surely entitled to assume that the words he utters into the mouthpiece will not be broadcast to the world."[40]

Thus, *Katz* is said to have rejected a formalistic, property-based definition of the Fourth Amendment, replacing it with a focus on privacy. The focus on privacy was even more apparent in the formulation of the Fourth Amendment's threshold offered by Justice John Harlan in his concurring opinion in *Katz*. There he stated that those seeking Fourth Amendment protection should have to demonstrate only two propositions: "first that a person have exhibited an actual (subjective) expectation of privacy and, second, that the expectation be one that society is prepared to recognize as 'reasonable.' "[41] This language, the second part of which has since become the accepted definition of the Fourth Amendment's threshold, was clearly meant to confer Fourth Amendment protection on Charlie Katz.

On the other hand, Justice Harlan wrote, "conversations in the open would not be protected against being overheard, for the expectation of privacy under the circumstances would be unreasonable."[42] The majority opinion made a similar observation when it stated that "[w]hat a person knowingly exposes to the public, even in his own home or office, is not a subject of Fourth Amendment protection."[43] This language made clear that the expectation-of-privacy concept was malleable, something subsequent cases would demonstrate beyond cavil.

Even so, *Katz* appeared to expand the scope of the Fourth Amendment. Certainly, the Court that decided it—the so-called Warren Court, named after Chief Justice Earl Warren—thought so. Thus, for instance, in *Berger v. New York,*[44] decided the same year as (although a term before) *Katz*, the Warren Court struck down New York's eavesdropping statute because it failed to require probable cause that a particular offense has been or is being committed, and also failed to require that the conversations sought to be intercepted be particularly described in the warrant. In doing so, the Court never paused to differentiate between surveillance that involved a physical penetration of premises and surveillance that did not; in either case, the Court made clear, electronic eavesdropping works an infringement of privacy.[45] It was against the backdrop of *Katz* and *Berger* that Congress passed Title III, requiring that all nonemergency electronic surveillance, federal and state, be authorized by a warrant meeting *Berger*'s requirements, and additionally providing that such warrants be issued only when there is cause to believe that "normal investigative procedures have been tried and failed or reasonably appear to be unlikely to succeed if tried or to be too dangerous."[46]

The year following the *Katz* and *Berger* decisions, the Warren Court handed down *Mancusi v. DeForte,*[47] which held that a union official should be able to expect privacy in his office even when he shares it with others. Justice Harlan wrote for the Court that, despite the multiple users of the space, "DeForte still could reasonably have expected that only those persons and their personal or business guests would enter the office, and that records would not be touched except with their permission or that of union higher-ups."[48] One year later, the Court concluded in *Alderman v. United States* that a person whose phone is tapped has standing to contest the tap even if he is not a party to the conversation, because when such surveillance occurs "officialdom invades an area in which the homeowner has the right to expect privacy for himself, his family, and his invitees."[49]

Within a few years of these decisions, the membership of the Court changed substantially. Earl Warren was replaced by Warren Burger as chief justice, and Justices Abe Fortas and William Douglas, also in the majority in all of these cases, departed as well, replaced by Justices Harry Blackmun and John Paul Stevens. Perhaps most important, the chair of Justice Harlan, who dissented in *Berger* and *Alderman* but played a crucial role in the majorities for *Katz* and *DeForte*, was taken by William Rehnquist.

In decisions handed down in the 1970s and 1980s, most of which all of the new justices joined, the Court indicated that in a whole host of situations, the expectation-of-privacy rubric does not necessarily provide any more protection than a property-based approach, and perhaps affords even less protection. For instance, the Court held that the Fourth Amendment is not implicated when police rummage through one's garbage,[50] inspect packages at an international border,[51] or trespass on "open fields" (that is, privately owned land beyond the "curtilage," or area immediately surrounding one's home).[52] In each of these cases, the Court concluded that even if the target had a subjective expectation of privacy in the area involved, any such expectation was unreasonable.

All these cases involved traditional searches. The Court's decisions directly addressing application of the Fourth Amendment to physical and transaction surveillance have been similarly restrained. That conclusion might seem to be contradicted by the most prominent recent Supreme Court case concerning surveillance, *Kyllo v. United States,*[53] decided in 2001. *Kyllo* did prohibit use of a thermal imager to detect heat differentials inside a home unless authorized by a warrant based on probable cause. But *Kyllo* also indicated that if the domestic spying relies on technology that is in "general public use," it may occur without any justification at all. As discussed in chapter 3, that aspect of *Kyllo* potentially opens a huge hole in the holding. In other decisions, the Court has concluded that Fourth Amendment protection also disappears whenever the physical surveillance monitors activities outside the home, regardless of the type of technology used. Thus, according to the Court, police may use beepers to track public travels,[54] planes to fly over backyards,[55] map-making cameras to survey business curtilage from the air,[56] dogs to sniff luggage,[57] and flashlights to look inside cars and barns,[58] all without worrying about the Fourth Amendment.

The same niggardly approach to Fourth Amendment protection is reflected in cases involving transaction surveillance. The most important case here is *United States v. Miller,*[59] decided in 1976 after Justices Warren, Fortas, Douglas, and Harlan had left the Court. In *Miller*, the Court, with Justices William Brennan and Thurgood Marshall dissenting, concluded that we have no reasonable expectation of privacy in information we surrender to our banks. Three years later, in *Smith v. Maryland,*[60] the Court similarly held, 6–3, that the Fourth Amendment is not implicated when the government seeks our phone records from the phone company. Read broadly, these decisions suggest that transaction surveillance is also immune from the restrictions of the Fourth Amendment.

IV. A Preview of the Book

This book criticizes all the post–Warren Court holdings described above, as well as the assumptions about privacy and the reach of government power that underlie them. The Court's willingness to declare that persons cannot reasonably expect their interactions with businesses and banks, their daily wanderings, and even some of their conduct at home to be free from suspicionless, warrantless surveillance by the government is contrary to societal mores and other legal norms. This book also criticizes the courts' failure to regulate other aspects of surveillance, ranging from maintenance and destruction of surveillance records to when and how notice of the surveillance should be communicated to its targets. Finally, it takes Congress and state legislatures to task for failing to rectify the Court's deficient case law and makes concrete proposals about what both courts and legislatures should be doing instead.

Chapter 2, the second chapter in this introductory section of the book, sets out an interpretation of Fourth Amendment doctrine that provides the springboard for these various criticisms and proposals. Most fundamentally, this chapter argues that when contemplating surveillance (or any other investigative technique), government should be required to provide justification proportionate to the intrusiveness of the surveillance and to seek third-party authorization in all nonexigent circumstances. These two basic precepts—what I call the proportionality and exigency principles—are consistent with the Court's general approach to search and seizure jurisprudence. In particular, they derive from the "balancing" analysis (i.e., weighing of government and individual interests) endorsed by the Court in the late 1960s and applied with a vengeance by the post–Warren Court. However, the similarities between my framework and the Court's are only skin deep. While I do not quarrel with balancing analysis per se, the remaining chapters demonstrate that the post–Warren Court's application of that analysis has attributed far too much weight to the government's interests and far too little to the individual's.

Part 2 of the book consists of three chapters, all concerning physical surveillance. Chapter 3 examines physical surveillance of the home. It argues that the Supreme Court's decision in *Kyllo*, which many hailed as a victory for privacy rights in our dwelling places, may not be as protective as it first appears. *Kyllo* not only announced the "general public use" exception but also declared that use of technology to view conditions that a naked eye observer could see from a public vantage point is not a search, even when the location viewed is the interior of the home. This chapter shows that both the general public use and the "naked eye" exceptions are inscrutable, conceptually incoherent, and normatively objectionable. It then argues that technological surveillance of the home should be regulated either through a proportionality approach, which varies the level of cause with the search's intrusiveness, or through a legislative approach, using Title III's regulation of communications surveillance as the model.

Chapters 4 and 5 take on physical surveillance outside the home. The primary thesis of these two chapters is that the advent of sophisticated technology that allows the government to watch, zoom in on, track, and record the activities of anyone, anywhere in public, twenty-four hours a day, demands regulation. A second thesis is that if the legislative and executive branches are unwilling to undertake that regulation, courts should step in, using the Fourth Amendment.

Chapter 4 builds the case for regulation, relying on philosophical and constitutional principles as well as on the results of an original empirical study investigating the reactions of ordinary citizens to public surveillance. Chapter 5 imagines what that regulation would look like. It builds on the Supreme Court's roadblock jurisprudence and the proportionality principle in defining when surveillance is permissible, and then addresses issues connected with implementing a public surveillance regime. On the latter score, it contends that politically accountable officials should decide where to place the cameras (an application of the exigency principle), that government should provide notice of the surveillance and regulate the disclosure and maintenance of surveillance records, and that enforcement of these rules requires both direct sanctions on violators and periodic dissemination of information about surveillance practices. Finally, the chapter briefly explores the role of the courts in bringing all of this to fruition. It suggests that courts set minimum guidelines and monitor police decisions to assure that public surveillance is conducted in a reasonable manner, but that most of the details be left up to the political process.

Part 3 of the book, discussing transaction surveillance, consists of two chapters. Chapter 6 analyzes the constitutional legitimacy of subpoenas, a subject that is crucial to understanding how transaction surveillance is currently regulated. Whether issued by a grand jury or an administrative agency, subpoenas are extremely easy to enforce, requiring only a demonstration that the items sought are "relevant" to an investigation. Yet today subpoenas and pseudo-subpoenas are routinely used to obtain not only business and other organizational records but also documents containing significant amounts of personal information about individuals, including medical, financial, and e-mail data. Chapter 6 explains why this regime is a historical accident, and why it is repugnant as a matter of policy.

Chapter 7 describes in more detail the current legal regulation of transaction surveillance, and then suggests how it can be improved. In contrast to physical surveillance, transaction surveillance has been the subject of significant legislative activity. However, this law is only minimally restrictive, and it is also confusing and contradictory; beyond the traditional subpoena, challengeable by the target of the investigation, current law recognizes a number of subpoena mutations that seem to have little rhyme or reason. The proposed reform recognizes, as does the current regime, that different sorts of records merit different (proportionate) levels of protection. But in contrast to current law, and bolstered by another empirical study of societal attitudes, I urge legislatures (or courts if legislatures fail to act) to increase the showing required to probable cause for private records obtained through target-driven surveillance and to reasonable suspicion for private records obtained through event-driven surveillance. I also recognize a category of quasi-private records that can be obtained only on reasonable suspicion if sought through target-driven surveillance. The relevance standard, which is the most demanding test that transaction surveillance must meet under current law, would be reserved for investigations seeking truly public records, records detailing the activities of businesses and other organizations, and data mining that does not access private records.

Chapter 8 summarizes the arguments made throughout the book and then explores a central implication of its proposals—that the traditional Fourth Amendment model requiring probable cause for all searches and backed by the exclusion remedy serves neither societal nor individual interests. Much relatively nonintrusive physical and transaction surveillance cannot be justified at the probable cause level and should not have to be; rather than recognizing this fact and adjusting Fourth Amendment law accordingly (through a proportionality approach), the Court has insisted that searches be based on individualized probable cause, which has created an incentive to forgo constitutional constraints on investigative techniques aimed at individuals and to defer to the government with respect to surveillance of groups. Nor is the suppression remedy always an effective deterrent in the surveillance context; at best it benefits an infinitesimally small number of people subjected to illegal surveillance, and in any event it is a poor remedial fit with the types of violations that public surveillance and much transaction surveillance are likely to involve. The dissonance between these types of investigative techniques and the individualized suspicion/exclusionary rule model suggests a need for rethinking both the type of justification and the type of accountability that the Fourth Amendment should require.

CHAPTER TWO

A Fourth Amendment Framework

This chapter lays the groundwork for a reconceptualization of the Fourth Amendment, a reconceptualization that drives both this book's critique of current law and its proposals for reform. While there are a number of nuances to this new way of looking at the Fourth Amendment, its key component can be stated very simply: a search or seizure is reasonable if the strength of its justification is roughly proportionate to the level of intrusion associated with the police action. I call this concept the *proportionality principle*.

As this book will demonstrate, the proportionality principle produces rules that are sometimes dramatically different from current law. But the principle is not without precedent in the Supreme Court's own case law. Almost forty years ago, in *Terry v. Ohio*,[1] the Supreme Court established a framework for analyzing the scope of Fourth Amendment protection that should still inform our analysis today. As the Court in *Terry* put it, "[T]here is 'no ready test for determining reasonableness other than by balancing the need to search (or seize) against the invasion which the search (or seizure) entails.' "[2] This book's approach to the Fourth Amendment and its application of the Fourth Amendment to surveillance are to a large extent an elaboration of this principle.

In *Terry* itself, the proportionality principle led to the holding that a stop and frisk need be justified only on reasonable suspicion rather than on the higher standard of probable cause required for more invasive arrests and full searches.[3] A number of subsequent cases purported to apply the principle to a wide array of other searches and seizures. If these cases had applied *Terry*'s proportionality framework in a consistent fashion and extended it to the entire Fourth Amendment universe, constitutional regulation of searches and seizures would be in much better shape than it is today. In particular, if the promise of *Terry* had been realized by the Court, the rules regulating physical and transaction surveillance would be more coherent and provide more protection of individual privacy.

Unfortunately, instead of treating *Terry*'s balancing formula as a serious principle that requires some hard thinking, the Court has used it as a smoke screen for an ad hoc agenda. Instead of applying the proportionality principle to all Fourth Amendment analysis, it has applied it only in connection with seizures and a few other isolated scenarios. Accordingly, Fourth Amendment law is a "mess," to use the elegant phrasing of Akhil Amar.[4] It is a mess not just descriptively, in the sense that police and courts have a hard time mastering it, but normatively, in the sense that it does not reflect society's core values.

As a predicate for explaining why current law about virtual searches is deficient and how it should be changed, this chapter makes the case for rejuvenating and restructuring *Terry*'s proportionality principle. The principle needs rejuvenation because its rationale—that the level of intrusiveness should drive the level of justification—seems to have been ignored even in cases purportedly applying *Terry*. It needs to be restructured because subsequent cases have been frustratingly vague about the government and individual interests involved. In the spirit of rejuvenation, section 1 lays out the positive case for the proportionality principle, in more detail than *Terry* and its progeny have done. As a beginning to the restructuring process, section 2 looks more closely at the two sides of the *Terry* balancing formula—invasiveness and justification—and fleshes out what assessment of them should entail. It also introduces what I call the exigency principle (essentially a requirement for ex ante review in nonemergency situations) and explains how it would work in conjunction with the proportionality principle.

Section 2 also defends this proposed regime against various attacks that have been leveled at *Terry*. From the left, these attacks include the argument that *Terry*'s balancing formula is a dangerous threat to individual freedoms because it undermines the probable cause standard and allows a pragmatic assessment of interests that inevitably favors the government.[5] From the right they include the contentions that the proportionality idea places restrictions on types of police actions that should not be subject to any constitutional regulation and that it mandates judicial activism in the Lochnerian mold. A principle that can inspire such an outcry from both sides must have something going for it.

But there is one criticism of the proportionality principle that has considerable punch. That criticism is that any effort to take *Terry*'s balancing formula seriously, which is what this book purports to do, is ultimately unadministrable. Section 3 acknowledges this problem and suggests ways of handling it.

I. The Case for Proportionality

Terry dealt with the constitutionality of a frisk. Basing its decision on the Reasonableness Clause of the Fourth Amendment, *Terry* held that police may conduct a pat down of the outer clothing if they have a reasonable suspicion that doing so will prevent harm to themselves or others.[6] This relaxation of the probable cause standard can be, and in large part was, justified on proportionality grounds: because a pat down is less invasive than a full search, the Court said, it does not require probable cause.[7]

The version of this proportionality idea that is advanced in this book is built on two propositions: (1) the interest the Fourth Amendment protects is security from unjustified government infringement on individuals' property, autonomy (in the sense of ability to control one's movements), and privacy; and (2) the greater the threat to that security, the greater justification the government should have to show. Both propositions are explored below.

The Security Model versus the Trust and Coercion Models

The first proposition—what I call the security model of the Fourth Amendment because of the amendment's use of the word "secure"—has been widely accepted by the courts and academics since *Katz v. United States.* Property and autonomy were already clearly protected by the Fourth Amendment at the time *Katz* was decided;[8] that case added privacy as a protected category. More recently, however, some commentators have attacked the security model, in particular *Katz*'s inclusion of privacy within it. Thus, it is worth emphasizing why privacy is a core value protected by the Fourth Amendment.

We can begin with the plain language of the amendment, which strongly suggests that its drafters, who were particularly bothered by indiscriminate intrusions into their possessions by British soldiers in search of uncustomed goods,[9] were trying to protect not only property and autonomy but the closely associated notion of privacy. The key part of the Fourth Amendment states that the people have a "right . . . to be secure in their persons, houses, papers and effects, against unreasonable searches and seizures." To search means "to look into or over carefully or thoroughly in an effort to find or discover something"[10] and to seize means "to take possession of" or to "lay hold [of] suddenly or forcibly."[11] When the government enters one's house to seize one's possessions, property interests are most directly implicated. When the government seizes one's person, autonomy interests obviously come into play. But when the government engages in a search—i.e., when it "looks into" one's house or effects or "looks over" persons or their papers in "an effort to find or discover something"—the interest most clearly implicated is not property or autonomy but privacy.

This is not to deny that all these terms, and in particular privacy, mean different things in different contexts.[12] Indeed, *Katz* itself emphasized that the Fourth Amendment "cannot be translated into a general right to privacy" and reminded us that "the protection of a person's general right to privacy—his right to be let alone by other people—is, like the protection of his property and of his very life, left largely to the law of the individual States."[13] But *Katz* also insisted that the amendment does protect "individual privacy" against "certain kinds of governmental intrusion," including government actions such as bugging and wiretapping that do not involve physical intrusion.[14]

As noted above, a number of commentators have questioned the conclusion that privacy should be the linchpin of Fourth Amendment search analysis. I cannot do justice to all these arguments, but I will briefly examine and counter two representative commentaries as a way of reinforcing why *Katz* is right. The first such critique comes from Scott Sundby, the second from William Stuntz (a third, from Morgan Cloud, is taken up in the final chapter of this book).

Professor Sundby contends that privacy is a problematic basis for regulating searches and seizures for at least three reasons. First, the ease with which privacy can be manipulated in this technological age makes it an unsteady, constantly diminishing basis for Fourth Amendment protection.[15] Second, the "right to privacy" rubric no longer convincingly justifies restriction of the government's crime prevention efforts; in these days of "anti-crime hysteria," those who advocate a criminal "right" will not get very far unless they are "prepared to explain how the protection benefits not only the individual claimant but all of society."[16] Finally, because privacy interests vary with the situation, reliance on privacy as the basis for Fourth Amendment protection has facilitated the demise of the unitary probable cause standard, which Sundby clearly prefers, in favor of a rudderless "reasonableness" analysis.[17] For these reasons, privacy is no longer the best lens through which to view the interests implicated by searches and seizures. In its stead, Sundby proposes that the Fourth Amendment be reconstrued as a means of maintaining mutual government-citizen trust[18] (an approach I call the trust model).

Professor Stuntz disfavors privacy as the animating feature of Fourth Amendment jurisprudence for somewhat different reasons. He notes that the modern regulatory state, ranging from tax laws to health and safety inspections, involves significant intrusions into privacy, some much greater than those associated with typical law enforcement searches that require probable cause.[19] Yet these regulatory searches could not take place if they were subject to Fourth Amendment warrant and probable cause requirements, and thus privacy interests do not govern this area of the law. At the same time, the Supreme Court's obsession with privacy has led it to neglect regulation of the force often associated with street searches and seizures. Bringing these two themes together, Stuntz suggests that rather than privacy, coercion (i.e., the extent to which a search or seizure involves a police-citizen encounter) should be the primary focus of the Fourth Amendment[20] (an approach I call the coercion model).

These two excellent analyses make a number of insightful points. Sundby is right about the potential malleability of the privacy construct, and his trust metaphor is a useful heuristic. Stuntz is correct that many regulatory actions would be stultified if they required probable cause and that the courts have neglected regulation of police coercion in the search and seizure context. But neither of these scholars provides a convincing substitute for privacy as a fundamental Fourth Amendment value.

Sundby's trust metaphor is an elucidating way of explaining why, even in an age when subjective expectations of privacy have been diminished substantially, the government must make some showing before it can act; for instance, covert government surveillance of the public streets does not infringe subjective privacy expectations (because we don't know it is occurring), yet it clearly suggests a lack of trust. As Sundby argues, the state should trust its citizens until it can produce proof that they do not deserve to be trusted. But the trust model doesn't help us figure out what that proof should be. For instance, both government intrusions into our houses and government spying on our public movements evidence a lack of trust and presumably should be regulated. But should both require probable cause? Under the trust model one would have to answer yes; otherwise one citizen is being trusted more than another. Some other referent for measuring the government's showing is needed in these very different types of cases.

The coercion model might provide that referent: a house search could be seen as more coercive than covert tracking, just as a street search is typically more coercive than a regulatory inspection (the paradigmatic comparison that Stuntz makes). However, these differences can be explained just as well by pointing to the lesser degree of intrusion associated with public surveillance and business inspections on one hand and searches of houses and an individual's person on the other.[21] Furthermore, the coercion model does not explain nearly as well as the security model why completely uncoercive searches such as electronic surveillance are regulated but very coercive searches such as subpoenas for documents or testimony are not regulated in any meaningful way.

Or consider *Terry* itself, assuming the correctness of its holding that frisks may be based on reasonable suspicion of danger. Which approach—the coercion model, the trust model, or the security model—best explains that holding? Put another way, which model best explains why a frisk requires only reasonable suspicion while a full search requires probable cause?

Under the coercion model, one would presumably argue that a search is more coercive than a frisk. But the sense in which a search is more coercive than a frisk is virtually identical to the sense in which it is more invasive; the coercion comes from the search's greater intrusion into privacy, its interference with more types of property, and its more prolonged insult to autonomy. In other words, the coercion model adds very little to the security model and, as a semantic matter, may not as accurately reflect the interests involved.

Under the trust model, as I suggested above, there may be no way to justify the different treatment of searches and frisks. Both actions imply a lack of trust, yet the trust metaphor does not immediately suggest why the government needs only a suspicion that the frisked person is not to be trusted while it must demonstrate probable cause before a search can take place. A frisk on less than probable cause is unlikely to make people accustomed to a probable cause standard feel they are sufficiently trusted unless the government can also point to the fact that the invasion visited on them is minor relative to a full search.

The Danger Exception

A second interpretation of *Terry* does not rest on a reconceptualized Fourth Amendment but rather on a very important practical concern: police safety. On this view, frisks on less than probable cause are permitted because stopping a suspect presents a danger to police that mitigates the usual justification standard. A number of commentators have suggested this rationale for *Terry* and, in doing so, effectively reject the proportionality rationale I am advancing to the extent they insist that danger should be the *only* reason the probable cause standard should be relaxed.

Prevention of imminent harm is clearly a legitimate government objective. In the post-9/11 era, the danger rationale for reducing the government's burden is particularly attractive. What is not clear, however, is why concern about danger should lead to an automatic relaxation of the government's justification without reference to the degree of invasion associated with the government action.

Most prosaically, a blanket danger exception does not explain the other "holding" in *Terry*, involving the constitutionality of the stop before a frisk occurs. On that issue, the Court declared that police may detain an individual based merely on reasonable suspicion that "criminal activity may be afoot."[22] Note that under this language (which was dictum in *Terry* but is now clearly the law), protection of the officer or others is *not* an objective of the initial encounter; otherwise a frisk would be authorized as soon as the officer approached the individual, without the inquiries and further development of suspicion of danger mandated by *Terry*. As the Court stated in moving from its analysis of stops to its treatment of frisks:

> We are now concerned with more than the governmental interest in investigating crime; in addition, there is the more immediate interest of the police officer in taking steps to assure himself that the person with whom he is dealing is not armed with a weapon that could unexpectedly and fatally be used against him.[23]

Commentators who like *Terry*'s indication that stops may take place on reasonable suspicion (which presumably includes every commentator who supports *Terry*'s holding about frisks) need to explain that preference on grounds other than officer safety. The most obvious explanation is that stops are not as intrusive as arrests.

A second and more important reason for distrusting a prevention-of-harm exception to probable cause is its potential for swallowing up the probable cause requirement entirely. The danger rationale has bolstered Supreme Court decisions permitting sub–probable cause searches of all custodial arrestees, no matter what the charge,[24] and of all cars whose occupants have been arrested, even if the occupants are nowhere near the car at the time it is searched.[25] The Court has also relied on that rationale to permit, in the absence of any suspicion, inspections of the area of the home immediately surrounding an arrestee[26] and forced disembarkment of car occupants.[27] Law enforcement officials, trained to be suspicious, are prone to see threats lurking everywhere, and the danger rationale in its current diffuse form has allowed the Court to cater to those tendencies.

Proportionality analysis would temper these results. A cursory sweep of a house solely for the purpose of finding confederates of an arrestee (whose home has already been invaded) is not particularly intrusive and might be justifiable on reasonable suspicion, as the Court has held. But a fuller search of the person, car, or personal possessions on less than probable cause is, contrary to the Court's insinuation, disproportionate, because these actions are more invasive than a frisk (which allows police only to feel objects, not look at their contents).

None of this is meant to imply that the need to prevent harm should be an irrelevant consideration in setting justification levels. The substantive criminal law's treatment of dangerousness is instructive here. As the relatively stringent actus reus and mens rea elements of attempt and conspiracy illustrate, usually the state must demonstrate a high degree of risk before conviction may occur. However, for some crimes, ranging from drunken driving to reckless endangerment, a low probability of risk does not preclude conviction if the risk is *significant* and *imminent*.[28] The same concept should apply in connection with searches and seizures. Thus, for instance, the carnage that would follow from a terrorist act on a plane justifies preventive steps at airports despite the extremely low likelihood that any one person boarding the plane is a hijacker.

As this book will emphasize, however, the boundaries of the danger exception to the proportionality principle must be strictly drawn; otherwise, the tendency will be to permit frisks of everyone the police encounter, searches of all cars whose occupants have been arrested, and surveillance of anyone making overseas calls. When the danger is not significant and imminent, any reduction below the probable cause standard ought to depend on intrusiveness considerations, not concerns about danger.

A Sliding Scale versus Probable Cause Forever

One response to these arguments for a flexible Fourth Amendment might be that, contrary to the assumption made above, *Terry*'s endorsement of a lower, reasonable suspicion standard is wrong. This suggestion leads to a more direct examination of the second proposition set out above—that the threat to security posed by the government action should determine the degree of justification, so that the greater the threat, the greater the justification the government must show, and the less invasive the action, the less authorization needed. Justice Douglas, for one, found this proposition specious. In his dissent in *Terry*, he argued that if the government action infringes privacy, property, or autonomy interests to an extent sufficient to call it a search or seizure, then it should always require probable cause, no more and no less.[29] This "probable cause forever" position has been endorsed by others as well.[30]

There are two problems with this position, one pragmatic, the other normative. First, it exerts enormous pressure on the courts to reduce the scope of the Fourth Amendment by narrowly defining "search" and "seizure." The probable-cause-forever position does not dictate that stops take place only on probable cause; a second option, apparently endorsed by the lower courts in *Terry* itself,[31] is to hold that stops do not implicate the Fourth Amendment at all. The latter holding would have been much more likely had the *Terry* Court felt compelled to require probable cause for all seizures. Calling a brief stop a seizure and requiring probable cause to justify it would either have made crime prevention on the streets much more difficult or have led to a vast expansion of "preventive crime" statutes, such as loitering and traffic laws, designed to give police probable cause for arresting those suspected of being up to no good. Combine the unattractiveness of these options with the fact, of which the *Terry* Court was painfully aware,[32] that the exclusionary rule does little to deter low-level preventive actions in any event, and a holding declaring stops to be nonseizures might well have seemed the best among bad choices.

Admittedly, a holding that a stop is not a seizure clearly does violence to the normal meaning of "seizure," which might have given the Court pause. But as already suggested in chapter 1, the Court's cases defining "search" for Fourth Amendment purposes have shown no compunction in mutilating that term beyond recognition. Because, as discussed in more detail below, the latter development is directly related to the Court's adherence to the probable cause standard in the search context, it is highly likely that, had *Terry* not adopted a sliding-scale approach in the seizure context, that threshold would bear even less semblance to common English usage than it does today.

Even if the Court had resisted this pressure—instead boldly calling the stop in *Terry* a seizure and insisting on probable cause for all seizures—it would have been wrongheaded in doing so. For one thing, such a holding would have been contrary to both the text and history of the Fourth Amendment, which indicate that reasonableness, not probable cause, is the touchstone of substantive Fourth Amendment regulation.[33] Just as importantly, the probable-cause-forever position cuts against the intuition, reflected throughout our jurisprudence, that the government's burden should *vary* depending on the effect of its actions on the individual.[34] The standard of proof in criminal trials is different from that in civil commitment proceedings because of the perceived differences in the deprivation of liberty that each brings.[35] Levels of scrutiny in constitutional litigation vary depending on whether the individual right infringed by the government is "fundamental" or not.[36] In the entitlements context, the degree of process due before benefits can be terminated depends on the effect of the termination.[37] Outside the constitutional setting, the same sort of thing holds true. In the tort context, for instance, many courts require greater proof for punitive damages than for compensatory damages.[38]

A probable-cause-forever standard thus cuts against a pervasive normative-legal intuition. If taken seriously, it also means that, just as we may not relax the required government justification, we also can't ratchet it upward. Thus, requiring something more than probable cause for electronic surveillance and serious bodily intrusions such as surgery, as the Supreme Court has done,[39] would be inconsistent with a unitary approach. Under the proportionality principle, on the other hand, such superprotection makes sense given the serious privacy invasions associated with such actions.

II. Revamping the Proportionality Principle

To say that *Terry*'s proportionality principle is the appropriate framework for Fourth Amendment analysis is not to say that the Court's version of that principle is acceptable. Indeed, the way the Court has manipulated *Terry*'s insight has usually been disingenuous. Even when it has adhered to the spirit of *Terry*, the Court has failed to develop any good framework for applying the balancing formula.

Refinement of that framework, or at least a start at doing so, is the goal of this part of the chapter. Both the assessment of invasiveness that the proportionality principle demands and the manner in which the government can justify its invasions require analytical schemes that have yet to find their way into the case law. Subsequent chapters will fine-tune the analysis in the surveillance setting.

Operationalizing Invasiveness

To implement *Terry*'s proportionality principle, some assessment of the invasiveness of the police action in question must be made. The Supreme Court's efforts in this regard have been abysmal. The Court has been remiss in three areas: defining the threshold of the Fourth Amendment, differentiating the various degrees of invasiveness, and incorporating into invasiveness analysis other constitutional considerations.

THE FOURTH AMENDMENT THRESHOLD. As many commentators have pointed out, the most obviously flawed Fourth Amendment decisions from the Court, alluded to in chapter 1, are those telling us what is *not* governed by that amendment: prosecutorial demands for bank records and phone number logs, use of undercover agents, trespassing on cornfields, flyovers of backyards, rifling through curbside garbage bags, using enhancement devices to conduct surveillance of public movements and business property, and so on. These decisions exempt a vast array of investigative techniques from the warrant and justification requirements in the Fourth Amendment. The Supreme Court is almost as unimpressive when it comes to telling us what is not a Fourth Amendment "seizure": interrogations on buses, chases of fleeing youths, pointed questioning about alienage at one's place of work, and requests for ticket and identification at airports.[40] Perhaps if people were told they had the right to terminate such encounters (which the Court insists they have)[41] and the police honored that right, then continued cooperation with the police could sensibly be said not to implicate the Fourth Amendment. But the Court does not require such a warning,[42] nor, if one were given, would it likely alleviate the inherent coercion of such confrontations.[43]

This line of decisions is the direct result of a twofold abuse of *Terry*. The first abuse is the implicit use of *Terry*'s proportionality principle to determine the threshold of the Fourth Amendment. Although the Court has never acknowledged as much, the only good explanation for the Court's unwillingness to regulate so many actions that are clearly searches and seizures is that it has decided that the cost to law enforcement of doing so outweighs the "minimal" intrusions involved.[44] Such an application of the balancing formula is barred by the language of the Fourth Amendment itself. That provision's prohibition on "unreasonable searches and seizures" applies the reasonableness test only *after* something has been labeled a search or seizure.

The second abuse of *Terry* in this context (which inevitably follows from the first) is the failure to apply its proportionality principle to actions that should have been designated searches and seizures. If the Court had been willing to recognize that some relatively less invasive "searches" and "seizures" can take place on less than probable cause, it would have felt much more comfortable broadening the definition of those two terms. Indeed, in many of the decisions in which the Court rejected application of the Fourth Amendment, the police had developed a degree of suspicion that might have justified the action under proportionality reasoning. For instance, in *Oliver v. United States,* which permitted trespass on private property outside the curtilage, the police were acting on "reports" that the defendant was raising marijuana on his farm.[45] In *California v. Ciraolo* and *California v. Greenwood,* respectively permitting suspicionless flyovers and rifling through garbage, the police were acting on tips about drug possession.[46] In *California v. Hodari D.,* holding that chases are not seizures, the police had seen the defendant flee before them.[47]

Although the police in these cases did not have probable cause, they may have had enough suspicion to justify, under a proportionality scheme, their relatively uninvasive actions. If so, the Court could have eaten its cake and had it too. It could have brought these actions within the compass of the Fourth Amendment and still approved them. Instead it has read vast domains of intrusive police action out of the Fourth Amendment.

ESTABLISHING A HIERARCHY OF INVASIVENESS. These examples lead to the next question about invasiveness that the Court has failed to answer satisfactorily: how should we gauge the relative intrusiveness of a police action that *is* considered a search or seizure? For instance, does it make sense to say that a trespass on "open fields" is more intrusive than surveillance on the public streets but less invasive than a search of the home? Without an answer to these types of questions, proportionality analysis is impossible.

A central assertion of this book is that the reference point for evaluating the relative invasiveness of different police techniques should be the same as it is for determining whether an action is a search or seizure in the first instance: *Katz*'s declaration that the Fourth Amendment protects expectations of privacy that "*society* is prepared to recognize as reasonable."

In other words, some assessment of societal attitudes about the relative intrusiveness of police actions should inform the analysis. As has already been suggested and will become clearer below, the Court has pretty much ignored this precept, with predictably anomalous results.

Society's views about privacy and autonomy can be gleaned in at least two ways. The first is to look at positive law—property, contract, and tort doctrine—for clues as to what we think is private.[48] From this perspective, it is hard to justify the Court's conclusions that no invasion of security occurs when police trespass on private property, fly in airspace that the Federal Aviation Administration has declared off-limits, or requisition records that the bank has promised will remain confidential.

When, as is often the case, the positive law is ambiguous or does not address a particular situation, a second method of determining when society expects privacy is to pose that question to its members. In a study reported in 1993, Joseph Schumacher and I presented fifty different scenarios, all based on Supreme Court cases, to 217 randomly selected individuals and asked them to rate the scenarios' intrusiveness on a scale of 1 to 100.[49] Chapters 4 and 7 report the results of two similar, more recent studies focused directly on surveillance techniques. Chapter 4 also addresses methodological concerns about this type of research, as well as the larger issue of whether empiricism can ever settle normative questions. Assuming, for now, that such research is relevant to Fourth Amendment issues, comparing what it tells us about society's privacy expectations to the Court's views on that matter is instructive.

Some of the Court's intuitions about invasiveness are borne out by our research. With respect to seizures, for example, the Court has told us that a *Terry* stop is less invasive than an arrest, and that a brief stop at a sobriety roadblock is less invasive than either a stop or an arrest.[50] With respect to searches, the Court has indicated that searches of houses and luggage are more invasive than searches of cars,[51] which in turn are more invasive than frisks,[52] drug testing in the school or workplace,[53] and most other searches in the latter two arenas.[54] It has also indicated that regulatory inspections of gun and liquor stores and the like are even less invasive.[55] Our survey results are consistent with these decisions. Identical or similar scenarios presented to our subjects yielded a similar hierarchy.

In many other cases, however, a wide chasm exists between the Court's holdings and our subjects' intrusiveness rankings. Not surprisingly, the gap between the Court's views and the views of the "society" we sampled is greatest in those cases in which the Court has held that police action does not implicate the Fourth Amendment. Relevant to the subject matter of this book, for example, our sample viewed undercover activity of intimates and government perusal of bank records, both of which the Court has left unregulated, as much more invasive than a *Terry* pat down.[56] A proportionality approach based on this research would not only denominate the former investigative activities as "searches" but might well require more than reasonable suspicion to justify them. Similarly, whereas flyovers of backyards and looking through garbage bags were not considered as intrusive as a pat down,[57] they were seen as much more intrusive than looking at the exterior of a car or using a magnetometer at an airport.[58] These findings suggest that under a proportionality rule, some credible reason for the former types of action is necessary.

Our research also calls into question some Court decisions about investigative techniques that the Court is willing to call a search or seizure. Take, for instance, the Court's assumptions that we expect appreciably less privacy at school and at work, in cases such as *New Jersey v. T.L.O.*[59] (holding that search of a pupil's purse for evidence of disciplinary infractions does not require probable cause), *Board of Education v. Earls*[60] (upholding suspicionless drug testing of students involved in extracurricular activities), and *National Treasury Employees Union v. Von Raab*[61] (upholding suspicionless drug testing of customs agents). A theoretical rationale for recognizing diminished privacy protection in these locales, obliquely suggested in these cases,[62] is that many of the searches conducted there are relatively benign, particularly when they can be characterized as administrative rather than criminal in objective. And indeed, our research suggests that when the motivation of a search or seizure *is* protective or facilitative rather than adversarial, the perceived intrusiveness of the action diminishes significantly. Illustrative is the finding that subjects viewed rummaging through luggage at an airport as no more intrusive than a dog sniff;[63] apparently, this result stemmed from the perception that this search is designed to prevent a serious danger that could not effectively be averted in other ways (and thus coalesces with the narrow danger exception described earlier). Equally low on the intrusiveness scale were searches of sixth grade lockers and inspections for the purpose of ensuring safe living and working conditions;[64] here the results may bespeak a willingness to accept a particular type of paternalism.

However, our research also suggests that when searches in these settings are not imbued with facilitative aims, people's privacy expectations, contrary to the Court's assumption, are heightened. Apparently, as far as our survey participants were concerned, searches of purses for contraband in the school (as in *T.L.O.*) and drug testing in the school and workplace (as in *Earls* and *Von Raab*) are not as easily encompassed by the "Family Model" of criminal procedure;[65] they are perceived as adversarial invasions rather than paternalistic. If that is an accurate assessment of society's expectations, the proportionality principle would demand greater justification than mere assertions that schools and workplaces have drug problems, which is the only justification, later discussion will show, that the Court provides in these cases. Because the judicial justification for some types of surveillance is often similarly vague, this aspect of proportionality analysis is particularly relevant to this book.

INCORPORATING OTHER INTERESTS INTO INVASIVENESS ANALYSIS. A third deficiency of the Court's case law is closely related to the second. As Professor Amar has pointed out,[66] the Court has failed to take into account the interests aside from privacy, property, and autonomy that are protected by other provisions of the Constitution. The First Amendment (in connection, for example, with searches of newspaper offices or diaries and other very private papers), the Sixth Amendment (in connection with subpoenas of attorney's files), the Equal Protection Clause (where race is involved), and the Due Process Clause (where police conduct shocks the conscience) all may independently add weight to the individual's side of the balance, thus requiring more by way of government justification. More will be said later in this book about how these supplementary considerations, in particular the First Amendment and the Due Process Clause, affect regulation of surveillance. Here the focus will be on the implications of the Equal Protection Clause for search and seizure law, because racial issues so pervade the government's efforts to investigate crime that they deserve special attention.

Some of the most provocative writing in this regard has come from Tracey Maclin. Professor Maclin provides convincing proof that minorities are targeted for stops and other police confrontations and that they have come to expect and resent such treatment.[67] From this observation he argues that in evaluating individual interests under *Terry*, the Court should take race into account; the added anxiety that people of color feel when confronted by the police or when they know they are singled out for surveillance should be considered in determining invasiveness.[68]

There is no doubt that a given investigative technique's potential for racially disparate impacts should be considered in figuring out how to regulate it. Government should not send the message that race can form the basis for discriminating among citizens, and thus should not single out racial or other groups (unless a known perpetrator with specific racial characteristics is being sought).[69] Police can also lessen the subjective sense of invasion that minorities feel during confrontations by explaining the basis for the police action; our research confirms that knowledge of the objective of a search reduces the sense of intrusion.[70]

Maclin's prescription, however, would seem to go further, by requiring that police contemplating a search or seizure demonstrate a greater degree of suspicion if their target is black rather than white. If so, it runs into a number of difficulties. An individual's reaction to a police search or seizure will vary widely with race, gender, age, and hundreds of other variables, including previous experiences. More important, perceptions of privacy among African Americans, or any other minority group for that matter, will vary immensely. Accurately assessing these variations and then fairly taking them into account in measuring invasiveness would be impossible. Furthermore, as the Court has noted on several occasions,[71] the police cannot be expected to perceive these types of sensitivities in most cases. As with other legal constructs, then, concepts such as privacy and intrusion probably should not be tailored to individual sensitivities. It is also worth noting that giving blacks more leeway to commit crime, the end result of Maclin's suggestion, would hardly improve the race problem.

Another partial solution to the race problem, one that Maclin himself proposes, is to overrule *Terry*. Because it eschewed probable cause, Maclin asserts, "the ruling in *Terry* was a significant setback in the fight against discriminatory police tactics."[72] But reversing *Terry*, which would mean giving up on the proportionality principle, goes too far, for three reasons.

First, reasonable suspicion is not a hunch; it requires an articulable belief that criminal activity is afoot. In *Terry*, the repeated casing of a store window by Terry and his colleagues gave Officer McFadden good reason to suspect they were planning a burglary. In contrast, some of the examples of discriminatory action that Maclin gives, such as the dragnet roundups of black youth in the wake of the Charles Stuart shooting,[73] are clearly not authorized by *Terry*. Maclin may be right that an officer who confronts a black man "knows that he has unchecked discretion to make the stop."[74] But that is not *Terry*'s fault; it is the fault of a society that does not make the officer obey *Terry*.

That observation leads to the second point. Maclin's target should not be *Terry* but the lack of remedies for discriminatory police action. As the *Terry* Court itself pointed out,[75] the exclusionary remedy is virtually useless in this situation because most stops never lead to a prosecution in which to invoke it. Other current sanctions—jury damages, injunctions, criminal penalties, internal sanctions—are unlikely to take care of this problem. Juries don't like taking money from cops or giving it to criminals; prosecutors aren't likely to bring criminal charges against the police for any reason, much less a bad stop; and, given their ethos and the pressure from the public to solve crime, police cannot be counted on to remedy this situation themselves.[76] Rather, as chapter 8 sets out in more detail, an administrative damages remedy operated by an ombudsman independent of the police—who can discern patterns of misbehavior better than attorneys with individual clients and who can make officers pay out of their own pocket for bad faith and discriminatory actions and make departments pay for failure to train members effectively on race issues—is a much more powerful remedial device than these traditional ones.

Third, once such an effective remedy is in place, the version of *Terry*'s proportionality doctrine advanced here is ultimately more likely than a probable cause standard to deter discriminatory action against African Americans and other people of color. One reason is that it avoids the pressure that a probable-cause-forever standard creates to enact low-level crime prevention statutes and to leave investigative stops (as well as casual police-citizen encounters) entirely unregulated. Another is that it does not, like a probable cause standard would, abandon preventive law enforcement. As Randall Kennedy has suggested, the latter outcome might well visit real discrimination on communities of color, given the fact that they tend to be victimized by crime much more often than other communities.[77]

Justification Schemes

Assessing the intrusiveness of an investigative action is the first step in proportionality analysis. The second step is determining when a particular intrusion is justified. Consistent with proportionality reasoning, *Terry* recognized that one justification standard was not enough for this purpose, and it created reasonable suspicion to help fill the void. The Court has since resorted to the reasonable suspicion standard in several search cases, especially in "special needs" situations that do not involve "ordinary law enforcement" (e.g., searches for disciplinary or workplace infractions, or drug testing for safety purposes). In some of these situations even reasonable suspicion is not required, but merely an assertion that government has a strong need to forgo the warrant and individualized suspicion requirements.[78] In other cases involving particularly invasive searches, the Court appears to require more than probable cause.[79] But in none of these cases has the Court attempted to delineate the relationship between these various standards.

To better protect privacy interests and implement the proportionality idea, I propose here a more explicit justification hierarchy, one that consists of four tiers and that applies across the board to all searches and seizures. To probable cause and reasonable suspicion should be added a higher standard of clear and convincing evidence and a lower standard of relevance. Below is a description of the four standards, along with an examination of when they would apply and a brief exploration of how this framework fits with the Warrant Clause of the Fourth Amendment.

THE FOUR TIERS. The probable cause and reasonable suspicion standards are well established and fairly well defined. Probable cause is often equated with a more-likely-than-not (51 percent) finding, or perhaps a level of certainty somewhat below that.[80] Reasonable suspicion, in contrast, has been associated with approximately a 30 percent level of certainty.[81] The quantification of these standards may seem artificial and even misleading, given the difficulty of translating percentages into anything police and magistrates can use on the street. But it is similar to the way we talk about standards of proof. For instance, the reasonable doubt standard is often discussed in terms of our willingness to let nine guilty people go free to ensure that one innocent person is not convicted. To get some idea of the type of justification we want to require for police actions, we need to think about analogous normative queries.

Pursuing this line of inquiry, it is clear that if proportionality reasoning is to be taken seriously, two levels of justification are insufficient. Some government actions such as bodily surgery, perusal of private diaries, and prolonged undercover operations are much more intrusive than an arrest or search of a home and thus should require more than probable cause as it is currently defined. Specifically, these more invasive actions should take place only if there is clear and convincing proof that the evidence thereby sought is crucial to the state's case, a standard that might be quantified at the 75 percent level of certainty.

At the other end of the spectrum are searches and seizures that are much less intrusive than the five- to ten-minute stops the Supreme Court has authorized based on reasonable suspicion; examples of these might be brief seizures at roadblocks, casual questioning, and searches of businesses. To regulate these government actions, a fourth justification level—the relevance standard—should be formally recognized under the Fourth Amendment. As chapter 6 details, the relevance standard is commonly associated with subpoenas and, under the evidentiary rules, it describes evidence that has any tendency to make a fact in issue more probable than not. This standard would simply require police or prosecutors to articulate a reason for believing their action has some tendency to lead to information that would help solve a crime or apprehend a suspect. Put statistically and arbitrarily, it might be equated with a 5 percent success rate. Using legal terminology, the relevance standard could require police to demonstrate an objective credible belief that a legitimate law enforcement objective will be achieved through the police action.[82]

The above prescriptions are not cast in stone; they are simply meant to illustrate how proportionality analysis might work. Under a proportionality approach, the animating inquiry in setting levels of suspicion should be how much explanation for a given intrusion is necessary to convince an innocent person subjected to it that the police acted reasonably. The innocent person who is arrested or the target of bedroom surveillance will expect a "damn good reason" for the inconvenience and intrusion. The innocent person who is stopped on the street for a brief interrogation or tracked by a public camera is likely to be satisfied with a less extensive explanation for the government attention. The official excuse for a mistaken action should be adequate, but need be no more than adequate, to dissipate the umbrage the action excites. This is the central insight of the proportionality principle: the justification for a search or seizure should nullify its intrusiveness, no more and no less.

THE MYTH OF INDIVIDUALIZED SUSPICION AND THE IMPORTANCE OF RATIONALITY REVIEW. The next aspect of the justification scheme that needs significant fine-tuning concerns the type, rather than the amount, of evidence the government must proffer in order to meet its justificatory burden. The courts often recite the idea that suspicion must be "individualized."[83] *Terry* itself appeared to endorse this position, stating that "in determining whether the officer acted reasonably . . . , due weight must be given, not to his inchoate and unparticularized suspicion or 'hunch,' but to the specific reasonable inferences which he is entitled to draw from the facts in light of his experience."[84] One consequence of this preference for particularized suspicion is frequent judicial expression of concern over police use of "investigative profiles" based on statistical information, particularly those relying on correlations between certain types of behavior or features and criminal activity (e.g., drug courier profiles).[85] To distinguish this nomothetic, or group-based, type of evidence from individualized suspicion, I will call it generalized suspicion.

The case against reliance on generalized suspicion appears to be premised on the idea that the use of profiles and the like undermines human autonomy and the notion of individualized justice.[86] But the distinction between individualized and generalized suspicion is, in all relevant respects, meaningless. To justify the stop he made in *Terry*, Officer McFadden needed the general knowledge about behavior of criminals that he had learned from his thirty-nine years on the force as much as his specific observations of Terry and his compatriots. Indeed, in the last half of the sentence quoted from *Terry* in the previous paragraph, the Court recognized precisely that fact. Put another way, had Officer McFadden taught a class of rookies how to identify potential burglars, those officers who later relied on his stereotypes and behavioral tips in nabbing their first Terry would not somehow be violating the Fourth Amendment.[87] If a profile can produce the success rate required by the proportionality principle, then the fact that it focuses on status or membership in a group should not be important (unless, for reasons discussed earlier, the group is defined by race or ethnicity).[88]

The hostility toward generalized suspicion is not only conceptually misguided but also pragmatically insidious. Without such a notion there can be no meaningful justification requirement in a vast number of search and seizure scenarios where separating the innocent from the guilty on an "individualized" basis is all but impossible. Consider that, as construed by the Supreme Court, the Fourth Amendment imposes virtually no limitations on roadblocks for the purpose of detecting illegal immigrants and drunken drivers, or on drug testing of customs workers and student athletes, or on regulatory inspections of residences and businesses, even though the Court concedes that all these situations involve searches or seizures.[89] Rather, leery of imposing difficult-to-meet individualized suspicion requirements in these situations, the Court has been satisfied with claims by the government that its action will address a "significant" criminal or regulatory problem;[90] once this allegation is made, the Court adopts a hands-off stance. In traditional constitutional jurisprudence terminology, the Court is at best engaging in rationality review, which is always extremely deferential to executive and legislative decisions[91] and is a recipe for pretextual actions—

the use of roadblocks, regulatory inspections, and other group searches and seizures for hidden purposes.

A proportionality regime that recognizes the generalized suspicion concept, in contrast, would significantly circumscribe this type of government power. Assume that the government wants to initiate drug and alcohol testing using urinalysis in a particular workplace. Assume also that the government cannot demonstrate individualized cause, that is, cause based purely on observation of individuals' behavior at work, either because drugged behavior is not easily observable or because it is too difficult to post observers over everyone. While the Court would probably permit the drug testing so long as there is some evidence that drug use could threaten health or safety,[92] a proportionality analysis would require more. Assuming that urinalysis testing is sufficiently invasive so that under the proportionality principle it requires probable cause (defined above as about a 50 percent level of certainty), the government would need to show that roughly 50 percent of the relevant employees are at risk for drug use. Only if it can demonstrate a generalized suspicion at the requisite level should it be able to conduct the test.

How, one might ask, is the government to generate the necessary showing if the testing program has yet to commence? Often the government has other ways of developing cause; after all, a rational agency will establish a drug testing program only after a conspicuous problem arises. Furthermore, by the time such programs are challenged in court, they have usually been in operation for some time and have produced relevant statistics. Thus, in *Skinner v. Railway Labor Executives' Association,* the government was able to show, from various sources, that at least forty-five of the train accidents and incidents that occurred between 1975 and 1983 were caused by drug- or alcohol-impaired employees.[93] If that number amounts to about half the incidents during that period, the requisite generalized suspicion would exist for anyone who causes or is involved in a train accident or safety violation. If it doesn't, individualized suspicion would typically need to be shown before a particular individual could be tested. Other examples of this type of analysis, involving surveillance, are provided later in this book.

If this justification scheme strikes the reader as artificial, technocratic, or too activist, consider the comments of Justice Antonin Scalia in his dissent in *National Treasury Employees Union v. Von Raab,* where the majority upheld drug testing of customs agents. Scalia was livid about the holding, calling it "a kind of immolation of privacy and human dignity in symbolic opposition to drug use."[94] Not normally associated with a fondness for detailed judicial oversight, Scalia nonetheless argued that the Court should have to find some "social necessity" before approving a drug testing program, and asserted that the majority provided no "real evidence of a real problem that will be solved by urine testing of Customs Service employees"; rather, the majority's holding was based on "nothing but speculation, and not very plausible speculation at that."[95] In support of this point, he noted that only 5 agents out of 3,600 customs employees had tested positive for drugs.[96] Thus, even Scalia recognizes that some type of concrete justification is needed before courts affirm government intrusions.

The difficulty, of course, is determining what sort of justification is necessary. For the sake of argument, let us assume that drug testing deters and detects dangerous drug use. Would a hundred positive tests have been enough to justify the drug testing program in *Von Raab*? Or would thirty have been sufficient? When is there "real evidence of a real problem"? The proportionality principle, working in tandem with the generalized suspicion concept, provides a way to answer these questions. Assuming, again, that the invasion associated with drug testing should require probable cause (and that there is no airport-like significant and imminent danger presented by drug-using customs agents), the Court in *Von Raab* should have demanded that roughly *half* of the 3,600 employees test positive in order to justify mass testing. That number may seem high, but then so is the intrusiveness of a drug test.

If one's intuition is still that a mass drug-testing program should not be so easily frustrated, consider the scenario from another perspective. About 7 percent of the American population as a whole, and 19 percent of those between the ages of 18 and 25, have used illegal drugs in the past thirty days.[97] If one believes, say, that a hundred positive tests in the *Von Raab* sample (3 percent of the total) represents a "real problem," then the Fourth Amendment would present no obstacle to nationwide drug testing (at least if one assumes that use of drugs by young adults can be just as dangerous as use of drugs by customs agents). That result would be offensive to most, including, I would guess, the majority in *Von Raab*.

In short, Fourth Amendment analysis should mimic equal protection rationality review "with bite," if not strict scrutiny. Courts evaluating the reasonableness of a search or seizure, whether it is in the street or regulatory in nature, or whether it is of an individual or a group, should demand from the government a specific showing of need that is proportionate to the invasion or, if that showing is not forthcoming, a good reason why the relevant information cannot be generated.[98] Courts should not allow what the Supreme Court has permitted: searches and seizures justified solely by vague assertions about the magnitude of whatever problem the government has targeted.

A caveat to this stance might arise when the authorization to conduct the group search or seizure comes from the legislature rather than a municipality, government bureaucracy, or police department. In such a case, political process theory would hold, courts are *obligated* to show deference to the democratically made decision.[99] It is noteworthy, however, that with one exception,[100] none of the group search cases considered by the Supreme Court involved legislative action; rather, the roadblocks, drug tests, and other actions at issue in those cases were triggered by executive officials or low-level deliberative bodies unrepresentative of the general polity. Furthermore, even legislative action does not deserve deference under political process theory if the legislature delegates all important discretionary decisions to executive officials or enacts a law that impinges on a discrete and insular minority having little or no say in the deliberative process.[101] Unfortunately, one or both of these conditions will likely be present in the typical case.

Thus, generalized suspicion review of group searches and seizures is normally warranted. Although this type of review is a throwback to Lochnerism (named after the case, *Lochner v. New York,* that most conspicuously involved the Court in a much-maligned series of decisions second-guessing legislators),[102] it is defensible for three reasons. First, there is the Court's famous exemption from Lochnerian analysis, in footnote 4 of *United States v. Carolene Products,* for government actions affecting fundamental rights.[103] Second, as Professor Amar has noted, the Fourth Amendment's prohibition on "unreasonable searches and seizures" appears to call explicitly for substantive due process analysis.[104]

Finally, as already suggested, any other approach could easily lead to emasculation of the Fourth Amendment's protections. In an article bemoaning the difficulty of applying the Fourth Amendment in the modern context, Michael Seidman illustrates the consequences of failing to adopt the approach advocated here with an example that directly implicates not only the *Terry* scenario but many types of surveillance discussed in this book.[105] As he notes, "[T]here is no constitutional right to sidewalks; in principle, walking on sidewalks could be treated as a highly regulated activity."[106] If so, he points out, the government could interrupt that activity at will, on the theory that people wishing to get from one place to another consent to such intrusions when they choose to use public walkways, just as gun dealers consent to random searches of their stores when they enter the weapons business. Noting that the Court has yet to explain how it would distinguish the two situations, Seidman concludes that "the rejection of *Lochner* makes it difficult to evaluate the justice of various background conditions."[107] He is right, and that is precisely why we should not reject *Lochner* in the Fourth Amendment context. Given the government's ability to manipulate our surroundings, immensely enhanced by the technological developments described in chapter 1, we might otherwise face the elimination of concrete justification requirements for any search or seizure.

THE WARRANT CLAUSE AND THE PROPORTIONALITY PRINCIPLE. Until now I have not touched on the role of warrants under a proportionality regime. *Terry*, of course, held that a warrant was not necessary to authorize a stop and frisk, a holding that made sense given the exigencies of the situation. But when there is no exigency, ex ante review of the search by some independent official should be preferred—a tenet this book will call the *exigency principle*. William Stuntz has noted that such review both eliminates the hindsight bias that can infect ex post review and makes perjury by the police difficult, given their ignorance about what they will find.[108] To these advantages a third can be added: ex ante review, at least meaningful ex ante review, prevents illegal searches and seizures and the breach of privacy and trust that goes with them. Research from the National Center for State Courts indicates that while magistrates have been known to rubberstamp warrant applications, the mere fact that they must be consulted significantly increases the standard of care among police and prosecutors pursuing an investigation.[109] Like doctors, police should seek a second opinion if there is time to do so.

If these reasons convince one to require pre-authorization in all nonexigent circumstances, a conflict between the text of the Fourth Amendment and the proportionality principle arises. The Fourth Amendment's Warrant Clause states that warrants shall issue only upon probable cause. Thus, if warrants are the vehicle for providing ex ante review, searches and seizures that the proportionality approach permits on less than probable cause, as currently defined, could not be authorized by a warrant.

There are three ways of handling this conflict, all sanctioned by one or more Supreme Court decisions. The first is to redefine probable cause to mean *the cause that makes probable the reasonableness of the intrusion occasioned by a given search or seizure*. This is essentially how *Camara v. Municipal Court*,[110] a Supreme Court decision handed down one year before *Terry*, looked at probable cause in connection with residential safety inspections. The Court there held that warrants for such inspections could issue based solely on a probable cause showing that the conditions of the area to be inspected merited the intrusion.[111] Under this sliding-scale definition, probable cause would subsume the four tiers described above, and a warrant could constitutionally authorize searches and seizures in a host of situations that do not require probable cause as it is presently defined.

If that gambit is considered too confusing, or too inconsistent with Fourth Amendment history,[112] a second alternative would be to develop other methods of ex ante review. The Supreme Court has recognized at least two contexts in which what might simply be called a "court order" could issue on less than probable cause. In *Hayes v. Florida*, the Court stated in dictum "that under circumscribed procedures, the Fourth Amendment might permit the judiciary to authorize the seizure of a person on less than probable cause and his removal to the police station for the purpose of fingerprinting."[113] In *United States v. Karo*, the Court indicated that court orders authorizing beeper tracking of items inside a residence might constitutionally be issued based on reasonable suspicion.[114]

Finally, of course, there is the tack the Court most commonly prefers: retain the unitary probable cause standard and insist that ex ante authorizations meet that standard. For the reasons given above, the first or second approaches are preferable to this one.

It must be admitted that even with the advent of telephonic warrants,[115] the costs of requiring ex ante review for all nonexigent searches and seizures would not be negligible in a regime that defines the scope of the Fourth Amendment as broadly as this chapter has. Those costs could be mitigated to some extent by permitting the review to be carried out by administrators rather than judges when the search takes place in an administrative context, an idea that is applied to some surveillance settings later in this book. In any event, the cost of ex ante review, whatever it may be, is worth the extra security. Law enforcement agents, even when acting in good faith, can easily get carried away in their pursuit of criminals. Ex ante review makes them think twice before barging in doors, planting tracking devices, or mining personal records.

III. The Proportionality Principle: An Unworkable Rorschach Blot?

Reacting to the proportionality idea six years after *Terry* was decided, Anthony Amsterdam made two comments. The first is one I have stolen for this book: "A sliding scale approach would considerably ease the strains that the present monolithic model of the Fourth Amendment almost everywhere imposes on the process of defining the Amendment's outer boundaries."[116] The second comment was far more critical: "Present law is a positive paragon of simplicity compared to what a graduated Fourth Amendment would produce."[117] He added that the sliding-scale approach would convert the Fourth Amendment "into one immense Rorschach blot."[118]

There is no doubt that the assessment of relative invasiveness and the multiple tiers of justification that the proportionality principle demands are complex. But this scheme is not necessarily muddier than the present one, at least as it has developed since 1974, when Amsterdam made his Rorschach jibe. Many of the Court's rulings since then have often required subtle evaluations of intrusiveness.[119] These rulings also demonstrate, contrary to Amsterdam's suggestion, that the courts are quite capable of dealing with the proportionality approach. Most obviously, they have been applying a graduated Fourth Amendment in the seizure context since at least *Terry v. Ohio.*[120] Further, despite what they say, courts often taken the same approach where searches are involved. Exhibit One is once again *Terry*, which held that a frisk requires only reasonable suspicion.

In any event, the justification hierarchy described here (as opposed to how it should be applied) is virtually identical to the Court's own template—the probable cause and reasonable suspicion standards are obviously firmly ensconced, the relevance standard is routinely applied in subpoena cases, and the clear and convincing standard is not that far removed from the requirements the Court has imposed in surgery and communications surveillance cases, where the government must demonstrate that the search is the only means of proving a crucial element of its case.[121] If there is a significant difference in clarity between current law and the rejuvenated proportionality principle advanced in this chapter, it may be in the other direction. The scheme proposed here makes more explicit how invasiveness is to be assessed and thus should provide a clearer picture of the relative intrusiveness of different types of police actions. It also defines more concisely the types of justifications the government must put forward.

Finally, the discretion granted police by the proportionality approach can be bounded in several ways. First, as has occurred over time with the amorphous language of the Fourth Amendment, application of the proportionality principle to recurring situations would undoubtedly lead to the development of relatively clear "rules," most of which, as this book will suggest, would be no different from today's rules, except that the level of certainty required for given actions would be more explicit and (sometimes) more demanding. Second, in developing these rules, only rough proportionality should be the goal: in some cases, individual (or state) interests may be sacrificed, at least marginally, to achieve greater clarity. Third, where clear rules do not develop, the police would at least have an easily remembered "standard of thumb" that will help fill in the gaps. Finally, if ex ante review is required in all nonexigent circumstances, as the exigency principle requires, then often an independent party, rather than law enforcement officials, would be applying the proportionality principle.

Conclusion

If the underlying rationale of *Terry* were dusted off and rejuvenated, the proportionality and exigency principles that emerged would provide a comprehensive yet flexible framework for regulating government investigative efforts. All government searches and seizures would be regulated, not just those that rise above some ill-defined level of intrusion. Investigations of groups and institutions, as well as of individuals, would require concrete justification proportionate to the invasion they perpetrate. Nonexigent searches would be subject to pre-authorization. All of this could be instituted without denying law enforcement the ability to be proactive, an ability that would be circumscribed under a more rigid approach requiring probable cause for all searches and seizures. Nor need ex ante review, when it is required, always involve a cumbersome judicial process.

It is now time to apply these concepts to the subject matter of this book. Under the proportionality and exigency principles, physical and transaction surveillance would no longer be outside the purview of the Fourth Amendment. At the same time, that amendment's probable cause and warrant language would apply in only a limited number of situations. The advantages to both individuals and government of a regulatory framework governed by these principles should become apparent in the following pages.

PART II
Physical Surveillance

CHAPTER THREE

Peeping Techno-Toms

In *Kyllo v. United States,*[1] the Supreme Court purportedly struck a blow for the sanctity of the home, in an age when technology threatens to destroy it. This chapter wonders whether *Kyllo* is a Pyrrhic victory. It also explains why various aspects of the decision offend the proportionality and exigency principles discussed in chapter 2 and how surveillance of the home would be governed by these principles.

Prior to *Kyllo,* the majority of lower courts had held that use of a thermal imaging device to detect heat sources within a house is not a Fourth Amendment search, either because the heat waves detected by such devices are "abandoned" and do not require physical intrusion to discern, or because they are too impersonal to warrant privacy protection.[2] In *Kyllo*, the Supreme Court rejected these rationales and concluded that the government may not mechanically measure the warmth of the home unless it demonstrates probable cause for doing so. The Court's decision could also be read to say that most other scientifically enhanced investigations of the domicile are searches as well, and thus might indicate a desire to put significant restrictions on all technological surveillance of our most private sanctuary.

If so, the ruling is a good one. But the Court left at least one loophole in its decision, a loophole that could become quite significant. Its precise holding stated that "where, as here, the Government uses a device *that is not in general public use*, to explore details of the home that would previously have been unknowable without physical intrusion, the surveillance is a 'search.' "[3] As the dissenters in *Kyllo* rightly pointed out, varying Fourth Amendment regulation of technology with the prevalence of that technology is troublesome, because "the threat to privacy will grow, rather than recede, as the use of intrusive equipment becomes more readily available."[4]

Much depends on how the Court defines "general public use." One might be comforted by the majority's insistence (indeed, it was "quite confident")[5] that despite its availability from more than half a dozen national companies,[6] the type of thermal imaging device at issue in *Kyllo* is not in general use. As this chapter will document, however, today's marketplace offers a wide array of much cheaper enhancement devices that are easily bought over the Internet and from nationwide chains and specialty shops. The march of progress guarantees that this trend will accelerate. Thus, the dissent's caution in *Kyllo* should be taken seriously.

The majority's sole response to this caution was the disquieting statement that the dissent's "quarrel . . . is not with us but with this Court's precedent."[7] Here it cited *California v. Ciraolo,*[8] which held, in the context of airplane flyovers, that the privacy protected by the Fourth Amendment is no greater than the privacy one can expect from the public at large—and a decidedly curious public at that (one composed, for instance, of members who look closely at plants growing in backyards from low-flying airplanes).[9] If that is to be the Court's approach to police use of technology, then the *Kyllo* dissent may be right in its suggestion that the general use exception will eventually swallow the Court's newly minted prohibition of technologically enhanced investigation of homes. That prediction is, if anything, strengthened by *Ciraolo*'s companion case, *Dow Chemical Co. v. United States.*[10] There the Court held that while "surveillance of private property by using highly sophisticated surveillance equipment not generally available to the public" might well require a warrant, use of a $22,000, high-magnification mapmaking camera to surveil the exterior of secluded business premises does not.[11]

Ciraolo and *Dow Chemical* both involved observation of curtilage, not the inner domain of the house. Perhaps the Court will define general public use differently depending on the target of the surveillance, and insist that police always obtain warrants to carry out technological searches of homes, as it did in *Kyllo* and in *United States v. Karo,*[12] which held that use of a beeper to discover the contents of a house is a search. But as I document below, the lower courts have not let walls get in the way of technological innovation. Several have held that observation of the home interior using flashlights, binoculars, and more sophisticated illumination and magnification devices is not always a search. Of course, flashlights and binoculars are much more common than the newer search enhancers. But as the *Kyllo* dissent implies, thermal imagers and beepers may be the flashlights and binoculars of tomorrow. More important, even the more mundane types of technology can visit significant intrusion on home dwellers.

In this chapter, I argue that the extent to which a particular technological device is used by the general public, and the related inquiries into whether it is generally available or highly sophisticated, should be irrelevant to Fourth Amendment analysis. On a more fundamental level, I argue that the Court's willingness to limit Fourth Amendment privacy to areas that are free from naked eye observation, a willingness that is apparent in many of the Court's cases and that appears to be codified in *Kyllo*, is inconsistent with the Fourth Amendment. Although the reasoning advanced here applies to all police investigative actions, the focus will be on the use of technology to investigate goings-on inside the home and similarly private locations. Use of technology to conduct surveillance of public areas is treated in the next two chapters.

Section 1 of this chapter summarizes the law regarding both the general public use exception and what I will call the "naked eye exception" as they are described in *Kyllo*, other Supreme Court decisions, and the lower courts. Section 2 explains why these concepts are unsustainable in theory and incoherent in practice. Section 3 proposes two solutions to the problems posed by technological searches. The first is based on the proportionality principle, which dictates that "search" be defined broadly for Fourth Amendment purposes (so that any intentional surveillance of a house would require some suspicion) but permits police to search on less than probable cause when their actions are not particularly intrusive. The second proposal is that Congress enact a statute prohibiting use of technological devices under circumstances analogous to those specified in Title III with respect to eavesdropping instruments.

The first proposal might strike some as a nonstarter, given the Court's grudging definition of search, on one hand, and its apparent insistence, on the other, that actions denominated as searches be based on probable cause. But the Court has yet to define reasonable expectations of privacy in connection with technologically enhanced house searches, so it is not too late to adopt an expansive view of "search" in this particular context. As for the probable cause dogma, the lower courts, which have to deal with the run-of-the-mill case on a daily basis, have often ignored it, something the Supreme Court has come close to doing as well.

If the proportionality approach is viewed as too radical in this context, the second proposal is offered as a worthy substitute. Generally, that proposal would criminalize nonconsensual technological surveillance of home interiors and similar locations by civilians. Visual surveillance devices would therefore never lawfully be in "general use" for the purpose of spying on homes and the like, and that reality would in turn render the general public use exception as applied to private areas irrelevant, even as technology becomes more prevalent.

I. The General Public Use and Naked Eye Exceptions

The general public use doctrine is of ephemeral origins. Perhaps as a result, its scope is very imprecise. Also unclear is how it interacts with other factors relevant to Fourth Amendment analysis, including the naked eye exception. These three matters are explored below.

Genesis

As noted in chapter 1, until the 1960s, the Fourth Amendment protected against government trespass in four areas: houses, persons, papers, and effects. The prevalence of technology the police used was irrelevant. The sole inquiry was whether operation of the technology required intrusion into a protected area. If so, a search occurred; if not, the Fourth Amendment was not implicated.

Katz supposedly changed all that. Trespass doctrine was discarded in favor of the expectation-of-privacy rubric. But, as chapter 1 also noted, *Katz* added that "what a person knowingly exposes to the public, even in his own home or office, is not a subject of Fourth Amendment protection."

In *Ciraolo*, the Supreme Court relied on that language in concluding that naked eye observation of a backyard surrounded by a fence ten feet high, from an airplane flying at one thousand feet, is not a search. In context, the Court's use of this aspect of *Katz* is instructive:

> The Fourth Amendment protection of the home has never been extended to require law enforcement officers to shield their eyes when passing by a home on public thoroughfares. Nor does the mere fact that an individual has taken measures to restrict some views of his activities preclude an officer's observations from a public vantage point where he has a right to be and which renders the activities clearly visible. . . . "What a person knowingly exposes to the public, even in his own home or office, is not a subject of Fourth Amendment protection."
>
> The observations . . . in this case took place within public navigable airspace, in a physically nonintrusive manner. . . . Any member of the public flying in this airspace who glanced down could have seen everything that these officers observed. On this record, we readily conclude that respondent's expectation

> that his garden was protected from such observation is unreasonable and is not an expectation that society is prepared to honor.[13]

The Court used the same reasoning in *Florida v. Riley*,[14] where it held that observing a backyard from a helicopter, this time only four hundred feet above the ground (but still in navigable airspace), is not a search. In both cases, the Court assumed that members of the public might engage in the type of behavior the police did, and reasoned from that assumption that the behavior did not offend reasonable expectations of privacy.

In neither *Ciraolo* nor *Riley* did the Court focus on the fact that the police were using technology (aircraft) to carry out their observations. In *Ciraolo*, however, the Court did state that "in an age where private and commercial flight in the public airways is routine, it is unreasonable for respondent to expect that his marijuana plants were constitutionally protected from being observed with the naked eye from an altitude of 1,000 feet."[15] It was this sentence that the Court would later cite in *Kyllo* in support of its general public use exception to technological surveillance of the home.[16]

Although a companion case to *Ciraolo*, *Dow Chemical*'s contribution to the general public use exception was formulated somewhat differently. In finding that the Environmental Protection Agency's use of a $22,000 mapmaking camera to photograph Dow Chemical's plant was not a search, the Court focused on the camera's availability and capabilities rather than its prevalence. Again, the relevant language is worth looking at in context.

> It may well be, as the Government concedes, that surveillance of private property by using highly sophisticated surveillance equipment not generally available to the public, such as satellite technology, might be constitutionally proscribed absent a warrant. But the photographs here are not so revealing of intimate details as to raise constitutional concerns. Although they undoubtedly give EPA more detailed information than naked-eye views, they remain limited to an outline of the facility's buildings and equipment. The mere fact that human vision is enhanced somewhat, at least to the degree here, does not give rise to constitutional problems.[17]

This language, like the opinion in *Ciraolo*, makes clear that the extent to which the public has access to a given technology is only one of many considerations in the Fourth Amendment calculus. More will be said about this multifactor approach below. For now, it is enough to observe that the foregoing cases represent the sum total of the Supreme Court's pronouncements on the general public use concept. On this score, the lineage from *Katz* to *Kyllo* is thin indeed.

The lower courts, in contrast, provide many pre-*Kyllo* and post-*Kyllo* examples of judicial reliance on the general public use rationale. For instance, in the pre-*Kyllo* decision *State v. Vogel,* the court held that police use of a camera with a zoom lens to photograph the interior of a residence was not a search, in part because there was "no showing that the cameras and lenses used [were] sophisticated visual aids" or "special equipment not generally in use."[18] In *State v. Rose,* the court concluded that use of a flashlight to aid peering into a mobile home is not a search, in part because a flashlight is "an exceedingly common device."[19] Several cases have used the same kind of language in concluding that no search occurs when police use zoom or other magnification lenses to observe curtilage just outside the home.[20] Finally, at least two post-*Kyllo* cases have said the same about police use of night scopes to observe home interiors or curtilage, despite the relative sophistication and expense of these devices.[21]

A number of other decisions have permitted enhanced observation of homes and curtilage, using devices ranging from binoculars to Star-Trons (night scopes with magnification capacity), without specifically mentioning the general public use concept. But they have either clearly assumed that such visual enhancement does not change the Fourth Amendment analysis[22] or noted that the use of more sophisticated devices might have changed the result.[23] Thus, the routine use and general availability notions briefly alluded to in *Ciraolo* and *Dow Chemical* have heavily influenced the lower courts.[24]

Definitions

Despite the number of cases mentioning the issue, the general public use concept remains amorphous. As noted above, a number of courts seem to believe that flashlights and binoculars, and perhaps night scopes as well, are in general public use. The Supreme Court has indicated that airplanes (in navigable airspace) and mapmaking cameras are also in general use but that thermal imagers are not; given the Court's decision in *Karo v. United States* requiring a court order when a beeper is used to discern activity within a home, tracking devices should probably be added to the latter category.[25] But no court has put forth a more general definition of the general public use concept. Until we get one, the thumbnail sketch of the case law provided above suggests three basic definitions, each of which is itself divisible into two or more versions.

The first basic definition focuses on whether the technology in question is generally available to the public—the language found in *Dow Chemical.* "Generally" means "usually" or "as a rule,"[26] while "general" means "applicable to the whole."[27] "Available" means "accessible" or "obtainable," or "ready for immediate use."[28] Accordingly, a generally available item is one that all or virtually all members of the public are able to obtain. Taken literally, this definition would exclude much surveillance technology, except perhaps the cheapest flashlights. It would certainly not encompass mapmaking cameras or low-flying airplanes, suggesting that this is not the definition the Court would endorse.

Moving to a broader definition of this first basic approach, general availability could be construed to mean that the item is available to a substantial portion of the public. Under this definition, indicia of general availability might be the number of items manufactured, the cost of the item, and the number of outlets carrying it. More colloquially, this definition could be dubbed the "Wal-Mart test." If the item is available at Wal-Mart, it is likely to be affordable to and accessible by a large segment of the public.

Flashlights are generally available in this sense. They are usually inexpensive (a high-beam version costs as little as $8, batteries included; a Cyclops 10 Million Candle spotlight goes for about $38) and can be purchased at nationwide stores such as Wal-Mart, K-Mart, and Target as well as numerous local stores. Binoculars are not as prevalent but are still relatively cheap, ranging from $30 for a pair with a magnification capacity of 10 (10x) to $197 for binoculars with 16x power. Cameras equipped with zoom lenses are also fairly easy to purchase, with Wal-Mart prices ranging from $60 to $100 for cameras with 2x to 4x magnification power. This much is common knowledge.[29]

What might be somewhat surprising is that Wal-Mart also offers inexpensive versions of highly powerful telescopes and night vision equipment. The Polaris 60EQ-A Telescope, described as "an extremely powerful, 60mm telescope that offers contrast-rich, high-resolution images not found in smaller scopes," can be purchased for $65. Night vision binoculars costing between $400 and $725 purport to permit magnified night viewing "even in total darkness." These devices may not be in every home, but they are certainly much more widely available to the general public and much less sophisticated than the $22,000 mapmaking camera in *Dow Chemical.*

The second, less expansive basic definition of the general public use concept adheres more closely to the words in that phrase rather than *Dow Chemical*'s "generally available" language: how often does the public *use* a particular type of technology? Generally available items may not be commonly resorted to. For instance, although most of the aforementioned devices are obtainable by a sizeable portion of the public, their use is quite varied; people rely on flashlights all the time, binoculars and zoom lenses somewhat less frequently, and telescopes and night vision equipment less frequently still.

At the same time, all these items are everyday paraphernalia to certain segments of the population, and are relied on at least as frequently as low-flying airplanes in carrying out certain types of endeavors. Birdwatchers, sports fans, hunters, and opera enthusiasts make avid use of binoculars. Tourists and loving families focus their zoom lenses on a daily basis. Telescopes are a favorite of stargazers, and night vision devices are popular with hunters. The number of these groupings and their size will only expand as time marches on. Also worth noting is the Court's apparent endorsement of this "subgroup" approach to the general use doctrine in *Dow Chemical*, where it emphasized that the device relied on in that case was "a conventional, albeit precise, commercial camera commonly used in mapmaking."[30]

That observation leads to a third, narrower basic definition—general public use for a particular purpose. Most of these devices, even if generally available and used by large segments of the public, are not usually used the way police use them. In particular, they are probably not normally employed to look into homes or curtilage.

As the Court demonstrated in *Riley*, there are several versions of this approach as well. A plurality of justices in that case (including Justice Scalia, author of *Kyllo*) adopted what might be called a positivist approach, finding the fact that planes could legally fly within four hundred feet of the ground dispositive of whether observation of curtilage from that height was a search.[31] This stance, as the *Riley* dissent pointed out, in essence asserts that "the expectation of privacy is defeated if a single member of the public could conceivably position herself to see into the area in question without doing anything illegal."[32]

The other five justices took an empirical approach to the issue. Justice Sandra Day O'Connor, in a concurring opinion, concluded that if overflights at four hundred feet are rare, then they should be considered searches even though technically in navigable airspace (although she ended up deciding they were not rare in the locale at issue, and thus joined the plurality in finding that no search occurred in *Riley*).[33] The four dissenters in *Riley* fine-tuned the empirical approach further, asking whether overflights at four hundred feet for the specific purpose of observing the contents of residential backyards are rare, and deciding that they were exceedingly so.[34]

Interaction with Other Factors

Besides the definitional ambiguity, another potential source of confusion about the general public use doctrine is that it is only one of many factors possibly relevant to the search issue. For instance, following *Dow Chemical*, a mapmaking camera aimed from an airplane is not a search if the target is business curtilage, but, as the Court suggested in *Dow Chemical* and *Kyllo*, it may become a search if the interior of the home is the focus. In fact, an examination of the Court's decisions reveals seven variables the justices have addressed in determining whether police use of technology is a search. In addition to the availability of the technology to the general public, they have considered (1) the nature of the place to be observed; (2) the steps taken to enhance privacy; (3) the degree to which the surveillance requires a physical intrusion onto private property; (4) the nature of the object or activity observed; (5) the extent to which the technology enhances the natural senses; and (6) the extent to which the surveillance is unnecessarily pervasive, invasive, or disruptive (i.e., because the police failed to take steps to minimize the intrusion).[35]

Ciraolo, *Riley*, and *Dow Chemical* illustrate application of each of the six factors. With respect to the nature of the area surveilled, all three cases emphasized that the home and surrounding curtilage are accorded the most significant privacy protection.[36] On the issue of privacy enhancement, *Ciraolo* noted that the ten-foot fence, although clearly meant to shield the backyard from street-level viewing, would not have barred observers on trucks or double-decker buses (!) from seeing the marijuana,[37] and the majority in *Dow Chemical* scoffed at Dow's assertion that keeping track of the identification numbers of overflights was an adequate precaution against this type of privacy invasion.[38] All three cases also emphasized that the overflight did not require physical intrusion onto the property.[39]

Concerning the nature of the activity observed, the majority opinions in *Dow Chemical* and *Riley* asserted that the helicopter observers did not see any "intimate" activities in the backyard.[40] With respect to the potency of the enhancement used, *Dow Chemical* distinguished the camera observation in that case from technological observation that can penetrate walls.[41] And on the issue of minimization, *Riley* noted that the helicopter caused no "undue noise" or any "wind, dust, or threat of injury."[42]

Post-*Kyllo*, courts will have to figure out how important the general public use factor is in relation to the other six factors. Fortunately, in contrast to its failure to define the general public use exception, *Kyllo* does a fairly good job of answering this question. First, as this chapter has already discussed at length, *Kyllo* indicates that the extent to which technology used by the police is also used by the public is very important; although technically dicta, two acknowledgments of the general public use exception occur in the opinion.[43] Second, *Kyllo* also clearly affirms that the interior of the home (factor 1 above) is normally accorded full Fourth Amendment protection.[44] Third, *Kyllo* indicates that when the area observed *is* the interior of the home (as opposed to the curtilage at issue in *Ciraolo*, *Dow Chemical*, and *Riley*), four of the other five factors are either of secondary importance or are entirely irrelevant in deciding whether a Fourth Amendment search has occurred.

To verify this last point, consider *Kyllo*'s treatment of factors 2 through 6. On steps taken to enhance privacy (factor 2),the *Kyllo* majority was at its most opaque, for it did not directly address the dissent's point that the defendant could have avoided the discovery of the heat waves by "making sure that the surrounding area [was] well insulated."[45] Perhaps the majority did not think the matter important enough to address. More likely, as explained below, this factor remains crucial.

In contrast, the majority forthrightly dismissed the dissent's argument that the imager "did not penetrate the walls of petitioner's home"[46] (factor 3), stating "we rejected such a mechanical interpretation of the Fourth Amendment in *Katz*, where the eavesdropping device picked up only sound waves that reached the exterior of the phone booth."[47] To the assertion that the thermal imager detected no intimate details (factor 4),[48] the majority once again minced no words: "In the home, our cases show, all details are intimate details, because the entire area is held safe from prying government eyes."[49] And the dissent's attempt to show—through its observations about the various other ways the heat inside *Kyllo*'s home could have been detected[50]—that the imager merely replicated what careful unenhanced surveillance would have discerned (factor 5) was "quite irrelevant" to the majority.[51] The majority continued:

> The fact that equivalent information could sometimes be obtained by other means does not make lawful the use of means that violate the Fourth Amend-

> ment. The police might, for example, learn how many people are in a particular house by setting up year-round surveillance; but that does not make breaking and entering to find out the same information lawful. In any event, on the night of January 16, 1992 [the date of the surveillance], no outside observer could have discerned the relative heat of Kyllo's home without thermal imaging.[52]

Although the final variable—concerning steps taken to minimize the surveillance—was left unaddressed by the *Kyllo* majority, presumably that factor too is irrelevant when the surveillance is of the home. If all activities therein are intimate, then no level of minimization suffices.

Before concluding, however, that general public use is the only factor relevant to deciding whether sense-enhanced surveillance of the home is a search, look again at the holding in *Kyllo*: "Where, as here, the Government uses a device that is not in general public use, to explore details of the home *that would previously have been unknowable without physical intrusion*, the surveillance is a 'search' . . ."[53] In an earlier phrasing of its holding, the Court stated, "We think that obtaining by sense-enhancing technology any information regarding the interior of the home *that could not otherwise have been obtained without physical 'intrusion into a constitutionally protected area'* constitutes a search—at least where (as here) the technology in question is not in general public use."[54] The italicized portions of these statements, taken together, announce that if the activity observed could be seen with the naked eye (or detected with other unenhanced senses) without physical intrusion into the constitutionally protected areas of home or curtilage, then police may exploit any technology—generally used or not—without implicating the Fourth Amendment (whereas if the activity *cannot* be directly detected with the naked senses in the absence of physical intrusion, the police may use only common technology to conduct warrantless enhanced surveillance).

This second exception to the general prohibition on enhanced surveillance of the home interior—the naked eye exception—suggests that in addition to the general public use idea, factor 2 is very important in assessing technological observation of the home. If one does not take steps to enhance one's privacy, such as drawing curtains over windows or fencing off one's yard, then naked eye observation of the interior of the home from outside the house is much more likely. And in those situations, *Kyllo* allows police use of any technology—not just common devices—to view the same details.

After *Kyllo*, then, the determination of whether technologically enhanced home surveillance is a search depends on two factors: whether the technology is in general public use and, if it is not, whether the technologically enhanced surveillance detects only details that would have been viewable without technology, from an area unprotected by the Constitution. If either the general public use or the naked eye exception applies, then no search has occurred.[55] It is now time to examine whether these various aspects of *Kyllo* make sense.

II. *Kyllo*'s Problems

To the extent it endorses the general public use concept or the naked eye exception, the ruling in *Kyllo* is seriously flawed. The following discussion demonstrates that conclusion from three perspectives. The first is pragmatic: both the general public use and the naked eye doctrines are virtually impossible to apply in a meaningful manner. The second perspective is theoretical: despite the courts' insinuation to the contrary, these two concepts cannot, as a logical matter, flow from *Katz*'s "knowing exposure" language. The third perspective is normative: society should be constitutionally entitled to expect that government will refrain from spying on the home in any manner—technological or otherwise—unless it can demonstrate good cause for doing so.

The Public Use/Naked Eye Quagmires

An earlier section of this chapter has already indicated the numerous possible meanings of "general public use." There are at least three broad definitions of that phrase (general availability, general use, and general use for a particular purpose), and each of those definitions can be subdivided into alternative definitions that vary widely. For instance, interpreting "general" to mean "of the whole," the general availability rubric might cover only the most common devices (such as flashlights or binoculars). In its Wal-Mart guise, however, it could also encompass zoom cameras, night vision equipment, and telescopes. And if one takes *Dow Chemical*'s use of the term seriously, then even $22,000 mapmaking cameras qualify. In contrast, the general use rubric, in its narrowest version, might not even include binoculars, because that item is probably not routinely used by *most* of the population. But "general use" could also fairly be construed to include binoculars as well as any other device used by a large subgroup of the population (including airplanes and zoom cameras).

Finally, the narrowest of the three definitions, general use for a particular purpose, could also encompass many devices—or it could exclude all of them, depending on whether a positivist or empirical approach is taken and on which purpose is at issue. As a matter of positive law, use of flashlights and binoculars on the public thoroughfares is permissible; thus, if one were to follow the plurality's approach in *Riley* (which apparently considered curtilage-viewing from any flight within navigable airspace near an air lane to be routine), such use might not be a search even if it happened to disclose activities inside the home. As an empirical matter, however, people may seldom use public vantage points to peer into others' homes, and fewer still use flashlights or binoculars, much less more sophisticated equipment, to do so; one could probably say such instances are "rare." Even home observation aided by the most widely adopted forms of technology—eyeglasses, for instance—might thus constitute a search.

In short, the possible permutations of the general public use doctrine are myriad and perhaps overwhelming. To this problem, which admittedly besets other legal doctrines as well, is added the vexing quandary alluded to by the *Kyllo* dissent: how are the courts to deal with the rapid pace of technological development in deciding whether something is in general public use? Although the Court has declared that thermal imagers do not fit in this category, it may have to change its stance in the future, given the increasing reliance on such devices.[56] Night vision equipment, although also relatively new, is even more widely used and much less expensive. If a declaration that these items are in general public use is hard to imagine, consider that the zoom camera—a device that at least two courts have considered generally available[57]—did not come into being until 1986.[58] And, as already noted, since *Kyllo* two other courts have declared that night scopes are in general public use.

In short, advanced technology can find its way into the average home very quickly (something the history of flashlights and binoculars verifies).[59] When that happens with devices such as night scopes and beepers—and perhaps thermal imagers—the courts will have to either change their stance, manipulate the meaning of the general public use doctrine, or ignore the doctrine altogether. None of these options is very palatable, either as an institutional matter for courts used to following precedent or as a policy matter for police, litigants, and citizens trying to organize their affairs.

Conscientious courts will also be flummoxed by *Kyllo*'s position on police use of technology that is not in general public use. Here they must determine whether the details seen with technology would also have been viewable with the naked eye without physically intruding into a constitutionally protected area. The first conundrum raised by this formulation is its inherently paradoxical nature. If naked eye viewing without physical intrusion could have occurred, why didn't it? If the answer is (as it often will be) that the police were worried they would be discovered, thus leading the targets to stop what they were doing or to hide it better, then the interior details arguably could *not* have been seen with the naked eye. The Court probably did not intend this investigative paradox. Assuming so, it has left courts with the puzzle of determining both the extent to which fear of detection should be factored into the analysis and how to discern whether that fear existed.[60]

Putting this problem aside would not end the difficulties associated with the Court's naked eye ruling. Again, that ruling holds that enhanced searches of the home are permissible if they merely duplicate naked eye searches from vantage points that are not constitutionally protected. Many imponderables will surely arise in making this determination. Is the curtilage always a constitutionally protected area? What if it "invites" the public onto it with sidewalks and similar arrangements? Do apartment buildings have curtilage? Assuming that the naked eye viewing could take place without physical intrusion on a protected area, are there any restrictions on how it could occur? Can it be hypothesized that police would have climbed trees, peered through cracks, and looked between half-drawn curtains in determining whether the naked eye would have spied the activities actually observed with the enhancement device?

Lower courts have already had trouble grappling with these types of questions in dealing with unenhanced viewing of the interior of the home. Although virtually all courts hold that looking through an open door or window from a public vantage point is not a search,[61] in other situations one court's sufficiency of precaution is another court's complete failure to take adequate steps to protect privacy. Cases often come down to whether curtilage is secluded enough, a fence high enough, a curtain drawn enough, or a crack in the door small enough.[62] Because it requires courts to speculate whether a *hypothetical* naked eye could have lawfully observed what the enhanced viewing detected in such circumstances, *Kyllo*'s formulation profoundly exacerbates an already difficult judicial task. Even more daunting is the possibility that the general use and naked eye exceptions could work together, so that no search occurs when police use novel technology to spy on activities that naked eye viewing *or* viewing with technology in general use could have observed. Because observation with generally used technology is apparently meant to be equated with naked eye observation in terms of privacy expectations, this bootstrapping of the two exceptions is not implausible.

Technologically Enhanced Observation and Knowing Exposure to the Public

The problems with the general public use and naked eye doctrines go much deeper than difficulties in pinning down their meaning. Ultimately neither doctrine is sufficiently grounded in Fourth Amendment theory, either as laid out in *Katz* or as a more general proposition.

This conclusion is particularly evident when one tries to connect these doctrines with *Katz*'s "knowing exposure" language. As section 1 of this chapter explained, in *Ciraolo* the Supreme Court relied on the statement in *Katz* that activities "knowingly exposed to the public, even in [the] home or office" do not deserve Fourth Amendment protection, and *Kyllo* later cited *Ciraolo* to bolster its adoption of the general public use exception. Yet the logical connection between this aspect of *Katz* and the Court's rules concerning technologically enhanced home surveillance is extremely tenuous. Almost by definition, activities in the home that are observed using enhancement devices are not "knowingly" exposed to the public. As suggested above, police usually use technology because they want to ensure the target does *not* know about the surveillance and because they believe naked eye viewing is not feasible.

The only cases cited by the *Katz* opinion to support its "knowing exposure" language were *Lewis v. United States*[63] and *United States v. Lee.*[64] Both involved scenarios quite different from enhanced observation of the home. In *Lewis*, the Court held that no search occurred when an undercover agent entered Lewis's home after Lewis had invited him there under the impression that the agent wanted to buy drugs.[65] In contrast to the person subjected to covert technological surveillance, Lewis knew he was disclosing information to a third party. In *Lee*, the Court held that no search occurred when government agents used a searchlight to discern cans of alcohol on the deck of Lee's boat. Whether or not Lee knowingly exposed these cans to public view (arguably he intended to hide them under cover of darkness), they were clearly positioned on the equivalent of the boat's curtilage, not in its interior, a point the Court seemed to find important when it stated, "[I]t is not shown that there was any exploration below decks or under hatches."[66] In *Lewis*, there was "knowing" exposure.

In *Lee*, the home interior was not involved. The *Kyllo* scenario differs from both.

Virtually all of the Court's post-*Katz* decisions finding that the Fourth Amendment is not implicated fit one of these two molds. Either the defendant knowingly revealed information to a third party, who turned the information over to the government,[67] or the exposure did not occur inside the home.[68] Taken together, the Court's cases stand for the proposition that covert (i.e., undetected) observation of activities within a domicile triggers the Fourth Amendment.

There is admittedly one post-*Katz* case involving government seizure of information from inside the home that does seem to have jettisoned the "knowing" requirement. In *Smith v. Maryland,*[69] the Court held that even if a person does not know that the numbers he calls are recorded by the phone company, he assumes the risk that they will be.[70] Similarly, it might be said, one assumes the risk that activities inside the home that can be seen with generally used technology or by a (hypothetical) naked eye observer from outside the home will in fact be viewed in those ways.

Assumption-of-risk reasoning in this context is vacuous, however. We only assume the risks of unregulated government intrusion that the courts tell us we have to assume. The most pertinent illustration of that fact is *Kyllo* itself. As noted at the beginning of this chapter, until the Supreme Court's decision in that case, most jurisdictions had settled that we *did* assume the risk that police would subject the interior of our houses to thermal imaging without obtaining a warrant or developing any level of suspicion that evidence of crime would be discovered. Ultimately, despite their constant citation by the lower courts and the Supreme Court, neither the knowing exposure language of the *Katz* majority opinion nor the modified (assumption of risk) version thereof poses the proper question. Rather, the correct inquiry is that suggested by Justice Harlan's concurring opinion in *Katz*: is suspicionless observation of the home interior using enhancement devices something that "society is prepared to recognize as 'reasonable' "? *Kyllo* itself accepted this point, and it is to that issue we now turn.

Technologically Enhanced Observation and Reasonable Expectations of Privacy

The *Kyllo* majority recognized that "the *Katz* test—whether the individual has an expectation of privacy that society is prepared to recognize as reasonable—has often been criticized as circular, and hence subjective and unpredictable."[71] Yet, the Court continued, at least "in the case of the search of the interior of homes—the prototypical and hence most commonly litigated area of protected privacy—there is a ready criterion, with roots deep in the common law, of the minimal expectation of privacy that exists, and that is acknowledged to be reasonable."[72] From this premise the majority reached its holding that enhanced surveillance, relying on technology that is not in general public use and that detects more detail than any lawful naked eye observation could have, is a search. "This," claimed the Court, "assures preservation of that degree of privacy against government that existed when the Fourth Amendment was adopted."[73]

Thus, the Court grounded its analysis of privacy expectations vis-à-vis enhanced home surveillance on historical assumptions. To the extent the Court believed history also supported the general public use and naked eye exceptions to its holding, however, it may well be wrong. In any event, if the scope of the Fourth Amendment as applied to technological surveillance depends on expectations "society is prepared to recognize as 'reasonable,' " as both *Kyllo* and this book assume, we ought to consult more recent sources than attitudes that predated the invention of flashlights and binoculars by more than a century (and most other technological surveillance techniques by almost two centuries). Modern law and empirical work suggest that society is not prepared to recognize either exception.

As far as history is concerned, there is not much to go on. The *Kyllo* majority quotes the famous statement from the seminal English case *Entick v. Carrington*[74] that "the eye cannot by the laws of England be guilty of a trespass."[75] Although that statement is irrefutably true, given that the common law of trespass required a physical intrusion, it does not answer the historical question posed in *Kyllo*, which is whether naked eye or nominally enhanced viewing of the home violated colonial notions of privacy. The one Supreme Court case that directly addressed this issue, decided in 1948, appeared to conclude that it did. In *McDonald v. United States,*[76] a government agent stood on a chair to look into McDonald's room through the door transom. In finding that this action was a search, the Court dismissed the argument, based on *Entick*, that "the eye cannot commit the trespass condemned by the Fourth Amendment." Despite the fact that trespass doctrine still governed Fourth Amendment jurisprudence, the Court stated that it would not "stop to examine [*Entick's*] syllogism for flaws" but instead would simply "reject the result" that *Entick*'s formulation would have required in *McDonald*.[77]

Other than the quote from *Entick*, the significance of which *McDonald* clearly undermined, *Kyllo* provides nothing in support of its view that eighteenth-century Americans were unfazed when strangers spied into their homes from a public vantage point. In contrast, we do know that the drafters of the Fourth Amendment were obsessed with protecting the security of the house. As John Adams put it,

> An Englishmans [*sic*] dwelling House is his Castle. The Law has erected a Fortification round it—and as every Man is Party to the Law, i.e. the Law is a Covenant of every Member of society with every other Member, therefore every Member of Society has entered into a solemn Covenant with every other that he shall enjoy in his own dwelling House as compleat a security, safety and Peace and Tranquility as if it was surrounded with Walls of Brass, with Ramparts and Palisades and defended with a Garrison and Artillery.[78]

Thomas Davies's comprehensive treatment of Fourth Amendment history confirms that at the time the Constitution was drafted, the law provided that "except for extraordinary circumstances, an officer could not justify 'breaking' (that is, opening) the outer door of a house unless he acted pursuant to a judicial warrant."[79] Further, as Professor Davies points out, "breaking" constituted virtually any interference with the home, including something as slight as "lifting up the latch."[80] If moving a latch was a search requiring a warrant in colonial times, peering into a window could easily have been considered one as well.

Substantiating that conjecture is the fact that civil lawsuits involving voyeurs were heard in New England as early as the seventeenth century.[81] Further, several American and English cases in the eighteenth century and the first half of the nineteenth century permitted criminal prosecutions for eavesdropping from a vantage point outside the home.[82] Although technically these prosecutions focused on "listening toms" rather than "peeping toms," at least one of them involved a defendant who also "was proved to have watched at the window of the chamber of the prosecutrix;" the claim was upheld because "no man has a right . . . to pry into your secrecy in your own house."[83] In any event, by the end of the nineteenth century, civil and criminal trespass law in leading jurisdictions clearly prohibited window peering.[84] As one decision in 1897 opined, "we cannot conceive of any conduct much more indecent and insulting than for a stranger to be peeking into the windows of an occupied, lighted residence, and especially at the hours of night when people usually retire."[85]

More important, this notion retains viability today. At least twenty-five states have statutes that criminalize looking into the home, under labels such as "voyeurism," "criminal surveillance," "criminal trespass," or simply "disorderly conduct."[86] Convictions under such laws, some of them quite recent, have often been based simply on evidence that the defendant was seen peering into a window, with intent to invade privacy inferred from the conduct.[87] Tort case law similarly indicates that "spying into windows of a home" can lead to compensable injury for invasion of privacy or the tort of intrusion.[88] These laws send the message that society is not prepared to accept unjustified spying on a residence.

Most of the criminal laws prohibiting voyeurism require trespass as an element of the offense.[89] But some do not. For instance, in Louisiana a peeping tom is defined as "one who peeps through windows or doors, or other like places, situated on *or about* the premises of another for the purpose of spying upon or invading the privacy of persons spied upon without the consent of the persons spied upon."[90] As the statute then makes clear, "it is not a necessary element of this offense that the 'Peeping Tom' be upon the premises of the person being spied upon."[91] At least five other states have similar statutes,[92] and several other jurisdictions construe their laws to cover nontrespassory surveillance[93] or define trespass very loosely.[94] Thus, in these states, naked eye viewing that does not involve physical intrusion into constitutionally protected areas can be a crime.

Even in states that require clear proof of trespass for a peeping tom violation, the kind of viewing *Kyllo* places outside the ambit of the Fourth Amendment might be a crime because many courts refuse to designate curtilage a "constitutionally protected area"[95] (a stance with which at least one member of the Supreme Court agrees).[96] In these jurisdictions, voyeurism by a person situated in the curtilage would not implicate the Fourth Amendment as construed in *Kyllo*. But it would still be a crime in trespass states, because curtilage is private property. Further, most of the peeping tom statutes that require trespass do not contemplate the possibility of home viewing using enhancement devices that obviate such an intrusion; the one statute that clearly does (California's) eliminates the trespass element in this situation.[97] This suggests that when states begin to focus on surveillance using enhancement equipment, the trespass requirement will go by the wayside.

Finally, there is some empirical evidence suggesting that society considers home surveillance using enhancement devices to be more intrusive than the Supreme Court seems to think. In the study that I conducted with

Professor Schumacher (described in chapter 2), the responses of our 217 subjects, averaged together, provided a hierarchy of intrusiveness, ranging from looking through foliage in a public park (R = 1) to a body cavity search (R = 50).[98] Most interesting for present purposes were the rankings assigned to the two scenarios that most closely relate to the current discussion—flying four hundred yards above a backyard in a helicopter (R = 10), and using binoculars to watch a person in a front yard (R = 33). The flyover was ranked roughly the same as two scenarios involving roadblocks (R = 9; R = 14), an action that the courts have held implicates the Fourth Amendment and that sometimes requires individualized suspicion.[99] Even more relevant, the scenario involving binocular surveillance of the front yard was ranked at roughly the same level of intrusiveness as examination of a car trunk (R = 29), a footlocker in a car (R = 32), and a garage (R = 37), all actions the courts consider to be searches requiring probable cause.[100] Although not included as a scenario in the study, the use of binoculars to look into a house would likely have been ranked as even more intrusive, and unenhanced spying on the home interior would probably have also been ranked as fairly intrusive, at least at the same level as binocular viewing of a front yard.

Thus, evidence from history, positive law, and social science casts significant doubt on *Kyllo*'s apparent conclusion that societal mores concerning privacy are not transgressed by suspicionless home surveillance carried out with devices that are in general public use or that can see what the naked eye could see from a lawful vantage point. This conclusion, especially when combined with the inscrutability of the general use and naked eye doctrines discussed earlier, argues for a different holding in *Kyllo*: peering into the home by government officials, at least when it relies on enhancement devices, should always be considered a Fourth Amendment search. The next section explores how this notion can be implemented.

III. Two Post-*Kyllo* Proposals

A rule that all technologically enhanced home surveillance is a search not only reflects society's expectations of privacy—whether defined historically or by today's standards—but also can be easily reconciled with the language of the Fourth Amendment. As noted in chapter 2, to "search" means "to look into or over carefully or thoroughly in an effort to find or discover something." The Fourth Amendment prohibits unreasonable searches of houses. Thus, as many others have pointed out (and even *Kyllo* intimated),[101] it does not stretch the Fourth Amendment in the slightest to say it is implicated when police look carefully or thoroughly for something inside a house, even when doing so does not involve a physical trespass or intrusion.

If that were the rule, then under current Fourth Amendment jurisprudence all governmental peering into houses—even naked eye viewing—would require probable cause, as well as a warrant in nonexigent circumstances. The obvious protest against this interpretation is that it would seriously hamper police investigation. Police with suspicion short of probable cause to believe that criminal activity is taking place inside a home would be unable to verify their suspicion through observation, either with or without a warrant. Indeed, a cynic might claim that it is this concern, not history or assessments of society's privacy expectations, that best explains *Kyllo*'s general public use and naked eye exceptions.

The regulatory approach proposed in chapter 2, however, would allow police the benefit of their observations, inadvertent and otherwise, without sacrificing individual privacy interests. Recall that under the proportionality principle, although "search" is broadly construed under this proposal, so too is "probable cause" (to mean "the cause that makes probable the reasonableness of the intrusion occasioned by a given search or seizure"). Thus defined, peering into the home interior might not always require the quantum of certainty associated with physical searches of the home. The full implications of this notion are discussed below.

Also discussed below is a quite different way of addressing the problems raised by *Kyllo*, patterned on Title III's prohibition of warrantless electronic communications surveillance. Analogous legislation banning particular forms of enhanced visual surveillance could in effect nullify both the general public use and naked eye exceptions.

The Proportionality Principle and Home Surveillance

Here is the first sentence of a twenty-first-century news story: "When Sgt. John Shupe went looking for a serial thief last month, he packed his car with the tools of his trade: a night-vision telescope, high-resolution binoculars, a camcorder and a shotgun."[102] The story goes on to note that Shupe's team had carried out more than 400 surveillance operations in the past year, which led to 127 arrests, although it does not describe how the various enhancement devices Shupe carries were employed. If Shupe had used any of these items to peer randomly into homes from his car, on the off chance he would spy the serial thief, would he be violating the Fourth Amendment? Very possibly not, after *Kyllo*. The camcorder and binoculars could easily be considered items that are in general public use, and the scope might be as well. Even if they are not, any activities that Shupe sees while using them that might also have been seen by the casual observer on the sidewalk could well be covered by the naked eye exception. A final resolution of these matters would depend on which definition of general public use is adopted and how easily naked eye viewing from a lawful vantage could be hypothesized.

Now consider another story, this one a description of the pre-*Kyllo* case of *United States v. Wright.*[103] At 4:20 p.m., police located the chassis of a stolen car under circumstances indicating that it had been stripped in that vicinity. During a systematic sweep of the surrounding area, they found nuts and bolts, as well as red rags similar to those found next to the car's carcass, in front of a three-car garage facing an alley. The sliding doors of the garage, although locked, were not completely closed because of the way they were constructed and their age. Officer Huffstutler shined a flashlight through the door gap to see the garage interior, where he observed parts that had been removed from the stolen car. The majority held that use of the flashlight was not a search, while the dissent emphasized that the garage doors were locked and stated, "certainly a flashlight is not standard equipment for 'any curious passerby,' particularly in the daytime."[104]

The actions of Officer Huffstutler, like Sergeant Shupe's hypothesized enhanced spying, are not easily characterized under *Kyllo*. On one hand, if flashlights are in general public use, which is the case under most definitions of that term, then the majority's holding seems to be more consistent with *Kyllo*. On the other hand, if one takes the empirical, general-use-for-a-particular-purpose approach adopted by the dissent, then perhaps the officer's actions did constitute a search. And there is even a third possibility: the inside of the garage was only "relatively dark" according to the court (meaning the flashlight was useful but not absolutely necessary), and the officer was kneeling on public property when he peered inside, so perhaps the naked eye exception would apply here.

Under the proportionality approach, the analysis of Shupe's and Huffstutler's actions would be both easier and more coherent. First, Shupe's surveillance of home interiors and Huffstutler's exploration of the garage would clearly be searches, because in both cases police were looking for evidence. Whether these searches were valid under the Fourth Amendment would depend on the level of justification and the level of intrusion. If Shupe randomly peered into houses "looking for something," then he would be violating the Fourth Amendment, because his suspicion is too minimal for even a slight intrusion into the home. The result would be different, however, if he is merely using his binoculars or night scope to scan rooftops, yards, and house exteriors for suspicious movement in a neighborhood thought to be a target of the serial thief; further, if he spies any such movement he should be able to focus on it long enough to ascertain its nature, even if viewing inside a window is involved. Similarly, Huffstutler's observation of the car parts and rags gave him sufficient cause, even if not probable cause, for a brief look at the interior of a garage with or without a flashlight (although the exigency principle would still require ex ante authorization for this act absent an emergency).

Under proportionality analysis, the ubiquity of the enhancement device the police use is irrelevant. So is any inquiry into whether the details observed through enhancement could have been viewed with the naked eye from a lawful vantage point. The only issues are the level of intrusion visited by the police action and the level of justification for it.

The two significant advantages of this approach should be apparent. First, it avoids the complications associated with the general public use and naked eye doctrines. Second, as pointed out in chapter 2, it avoids the strains placed on courts and the police by the rigid probable-cause-forever precept. Under the monolithic approach, courts are encouraged, as the majority was in *Wright*, to declare searches to be nonsearches. That result leaves a huge range of intrusive police actions completely unregulated by the Fourth Amendment, including, most probably, use of flashlights and binoculars to look inside homes. At the same time, under current rules no search, even a relatively unintrusive one, can take place unless police have full-blown probable cause. That result runs counter to legal reasoning in a number of other constitutional and nonconstitutional domains, where the required justification need be proportionate only to the impact of the government intervention.

The usual criticism of the proportionality idea—that it converts the Fourth Amendment into "one immense Rorschach blot," to use Professor Amsterdam's phrase—was also countered in chapter 2. The only riposte that will be repeated here is the observation that, whatever they may say they are doing, courts routinely apply proportionality reasoning, even in connection with home searches. Consider first the Supreme Court's other enhancement device case involving the home, *United States v. Karo.*[105]

There the Court held that use of a beeper to detect movement inside a house is a search, but also indicated that a "court order" authorizing such a search might be valid even if based on reasonable suspicion rather than probable cause. Although not provided by the Court, the rationale for allowing a lower level of suspicion could easily be that a beeper does not reveal the detail that direct visual observation does. As *Kyllo* held, the precise capacity of the device used is not relevant to whether a search occurs when the target is a house interior, but it might help define the level of justification necessary for such a search under proportionality analysis.[106]

The lower courts also routinely engage in proportionality analysis when analyzing home surveillance. For instance, in *Wright*, the majority gave as an alternative ground for its holding the fact that although the police may not have had probable cause, they had developed sufficient cause to look into a garage.[107] Similar holdings are found or implied in a number of other decisions.[108]

Kyllo does not necessarily reject the proportionality approach in the context of enhanced home surveillance. Both the general public use and naked eye doctrines could be characterized as dicta.[109] Or both doctrines might be defined so narrowly that they have no practical impact. For instance, if general public use were defined to apply only to technology used by the entire population to carry out the type of observation in question, it would have no application in connection with home surveillance. If the naked eye doctrine were defined to require clear proof that all the activities and items seen with the enhancement device could also have been seen with the naked eye from a public vantage point (e.g., sidewalks, but not curtilage or other areas abutting the home), then it too would have little purchase.

At the same time, following the suggestion in *Karo*, searches of houses (enhanced or not) that by their nature are not particularly intrusive could be justified on something less than probable cause as traditionally defined. In this regard it is fruitful to revisit the explicit *Kyllo* holding. The primitive thermal imager in that case detected only heat waves and could not tell the police the source of the temperature differential they observed; other information was necessary to convince them that the heat escaping from Kyllo's house came from halide lights used to grow marijuana.[110] It is true, as the majority pointed out, that thermal imaging, along with other information, might also tell government officials when the occupants are cooking or the "hour each night the lady of the house takes her daily sauna and bath";[111] thus, one should conclude, as Scalia did for the majority, that "in the home . . . all details are intimate details" and that use of the imager was a search. But that conclusion does not necessarily dictate that *probable cause* is needed to use devices that detect only heat waves and do not reveal their source.[112]

The same approach could be taken with respect to technological searches of persons and effects, two of the other three categories mentioned in the Fourth Amendment (the fourth category—papers—is the topic of chapters 6 and 7). The technology most relevant here is the type of detection device, described in chapter 1, that permits police to see "through" clothing and opaque containers. Generally probable cause should be required to use this type of device. Not only has the Court typically treated persons and effects as protectively as it has houses,[113] but the general public use and naked eye exceptions are unlikely to apply where persons and effects are involved, given the sophistication of the technology and the opaqueness of the targets.

However, both the Court's case law and proportionality analysis might dictate a different result for certain types of detection devices. To the extent a device detects *only* contraband (such as drugs or explosives) or *only* weapons (in jurisdictions where weapons concealment is a crime), then the Court has intimated that the Fourth Amendment does not apply. For instance, *Place v. United States* held that a dog sniff of luggage is not a search, in part on the assumption that the dog responds only to the presence of drugs,[114] and *Jacobsen v. United States* concluded that a test that detects only the presence of cocaine does not implicate the Fourth Amendment because it compromises "no legitimate interest."[115] Assuming that use of a detection device (1) does not require a seizure or is used only after a legitimate seizure, (2) does not harm the person or the contents of the container involved, and (3) is truly contraband specific or weapon specific, proportionality analysis might in effect reach the same conclusion, on the ground that, although a search, such an intrusion is trivial.

A Legislative Approach

As noted in chapter 1, federal legislation has regulated electronic communications surveillance since 1968, when Congress passed the Omnibus Crime Control and Safe Streets Act, which most courts designate simply Title III.[116] Similar federal legislation regulating enhanced visual surveillance—a sort of national "peeping techno-tom" law—might have much the same effect on *Kyllo*'s general public use and naked exceptions as the proportionality approach. Consider the following description of how Title III might serve as a model for that purpose.

Title III deals with interception of oral, wire, and electronic communications, but for present purposes the provisions regarding oral communication are most pertinent. Title III defines the latter type of communication as "any oral communication uttered by a person exhibiting an expectation that such communication is not subject to interception under circumstances justifying such expectation"[117] and defines "intercept" to mean "the aural or other acquisition of the contents of any . . . oral communication through the use of any electronic, mechanical, or other device."[118] It then prohibits all "intentional" interceptions of oral communications, so defined, unless they are judicially authorized or one of the parties to the communication consents to the interception.[119] Violations can lead not only to exclusion of evidence but to civil and criminal penalties.[120]

One important effect of these provisions is that they criminalize all nonconsensual electronic eavesdropping by civilians. Other parts of Title III reinforce this prohibition by banning the manufacture and sale of "any electronic, mechanical, or other device [that is] primarily useful for the purpose of the surreptitious interception of . . . oral . . . communications."[121] Although ordinary interception devices such as tape recorders are not covered by this provision, hidden recorders or microphones may be.[122]

With important modifications, these provisions can be applied in the visual surveillance context. First, just as unauthorized interceptions of oral communications are prohibited, the proposed statute would ban nonconsensual, warrantless "visual surveillance" of "private locations."[123] The latter term could be defined as "the interior of the home and all other areas in which activities are carried out or items possessed by people exhibiting an expectation that such activities or items are not subject to surveillance under circumstances justifying such an expectation." This definition would encompass car trunks, luggage, and areas underneath clothing as well as homes. "Visual surveillance" could be defined as "the viewing of activities or items in a private location using any electronic, mechanical, or other device." If that definition is viewed as too broad (it would include viewing private locations with eyeglasses as well as with cameras, thermal imagers, and detection devices, for instance), the phrase "that enhances normal (20/20) vision" could be appended to it. Any intentional visual surveillance, so defined, would be prohibited unless judicially authorized or at least one of the parties under surveillance consents to it.

Another aspect of the proposed statute would, like Title III, seek to limit the proliferation of surveillance devices. Unauthorized manufacture, sale, or possession of visual surveillance equipment that is "primarily useful for the purpose of the surreptitious visual surveillance of private locations" could be prohibited. Devices that could see images through walls and video cameras that are designed to be secreted in briefcases and clothing clearly fall in this category, while flashlights, binoculars, night scopes, and telescopes clearly do not. Devices such as thermal imagers and beepers are less easily categorized. Perhaps with respect to these types of devices, legislation could place limitations on their purchase and possession similar to those that exist with surreptitious listening devices.[124]

Because it bans warrantless, nonconsensual technological surveillance of "private locations," defined to include the interior of residences, this statute should render virtually irrelevant both the general public use and naked eye exceptions to the extent they allow suspicionless, covert technological surveillance of the home. In this regard it is worth noting that analogous exceptions under Title III have been rejected. For instance, although Congress amended Title III in 1986 to remove protection for conversations on cordless phones on the theory that they could be intercepted using "readily available technologies" such as an AM radio,[125] eight years later it reversed itself,[126] presumably for reasons similar to those advanced here against the general public use exception in visual surveillance cases. Courts have also found that electronically monitoring conversations that take place in private places violates Title III even when the conversations could also have been heard from an adjacent public area without eavesdropping equipment.[127] Parallel reasoning in the visual surveillance context would make the naked eye exception untenable. In other words, under Title III privacy does not disappear simply because the technology used to conduct surveillance is generally available or picks up conversations in private areas that could be heard with the naked ear.

The proposed statute would not, of course, "reverse" the part of *Kyllo* that adopts the general public use and naked eye exceptions, because they are interpretations of the Constitution. As a consequence, if the statute did not provide for an exclusionary remedy (such as occurs under Title III with respect to computer communications, for instance),[128] then evidence obtained when these exceptions apply, although observed in violation of the statute, could still be used in court. But even in this situation the statute would have an impact. Because the statute would prohibit covert civilian use of any technology—including commonly available devices such as flashlights and binoculars—to spy into homes, courts would be hard put to find that such items are in general public use for that purpose, whether they consider the issue empirically or as a matter of positive law. That position, in turn, should nullify *Kyllo*'s general public use exception (unless the Court insists on defining the exception in terms of general use for *any* purpose). Moreover, because the statute would prohibit civilian *purchase and possession* of technology made primarily for covert spying of private locations, that type of technology would never become "generally used."

The statute's effect on *Kyllo*'s naked eye exception would be more ambiguous. Although Congress could perhaps pass a national peeping tom statute,[129] the proposed legislation does not directly regulate unenhanced observation of home interiors. Thus, under the reasoning of *Kyllo*, the government might still be able to avail itself of the naked eye exception when its technological surveillance discerns only what such viewing would discern. However, courts might find that enhanced viewing of activities that would also have been visible to a naked eye observer are nonetheless, under the statute, "carried out . . . by people exhibiting an expectation that such activities . . . are not subject to surveillance under circumstances justifying such an expectation." If so, the naked eye exception would lose any moral force it might otherwise have had.

Conclusion

The drafters of the Fourth Amendment believed the house should be sacrosanct. *Kyllo* leaves that fundamental principle in doubt. Its general public use and naked eye exceptions to the general prohibition against enhanced visual observation of the home interior represent potentially huge loopholes in the Fourth Amendment's protection. Unless very narrowly defined, they are difficult to apply. More important, they would allow police to violate our reasonable expectations of privacy, whether defined by what we knowingly expose to the public, by history, by positive law, or by empirical investigation of societal mores.

The better approach is to designate all house surveillance a search, but modulate the cause necessary to carry it out. At the same time, the legislature should outlaw unauthorized use of technology to view the home, thereby ensuring that it never becomes routine. Otherwise, our most private sanctuary will become progressively less private.

CHAPTER FOUR

Public Privacy: Surveillance of Public Places and the Right to Anonymity

In London, police say that every worker or shopper is caught on at least 300 cameras every day. — *The Straits Times* (Singapore) (2001)

[In the United States] there are 29 million cameras videotaping people at airports, government buildings, offices, schools, stores and elsewhere, according to one widely cited estimate in the security industry. — *Wall Street Journal* (2004)

There was of course no way of knowing whether you were being watched at any given moment. — George Orwell, *1984* (1949)

If . . . dragnet type law enforcement practices should eventually occur, there will be time enough then to determine whether different constitutional principles may be applicable. — *United States v. Knotts* (1983)

The advent of sophisticated technology that allows the government to watch, zoom in on, track, and record the activities of anyone, anywhere in public, twenty-four hours a day, demands regulation. Yet to date no meaningful constraints on this type of surveillance exist. The constant drumbeat of the "war on crime," louder than ever since the terrorist attack on September 11, 2001, has drowned out calls for greater control over technological surveillance of the streets. This chapter argues that the Fourth Amendment requires courts to regulate such surveillance—in particular, camera surveillance of public activity—if the legislative and executive branches are unwilling to do so.

The primary obstacle to this agenda is the United States Supreme Court decision in *United States v. Knotts,*[1] which considered the Fourth Amendment's application to the practice of tracking a car's movements with an electronic beeper. There the Court held that "a person traveling in an automobile on public thoroughfares has no reasonable expectation of privacy in his movements from one place to another."[2] Even more significant, it concluded that the fact that such movements might be detected through use of a beeper rather than via visual surveillance "does not alter the situation."[3] If the Fourth Amendment is not implicated by technological surveillance of a car traveling on public thoroughfares, it is unlikely to apply to enhanced surveillance of a person walking the streets.

As the portion of *Knotts* highlighted at the outset of this chapter indicates, however, the Court did broach a caveat to its conclusion—perhaps a tiny one, but nonetheless one that is very pertinent today. Knotts had argued that beeper tracking should be considered a Fourth Amendment search because otherwise "twenty-four hour surveillance of any citizen of this country will be possible, without judicial knowledge or supervision."[4] Although the Court considered this observation irrelevant to the case at hand, where the beeper had been used merely to relocate the receptacle in which it had been placed after police lost visual contact,[5] the Court also acknowledged that the type of "dragnet" practices conjectured by Knotts might raise constitutional issues.[6]

That concession is important because in many urban and even some suburban areas today, full-time technological surveillance of the public is the norm. While tracking devices comprise one aspect of this surveillance, it is cameras, positioned on buildings and telephone poles, that pose the bigger threat in this regard. The traditionally grainy video image, accessible at the time it is captured only by the camera operator, is rapidly being replaced by digital technology that produces top-quality images available in real time to police and to others at remote locations, including command centers and patrol cars. Digitization allows much easier long-term storage than bulky videotape, thereby increasing the potential that images will be around longer and viewed by more people, and it also makes possible identification of those captured on camera through computer-based matching programs that use biometric technology.[7] Most important, the vast expansion of camera networks, most advanced in the United Kingdom but occurring in parts of this country as well, means that twenty-four-hour monitoring of public activities is now possible in many urban areas. Dragnet surveillance is upon us.

The Court's unwillingness in *Knotts* to announce definitively that all public surveillance is unregulated by the Constitution may reflect an intuition that at some point this type of surveillance amounts to a serious infringement of reasonable expectations of privacy. If so, the Court's hesitancy in implementing this intuition probably stems not only from traditional judicial parsimony but also from the Court's perplexity over how one can possess "privacy" in public. When one's every movement is readily observable by others, how can one expect constitutional protection of those movements?

This chapter answers that question from a number of perspectives, summed up in the notion that we all possess a right to anonymity, even in public. Continuous, repeated, or recorded government surveillance of innocent public activities that are not meant for public consumption is neither expected nor to be condoned, for it ignores the fundamental fact that we express private thoughts through conduct as well as through words. The Fourth Amendment should be construed to recognize the right to public anonymity as a part of the privacy expectations that, to use the Supreme Court's expression, "society is prepared to recognize as 'reasonable.' "

The first section of this chapter sets the stage for this argument by describing in more detail the extent of camera surveillance and the deficiencies in the way legislatures and courts have reacted to it. The second and third sections develop the basis for the right to public anonymity. They draw from a number of different commentators and court decisions, as well as from an empirical study that demonstrates the extent to which ordinary citizens value the ability to walk and drive the streets without having to contend with constant technological monitoring. Chapter 5 then explores the implications of the right to anonymity.

I. Camera Surveillance of the Public Now and in the Near Future

The government uses cameras to watch us in all sorts of venues, ranging from private stores to public restrooms, from government-owned buildings to public streets, from traffic intersections and parking lots to traffic stops by state troopers. This book will focus on government camera surveillance of pedestrians in public streets, as distinguished from video monitoring of building interiors and motorist stops. Thus, this chapter's use of the phrase "public camera surveillance" and its commonly accepted abbreviation, "CCTV"—for closed-circuit television—will refer only to surveillance of public streets, parks, and the like. Even when defined in this narrow sense, public surveillance using camera technology is increasing at an exponential rate. As in other areas of technological development, the law has not kept up.

The Surveillance Dragnet

The future has arrived in Washington, D.C., in the wake of the terrorist attacks of September 11. Hundreds of government cameras are trained on streets, subways, school hallways, and federal facilities, in a project that "makes Washington the first U.S. city to be able to peer across wide stretches of the city and to create a digital record of images."[8] State-of-the-art cameras allow operators to take advantage of "satellite-based optics" that enable them to see in the dark, capture words on a printed page from hundreds of feet away, and peer into buildings. Numerous private cameras are also added into the mix. In 2002, the head of the project stated, "I don't think there's really a limit on the feeds [the system] can take"; further, he noted that the system has the "capability to tap into not only video but databases and systems across the region"[9] and could expand into schools, businesses, and suburban neighborhoods.[10] All this is accomplished through a $7 million central control facility, which relays the feeds to nearly one thousand squad cars.[11]

Washington's cameras are supposedly activated only during major events and emergencies, and recordings are kept for only ten days. But pressure is building to monitor the devices 24/7.[12] And other cities, bolstered by tens of millions of federal dollars, are not so hesitant about using their cameras. By the end of 2006 Chicago had networked more than 2,200 video cameras—at a cost of more than $8 million in federal and municipal funds—that are turned on night and day, every day of the week. Many of the cameras are hidden, and all are patched into the city's $43 million operations center, so that a dispatcher can send video images from the camera located closest to the scene of a reported incident.[13] Baltimore's system is also running continuously and is linked to cameras in four surrounding counties.[14]

The camera systems in Washington, Chicago, and Baltimore are among the most extensive and sophisticated, but many other American cities have installed camera complexes that are far from antiquated. For instance, Newark, Tampa, Virginia Beach, and Memphis all have cameras, ranging in number from six to seventy-two, that cover large areas of public real estate and that can rotate 360 degrees, pan and tilt, and zoom in on subjects.[15] In 2001, Tampa added several dozen cameras equipped with face recognition technology that purportedly matched captured faces with criminal arrest records (although the city discontinued the program when it failed to produce any arrests).[16]

Many smaller cities and towns are following suit in one way or another. Cicero, Illinois (population 83,000), Newport, Rhode Island (86,000), and St. Bernard Parish, Louisiana (66,000), have each spent well over $100,000 installing camera systems since 2004.[17] A 2001 study by the International Association of Chiefs of Police found that 80 percent of the 207 responding American law enforcement agencies have deployed some sort of closed-circuit television and that another 10 percent will soon do so.[18] Much of this technology is "in-car" video designed to record police detention activities, or is placed at traffic intersections or in government buildings. But about half the agencies surveyed in the study use cameras in high crime areas, 25 percent use them on streets, and 15 percent use them in parks.[19] Even small towns have set up cameras for this purpose. An informal survey conducted in 2006 found that seventeen small police departments (with fewer than one hundred officers) have a surveillance system or plan to establish one soon.[20] It should also be noted that some traffic camera networks, although primarily designed to photograph the license plates of speeders, can peer inside a vehicle, at areas outside the intersection, and even into homes and offices alongside the targeted thoroughfares.[21]

All these cameras are owned by the government, although in some locales they are operated by "volunteers" from the community.[22] In the private sphere, camera use is even more widespread. A nationwide survey of a variety of companies, taken more than ten years ago, found that 75 percent use CCTV surveillance.[23] That fact becomes important even if the focus is solely state action, given the above-mentioned capacity to link these cameras to government command centers.

When it comes to government-operated camera surveillance, however, the United States can't hold a candle to the United Kingdom, the champion of CCTV. Well over eight hundred public video surveillance programs operate locally in the United Kingdom, involving between three and four million cameras and creating more video images per capita than any other country in the world.[24] Between 200,000 and 400,000 of these cameras monitor public areas;[25] many are equipped with zoom lenses that can read the wording on a cigarette packet at one hundred yards and bring nighttime images up to daylight level.[26] And the installation of cameras is likely to continue unabated. Researcher Clive Norris concludes that "in the first decade of the new millennium, when average Britons leave their homes what will be remarkable is if their presence is not seen, their behavior not monitored and their movements not recorded by the omni-presence of the cameras, CCTV operators, and video recorders."[27] Most of these programs are jointly operated and managed by law enforcement and the private sector. Almost all are linked to police stations, but quite a few are also monitored by private security guards.[28] Many other European countries have similar systems.[29]

Today, these cameras are operated primarily by people. But the camera systems of the not-so-distant future will be much more automated. Motion detection systems will be able to discern when movements are out of the ordinary and then alert human assessors, who are thereby spared sifting through mountains of data.[30] License plate recognition systems, already in operation in London and some other parts of the United Kingdom, will be able to identify cars that enter unauthorized areas or that move in the wrong direction, and automatically keep track of every car's movement.[31] Facial and "swagger" recognition systems, more sophisticated than the one used in Tampa, will trigger a signal when people with criminal records, outstanding warrants, or lack of authorization are spotted.[32] There is no technological reason why cameras could not also be equipped with "see-through" technology that can detect when an individual is carrying a gun.

The Efficacy of CCTV

The huge investment in CCTV technology here and abroad is based on two premises. The first assumption, of course, is that it enhances public safety. The second is that it does so less expensively than any equally effective alternative. Both premises are subject to some doubt.

Reports abound of prodigious camera-induced drops in street crimes, in the 50–70 percent range.[33] But these accounts are of questionable accuracy, at least when they purport to describe crime reduction caused by *street-based* CCTV.[34] One commentary on the reports about the United Kingdom's CCTV system describes the glowing statistics as "post hoc shoestring efforts by the untrained and self-interested practitioner."[35] More neutral analysis of the efficacy of public surveillance paints a different picture. A meta-review of thirteen of the better-conducted studies carried out in the United Kingdom through 2000 concluded that "the criminological evidence as to CCTV's effectiveness in reducing crime does not support the almost exponential increase in cameras on British streets as a crime prevention measure."[36] An even more recent meta-analysis of the twenty-two most carefully conducted studies in the United Kingdom and North America indicated that while half of the studies found a "desirable effect on crime," five found an "undesirable" effect, and six found no effect or an uncertain effect on crime; ultimately, "the average overall reduction in crime was a rather small four per cent."[37] Similarly, a multisite study of camera surveillance in Australia completed in 2006 found that CCTV had "no significant impact" on crime rates, whether the crimes were against person or property, although it also concluded that CCTV might be "effective at detecting violent offending and/or may result in increased reporting" of such activity.[38]

A more specific example of such research comes from Glasgow, one of the first major cities to adopt CCTV. There, a three-year study conducted by criminologists found that although crime was reduced in "certain categories, . . . there was no evidence to suggest that the cameras had reduced crime overall," and "the cameras appeared to have little effect on clear up rates for crimes and offences."[39] Glasgow citizens also reported feeling *less* safe in the city center, perhaps because the cameras generated publicity about crime in downtown areas.[40] Anecdotal statistics from the more recent past are equally disappointing. In London, where cameras abound, even street robberies—the crime CCTV is supposed to be best at deterring—increased in 2002.[41] In Sydney, a relatively new camera system produced only one arrest every 160 days.[42]

American cities have had similar experiences. Early systems set up in five cities—Hoboken, New Jersey; Mount Vernon, New York; Miami; Charleston; and Detroit—were discontinued because they were not cost effective.[43] In the mid-1990s, cameras in Times Square were dismantled after producing fewer than ten arrests in twenty-two months.[44] These failures might be attributed, at least in part, to the primitiveness of the technology used. However, Oakland, California, more recently ended its three-year experiment using high-definition cameras—able to read a flyer hundreds of yards away and a license plate more than a mile away—because it had no "conclusive way to establish that the presence of video surveillance cameras resulted in the prevention or reduction of crime."[45] As of March 2006, the worst offense captured on Washington, D.C.'s sophisticated camera system was a car break-in, and that was in 2001.[46] "Mostly people drinking beer in public, or popping pills" is how one camera monitor describes the criminal incidents viewed by cameras in Baltimore.[47]

There are many reasons why cameras might not be effective at reducing crime in the areas on which they are trained. Consider the three ways cameras can, in theory, be useful: (1) they might help spot incipient crime that can be prevented, or at least solved, through immediate action; (2) they might create a record of crime that can be used in identifying and convicting perpetrators at some later time; and (3) they might deter crime. In each of these three areas, obstacles to smooth functioning exist.

The ability of cameras to help nab perpetrators at the time of their crime or prevent crime by those about to carry it out is circumscribed by a number of factors. Camera operators may not observe the conduct because the cameras have been destroyed or tampered with (as one detective said, gang members "break them, . . . turn them . . . shoot them up.").[48] Bad lighting or obstacles also often prevent good viewing; one British official admitted, for instance, that despite all the cameras in his country, "there are hundreds of thousands of nooks and crannies left" and that criminals "target[ ] luxury cars on the move so that any view the cameras gets of them is fleeting at best" or conceal "their street muggings by grabbing their targets in a clinch that, on CCTV, looks like nothing more than a romantic hug."[49] Even when an event is in full view, it may not be observed; operators get distracted or bored, or are simply unable to recognize what is happening in ambiguous situations.[50] If operators do see something suspicious, their distance from the scene sometimes makes them overcautious in concluding a crime is occurring.[51] And even when incipient crime is clearly identified, police will not necessarily be deployed. A dearth of sufficiently proximate officers (created in part by the belief that fewer police are needed when cameras are present),[52] lack of or poor communication between the control room and those in the street,[53] and even police fear of being caught on camera and having their actions misinterpreted can limit law enforcement response.[54] All these problems have their analogs in systems that are more fully automated. Alarms may not sound because of technological flaws,[55] or deployments may not occur because of human ones.

Attempts to memorialize the crime and the perpetrator on tape can also run into difficulty. Sometimes tapes are destroyed before authorities realize they may be helpful in solving crime.[56] Nor does retention of the tapes guarantee identification. Recordings are sometimes of poor quality[57] (although, as noted earlier, digitalization has gone a long way toward rectifying this problem), images caught on tape are always subject to interpretation (think of the Rodney King video),[58] and perpetrators are hard to identify even with good images (with some research finding that matching unfamiliar faces is "highly error-prone" even when carried out by experienced law enforcement agents).[59] Even if tapes are preserved and human error is set aside, obtaining the relevant frames can consume days of effort by the police.[60]

Finally, cameras cannot be effective deterrents if their presence is not made known, which apparently is often the case.[61] And even when the cameras' presence is conspicuous, certain types of offenders are too preoccupied or dense to notice, or are oblivious (as with rowdy revelers)[62] or uncaring (as with nighttime prowlers who wear masks, wigs, or other disguises).[63] A 1995 study reported that criminals believe the presence of cameras is the least of their concerns in considering whether to rob businesses.[64] Also of note is the unintended consequence of reducing surveillance by citizens, who assume that the cameras will do the job.[65]

Findings that crime has dropped in areas exposed to cameras must also be tempered by two facts. In some studies, part of the crime reduction was undoubtedly a result of other factors, including additional crime control measures undertaken at the time the cameras were installed and decreasing crime rates overall.[66] Second, many of these studies did not take into account the possibility that any crime that surveillance does deter is simply pushed into an area that does not have cameras.[67]

These observations should not lead to the conclusion that public video surveillance has little or no impact on crime. For instance, cameras made identification of those who carried out the London bombings of July 7, 2005, much easier, although they did not, of course, prevent the carnage.[68] And although law enforcement statistics are probably inflated (on those few occasions when they exist),[69] it must be acknowledged that even more careful, privately conducted studies indicate that some cities experience a noticeable reduction in offense rates after camera installation. For instance, the town center of Airdrie, Scotland, experienced a 21 percent drop in crime over the two-year period after cameras were set up, with no obvious evidence of displacement and after factoring out other explanatory variables such as a drop in overall crime rates.[70] Newcastle experienced significant drops in particular crimes: 35 percent in criminal damage, 50 percent in motor vehicle theft, and 56 percent in burglary, compared to 25 percent, 39 percent, and 39 percent reductions for the same crimes in the control areas.[71] A third United Kingdom study found a 25 percent drop in crime sustained over a two-year period, with no displacement effects.[72] Although these figures are significantly lower than initial law enforcement claims,[73] they are nonetheless impressive.

When all the data are looked at closely, a fair conclusion is that well-positioned, sophisticated cameras run by competent staff might be able to reduce some types of street crime, particularly theft, by 10–25 percent in high crime areas, compared to similar public areas that have no cameras, with only a small displacement effect.[74] As noted earlier, the second question that must be answered by careful policymakers is whether this reduction is cost-effective. Could other alternatives, such as more patrols, better lighting, and greater community participation in law enforcement, achieve equal or better results at less cost?

That question will not be answered definitively here. Some information about the cost of CCTV can provide a useful starting point, however. In the United Kingdom, a number of local authorities have yearly operating budgets of well over $500,000 for camera systems that cover downtown areas.[75] The annual budget of each of the several hundred-camera systems in New York City housing projects in 2001 was approximately $850,000 just for staffing (i.e., not including the upfront costs of the cameras, their maintenance, new tapes, tape storage, and associated expenditures).[76]

Whether equally effective alternatives would be cheaper is harder to calculate.[77] But it can be noted that even a relatively successful CCTV system may not pay for itself. One study indicated that although good CCTV systems can make significant dents in shoplifting, the value of merchandise retained would not equal expenditures on such a system for nearly five years;[78] as one researcher noted, "it might be more rational to just accept the losses."[79] Where violent crime is concerned, that kind of reasoning is less palatable, and expensive surveillance systems might be endorsed if even a few such crimes would be prevented or detected.[80] Unfortunately, however, violent crimes are probably the most difficult offenses for cameras to prevent or deter, given the often spontaneous nature of the crimes.[81] Several studies from the United Kingdom suggest that putting more officers on the streets is at least as effective as a camera system.[82]

In sum, it is not clear that public camera surveillance is always a worthwhile investment from a public safety perspective. That conclusion is unlikely to slow the continued proliferation of such surveillance, however. "Common sense" judgments, which view the efficacy of camera systems as a foregone conclusion, are likely to dominate any debate on the matter.[83] Politicians will continue to point to cameras as a "silver bullet" method of crime prevention.[84] Recent terrorist attacks here and in Europe will only add to the pressure to provide protection through surveillance.[85] Although, as noted above, some cities have terminated CCTV programs that have failed to reduce crime, there is also the possibility that once the newer, more expensive systems are set up, inertia will prevent their disassembly even in the face of proven ineffectiveness. The primary question is not whether such systems will be installed or maintained, but whether and how their use will be regulated.

Current Legal Regulation of Public Camera Surveillance

Meaningful legal strictures on government use of public surveillance cameras in Great Britain, Canada, and the United States are nonexistent. Great Britain's Code of Practice sets out operating standards "but has no mechanism for accountability or enforcement."[86] Similarly, while governments in Ontario, British Columbia, and Alberta, Canada, have adopted very extensive guidelines governing camera and tape use, storage, training, and the like—all of which are framed in terms of what governments "must" or "should" do—ultimately they are merely precatory; no administrative, civil, or criminal sanctions attach if they are breached.[87] A few American cities have adopted these types of nonbinding rules as well, again none of them enforceable in court or through a citizen-driven grievance procedure.[88] In a 2000 meeting of the International Association of Chiefs of Police, relatively comprehensive model rules were drafted, but the premise of the meeting was that "voluntary guidelines" are sufficient.[89] A majority of jurisdictions don't even have those.[90]

A number of American jurisdictions do criminalize nonconsensual video surveillance of certain types of activities, but these provisions will rarely implicate government use of public cameras. Arizona's statute is typical. It classifies as a misdemeanor the filming or recording, without consent, of any person who is "urinating, defecating, dressing, undressing, nude or involved in sexual intercourse or sexual contact" in a bedroom or bathroom or any other area "where the person has a reasonable expectation of privacy."[91] Given its predicate examples (bedroom, bathroom), surveillance of most public areas is unlikely to be covered by this law. Several states do prohibit viewing "intimate" or "personal" areas (e.g., under a woman's dress) in a public space.[92] But none purport to regulate other types of video surveillance in public.[93]

A principal reason for the virtually unanimous resistance to a tougher stance on public video surveillance in the United States is the assumption that courts are not likely to find it inimical to the Constitution or any other established body of law. For reasons developed in the previous chapter, video surveillance of the home interior and similar areas is probably governed by the Fourth Amendment.[94] But all courts that have considered application of the Fourth Amendment to cameras aimed at public streets or other areas frequented by a large number of people have declared that such surveillance is not a search, on the ground that any expectation of privacy one might have in these areas is unreasonable.[95] A few courts have noted that particularly intrusive public surveillance might implicate the Fourth Amendment, but all have shied away from so holding.[96] Similarly, some courts have held that Title III, which governs electronic eavesdropping, applies (with some modifications) to video surveillance of the home and similarly private locations,[97] but none has held that it also applies to surveillance of public activities.

It is worth noting that no court has considered a Fourth Amendment challenge to a CCTV *system*, and that most of the decisions holding that the Fourth Amendment does not apply to shorter-term, spot surveillance have involved covert rather than overt camera use. But the bottom line is that legislatures have not enacted meaningful regulation of public video surveillance by the government, and the courts have been unwilling to nudge them in that direction. That should change.

II. The Right to Public Anonymity

> Suppose that the local police in a particular jurisdiction were to decide to station a police car at the entrance to the parking lot of a well-patronized bar from 5:30 p.m. to 7:30 p.m. every business day for the purpose of making a list of the license plates of cars that were driven in and parked in the lot during that time. . . . If we assume that the bar has the necessary liquor license to sell drinks, that nothing more is known about the individuals patronizing the bar than that they happen to drive into its parking lot at this hour, and that there are no other special circumstances present, I would guess that the great majority of people who might have the question posed to them would say that this is not a proper police function. . . . There would be an uneasiness, and I think a justified uneasiness, if those who patronized the bar felt that their names were being taken down and filed for future reference. . . . This ought not to be a governmental function when the facts are as extreme as I put them.[98]

These words were written by William Rehnquist, not long after he was appointed to the United States Supreme Court in 1972. He was right that overt police monitoring of the comings and goings of individuals for no apparent reason is not an appropriate government function; as he stated later in his article, the "interest in not having public activities observed and recorded may prevail in the absence of any governmental justification for the surveillance."[99] The only thing wrong about the passage set out above is that the hypothesized facts are not "extreme." They describe a practice that would be quite feasible and even routine with any video surveillance system that openly records public activity.

Rehnquist also asserted that the individual interest involved in this situation, although deserving of protection, is not "privacy," because the observed action "is not intended to be concealed or confidential and is not in fact concealed or confidential."[100] It is true that no particular trip to the bar is concealed. But it is also true that those who make trips to the bar think that their observers either will not know or care who they are, or will be acquaintances or other bar patrons readily distinguishable from impersonal government observers bent on collecting information. Those who patronize bars or any other establishment both expect, and normally can count on, concealment from the latter type of observation. If the "uneasy" reaction to which Rehnquist refers is not based on a sense of privacy invasion, it stems from something very close to it—a sense that one has what I call a right to public anonymity.

Anonymity is the state of being unnamed.[101] The right to public anonymity is the assurance that, when in public, one is presumptively nameless—unremarked, part of the undifferentiated crowd—as far as the government is concerned. The right is surrendered only when one does or says something that merits government attention, which most of the time must be something suggestive of criminal activity, although it might involve a noncriminal emergency or accident.

The association of public anonymity with privacy is not new. In his seminal study of privacy, Peter Westin years ago described anonymity as a "state of privacy" that "occurs when the individual is in public places or performing public acts but still seeks, and finds, freedom from identification and surveillance."[102] Westin continued:

> He may be riding a subway, attending a ball game, or walking the streets; he is among people and knows that he is being observed; but unless he is a well-known celebrity, he does not expect to be personally identified and held to the full rules of behavior and role that would operate if he were known to those observing him. In this state the individual is able to merge into the "situational landscape."[103]

While most would probably share the intuition of Rehnquist and Westin that we expect some degree of anonymity in public, the burden of this discussion is to establish a constitutional right to such anonymity. I do so from three perspectives. First, I show how indiscriminate technological public surveillance seriously undermines the way we would like our society to function, because of its effect on public anonymity. Second, I argue that a number of constitutional principles, while not explicitly recognizing a right to public anonymity, provide solid groundwork for it. Finally, I report the results of an empirical study suggesting that American citizens feel public camera surveillance by the government is more intrusive than a variety of other police actions that the Supreme Court has labeled a "search" or "seizure," a finding that bolsters the case for folding the right to anonymity into the Fourth Amendment's protections.

The Impact of Losing Public Anonymity

Anonymity in public promotes freedom of action and an open society. Lack of public anonymity promotes conformity and an oppressive society. These sentences summarize the conclusions of a host of thinkers about public privacy.

THE PANOPTICON ANALOGY. The antithesis of public anonymity is the Panopticon, a model prison first imagined by Jeremy Bentham.[104] The Panopticon is circular, with the prison cells and walkways placed around the perimeter and the guard station perched on top of a tower in the middle, an arrangement enabling a large number of prisoners to be watched by just a few guards.[105] In theory, every movement of every convict could be monitored in such a building.

But the genius of this construction is that the guards, who are hidden by venetian blinds, do not actually have to watch in order to enforce order. The mere knowledge that one could be observed converts every prisoner into his or her own warden. This latter observation is a key point of emphasis for Michel Foucault, the renowned philosopher and historian, who elaborated extensively on the modern implications of the Panopticon.[106] As he recognized, "[H]e who is subjected to a field of visibility, and who knows it, assumes responsibility for the constraints of power; . . . he becomes the principle of his own subjection."[107]

Of course, prisoners are subject to rigid rules of discipline, violation of which can result in serious punishment. "Self-subjection" might not work as well when those in charge of the surveillance do not have reprisal power analogous to prison officials. Foucault asserted, however, that modern society increasingly functions like a super Panopticon, one that "assures the automatic functioning of power" by rendering "its actual exercise unnecessay."[108] As both public and private entities pour more resources into methods of monitoring people and architecture that facilitates it, Foucault felt, ordinary citizens aware of this monitoring are likely to feel increasing pressure to conform to whatever norms the observers are perceived to endorse.[109]

For Foucault, this "panopticism" was not necessarily a bad thing, at least compared with other methods of exercising control. He described it as "a functional mechanism that . . . improves the exercise of power by making it lighter, more rapid, more effective" than the older, balder ways of ensuring appropriate conduct.[110] Through the "subtle coercion" of panopticism, people can be led to be more productive, efficient members of society.[111] In the workplace, hospital, or school, the types of situations Foucault had in mind, one can see some logic in this conclusion. In those locations, specific rules govern people's actions, rules that might be enforced most efficiently through surveillance.

To the extent such "subtle coercion" operates on those in the public byways, however, it can do serious damage to cherished values. To see why, consider first Justice Douglas's comments in *Papachristou v. Jacksonville* about public vitality in America:

> Walking and strolling and wandering . . . are historically part of the amenities of life as we have known them. . . . These unwritten amenities have been in part responsible for giving our people the feeling of independence and self-confidence, the feeling of creativity. These amenities have dignified the right of dissent and have honored the right to be nonconformists and the right to defy submissiveness. They have encouraged lives of high spirits rather than hushed, suffocating silence.[112]

Quoting Walt Whitman and Henry David Thoreau, among others, Douglas painted a picture of a society that thrives on free-spiritedness in public.[113]

Now consider, in contrast, some of the effects that Foucault ascribes to the "discipline" that he says comes from panopticism. He tellingly calls this discipline "an anti-nomadic technique."[114] Because it inhibits behavior, it "arrests or regulates movements and dissipates compact groupings of individuals wandering about the country in unpredictable ways. . . ."[115] It also can "neutralize the effects of counter-power that spring from [the multiple organizations in society] and which form a resistance to the power that wishes to dominate it: agitations, revolts, spontaneous organizations, coalitions—anything that may establish horizontal conjunctions."[116] These effects are inconsistent, to put it mildly, with Douglas's vision of the conditions that a democratic, open society wants to nurture in its public spaces.

THE EFFECTS OF BEING WATCHED. How, more specifically, does panopticism undermine public openness? Foucault does not answer this question in detail. Others have, in ways that are directly relevant to public camera surveillance. Shoshana Zuboff writes about the phenomenon of "anticipatory conformity" among persons who believe they are being watched.[117] Similarly, philosopher Jeffrey Reiman states that "when you know you are being observed, you naturally identify with the outside observer's viewpoint, and add that alongside your own viewpoint on your action. This double vision makes your act different, whether the act is making love or taking a drive."[118] These observations suggest that any number of individuals—ranging from political demonstrators[119] to couples in love and carefree teenagers[120]—could be inhibited by the knowledge that their actions may be captured on camera.

Double vision is even more likely when the surveillance involves not just observation but recording of one's activities. For then, Richard Wasserstrom notes, "no matter how innocent one's intentions and actions at any given moment . . . persons would think more carefully before they did things that would become part of the record. Life would to this degree become less spontaneous and more measured."[121] As Daniel Solove has noted, the behavioral impact of surveillance is heightened by the reasonable surmise that one's recorded actions are easily susceptible to aggregation and use by a faceless bureaucracy.[122] Nicolas Burbules similarly notes that "as people accept the inevitability of being observed and recorded, their habits change; they change." He goes on to assert that these changes are even more pervasive than we might think, because "people carry many of the attitudes and self-imposed restrictions of activity from the surveyed public into their private life."[123]

The stultifying effect of public surveillance has been noted by many others.[124] But spontaneity is not all that could be hindered by routine public surveillance. As Richard McAdams notes, "[T]he problem drinker who goes to an Alcoholics Anonymous meeting, the patient who drives to his psychiatrist's office, the homosexual who visits a gay bar, the spouse who has a rendezvous with another lover, the teenager or adult who skips school or work to go fishing, would all be exposed if someone constantly tracked their public movements."[125] The practice of seeking secret solace in parks and other public places may also be circumscribed.[126] None of these activities is illegal, but it is easy to imagine why those who engage in them might want to keep them secret.

In addition to its effect on behavior, CCTV might trigger a number of unsettling emotional consequences. Relying on the work of Erving Goffman, Jeffrey Rosen notes that "it's considered rude to stare at strangers whom you encounter in public."[127] Staring, whether it occurs on an elevator, on public transportation, or on the street, violates the rules of "civil inattention."[128] The cyclopsian gaze of the camera eye may be equally disquieting, and perhaps more so, given the anonymity of the viewer and the unavailability of normal countermeasures, such as staring back or requesting that the staring cease.

The small amount of social science research specifically aimed at assessing the impact of concerted surveillance tends to verify that these and other psychological and behavioral effects can occur. For instance, empirical investigations of the workplace—one of the contexts Foucault thought might *benefit* from panopticism—indicate that even there surveillance has a downside. Monitored employees are likely to feel less trusted, less motivated, less loyal, and more stressed than employees who are not subject to surveillance.[129] The extent to which these findings would be duplicated in the context of public surveillance is not clear.[130] But one could plausibly infer from them that many citizens on the street who are subject to camera surveillance will experience less confidence in their overall freedom to act, as well as somewhat diminished loyalty to a government that must watch its citizens' every public movement. Roger Clarke also calls attention to the latter possibility in his study of the effects of widespread surveillance. Among the many consequences of "dataveillance," as he calls it, are a prevailing climate of suspicion, an increase in adversarial relationships between citizens and government, and an increased tendency to opt out of the official level of society.[131]

To capture the core of these disparate observations, consider again Rehnquist's example of police observing patrons of a bar. The people entering the bar will feel less trusted and more anxious and may even stop going there. Or try another simple thought experiment. Virtually all of us, no matter how innocent, feel somewhat unnerved when a police car pulls up behind us. Imagine now being watched by an officer, at a discreet distance and without any other intrusion, every time you walk through certain streets. Say you want to run (to catch a bus, for a brief bit of exercise, or just for the hell of it). Will you? Or assume you want to obscure your face (because of the wind or a desire to avoid being seen by an officious acquaintance). How about hanging out on the street corner (waiting for friends or because you have nothing else to do)?

In all these scenarios, you will probably feel and perhaps act differently than when the officer is not there. Perhaps your hesitancy comes from uncertainty as to the officer's likely reaction or simply from a desire to appear completely law-abiding; the important point is that it exists. Government-run cameras are a less tangible presence than the ubiquitous cop, but they are better at recording your actions. A police officer in Liverpool may have said it best: a camera is like having a cop "on duty 24 hours a day, constantly taking notes."[132]

THE GOVERNMENT'S USE OF SURVEILLANCE. These inhibitory consequences can be produced simply by setting up a camera system. If the government acts on what the camera sees, those effects can be significantly enhanced. Of course, that is all to the good if the result is prevention of serious criminal behavior. But sometimes government uses surveillance to achieve more ambiguous ends. In the United Kingdom, many of the crimes "solved" through CCTV are very minor offenses that are highly subject to discriminatory prosecution, such as littering, urinating in public, traffic violations, drunkenness, loitering, failing to pay parking meters, and even underage smoking.[133] Indeed, camera use in publicly accessible malls in Britain triggers law enforcement interventions even when there is no infraction of the criminal law; rather, the decision is often based on "commercial considerations" that characterize certain people (beggars, street entertainers, and groups of youth) as "flawed consumers."[134] Research suggests that in other public areas as well, the impact of surveillance tends to be the straightforward exclusion of disfavored groups rather than apprehension or deterrence of criminals.[135]

Thus, Rosen concludes, CCTV's primary use in Great Britain today is not to thwart serious crime but "to enforce social conformity."[136] One consequence, he reports, is that the cameras are "far less popular among black men than among British men as a whole."[137] That should be no surprise to those familiar with the American experience with loitering laws, stop and frisk practices, and "aggressive patrolling."[138] Others view CCTV as one of the most powerful forces pushing toward the "purification" of city spaces and their destruction as a stage for the "celebration of difference" and disorder. The result is that public spaces are becoming less public.[139]

Government may also rely on cameras to observe (intimidate?) political activists. On several occasions between 2000 and 2002, Washington, D.C.'s street cameras were trained on individuals engaged in political demonstrations. In 2003, Milwaukee police videotaped protesters outside President George Bush's fundraisers. Recent evidence that the FBI has directed local law enforcement agencies to collect extensive information about the tactics, training, and organization of antiwar demonstrators suggests the various ways cameras and other methods of surveillance government can use to monitor noncriminal activity it doesn't like.[140]

Automated systems that do not depend on human operators have been hailed as a method of avoiding these biases.[141] But they do not necessarily eliminate racist and other undesirable tendencies, since discretion is still exercised once the alarm is triggered. Facial recognition systems that are based simply on whether a person has previously been labeled a shoplifter or car thief (sometimes erroneously)[142] are likely to exacerbate these tendencies. If one tries to remove the impact of human flaws through full automation, as with the motion detection systems described earlier, the result is even more disturbing. Such systems are based on rigid categorizations of behavior. As Norris notes, "[T]hey utilize no other logic than whatever is programmed into their software, and the end point of such processing is the creation of a binary system of classification: access is either accepted or denied; identity is either confirmed or rejected; behavior is either legitimate or illegitimate."[143]

The implications of these various considerations should not be overstated. Contrary to the dire predictions of some privacy advocates, the potential effects of public surveillance are not Orwellian in magnitude. A principal feature of the society depicted in *1984* was the ever-present telescreen that relayed citizens' words and conduct back to an omniscient "ministry."[144] But the dread that was rampant in Orwell's fictional Oceania resulted primarily from the perception that the government was obsessed with severely punishing amorphously defined "thoughtcrimes" and "facecrimes," often with death.[145] In the real world today, in contrast, the norms likely to assume importance because of camera surveillance come from the conscience of the mainstream and the business class, the imagination of pedestrians and the calculations of technicians, and they are more likely to result in exclusion from certain areas than any significant formal punishment.

At the same time, in a society that wants to promote freedom of action, camera surveillance—more specifically, concerted, overt public surveillance using cameras with recording capacity—is clearly not an unalloyed good, even if it does significantly reduce crime. People who know they are under government surveillance will act less spontaneously, more deliberately, less individualistically, and more conventionally. Conduct on the streets that is outside the mainstream, susceptible to suspicious interpretation, or merely conspicuous—even if perfectly harmless—will diminish and perhaps even be officially squelched. Some people subject to public camera surveillance, perhaps in particular those from minority groups, will feel significant anxiety and discomfort although innocent of any crime, and some may react with disdain for government, again despite and probably because of their innocence. Public camera surveillance undermines an open society because it circumscribes out-of-the-ordinary behavior and makes everyone—including the ordinary—more conscious of the government's presence, at least until behavior is suitably conformed and the cameras forgotten.[146] In short, CCTV accelerates the "disappearance of disappearance."[147]

The Constitution and Public Camera Surveillance

Do the potential effects of public camera surveillance on public anonymity raise constitutional concerns, or are they merely subconstitutional matters that policymakers can either take into account or dismiss at their discretion? Camera surveillance is certainly not as physically intrusive as an arrest or stop or as invasive as a search of houses or belongings, the paradigmatic government actions addressed by the Fourth Amendment. But its aggregate impact can be equally significant because it affects a much larger number of people. It also evokes a particularly powerful image, of a government that panoptically observes, records, and categorizes our every movement in public.

As Laurence Tribe has emphasized, the Constitution should be interpreted with the "constitutive dimension of government action" in mind.[148] We should think about the issues raised by public camera surveillance "in terms of what they say about who and what we are as a people and how they help to constitute us as a nation."[149] As it turns out, not just the Fourth Amendment but a number of other provisions in the Constitution are relevant to that endeavor.

FREEDOM OF SPEECH AND ASSOCIATION. The First Amendment guarantees freedom of speech and association. Recall Justice Douglas's words in *Papachristou* linking wandering and strolling with the right to dissent, nonconformity, and defiance of submissiveness. Building on that language, one might argue for a First Amendment right to be free of the inhibiting effects of camera surveillance in public unless the government can proffer some justification for it.

Under the Supreme Court's case law, however, neither the speech nor the association guarantees are likely to provide a basis for constitutional regulation of most public surveillance, at least when it is only visual. While conduct alone can be expressive, the type of conduct normally captured by cameras apparently does not fit in this category. As the Court stated in *City of Dallas v. Stanglin*, "[I]t is possible to find some kernel of expression in almost every activity a person undertakes—for example, walking down the street, or meeting one's friends at a shopping mall—but such a kernel is not sufficient to bring the activity within the protection of the First Amendment."[150] Similarly, government inhibition of association is generally not a violation of the First Amendment unless the group is engaged in some type of speech activity.[151]

However, if public conduct *is* expressive—for instance, a speech at a park rally—and public associations are speech related—such as joining the rally—then the First Amendment should be implicated by camera surveillance. That is because, as the previous section suggested, such surveillance can chill conduct even though the conduct takes place in public and is meant to be seen by others.

Admittedly, the Supreme Court rejected a similar claim in *Laird v. Tatum*.[152] There the plaintiffs contended that their antiwar activities were inhibited by knowledge that the army was constructing dossiers on those involved, allegedly as a means of averting potential civil disorder. Construing the question to be "whether the jurisdiction of a federal court may be invoked by a complainant who alleges that the exercise of his First Amendment rights is being chilled by the mere existence, without more, of a governmental investigative and data-gathering activity that is alleged to be broader in scope than is reasonably necessary for the accomplishment of a valid governmental purpose,"[153] the Court dismissed the case. According to the five-member majority, the plaintiffs had no standing because they failed to allege any specific, foreseeable harm, other than an inchoate fear that the information would somehow be used against them.[154]

The Court has since indicated, however, that a government action the sole effect of which is to chill speech is justiciable under some circumstances.[155] *Tatum* thus does not necessarily foreclose a First Amendment argument against camera surveillance. The latter method of data collection is, in any event, distinguishable from the surveillance in *Tatum*. The government's efforts in *Tatum* consisted of perusing published material and public records and surreptitiously attending meetings;[156] furthermore, the plaintiffs in *Tatum* alleged no specific acts by the army against them[157] and may not even have been "chilled" in carrying out their activities.[158] In short, *Tatum* did not involve overt surveillance. The conspicuous presence of cameras aimed at participants engaging in First Amendment activity, in contrast, is closer to the more confrontational inhibition of speech that has concerned the Court in cases where it has found violations of the First Amendment.[159] Although many lower courts have nonetheless been hostile to First Amendment claims directed at camera surveillance (at least when the surveillance consists solely of photography),[160] several have upheld standing claims when such surveillance targets or intimidates individuals or causes a fall-off in attendance or membership in an organization,[161] or when the results of the surveillance are released to non-law-enforcement entities.[162]

The chilling phenomenon has also long been recognized in other settings, particularly in labor cases involving suits under the National Labor Relations Act against employers who have photographed or videotaped employees engaging in authorized strikes and demonstrations. In *F.W. Woolworth Co.*,[163] a representative example, the National Labor Relations Board concluded that "absent proper justification, the photographing of employees engaged in protected concerted activities violates the Act [specifically, its provision prohibiting employer actions that have a "tendency to coerce"] because it has a tendency to intimidate."[164] More so than mere observation, "pictorial recordkeeping tends to create fear among employees of future reprisals."[165]

As this last statement indicates, these holdings are bound up with the notion that employers exercise power over employees, power that might seem more palpable than the influence government exerts over citizens on the public byways. But that fact does not distinguish the labor cases from the public surveillance context. By definition, employer reprisals against those who engage in "protected concerted activities" are prohibited; yet the law recognizes that regardless of its actual impact on the employee's labor status, the photography can have an intimidating effect on employees so engaged. Likewise, speech and association in public are protected activities that should not result in government reprisal. But, understandably, people might not believe that is so when they know or think government cameras will be trained on them if they participate: if the activities are protected, why does the government need cameras?

Another way that public camera surveillance trenches on First Amendment rights of speech and association is its facilitation of the government's ability to pierce the anonymity of those engaging in expressive conduct. The Court has declared that absent a significant government justification, a person who writes a pamphlet[166] or collects signatures for a petition[167] cannot be required to reveal his or her name. It has also held that membership lists of organizations need not be revealed.[168] As Justice Stevens stated in *McIntyre v. Ohio Elections Commission,* whether "the decision in favor of anonymity is motivated by fear of economic or official retaliation, by concern about social ostracism, or merely by a desire to preserve as much of one's privacy as possible . . . it is an aspect of freedom of speech protected by the First Amendment."[169]

People who engage in expressive conduct in public know they will be observed. But they may choose, like the pamphleteer or the petitioner, not to reveal their identity, for all sorts of reasons. Camera surveillance virtually nullifies that effort. Because the camera's recorded images are far better identifiers than an informer's memory, it vastly improves government efforts to link visages with names. Furthermore, as one commentator points out, "surveillance of a person's movements could, over time, reveal associational tendencies as thoroughly as a membership list."[170] These facts can only inhibit the public conduct of those who want to remain anonymous.

There is little doubt that public camera surveillance can infringe First Amendment values. When those values are implicated, government should have to justify the presence of the cameras on a meaningful law enforcement ground; indeed, even cases that reject First Amendment arguments against camera surveillance seem reluctant to do so in the absence of a legitimate government objective.[171] Again, however, that conclusion provides constitutional protection only for expressive conduct, a category that the Court has defined rather narrowly. Other case law broadens that protection considerably.

FREEDOM OF MOVEMENT AND REPOSE. Derived from the Due Process Clause, the right to travel is another fundamental right that might be compromised by public camera surveillance. As the Supreme Court stated nearly a century ago, "Undoubtedly the right of locomotion, the right to remove from one place to another according to inclination, is an attribute of personal liberty, and the right, ordinarily, of free transit from or through the territory of any state is a right secured by the 14th Amendment and by other provisions of the Constitution."[172] Fifty years later that sentiment was echoed in *Kent v. Dulles,*[173] a case that dealt with restrictions on travel overseas but used language relevant to domestic travel as well:

> Freedom of movement across frontiers in either direction, and inside frontiers as well, was a part of our heritage. Travel abroad, like travel within the country, may be necessary for a livelihood. It may be as close to the heart of the individual as the choice of what he eats, or wears, or reads. Freedom of movement is basic in our scheme of values. . . . Outside areas of plainly harmful conduct, every American is left to shape his own life as he thinks best, do what he pleases, go where he pleases.[174]

As this language suggests, the "right of locomotion" is not limited to expressive actions. In contrast to the First Amendment, this right is important for economic and social reasons as well as political ones. The *Kent* Court went on to state explicitly that "freedom of movement also has large social values," including support of activities "close to the core of personal life [such as] spending hours with old friends."[175] More recently the Court has reaffirmed the right to travel as a guarantee implicit in the Privileges and Immunities Clause of the Fourteenth Amendment.[176]

Closely related to the right to freedom of public movement is the right to repose, or stasis, in public. In *Chicago v. Morales,* a four-member plurality of the Court stated that "the freedom to loiter for innocent purposes is part of the 'liberty' protected by the Due Process Clause of the Fourteenth Amendment. . . . Indeed, it is apparent that an individual's decision to remain in a public place of his choice is as much a part of his liberty as the freedom of movement inside frontiers that is 'a part of our heritage,' or the right to move 'to whatsoever place one's own inclination may direct' identified in Blackstone's Commentaries."[177] The Court has been emphatic about striking down vagrancy statutes that trench on this right to repose.[178]

How might these interests in locomotion and stasis—the "freedom to walk, stroll, or loaf"[179]—be affected by the panoptic eye of the camera? Although no courts have directly addressed this issue, the few that have dealt with analogous facts are wary of camera use that affects these interests, at least when there is also proof of some animus. In *Goosen v. Walker,* for instance, a Florida court enjoined the defendant from further videotaping of his neighbors (with whom he had previously had altercations), concluding that his videotaping of them in their yard and adjoining areas, on two to four occasions over a four-month period, constituted "stalking."[180] In *State v. Baumann*, the court upheld an order that permanently enjoined thirty-two individuals from photographing or videotaping people entering and leaving an abortion clinic under circumstances that exhibited "an intent to harass, intimidate or interfere with any person seeking access to or departing from such facility."[181]

Even the media, normally left unrestrained by courts concerned about freedom of the press, can go too far. In *Wolfson v. Lewis,* for instance, the court held that "a persistent course of hounding [by reporters], even if conducted in a public or semi-public place, may nevertheless rise to the level of invasion of privacy based on intrusion upon seclusion."[182] It then issued an injunction against investigative news reporters who had repeatedly sought to videotape and eavesdrop on a business executive and his family in and outside their home and place of work.[183]

In *Goosen* the videotaping inhibited repose (in the targets' backyard), in *Baumann* it inhibited movement (to and from the abortion clinic), and in *Wolfson* it inhibited both (around the house and workplace and going to and from those locations). In all three, the videotaping was actionable. That suggests that public surveillance, even when targeting actions not protected by the First Amendment, can infringe interests in locomotion and stasis to a legally cognizable degree.

At the same time, all three courts required proof that those who wielded the cameras intended to harass. That type of motivation will usually be absent when government watches with public surveillance cameras. Using the terminology of these cases, to say that the government's camera surveillance of people walking the streets constitutes the malicious-sounding acts of "stalking," "intimidation or interference," or "a persistent course of hounding" will normally be an exaggeration.

A crucial fact about these three cases, however, is that the defendants were claiming a First Amendment right of their own—a right to videotape public events. Thus, the courts had to find a compelling justification—illegitimate harassment—for the injunctions they issued.[184] Unlike its citizens, the government does *not* have a First Amendment right to train cameras on the populace. Accordingly, an absence of ill will on the part of government agents who operate the cameras should not immunize them from scrutiny. Instead, the issue should be, straightforwardly, whether government camera surveillance trenches on the right to movement or repose.

It clearly does, for reasons stated in the first section of this chapter. People ogled by cameras may choose to walk rather than run, move on rather than loiter, or even avoid going where they would like to go altogether. While government surveillance may not amount to intentional stalking or hounding, it is not innocuous. Indeed, whatever its intent, it can have a similar effect to stalking, given its inhibition of public locomotion.

That conclusion does not dictate that such surveillance be prohibited, of course. It simply requires, again, that the government demonstrate a legitimate reason for its actions. As the Supreme Court has said, "[R]estrictions on the right to travel . . . may not be achieved by means which sweep unnecessarily broadly and thereby invade the area of protected freedoms."[185]

THE RIGHT TO PRIVACY. A third constitutional basis for regulating CCTV comes from the general right to privacy, which is found, depending on the decision announcing the right, in the penumbras of the First, Third, Fourth, and Fifth Amendments, the Fourteenth Amendment's Due Process Clause, or the Ninth Amendment's reservation of rights to the states.[186] The Supreme Court has relied on this right (which in the case law is often subsumed under a "due process right to liberty") in striking down laws banning abortion,[187] interracial marriage,[188] purchase and use of contraceptives,[189] and the like. As with the rights to freedom of movement and repose, the right to privacy is not limited to protection of expressive conduct.

There are at least two versions of the right to privacy, one focusing on protection of personhood and the second on freedom from normalization. The personhood version views the right to privacy as a means of ensuring that individuals are free to define themselves. It protects against state interference in decisions that are "central to the personal identities of those singled out."[190] The antinormalization version, in contrast, focuses on the extent to which the government action standardizes lifestyles.[191]

The manner in which public camera surveillance affects our ability to define ourselves has already been suggested, but observations from Andrew Taslitz flesh out the analysis. Privacy, Taslitz notes, enables us to present to others only the parts of ourselves that we want them to see.[192] That in turn enables us to put forth different versions of ourselves in different contexts, with those at the job seeing one side, those at home seeing another, and those at social events or athletic competitions seeing still another. Even in public, we expect privacy to play its role as a facilitator of self-definition. Taslitz quotes Michael Riesman's observation that "people may look, but they are expected to look at those parts that the owner of the exoself wants them to look at, at appropriate times and following certain procedures."[193] Ogling, staring, or merely paying more than fleeting attention to strangers in public is considered impolite and uncivil, because it crosses personal boundaries and requires us to reveal more of ourselves than courtesy dictates. Such conduct prevents us from retaining control over how we present ourselves.

Thus, Taslitz summarizes, "who looks at us, how, how long, and for what purposes matter."[194] On camera surveillance in particular, he concludes:

> [W]hen technology enables the government to stare with an ever-vigilant and suspicious eye, the boundaries of the self may partly dissolve, reconstructed in the image chosen by Leviathan. . . . Regulation [of this technology] preserves the idea of a diverse, noisy America, where citizens are free to get lost in the crowd and where their sense of self stems from their chosen affiliations and actions rather than from the all-seeing gaze of the state.[195]

As the last sentence suggests, because a substantial part of our personality is developed in public venues through rituals of our daily lives that occur outside the home and outside the family, cameras that stultify public conduct can stifle personality development. The Supreme Court itself has said that anonymity "safeguards the ability independently to define one's identity that is central to any concept of liberty."[196]

The second version of the right to privacy, championed by Jed Rubenfeld, pushes toward the same conclusion but from a different direction. Rubenfeld argues that the Court's privacy cases most directly protect "the fundamental freedom not to have one's life too totally determined by a progressively more normalizing state."[197] A prohibition on abortion and use of contraceptives is unconstitutional, he says, not because decisions about those issues are necessary to self-definition, but because together they force women to be mothers; a prohibition on interracial marriages is unconstitutional not because it infringes one's autonomy to do what one wants, but because it coerces people into having homogeneous children. The danger of such laws, Rubenfeld states, "is a particular kind of creeping totalitarianism, an unarmed occupation of individuals' lives. That is the danger of which Foucault as well as the right to privacy is warning us: a society standardized and normalized, in which lives are too substantially or too rigidly directed. That is the threat posed by state power in our century."[198]

Note in particular Rubenfeld's use of Foucault, who was concerned about the modern state's ability, "through expanded technologies and far more systematic methods of acculturation, . . . to watch over and shape our lives, to dispose and predispose us, and to inscribe into our lives and consciousnesses its particular designs."[199] Although Rubenfeld does not speak of government surveillance directly, his argument that the right to privacy has been and should be ranged against government actions that promote "normalization" has significant implications for that particular type of state action. As Simon Davies commented in describing the effect of CCTV and other forms of technological surveillance, "the society we are developing now . . . is a Brave New World dominated not so much by tyranny as by a deadening political and cultural phenomenon that Ralph Nader calls 'harmony ideology' [the coming together of opposing ideologies and beliefs into manufactured consensus]."[200] If CCTV contributes to that effect—and the literature linking panopticism and anticipatory conformity suggests it does—it impinges directly on the privacy right that Rubenfeld believes the Court's decisions establish, and should be regulated accordingly.

FREEDOM FROM UNREASONABLE SEARCHES AND SEIZURES. None of these arguments about a constitutional basis for regulating government camera surveillance rely directly on the Fourth Amendment. Surely if CCTV implicates the First Amendment, the due process rights to movement and repose, or the general right to privacy, it ought to implicate the Fourth Amendment as well. Yet the Supreme Court's case law construing the scope of that amendment leaves little room for such a position.

The first obstacle in this regard is *Katz* itself, which baldly stated that "what a person knowingly exposes to the public . . . is not a subject of Fourth Amendment protections." This was also the sentiment informing the Court's reasoning in *Knotts* when it held that use of a beeper to monitor movement on the public highway is not a search. Application of this formulation to CCTV is likely to produce the same result. One might argue that people do not always "know" that certain public conduct was exposed to the camera, but that strategy is unlikely to work under most circumstances. First, we are talking about overt, not covert, camera use, accompanied by signs announcing its presence. Second, recall from chapter 3 that according to the Court, the government need not show actual knowledge of surveillance to nullify Fourth Amendment protection.[201] All that need be shown is that the target *should* have known public exposure might occur; if it does, the Court has held, the individual assumes the risk of such exposure and loses Fourth Amendment protection.

That's not all. Time and again, as chapter 3 documented, the Court has emphasized the distinction between mere observation and physical intrusion.[202] Thus, according to *Ciraolo* and *Dow Chemical*, police observation from a public vantage point is not a search even if the area observed is the curtilage, traditionally considered to be part of the home. Indeed, even if the target is the home itself, the degree of physical intrusion plays an important role, as the naked eye exception announced in *Kyllo* demonstrates. Thus, to the extent CCTV merely replicates naked eye viewing from a public vantage point, it is unlikely to merit Fourth Amendment protection either.

Similarly, despite CCTV's inhibition of the right to movement, it is unlikely to amount to a Fourth Amendment seizure under the Court's cases. Such a seizure occurs when the government, "by means of physical force or show of authority, has in some way restrained the liberty of a citizen"[203] or at least when "a reasonable person [would not be] at liberty to ignore the police presence and go about his business."[204] Although the latter formulation could in theory encompass the effects of CCTV, which may well retard people's ability to go about their business, the Court has twice held that police do not effect a seizure if they conspicuously follow or chase an individual without bringing the individual to a stop.[205] Under this case law, it would be difficult to argue that monitoring an individual with a camera is a seizure.

But what about the fact that CCTV allows recording of one's public activity? It has been argued that even if we assume the risk that others will view our public conduct, we do not assume the risk that our public actions will be reduced to a photograph or film that can be "scrutinized indefinitely and disseminated to an unintended audience" and that "allows the viewer to discern details that would not have been apparent to a casual observer."[206] This argument too is plausible, but once again the Court's cases are very unhelpful as support. In *On Lee v. United States,* decided before *Katz*, the Supreme Court held that the Fourth Amendment is not implicated when the government overhears and records an individual's conversation with an informer through a body bug worn by the informer,[207] a holding it affirmed post-*Katz*.[208] If we have to assume the risk that our acquaintances are secretly recording our private conversations, we probably also have to assume the risk that overt CCTV will be recording our public conduct.

There are three lines of attack against this view of the Fourth Amendment's (non)application to CCTV. The first, of course, is to distinguish CCTV and other types of public surveillance from the Court's cases to date. One might insist, for instance, that CCTV *does* result in a seizure because of its effect on movement or because it records and preserves our images. Or one might argue that it *does* constitute a search because people who have to go into public spaces (i.e., virtually everyone) don't meaningfully consent to public surveillance, or because being watched throughout the day is not a risk we assume when we go out in public. The futility of these types of arguments has already been suggested, and in any event will not be pursued here.

The second method of combating judicial acquiescence to unregulated public surveillance is to proffer some alternative to privacy as the focus of Fourth Amendment analysis. But despite much intriguing scholarship along these lines (some of it canvassed in chapter 2), the Court has refused to reconsider *Katz*. Moreover, as should be clear by now, what is misguided is not the Court's insistence on privacy as the linchpin of Fourth Amendment jurisprudence but its equation of Fourth Amendment privacy with the assumption-of-risk and public-exposure concepts.

That takes us to the most powerful line of attack, which involves explicitly switching from an analysis based on these latter concepts to an analysis grounded on the Court's alternative, and arguably more fundamental, admonition that the Fourth Amendment's scope be defined according to expectations of privacy that "society is prepared to recognize as 'reasonable.' " This language strongly suggests that society's views, not the Court's, are the most important determinants of the privacy afforded by the Fourth Amendment, and it begs for an empirical inquiry into those views. The next section briefly describes one effort at such an inquiry, which resulted in findings that support the Fourth Amendment's application to CCTV.

III. An Empirically Based Case for Fourth Amendment Regulation of CCTV

Basing Fourth Amendment protection on society's expectations of privacy requires answering several questions. First, how can we discover these expectations? Second, what are they? Third, in what sense are they relevant to Fourth Amendment analysis?

Sources of Society's Privacy Expectations vis-à-vis CCTV

How does one determine society's views about whether CCTV threatens privacy? Two sources come to mind. The first is the positive law governing public camera surveillance by entities other than the government. If such surveillance is a crime or a tort, then it might be said to infringe on expectations of privacy considered important by society.

At first glance, both case law and statutory law appear to indicate quite the opposite. As noted previously, the few court decisions that address overt videotaping of public activity by private actors generally require a significant degree of maliciousness before relief will be granted.[209] Statutory law regarding public camera use is also sparse. Recall that no statutes regulate nonprurient videotaping of public areas, in contrast to the many state laws that prohibit or significantly limit use of cameras to capture activities within the home.

The paucity of positive law regulating public camera use probably says little about society's attitudes toward CCTV, however, because nothing like CCTV exists in the private sector. No entity other than the government engages in concerted, overt surveillance of the public streets using cameras. If private companies or individuals began sharing round-the-clock recordings of all public spaces in an effort to discern, say, people's shopping, exercise, eating, and drinking patterns, both tort and statutory regulation would probably be forthcoming, just as has occurred in the transaction surveillance area now that private companies have begun accumulating data from our personal records (as to which, see chapter 7).[210]

A second source of information about society's views concerning the intrusiveness of CCTV comes from polls directly asking about attitudes toward CCTV. Although to date there are few polls of that type in the United States,[211] researchers in the United Kingdom have conducted several. All of them show significant public support for CCTV, well above 60 percent.[212] Yet the most sophisticated poll of this type also indicated significant concern about the practice, despite its prevalence. More than 50 percent of the respondents felt that some entity other than the government or private security firms should be responsible for the installation of CCTV in public places, 72 percent agreed that "these cameras could easily be abused and used by the wrong people," 39 percent believed that the people in control of these systems could not be "completely trusted to use them only for the public good," and 37 percent felt that "in the future, cameras will be used by the government to control people."[213] More than 10 percent of the respondents believed that CCTV cameras should be banned.[214] Americans, who tend to be more concerned about government power than the British, would probably be even more hostile to CCTV.

More important, poll results showing favorable attitudes toward CCTV fail to distill feelings about intrusiveness from feelings about security.

Those who say they do not mind government camera surveillance may be allowing its perceived effectiveness at preventing crime to submerge their discomfort about being watched. That attitude makes sense; indeed, if the threat of harm to be prevented is high, a wide range of people will welcome policing techniques much more intrusive than camera surveillance, as reactions to the events of September 11 showed. Under the Fourth Amendment, however, that type of balancing/reasonableness calculus is not supposed to inform the initial question whether something is a search or seizure, but rather, as chapter 2 pointed out, only whether something that is a search or seizure is justified.

To isolate the intrusiveness question more cleanly with respect to CCTV, I conducted a study using the same methodology that Professor Schumacher and I developed for the research described in chapter 2. In that study, we asked people how they rated the intrusiveness of a *number* of police investigative techniques. That approach permits a better assessment of how people feel about the effect each technique has on privacy, because it produces a hierarchy of perceived intrusiveness; even people who are willing to sacrifice most or all of their privacy interests to fight crime evaluate the privacy-invading impact of different crime-fighting techniques differently. Thus, for instance, on average our subjects rated a body cavity search as the most intrusive of the scenarios and a search of a public park as the least, and a search of a bedroom as more intrusive than a frisk. From these types of results, one can draw useful conclusions about the relative magnitude of people's expectations of privacy with respect to a given technique such as CCTV.

Unfortunately, the fifty scenarios in our earlier research did not include any involving camera surveillance. The empirical effort reported here fills that gap.

The Study

The survey form developed for this study was similar to the form used in the earlier study, with a few notable exceptions. First, it contained only twenty relevant scenarios,[215] not fifty. Second, it included either two or three scenarios (depending on which of three survey versions the subject received) describing various forms of camera surveillance. The camera surveillance scenarios involved police use of cameras (all with zoom capacity) to view (1) national monuments, (2) stores, (3) airports and other transportation centers, and (4) public streets (with the latter involving cameras placed every three hundred yards). The public street scenario had two variations: overt versus hidden cameras, and destruction of records within ninety-six hours versus indeterminate retention of records that could be released to government agencies and the media as needed. Also new with this survey form were scenarios involving other types of technological physical surveillance (i.e., beepers and "see-through" devices) and a scenario describing a police officer following an individual on the public street.

The survey was completed by 190 people called for jury duty in Gainesville, Florida. Because Florida jury pools are randomly selected from driver registration lists, this sample was a relatively diverse group of people. As in the earlier study, the subjects were told to assume that in each scenario, the police were looking for evidence of crime but that the target of the police action had not engaged in any criminal activity. In other words, the subjects were told to assume the individuals in the scenarios were innocent, an assumption that is consistent with the Supreme Court's definition of search and seizure for Fourth Amendment purposes.[216] Then, as in the earlier study, the subjects were told to rate each scenario in terms of intrusiveness on a scale of 1 to 100, with 1 representing "not intrusive" and 100 representing "very intrusive."

Using these ratings from the participants, an average intrusiveness rating for each scenario was calculated, along with the standard deviation so that the statistical significance of any differences between averages could be computed. As with the previous study, several such differences resulted. The table below reports the mean intrusiveness rating of the twenty scenarios, together with their confidence intervals (a figure that, when added to or subtracted from the mean, indicates the extent to which a given difference between means is statistically significant).[217] The following discussion will focus on the findings most relevant to understanding what the subjects thought about camera surveillance.

The most important finding of the study for purposes of this chapter was the relative rating of the scenario involving cameras overtly positioned along the street, with recordings destroyed within a short period of time (the typical arrangement in many American cities). As can be seen from the table above, that scenario (13) received an average intrusiveness rating of 53 (M = 53). This rating was significantly lower (as a statistical matter) than the rating for bedroom searches (M = 76), body cavity searches (M = 75), and electronic eavesdropping on conversations in public (M = 70), all of which require probable cause,[218] as well as lower than the rating for overt camera surveillance resulting in a *permanent* record (M = 73). The rating

Mean Intrusiveness Ratings of Twenty Scenarios (Physical Surveillance)

Scenario	Mean	Confidence Interval
1. Looking in foliage in park	8	+4
2. Conducting health and safety inspection of factory	14	+4
3. Monitoring cameras at national monuments	20	+7
4. Monitoring cameras at government buildings, airports, train stations	20	+7
5. Inspecting a coal mine	25	+5
6. Monitoring cameras at stores	26	+8
7. Stopping drivers at roadblock for fifteen seconds	35	+5
8. Monitoring covert street cameras that have zoom capacity	42	+9
9. Flying helicopter four hundred feet over backyard	50	+5
10. Conspicuously following person down street	50	+5
11. Going through garbage cans at curbside	51	+5
12. Searching a junkyard	51	+5
13. Monitoring overt street cameras; tapes destroyed after ninety-six hours	53	+8
14. Monitoring a beeper on a car for three days	63	+5
15. Using a device that can see through clothing to detect outline of items	67	+5
16. Conducting a pat down of outer clothing; feeling for weapons	68	+5
17. Using a video camera to overhear a conversation on the street	70	+5
18. Same as 13 above, but tapes not destroyed	73	+8
19. Searching body cavities at border	75	+5
20. Searching a bedroom	76	+5

for overt surveillance resulting in a short-term record was also significantly lower than the rating for either a traditional (M = 68) or electronic frisk (M = 67), both of which require reasonable suspicion.[219] At the same time, it was significantly higher than the average intrusiveness ratings for a health and safety inspection of a factory (M = 14), an inspection of a coal mine (M = 25), and a fifteen-second stop at a roadblock (M = 35), and similar to the rating for a junkyard search, all government actions that the Supreme Court has declared are governed by the Fourth Amendment.[220]

The intrusiveness ratings for the other scenarios involving cameras fell within the range demarcated by the latter three scenarios, with one exception. While camera surveillance of national monuments (M = 20), transportation centers (M = 20), and stores (M = 26) received relatively low intrusiveness ratings, *covert* camera surveillance of public streets (M = 42) received a significantly higher rating. At the same time, that rating is significantly lower than the rating for overt camera surveillance. Apparently, knowledge that cameras are present triggers a greater feeling of intrusion than knowledge that cameras might be present.

Also of note are the intrusiveness ratings of three government actions the Court has declared are not searches: helicopter overflights four hundred feet above the backyard (M = 50), being followed by a police officer (M = 50), and curbside searches of garbage (M = 51).[221] These three scenarios were perceived to be as intrusive, statistically speaking, as public camera surveillance resulting in a short-term record and significantly more intrusive than the administrative inspections and the roadblock.

Should these last three findings call into question the Court's determinations that administrative inspections and roadblocks are Fourth Amendment events, or instead lead us to question the holdings that helicopter overflights, police tailing, and garbage scavenging (and, by implication, public camera surveillance) are not? Consistent with the thesis of this book, I believe we should be more concerned about the second set of Supreme Court holdings, for two reasons. First, all these scenarios were rated as more intrusive, by a very large margin, than the paradigmatic situation in which privacy is nonexistent, i.e., searching through foliage in a public park (M = 8). Second, the survey participants are better representatives of society than the members of the Court, and thus their opinions are more probative regarding expectations of privacy society is prepared to recognize as reasonable. Of course, both of these reasons rely on the findings of the survey, a reliance that requires further justification.

The Relevance of Empirical Findings

As Professor Schumacher and I noted in connection with the previous study, there are several potential methodological problems with this kind of survey.[222] These internal and external validity issues will not be rehearsed in detail here. With respect to internal validity, it suffices to say that, despite some reservations, we concluded in the earlier work that this type of survey "accurately measured how people rank the intrusiveness of various search and seizures."[223] More suspect is the external validity of this study, given its paper-and-pencil nature. But note that the justices of the Supreme Court also decide Fourth Amendment questions in the abstract (that is, without experiencing the actual police-citizen interaction). Furthermore, they are much further removed from the reality of those interactions than the study participants, who, as noted above, are also much more representative of the community.

Assuming no significant methodological problems, then, it is still important to revisit one central issue: why should we care, for constitutional purposes, what ordinary people think about the intrusiveness of various police actions? One easy answer is the one already given: the Court has told us that society's views are relevant by defining the Fourth Amendment in terms of expectations of privacy that "society is prepared to recognize as 'reasonable.' " But perhaps this language should not be interpreted literally. There are at least three reasons why it may be a bad idea to do so. These reasons are all complicated, but they deserve at least a brief description here.

One possible reason to avoid a literal reading of *Katz* is the variability and manipulability of public attitudes. Technology and modern social practices are rapidly reducing everyone's privacy, as well as everyone's expectations thereof, with the result that a literal construction of *Katz* would produce an ever-shrinking Fourth Amendment. Resort to empirical data about society's attitudes in defining the Fourth Amendment's scope would probably accelerate that trend, and destabilize search and seizure law at the same time.

Research such as that described here, however, only provides information concerning society's views about *relative* intrusiveness. It does not tell the Court where to position the Fourth Amendment threshold (e.g., at a mean of 15 or 50 on a 100-point intrusiveness scale). The decision as to the level at which privacy expectations are accorded constitutional protection can still be a judicial, normative one that has precedential impact. Nor are society's views likely to change once the Court sets the Fourth Amendment threshold, because the Court's pronouncement will reinforce those views. If, however, those views nonetheless change substantially—for instance, if twenty years from now, government-run CCTV is seen as much less intrusive than searching foliage in a public park or much more intrusive than a frisk—then Fourth Amendment analysis should probably change with them. After all, that is what happened when *Katz* declared nontrespassory electronic surveillance a search after forty years of precedent saying otherwise.

A second objection to a literal interpretation of *Katz*'s expectation-of-privacy language is that at the margins it might render nugatory the language and history of the Fourth Amendment. Consider overt CCTV systems as an example. One could argue, as suggested earlier, that CCTV does not constitute either a search or a seizure of persons, papers, houses, and effects as those terms are normally understood. One could also plausibly contend that it is not the type of government activity that even remotely concerned the framers. These points, the constitutional theorist might say, far outweigh data on community sentiments about CCTV's intrusiveness.

Of course, there are also nonempirical arguments that rebut these points and are consistent with the survey findings. As indicated in chapter 2, close scrutiny of a person, whether in public or private, by camera or the naked eye, can easily be called a search. And while it is true that physical searches, particularly of homes, were the main concern of the framers, surveillance of the streets by British soldiers was also a major irritant for the colonists.[224] Ultimately, however, the strength of this second objection depends on how important plain meaning and original intent are to Fourth Amendment analysis and on what these phrases mean, topics that are the subject of much debate and outside the scope of this book.[225]

A related and final objection to taking *Katz* literally is that courts should consider *only* these latter types of factors—plain meaning, original intent, philosophical principles—and never look at community views, because courts are, by tradition if not by definition, nonmajoritarian institutions. While some constitutional issues—the definition of obscenity comes to mind[226]—largely reflect the community's conscience, most such issues—compulsion for Fifth Amendment purposes,[227] speech under the First Amendment,[228] probable cause for Fourth Amendment purposes[229]—do not. As the Supreme Court has said, "One's right to life, liberty, and property, to free speech, a free press, freedom of worship and assembly, and other fundamental rights may not be submitted to vote; they depend on the outcome of no elections."[230] At the least, shouldn't the courts ignore community norms that are inconsistent with principles derived from other sources when determining the scope of core constitutional concepts?

This question is also huge and difficult, and the answer depends much on context. Robert Post, a noted scholar on privacy issues, provides the beginning of a response, a response pertinent to the other two objections as well. Post describes three "concepts of privacy": privacy as the control of knowledge, privacy as a protector of dignity, and privacy as a means of implementing freedom.[231] The first concept, he argues, does not really raise a privacy question at all, because it has more to do with disclosure of information than with intrusion, and the third he sees as "an argument for liberal limitations on government" such as those imposed by cases such as *Roe v. Wade*.[232] The form of privacy he views as most relevant to Fourth Amendment issues is privacy as dignity, which grounds privacy "in social forms of respect that we owe each other as members of a common community" and "locates privacy in precisely the aspects of social life that are shared and mutual."[233] He asserts that when privacy "is understood as a form of dignity, there can ultimately be no other measure of privacy than the social norms that actually exist in our civilization."[234] If that is so, then Fourth Amendment privacy depends on measurements of societal norms regarding privacy expectations, which is what the survey described above attempts to measure.

There is also an institutional reason to align Fourth Amendment expectations of privacy with society's views on the matter. As stated in the article describing our first study, "assuming valid data showing that the community and the Court think differently, the Court's continued adherence to its own views, through what has aptly been called normative constitutional fact-finding, would further strain its credibility."[235] Ultimately, ignoring such data and the community views the data represent undermines the Court's legitimacy.[236]

Conclusion

A good case can be made for the conclusion that overt CCTV operated by the government in public spaces ought to be subject to constitutional regulation. The source of such regulation could be the First Amendment, the right to travel found in the Due Process Clause, the general right to privacy, or the Fourth Amendment. CCTV can intimidate those engaging in political expression, inhibit public movement and repose, affect one's public personality, accelerate normalization, and, if the empirical study reported here is any indication, be as intrusive as police actions that the Supreme Court has said implicate the Fourth Amendment. Although the interests infringed by CCTV are somewhat disparate, they can all be subsumed under the umbrella interest in public anonymity—the right to be free of intensive government scrutiny, absent suspicious conduct, even in public.[237]

Of the various constitutional bases that could implement this right to anonymity, I prefer the Fourth Amendment, for two related reasons. First, it is the amendment that traditionally has been applied to police investigation techniques, and CCTV is such a technique. The Court has suggested that when two or more constitutional provisions are applicable, the one most directly implicated should apply.[238] Second, Fourth Amendment analysis provides a better framework for regulating CCTV than the other constitutional doctrines. If a government action infringes the First Amendment, the Due Process Clause, or the general right to privacy, its permissibility depends on whether the government has a "compelling" or "substantial" interest in pursuing the action, concepts that are very ill-defined. Depending on the interest involved, the action's legitimacy may also hinge on how "necessary" it is to accomplish that interest, again a nebulously defined inquiry.[239] Although essentially the same analysis occurs under the Fourth Amendment, its greater flexibility and its better developed substantive and procedural rules provide a more concrete regulatory template, as the next chapter demonstrates.

CHAPTER FIVE

Implementing the Right to Public Anonymity

The conclusion that public surveillance must be subject to constitutional strictures does not necessarily mean that the usual Fourth Amendment jurisprudence—involving warrants, probable cause, and so on—applies. Relying on the proportionality concept, this chapter argues that the courts should set minimal guidelines and monitor police decisions to ensure that such surveillance is conducted in a reasonable manner. Given its relatively unintrusive nature, however, most public surveillance of individuals does not require probable cause in the traditional sense. At the same time, rules regarding who is involved in the targeting decision, the execution of the police action, and subsequent record-keeping and disclosure should assume much more significance here than in connection with the classic police search.

More specifically, I propose that constitutional regulation of government efforts to pierce public anonymity through CCTV consist of four components. First, law enforcement should have to justify both the establishment of a particular camera system and its use to scrutinize particular individuals. Second, it should have to develop policies regarding the procedure for conducting camera surveillance. Third, it should have to develop policies regarding storage and dissemination of recorded materials to other entities. Finally, and most important, it should be accountable to entities outside law enforcement when it fails to follow these three requirements.

Even this bare-bones description of the regulatory scheme sounds decidedly legislative in nature and therefore arguably something the judiciary is not equipped to fashion. But as the following discussion makes clear, the judicial objective should be merely to establish the regulatory framework; law enforcement agencies and political actors can fill in the details. Erik

Luna has described the phenomenon of "constitutional roadmapping," in which the courts, in striking down governmental laws or censoring conduct of government agents, suggest constitutionally permissible alternative courses of action.[1] The idea behind such decisions is to encourage a dialogue with the executive and legislative branches as well as the citizenry.[2] As Professor Luna says, road maps "openly share constitutional concerns with those institutions charged with making and enforcing law, refracting issues with judicial insight rather than merely reflecting them back to the political branches."[3] Although Luna believes that judicial resort to these quasi-legislative pronouncements should be rare, he also states that they are most likely to be useful in individual rights cases involving new practices where the need for clear rules is high, a scenario that resonates with the advent of CCTV.[4] The discussion below sets out a constitutional road map for public camera surveillance, relying on Fourth Amendment precedent for guiding principles and the ABA's Standards on Technologically-Assisted Physical Surveillance for slightly more specific recommendations that might be followed by legislatures.[5]

I. Justification

The government should be required to justify its use of cameras in two ways. First, it should have to justify the placement of the cameras it seeks to install. Second, it should have to account for the use of the cameras to inspect particular individuals. Precedent for requiring both justifications comes from the Supreme Court's cases on roadblocks, which were viewed by the subjects in the study reported in the previous chapter to be significantly less intrusive than CCTV.

Justifying Camera Location

One might think that the cost of camera systems alone would keep CCTV from spreading beyond areas with the highest crime rates. But if Great Britain's experience is any indication, cameras are likely to be seen as a cheap, effective method of deterring and detecting crime, whether or not that is actually the case. Thus, their proliferation beyond the most dangerous areas is inevitable unless limitations are imposed.

The precedent for limitation comes from an unlikely source: the Supreme Court's roadblock jurisprudence.[6] In the five cases in which the Court has pronounced on the constitutionality of roadblocks, the government has prevailed four times. In *United States v. Martinez-Fuerte,*[7] the Court upheld checkpoints established near the Mexican border that were designed to deter and detect illegal immigration. In *Michigan Department of State Police v. Sitz,*[8] it sanctioned roadblocks to deter drunken driving. In between these two cases, the Court decided *Delaware v. Prouse,*[9] where it indicated in dictum that license checkpoints would be constitutional as well (in the course of holding that random license checks of individual cars are unconstitutional). And just a few terms ago, in *Illinois v. Lidster,*[10] the Court sanctioned a checkpoint at the location of a hit-and-run accident in an effort to identify possible witnesses to the accident.

In a case decided in 2000, however, the Court drew the line at roadblocks that are set up merely to help the government catch more criminals. In *City of Indianapolis v. Edmond,* the Court held unconstitutional a "narcotics checkpoint," stating, "we have never approved a checkpoint program whose primary purpose was to detect evidence of ordinary criminal wrongdoing."[11] *Martinez-Fuerte*, Justice O'Connor wrote for the Court, was grounded on the "formidable law enforcement problems" connected with "effectively containing illegal immigration at the border," the "impracticality of the particularized study of a given car to discern whether it was transporting illegal aliens," and the traditional leeway given the government's efforts to protect the "integrity of the border." The sobriety checkpoints in *Sitz* were permissible because they were aimed at reducing "the immediate vehicle-bound threat to life and limb" posed by the presence of drunken drivers on the highways. And license checkpoints of the type discussed in *Prouse*, O'Connor stated, are meant to maintain highway safety through ensuring that drivers are qualified and that their vehicles are fit for safe operation.[12] In *Lidster,* decided after *Edmond*, the Court similarly emphasized that the purpose behind the roadblock there was to seek information from possible witnesses to a death rather than gather evidence against those stopped.[13] None of these roadblock variants, the *Edmond* majority stressed and *Lidster* reiterated, are established to further the government's "general interest in crime control."[14] In the latter situation, an "individualized suspicion" requirement prevails.[15] Otherwise, "the Fourth Amendment would do little to prevent such intrusions from becoming a routine part of American life."[16]

There is no doubt that the primary purpose of CCTV is to implement the government's general interest in crime control. If we assume, as concluded above, that CCTV is regulated by the Fourth Amendment, *Edmond*'s rationale could be read to prohibit government use of cameras unless there is individualized suspicion or one of the circumstances identified in *Martinez-Fuerte*, *Sitz*, or *Lidster* exists (*Prouse* is set aside for the moment). In other words, in the absence of individualized suspicion, CCTV should be permitted only where it can be shown that there is a "formidable law enforcement problem" associated with using traditional methods of investigation (as in the case of discerning illegal immigrants in cars), an immediate hazard to life and limb posed by a specified group of potentially dangerous people (as with drunken drivers), or a need to obtain information about a serious crime (as occurred in *Lidster*).

The third situation is self-explanatory. But when might the first two circumstances exist? Areas with a high magnitude of serious crime are the best candidates. A significant amount of crime suggests that traditional law enforcement methods are not working, and if much of the crime being committed is violent or similarly serious, it presents an immediate hazard proportionate to that posed by drunken drivers. Using the terminology introduced in chapter 2, CCTV should be limited to those areas associated with a "generalized suspicion" of serious crime.

Taking a cue from the Court's cases, it is possible to specify even more exactly the degree of harm necessary to justify brief suspicionless surveillance. In *Sitz* the Court said that the checkpoint there was reasonable in part because 1.6 percent of the drivers who went through the roadblock were drunk; the Court also noted that .12 percent of those stopped at the checkpoint in *Martinez-Fuerte* were illegal immigrants.[17] The latter percentage might presumptively be considered the threshold at which government can act, for two reasons. First, in *Martinez-Fuerte* it justified only the barest of seizures, one that lasted at most five seconds and that often consisted merely of getting the vehicle to slow down so that border agents could look inside.[18] Anything less intrusive would probably not have implicated the Fourth Amendment at all; anything more should require at least as much justification as the government proffered in *Martinez-Fuerte*. Second, the Court has indicated it is leery of suspicionless seizures that inconvenience large numbers of individuals for very little gain. In finding unconstitutional the random license checks at issue in *Prouse*, it noted that "the percentage of all drivers on the road who are driving without a license is very small and . . . the number of licensed drivers who will be stopped in order to find one unlicensed operator will be large indeed."[19] Although *Prouse* went on to sanction nonrandom roadblocks for license check purposes, this type of seizure, *Edmond* held, is permitted only when it is directly related to highway safety, not crime control. In the latter instance, *Prouse* and *Edmond* in combination would seem to say that hit rates lower than those obtained in *Martinez-Fuerte* cannot justify searches or seizures by the government.

In somewhat arbitrary "generalized suspicion" terms, then, CCTV might be permitted only in areas where more than one person in a thousand surveilled will commit some type of serious crime.[20] It might also be permissible in more idiosyncratic circumstances. For instance, as *Edmond* itself suggested and consistent with the danger exception outlined in chapter 2, cameras might be positioned in areas that are not particularly crime-ridden but are predicted to be the focus of some imminent, serious threat to life and limb, such as terrorism.[21] In such locations, or where crime fluctuates, cameras might be set up but switched off except during particular times or events, as occurs in Washington, D.C. Ideally these kinds of decisions would be made after studying crime patterns that identified locales particularly likely to attract certain types of serious criminal activity or harbor dangerous criminals.

An equally important aspect of the justification inquiry is determining who decides whether crime in a given area is of sufficient magnitude to warrant CCTV—the police, a court, a legislature, or the public. The Court's cases suggest the decision should be left up to law enforcement. For instance, in rejecting the argument that courts should determine the propriety of sobriety checkpoints, the Court in *Sitz* stated it would not "transfer from politically accountable officials to the courts the decision as to which among reasonable alternative law enforcement techniques should be employed to deal with a serious public danger."[22] It went on to conclude that "for purposes of Fourth Amendment analysis, the choice among such reasonable alternatives remains with the governmental officials who have a unique understanding of, and a responsibility for, limited public resources, including a finite number of police officers."[23]

While this language appears to leave quite a bit up to police discretion, it also endorses two significant limitations on that discretion. First, courts are not left out of the picture entirely. They are still permitted to intervene when the alternative chosen by the police is not reasonable. This overview role accords with the dictates of political process theory discussed in chapter 2; unless a legislature has authorized the surveillance and provided fairly precise parameters for executive officials, courts should be involved in supervising the decision-making process. The generalized suspicion concept can help courts determine whether police decisions are reasonable.

Second, *Sitz* makes clear that the police who make the frontline decision should not be the cop on the beat but politically accountable officials who have "responsibility for limited public resources." In other words, the chief of the department ought to be in charge of making these decisions. That conclusion makes sense, for a number of reasons. First, it is consonant with the exigency principle, which, as chapter 2 explained, dictates that a government official other than the executing officers determine the reasonableness of a search. Second, a high-level official is likely to have better access to the relevant statistics. And third, lower-level officers should not be making decisions affecting the large number of people who would be subject to public surveillance.[24]

All of these reasons, but especially the third, also might lead one to query whether the *public* should be involved in decision making. The Court has not specifically addressed this question. But William Stuntz has argued that *Sitz* stands for the proposition that the public should be directly involved in such cases.[25] More specifically, he posits that *Sitz* indicates that the Court is willing to abandon the individualized suspicion model of the Fourth Amendment in favor of what he calls a "politics model" when searches or seizures affect large groups of people, because a group, unlike the solitary suspect who is usually the target of searches and seizures, can "throw the rascals out" if it does not like a particular technique.[26]

If Professor Stuntz is right about the Court's underlying motivation in *Sitz*, the practical problem becomes how to implement this politics model. The typical electoral process, which is likely to revolve around many issues, is not an effective way for the group to make its attitudes toward a particular police action known. A more satisfactory implementation of the model would be to require direct input on the establishment of camera systems from those who will enjoy the benefit and bear the brunt of the surveillance. Such input can also provide the police with information about specific crime problems and the type of surveillance that might prove most useful.[27] It is instructive that several participants at the International Association of Chiefs of Police meeting on CCTV were adamant about involving the affected community in decisions involving cameras.[28]

The American Bar Association's Standards on Technologically-Assisted Physical Surveillance address all these concerns about the decision to install cameras. They state that CCTV "is permissible when a politically accountable governmental authority concludes that the surveillance will not view a private activity or condition and will be reasonably likely to achieve a legitimate law enforcement objective."[29] The latter phrase is defined to require "articulable reasons" for concluding that the surveillance will lead to the detection, deterrence, or prevention of crime,[30] which, after *Edmond*, should usually require a demonstration that a significant violent crime problem will be addressed by the surveillance. The ABA Standards also require that "where deterrence rather than investigation is the primary objective, the public to be affected by the surveillance . . . [should have] the opportunity, both prior to the initiation of the surveillance and periodically during it, to express its views of the surveillance and propose changes in its execution, through a hearing or some other appropriate means."[31] These are the kinds of general guidelines the courts can fashion based on Fourth Amendment principles.

A second method of protecting the right to anonymity in public spaces is technological rather than legal. The "Respectful Cameras" project at the University of California is developing a method of obscuring the faces of everyone within the camera's scope with an opaque oval.[32] Using this innovation, cameras could conceivably be set up everywhere without infringing public anonymity; operators could be told not to remove the technological mask unless and until the requisite suspicion, as discussed in the next section, develops. It remains to be seen, however, whether a program that blocks only faces protects anonymity and whether covering visages undermines camera operators' ability to detect criminal activity.

Justifying Individualization of Surveillance

If the *Edmond* standard is met for a particular area, then CCTV cameras can be installed there consistent with the Fourth Amendment. Randomly panning the camera to scan the streets ought to be permissible on the same showing, just as the brief initial stops in *Martinez-Fuerte* and *Sitz* were permitted without individualized suspicion. But what if the camera operators want to record or closely observe a particular person's actions, using zoom capacity or via prolonged or repeated surveillance? The only comprehensive study of CCTV operator behavior found that this scenario occurs frequently. In approximately six hundred hours of observation, almost nine hundred "targeted surveillances" of more than a minute occurred, with roughly one-third lasting between two and six minutes, and one-quarter lasting longer than six minutes.[33]

Here again, the roadblock cases, supplemented by proportionality analysis, lead the way. In *Sitz*, the Court cautioned that it was addressing "only the initial stop of each motorist passing through a checkpoint and the associated preliminary questioning and observation by checkpoint officers. Detention of particular motorists for more extensive field sobriety testing may require satisfaction of an individualized suspicion standard."[34] Similarly, in *Martinez-Fuerte*, the Court felt it important to note that the percentage of illegal immigrants discovered at the "secondary checkpoint" to which motorists were sent after the initial stop was close to 20 percent,[35] a figure that demonstrates a relatively high level of suspicion associated with this seizure, which amounted to a five-minute document check.[36]

These cases suggest that something more than an inchoate hunch ought to form the basis for intense scrutiny of individuals. Certainly use of audio capacity to eavesdrop on private conversations on the street ought to be based on individualized suspicion, presumably at the probable cause level. Likewise, if the camera is used to intrude into the interior of the home, probable cause should be required.

Short of these two situations, determining precisely when surveillance progresses from random scanning or casual surveillance to observation intense enough to warrant individualized suspicion may be difficult. But it will not be any more difficult than defining when a nonseizure becomes a seizure, or determining when a stop requiring reasonable suspicion becomes an arrest requiring probable cause, issues with which the Supreme Court has grappled on several occasions. Two factors that ought to be relevant here, according to the ABA Standards, are "the extent to which the surveillance technology enhances the law enforcement officer's natural senses" and "the extent to which the surveillance of subjects is minimized in time and space."[37] If the camera's zoom or recording capacity allows operators to obtain information that would be difficult for an observer on the street to discern (such as a title on a book cover or a biometric match with official records), then reasonable suspicion ought to be required; the same standard ought to be met if the cameras intentionally follow an individual for a prolonged period of time (say, more than the five minutes involved at the secondary checkpoint in *Martinez-Fuerte*) or on several separate occasions (analogous to Rehnquist's bar example described in chapter 4). Even a targeted surveillance lasting only a minute should require an articulated reason beyond mere curiosity (such as a signal from one of the automated systems described in the previous chapter). The amount of individualized scrutiny permitted should be roughly proportionate to the amount of individualized suspicion the government has developed.

These proposals may appear to go well beyond what the Fourth Amendment requires, given the Court's decision in *Knotts* permitting suspicionless tracking of public movements using a beeper. But the beeper in *Knotts* indicated only the location of an object or person; video surveillance provides government with much more. More important, unlike the beeper, CCTV is overt, and thus it generates a much greater panoptic effect.

In any event, the fact that beeper use is covert and reveals only the whereabouts of an individual should not necessarily suggest that *all* such monitoring is exempt from constitutional strictures. Over a prolonged period of time, this type of tracking can reveal an enormous amount of information about an individual—in particular, whom or where he or she visits and for how long—much more economically and conveniently than mere visual surveillance. Note also that according to the table in chapter 4, using a beeper to monitor travel for three days was rated as almost as intrusive as a frisk, suggesting that members of the public believe that prolonged tracking with a beeper is a significant invasion. Had the tracking in *Knotts* been longer (in fact, it lasted only about an hour and revealed only that the driver had visited one location),[38] a different result might have been warranted, as several commentators have suggested.[39]

II. Execution Issues

A search or seizure must not only be justified but be executed in a reasonable manner. Based on the Court's case law, three execution issues associated with CCTV might rise to the constitutional level. They concern notice of the surveillance, the types of individuals to be observed, and termination of the surveillance.

Notice

If the point of CCTV is deterrence, as its advocates claim, then notification of those subject to camera surveillance is imperative. Independent of this government interest, the Fourth Amendment also imposes a notice requirement. One of the primary reasons the Court gave in *Martinez-Fuerte* for finding the intrusion associated with the roadblocks in that case "minimal" was that, given the signs announcing the existence of the roadblocks, motorists were "not taken by surprise"; further, because of this notification, they knew, or could "obtain knowledge of, the location of the checkpoints" and would "not be stopped elsewhere."[40] The Court also stated that the intrusion was further minimized because the checkpoints appeared to be "duly authorized,"[41] another function signs can carry out.

Other Court decisions upholding suspicionless government actions have reaffirmed that notice is an important means of meeting Fourth Amendment requirements. For instance, in *Von Raab v. United States,* the case involving drug testing of people who applied and worked for the customs service, the Court emphasized that "employees are . . . notified in advance of the scheduled sample collection, thus reducing to a minimum any 'unsettling show of authority' that may be associated with unexpected intrusions on privacy."[42] In *Wyman v. James,* in which the Court permitted suspicionless inspections of a welfare recipient's home, the Court reasoned that advance notice of the inspection minimized the intrusion on privacy occasioned by the visit.[43]

A number of Court cases also suggest that suspicionless searches are more palatable when the targets "consent" to them ahead of time, which is impossible without some sort of notice.[44] Of course, as already suggested, the notion that people consent to public surveillance simply because they proceed with their business after having been notified that cameras are present is disingenuous at best. Consent implies that realistic alternatives exist, which is simply not true in places like London, where cameras are trained on almost every foot of public space. The purpose of notice in this context is not to obtain consent but purely to alert passersby that they are being watched so that they can act accordingly.

Avoiding Discriminatory Surveillance

The second execution issue of possible constitutional significance arises when government uses cameras to monitor only some of those who can justifiably be observed. Because no suspicion is required for camera surveillance as it is practiced today, significant potential for discrimination exists. Indeed, research in the United Kingdom indicates that bias against minority groups is widespread among camera operators. Norris and Armstrong report, for instance, that the CCTV practices they observed involved a "massively disproportionate targeting of young males, particularly if they are black or visibly identifiable as having subcultural affiliations."[45] This differentiation, they concluded, was "not based on objective behavioural and individualised criteria, but merely on being categorised as part of a particular social group."[46]

In the regime proposed here, discretionary targeting is reduced considerably because some degree of suspicion is required for any prolonged surveillance. But those who operate the cameras might still use race as a criterion for selecting from among those for whom the requisite suspicion exists. Such practices are probably unconstitutional. In *Whren v. United States,* for instance, the Supreme Court signaled that searches and seizures resulting from intentional racial discrimination could violate the Fourteenth Amendment's Equal Protection Clause.[47] Although proof of such intent is notoriously difficult, every step possible should be taken to ensure that, in the words of the ABA Standards, targets are not selected "in an arbitrary or discriminatory manner."[48]

Termination of the Surveillance

The final execution issue that might trigger constitutional analysis concerns the termination of individual surveillance. The Supreme Court has frequently emphasized, in a way that is consistent with proportionality reasoning, the importance of durational limitations. In upholding the checkpoints in *Martinez-Fuerte*, for instance, the Court pointed out that the initial stop was extremely brief and that the secondary documentary check lasted only about five minutes.[49] In *Sitz* as well it found the initial stop, which averaged twenty-five seconds, to be a "minimal" intrusion, as "measured by the duration of the seizure and the intensity of the investigation."[50] The Court has also indicated, in *United States v. Sharpe,* that stops based on reasonable suspicion should not last much longer than five minutes in the absence of extenuating circumstances such as delays caused by the target.[51]

When it comes to CCTV, these cases suggest that, in the ABA's language, the "surveillance should be limited to its authorized objectives and be terminated when those objectives are achieved."[52] And, for regulatory bodies so inclined, these cases could be mined for even more specific guidelines. Parallel to *Martinez-Fuerte* and *Sitz*, and consistent with the discussion concerning individualization of surveillance, camera operators could be required to terminate targeted surveillance of a particular individual after a minute or so, unless reasonable suspicion develops.[53] In cases where such suspicion develops they could be required, parallel to *Sharpe*, to cease surveillance if probable cause doesn't develop within the next five to ten minutes, unless extenuating circumstances are present. These rules would have significant impact, since research indicates that CCTV surveillance can last well over five minutes even in cases where no deployment or arrest results.[54]

Storage and Dissemination of Recordings

A principal feature of CCTV that distinguishes it from ordinary, nontechnological surveillance is the capacity to record observations. That capacity, plus the potential for abuse of the information so generated, is apparently of major concern to the public. The British survey quoted in chapter 4 indicated that many of the people questioned were very worried about misuse of the images recorded on CCTV, an anxiety that is well founded, given the fact that tapes showing people in compromising situations have been publicly released in the United Kingdom on several occasions.[55] In my study as well, the scenario in which the tapes are not destroyed and instead are made available to the media and other government agencies "as needed" received a much higher intrusiveness rating (M = 73) than the scenario in which tapes are destroyed within ninety-six hours (M = 53). Indeed, the former rating is statistically indistinguishable from the ratings associated with the search of a bedroom, an action that requires probable cause.

The Supreme Court has never addressed this particular type of privacy invasion as a Fourth Amendment matter. The closest it has come was in *Wilson v. Layne,*[56] where it held that the Fourth Amendment was violated by a "media ride-along" in which a newspaper reporter and photographer accompanied police on a search of a house. There, however, the issue was solely whether the presence of the media at the time of the search was unconstitutional; because the ride-along was not "in aid" of the search's execution, it unconstitutionally infringed on the privacy of the search's target.[57] *Layne* did not address the lawfulness of later dissemination of information about the search, whether acquired by the media at the time it occurs or from police at some later point. In the CCTV context, then, *Layne* at most would ban the media and other non-law-enforcement entities from being present during the surveillance.

Other Supreme Court decisions, however, suggest the Constitution requires law enforcement to keep a tight rein on information it accumulates. In *Whalen v. Roe,*[58] the Court considered a Fourteenth Amendment privacy challenge to a state statute that required physicians to submit information about patients' drug use to a state agency. Although the Court upheld the statute, it made much of the state's efforts to maintain security over the information submitted and the fact that the records were destroyed after five years.[59] At the end of its opinion, it also noted "the threat to privacy implicit in the accumulation of vast amounts of personal information in computerized data banks or other massive government files" and stated that "in some circumstances" a "duty to avoid unwarranted disclosures . . . arguably has its roots in the Constitution."[60] Citing *Whalen*, the Court in *Ferguson v. City of Charleston* concluded that "the reasonable expectation of privacy enjoyed by the typical patient undergoing diagnostic tests in a hospital is that the results of those tests will not be shared with nonmedical personnel without her consent."[61] Also relying on *Whalen*, the Court in *Department of Justice v. Reporters Committee for Freedom of the Press* stated that "the fact that an event is not wholly 'private' does not mean that an individual has no interest in limiting disclosure or dissemination of the information."[62] That case went on to hold that under the Freedom of Information Act (FOIA), government-maintained rap sheets on criminals need not be disclosed to the press because they did not further the FOIA's "central purpose" of exposing to public scrutiny official information that sheds light on an agency's performance of its statutory duties.[63]

These cases indicate that the Court is willing to interpret the Constitution and statutory mandates to circumscribe disclosure of private information gathered by the government. In the CCTV setting, the content of these rules might vary widely. With respect to storage of information, a jurisdiction might require that all recordings not relevant to a criminal investigation be destroyed within a short period of time (the ninety-six-hour limitation used in the survey reported in chapter 4 comes from Baltimore's policy).[64] Or it could opt for a much longer maintenance period, in the belief that the usefulness of particular tapes, either to inculpate or exculpate, may not become apparent until significant time has elapsed. The important feature here is to ensure the security of the recordings. With respect to dissemination, the Court's cases suggest that allowing information to be used for non-law-enforcement purposes ought to be permitted only under compelling circumstances, if at all. The ABA Standards recommend that "disclosures be prohibited unless affirmatively authorized by statute, judicial decision, or agency rule."[65] That language echoes the *Sitz* mandate that decisions affecting large segments of the public be left to politically accountable officials.

Before leaving this subject, mention must be made of a provocative proposal from Professor Stuntz. I have argued here that in addition to rules regarding disclosure, we need rules concerning justification and implementation. Stuntz suggests that when government engages in "secret searches," we might profitably consider focusing *solely* on disclosure rules.[66] More specifically, he proposes that government be allowed to carry out such searches randomly, without having to demonstrate any suspicion, on condition that the information thus obtained be used only in prosecutions for serious, violent crimes. That approach, he asserts, "would allow us to give both the police and private citizens more of what they value—easier evidence-gathering and reduced risk of embarrassment or harassment."[67]

Although CCTV, as defined for purposes of this discussion, is not conducted secretly, it could be. For instance, a CCTV system in Hull, England, uses "tiny cameras disguised in street lamps or concealed on buildings to transmit pictures to a monitoring center around the clock."[68] Stuntz would allow such covert use at the whim of the police so long as his limited disclosure rule is followed. People would not know that their right to anonymity had been invaded unless and until they are prosecuted for a serious crime. Why not institute this regime rather than bother with the elaborate justification rules discussed to this point?

One concern raised by Stuntz's proposal focuses on whether government can be trusted to limit its use of the information it obtains through covert CCTV to prosecutions of serious crimes. Given the secret nature of these searches, finding the "poisonous tree" in prosecutions for nonserious offenses may be difficult. Furthermore, of course, barring use of surveillance results in court does not provide any disincentive to police who intend to use CCTV feeds solely to harass "flawed consumers" or take other actions they know will not lead to charges being filed.

The more important problem with the elimination of justification and execution rules, however, has to do with the right to anonymity. Stuntz's proposal might not openly infringe that right for those not prosecuted, but it insidiously trenches on *everyone's* right to avoid suspicionless government scrutiny. Indeed, in the CCTV context, once the public becomes aware that random covert surveillance is occurring, as it inevitably would after a few prosecutions in which the covertly gleaned information is used, the panoptic effect of this regime will be greater than occurs with overt CCTV. The survey results reported in the previous chapter may appear to suggest otherwise, because the covert camera scenario ranked significantly lower than the overt scenario (albeit still significantly higher than the roadblock). However, the covert scenario used in the survey implied that the surveillance was limited to one location.[69] In Stuntz's society, by contrast, we would assume that secret surveillance was pervasive, not just incidental. That would move us one step closer to an Orwellian society, because we would no longer know when and where government is attempting to find out what we are doing in public; in other words, we would not know when or how to protect against invasion of our public anonymity. Probably no passage in Orwell's *1984* is more chilling than the one partially excerpted at the beginning of chapter 4: "There was of course no way of knowing whether you were being watched at any given moment. . . . It was even conceivable that they watched everybody all the time."[70]

III. Accountability

Unless we know precisely when publicly placed cameras are being used to watch us, for how long, and with what level of justification, enforcement of the rules described above is not possible. Even if this information is available, reliance on the police to hold themselves accountable for a violation of the rules, which is the current approach, is unlikely to ensure full compliance. Finally, even good faith efforts at full compliance with the rules will not achieve their ultimate goal so long as people still feel significant panoptic effects. All three of these concerns deserve some attention.

Watching the Watchers

The rules concerning individualization, discrimination, and termination comprise what could be called "conduct of surveillance" rules, since they have to do with the actual operation of the cameras. Ensuring accountability depends first on figuring out whether these conduct rules are being followed. How can we know when camera operators are scrutinizing a particular individual for a prolonged period of time despite a lack of articulable suspicion? How do we make sure that the police refrain from using cameras in a discriminatory fashion?

Self-reports probably will not work. Operators may not even recognize their discriminatory practices, and if they did, they are hardly likely to confess them. Furthermore, suspicion about targets of surveillance is always easy to manufacture in hindsight if the searcher has control of the facts.[71] As the ABA Standards admonish, police must develop "administrative rules which *ensure* that the information necessary for . . . accountability exists,"[72] a sentiment that is not inconsistent with Fourth Amendment tenets, which at the least are violated when the police conceal information relevant to determining the validity of a search.[73]

How might we ensure access to the information necessary for accountability? David Brin has argued that the best way to control the government (and everyone else) in a surveillance-happy "transparent society" is to watch the watchers.[74] That idea could be implemented in the CCTV context in at least two ways. Camera tapes could be audited periodically and randomly by independent reviewers to determine whether operators are violating any of the rules. Or the watchers really could be watched, by cameras. That method would not only capture the facts necessary to determine whether conduct of surveillance standards are obeyed, but also bring home to operators the panoptic effects their surveillance has on others, thus perhaps curbing voyeuristic and other unnecessary observation.

Assuring Compliance

Assuming a violation is discovered, what should be done? As noted in the previous chapter, police favor voluntary guidelines, by which they appear to mean rules that they not only develop but also enforce. But police are reluctant to punish their own for violations that involve balancing abstract concepts like privacy against law enforcement needs.[75] Some other accountability mechanism is necessary.

In the Fourth Amendment context, that mechanism has usually been exclusion of illegally obtained evidence.[76] Certainly that sanction should be invoked when it applies. But it is unlikely to be a potent deterrent in connection with the types of rules at issue here, for a number of reasons.

Take first the rules concerning individualization, discrimination, and termination—the conduct-of-surveillance rules. The most important reason exclusion does not do a good job encouraging compliance with these types of rules is that the vast majority of people subject to camera surveillance, and therefore most people whose activities are observed in violation of the rules, will never be prosecuted, either because they are completely innocent or because they commit infractions that are taken care of on the street. According to one study conducted in the United Kingdom, for instance, more than three-quarters of those stopped by police as a result of camera surveillance receive no more than a warning, and only just over 1 percent are arrested.[77] In short, most violations of the right to public anonymity will not be redressed through exclusion. That is not a good prescription for ensuring deterrence.

Moreover, when police do want to prosecute crimes illicitly discovered through camera surveillance, they will frequently be able to avoid exclusion. First, exclusion may not be required if the field officer who makes an arrest based on information from a camera operator acts in a good faith belief that no rules were violated by the operator.[78] Second, police know that if they can track down eyewitnesses, through the camera tapes or otherwise, the eyewitness's testimony will usually be admissible even if the testimony of the camera operator and field officer is tainted by illegal surveillance.[79] Only if the prosecution of crimes were barred outright whenever they are discovered through a violation of CCTV rules would the threat of exclusion pose a serious deterrent. But even then, resourceful operators can hide the poisonous tree through untracked calls to a field officer.

As a supplement to exclusion, a more direct sanction is necessary when conduct-of-surveillance rules are violated. In theory, criminal sanctions, damages actions, and administrative penalties are far superior to exclusion because they would not be dependent on whether prosecution—or indeed on whether any government action at all—is based on surveillance results. Criminal prosecutions would probably be considered too draconian or too difficult to bring, however.[80] And given the many limitations on constitutional damage actions that have been imposed by the courts, that method of deterring violations would not work well either, at least as it is currently structured.[81] The best sanctioning system, developed in more detail in chapter 8, may well be an administrative penalty, such as a suspension or a dock in pay, that is sought by an entity independent of the police and enforced by the courts.

The other three rules proposed above address camera placement, notice of camera placement, and disclosure of recordings. Here again the exclusionary sanction is not a particularly good fit. If the placement or notice rules are violated, exclusion of all evidence garnered through the subsequent surveillance would be overkill, at least if the other rules are followed, and in any event would not necessarily stop surveillance aimed at "flawed consumers." And unlawful disclosure to non-law-enforcement entities does not even involve a proceeding at which evidence can be excluded. For violation of placement or notice rules, the better remedy would be an injunction ordering installation to desist or notice to be provided, which courts could grant when politically accountable officials fail to provide a reasonable explanation for their decisions on these matters.[82] With respect to impermissible disclosure of recordings, damages remedies are a perfect fit, given the tort-like harm incurred,[83] although judicially backed administrative sanctions are probably necessary as well.

Beyond Sanctions: Accountability through Information

Will any of this do any good? After all, cameras will still be lawfully installed in some locations. In those areas, won't people still feel watched, regardless of whether the conduct-of-surveillance and disclosure rules are followed? If so, why bother with any of these rules?

These are good questions. At most, the panoptic effects of lawfully placed cameras can only be mitigated, not eliminated. To maximize mitigation, the conduct-of-surveillance rules should be promulgated widely, and any sanctions imposed as a result of their violation should be publicized as well.

Two other proposals, both recommended by the ABA, are worth consideration. First, "periodic review by law enforcement agencies of the scope and effectiveness of technologically-assisted physical surveillance" ought to occur.[84] Second, the government should "maintain[ ] and [make] available to the public general information about the type or types of surveillance being used and the frequency of their use."[85] Right now, most police departments take neither of these steps. That should be rectified. Periodic internal review would ensure that the government pays attention to whether the cameras are achieving the crime reduction goal it seeks and might even result in the disassembly of some cameras. Review would also provide information about the nature, frequency, and success of camera surveillance that could be disseminated to the public, which could then reach its own conclusions about the scope of surveillance.

Ideally, dissemination of information about CCTV that is conducted under the rules proposed here will lead to the realization that most of us are of no interest to camera operators. Fear that our public actions, or images of those actions, will be scrutinized by faceless bureaucrats or government agents with a suspect agenda should be allayed. Similar to the apparent impact of Title III's imposition of strict judicial control over and disclosure of government wiretapping and bugging practices,[86] we should be able to rest assured that camera operators will not watch us simply because they can.

The constitutional basis for these review and publication rules is again the Fourth Amendment. As chapter 2 noted, that amendment guarantees a right to be secure from unreasonable searches and seizures.[87] Knowledge that government has enacted rules limiting its surveillance powers, that the rules are being enforced, and that periodic reports on the implementation and success of the surveillance will be made public is the surest way to enhance a sense of security in an age when technology threatens our anonymity.

Conclusion

The fundamental question addressed in this chapter and the previous one is whether government use of cameras to observe the public activities of its citizens is a concern of constitutional dimension. CCTV might implicate several constitutional doctrines, among them the First Amendment, the right to freedom of movement, and the general right to privacy. But if one provision has to be selected as a constitutional basis for regulating this type of surveillance, it should probably be the Fourth Amendment, the primary source of limitations on police investigative techniques.

Admittedly, the Supreme Court's Fourth Amendment case law does not form a solid basis for the conclusion that CCTV constitutes a search or seizure. Yet as a linguistic matter, once camera operators shift from scanning crowds to targeting individuals, they are certainly engaging in a search, even the narrowest definition of which involves looking "into or over carefully or thoroughly in an effort to find or discover something." A less literal reading of the Fourth Amendment's threshold should lead even more readily to the same result. Whether framed in the Court's language—in terms of expectations of privacy society is prepared to recognize as reasonable—or in mine—in terms of a right to anonymity that protects against unnecessary government scrutiny—that threshold is crossed when government trains cameras on its citizens, because of the panoptic atmosphere such surveillance creates, an atmosphere that the empirical research reported here suggests is more intrusive than many other government actions that are clearly governed by the Fourth Amendment. If the federal constitution cannot be read to place restrictions on CCTV, then state constitutions, which are less encumbered with negative precedent, should be so construed.[88]

The same approach should be taken toward other types of government spying on public activities, whether they involve global positioning devices, satellite cameras, radio frequency identification, or handheld detection devices. Regulation of these surveillance practices is crucial to ensure that government intrusion into our lives does not grow with technological developments. "Dragnet law enforcement practices," to use *Knotts*'s terminology, should be the province of the Fourth Amendment.

PART III

Transaction Surveillance

CHAPTER SIX

Subpoenas and Privacy

We turn now from physical surveillance—the real-time visual observation of our activities—to transaction surveillance—the accessing of records about activities that have already occurred. In terms of volume, transaction surveillance dwarfs physical surveillance. The recent revelations about the National Security Agency's designs on the phone logs of millions of American citizens and the government's efforts to obtain hundreds of thousands of bank and credit records, both programs commenced at least as far back as September 2001, provide a dramatic illustration of the point.[1] Outside the national security context as well, government investigators are constantly and routinely seeking access to digital and hard copy documents.

Many of the documents obtained through transaction surveillance, particularly those sought in connection with regulatory investigations, describe the transactions of corporations and other businesses. But a significant proportion of these records contain more personal information. Housed in private businesses, government agencies, and other institutions, they include reports on our medical status and financial condition; data about our purchases, rentals, real estate holdings, licenses, and memberships; logs listing the destination of our e-mails, our Internet wanderings, and phone calls; and countless other bits of individual descriptors, ranging from salary levels to college grades to driver's license numbers. These records can sometimes be obtained directly, using snoopware or arrangements with service providers such as AT&T, Verizon, and America Online, or indirectly, through commercial data brokers for a price.

Whether the records memorialize our own version of personal activities or are created by the recordholder itself, they usually come into existence on the explicit or implicit understanding that the information they contain will be viewed by a limited number of people for circumscribed purposes. In other words, we consider the contents of most of these records private vis-à-vis most of the world. Thus, one might assume that the Fourth Amendment, which is meant to protect "reasonable expectations of privacy" in "papers" as well as houses, persons, and effects, applies here with full force.

Yet that is not the case. Law enforcement officials can, perfectly legally, gain access to all these records much more easily than they can search our houses or even our cars. While the latter types of actions require probable cause, government can obtain many of the records just described simply by asking (or paying) for them. And, at most, all the government needs to show in order to get any of these records is that they are relevant to a government investigation—a much lower, and much more diffuse, level of justification than probable cause.

This state of affairs might make sense when the records sought are truly public in nature. It might also be justifiable when the records involve an entity such as a corporation, professional service provider, or government department and are sought in an effort to investigate the entity and its members. But today, facilitated by the computerization of information and communication, government routinely obtains individual medical, financial, and e-mail records in connection with investigations that have nothing to do with business or governmental corruption. That practice is much more questionable.

To understand why this practice persists, one has to understand the subpoena, because it is the primary mechanism for acquiring records. A subpoena is a formal demand for tangible items and traditionally has come in one of two forms (although recently other versions have sprung up). Subpoenas *duces tecum* are controlled by the grand jury or the prosecutor, with the courts determining their validity when they are resisted by the target.[2] Administrative subpoenas or summonses are issued by government agencies, such as the Internal Revenue Service, the Federal Trade Commission, and the Department of Justice, and are also enforced by the courts.[3]

Although both types of subpoenas can be challenged by the recipient before any documents are handed over,[4] both are also extremely easy to enforce. There are essentially three grounds for resisting a subpoena: privilege, burdensomeness, and irrelevance. A successful privilege claim is rare; as explained in some detail later in this chapter, the Fifth Amendment privilege against self-incrimination is usually unavailable and the attorney-client privilege is coextensive with that privilege. Objections that the task of assembling the records demanded by a subpoena is too burdensome or expensive are also, in the words of a leading criminal procedure text, "almost always doomed to failure."[5] And an irrelevance challenge is usually equally unavailing. In the federal grand jury context, for instance, subpoenas are quashed as irrelevant only when "there is *no* reasonable *possibility* that the category of materials the government seeks will produce information relevant to the *general subject* of the grand jury's investigation."[6] The relevancy standard in the administrative subpoena context is similarly lax. The Supreme Court has indicated that constitutional requisites are met even when a subpoena seeks to satisfy "nothing more than official curiosity,"[7] and some lower courts have concluded that the standard is even more deferential than the "arbitrary and capricious" test applied in administrative law cases.[8]

No nationwide tally of the extent to which law enforcement uses document subpoenas exists. But the federal government alone issues thousands of such subpoenas every year.[9] As noted above, today subpoenas and pseudo-subpoenas are routinely used to obtain not only business records and the like but also documents containing significant amounts of personal information about individuals, information that can be extremely revealing. For instance, a subpoena is the only authorization the federal government needs to obtain medical and financial records. The contents of "stored" e-mail messages and phone company and Internet service provider (ISP) logs can also be acquired pursuant to a subpoena. And other types of information—ranging from the phone numbers and e-mail addresses one contacts, to the contents of records kept by government agencies—can be obtained simply upon the certification of a law enforcement official that the information will be useful to a government investigation.

Thus, as an investigative tool and as a means of discovering ostensibly private facts, subpoenas and their progeny are far more important than physical searches of homes, businesses, and effects. Yet very little literature on the history or rationale of the subpoena exists. This chapter helps fill that void, as a predicate for chapter 7's detailed discussion of current subpoena law and how it should be reformed.

Section 1 of this chapter looks at the history of the subpoena in an attempt to understand how the currently lax approach to transaction surveillance developed. An important, and surprising, part of the story is that throughout the nineteenth century, courts looked to the *Fifth* Amendment, not the Fourth Amendment, in analyzing the validity of subpoenas; furthermore, most courts held that the Fifth Amendment's injunction against compelling a person to testify against himself or herself *prohibited*, not merely limited, government attempts to obtain incriminating documents from a suspect. Late in the nineteenth century the Supreme Court expanded on this notion by holding that such compulsion violated the Fifth Amendment *and* the Fourth Amendment's restriction on unreasonable searches and seizures.

At the turn of the twentieth century, however, the Court appeared to reverse itself, removing virtually all Fourth Amendment strictures on document subpoenas and, when the documents were corporate in nature, eliminating Fifth Amendment limitations as well. This dramatic shift in the Court's posture was refined during the first three quarters of the twentieth century and remains good law today. The point emphasized in section 1 of this chapter, however, is that the Court's pre-1975 deregulation of subpoenas came in cases involving government attempts to regulate businesses; not a single one of them involved searches of personal papers. Because, as far as the Court was concerned, personal records held by the target of the subpoena—in those days, most personal records—remained protected by the Fifth Amendment's prohibition on compelled testimony, the virtual elimination of Fourth Amendment protection against subpoenas had no impact in that area.

Two relatively recent developments, also described in section 1, have changed all that. First, within the past three decades, the Supreme Court has radically altered its approach to the Fifth Amendment privilege: today, personal records held by the target are, in the run-of-the-mill case, almost as unprotected as corporate records as far as that constitutional provision is concerned. Far more important, the modernization of society has rendered the Fifth Amendment's application to personal records largely irrelevant in any event. Today, in contrast to the nineteenth century, most of our personal information is recorded and held by third parties. When third parties are ordered to produce information via a subpoena, they cannot, under any plausible interpretation of the Fifth Amendment, be said to be incriminating themselves. Thus, when the government compels production from a third-party recordholder—whether the recordholder is a hospital, an ISP, or another government agency—it is not violating the target's Fifth Amendment right.

Since today most subpoenas for personal documents are aimed at third-party recordholders, the upshot of these developments is that the government is almost entirely unrestricted, by either the Fifth or Fourth Amendment, in its efforts to obtain documentary evidence of crime. Section 2 of this chapter examines the various rationales for this regulatory regime.

More specifically, it identifies six possible reasons why subpoenas need not meet the probable cause standard even when aimed at obtaining personal information, the first and last of which apply to all subpoenas, and the rest of which are relevant only to third-party subpoenas. The first justification, offered by the Supreme Court more than a century ago, is that subpoenas are not searches under the Fourth Amendment because they do not involve physical intrusion. The second, put forward by the modern Court, is that third-party subpoenas are not searches because the information they seek is already exposed to others, and therefore they are not associated with a reasonable expectation of privacy. The next three reasons are not as clearly stated in Supreme Court opinions but are implicit in the Court's language or are found in lower court decisions: the records obtained through third-party subpoenas belong to the third party, not the target; third-party recordholders are no different from third-party witnesses who have information about a suspect; and third parties have an obligation to provide information to the government. The final reason courts give for leaving subpoenas essentially unregulated is also the most common: imposition of rigorous Fourth Amendment requirements on subpoenas would stymie important government investigations.

The conclusions that section 2 reaches with respect to these six rationales turn on the historical distinction between corporate and personal records described in section 1. Many of the rationales for deregulating subpoenas are persuasive in the context that most commonly triggers the use of subpoenas and in which constitutional subpoena law developed—the investigation of corporate crime. But none of these rationales is convincing when applied to demands for personal records.

If these conclusions are correct, then distinguishing between impersonal and personal records is important. That is the task of section 3. Ironically, this part of the chapter borrows heavily from the Court's old Fifth Amendment jurisprudence, which justified protection of records based largely on a desire to create a "zone of privacy." The irony stems from the fact that today, of course, the Fifth Amendment is not about privacy at all but rather about coercion. The fact that the Court's early Fifth Amendment decisions were focused on protection of privacy suggests that if the Court of one hundred years ago had known its Fifth Amendment jurisprudence would be jettisoned, its Fourth Amendment jurisprudence might have been much more protective of documentary evidence that is personal in nature.

I. A Constitutional History of Subpoenas

There are three legal processes for obtaining documents. The first, of course, is the search warrant, issued ex parte and executed by government agents.[10] The second is a subpoena ordering the person or entity whose activities are described in the documents to produce them (a first-party or target subpoena). The third is a subpoena directing a person or entity who is not a target of an investigation, but who happens to hold records relevant to it, to produce them (a third-party subpoena).

Subpoenas are the preferred method of obtaining documents, primarily because they are usually valid so long as the documents they demand are relevant to an investigation, a much lower standard than the probable cause required for a search warrant. The one supposed advantage a warrant has over a first-party subpoena is that it is executed when it is served and thus can prevent destruction of evidence by an alerted suspect. But that threat is minimal in most cases. Where business records are involved, document destruction seldom occurs after receipt of a subpoena because the documents are needed to run the business and because so many people know of their existence that obstruction of justice charges are a real possibility if destruction occurs. Shredding of documents is a more likely response to a first-party subpoena aimed at an individual's personal records, but even here obstruction penalties tend to inhibit it.[11]

More important, personal information can usually be obtained via a third-party subpoena, which of course eliminates the possibility that the target will destroy the evidence. In many settings, this investigative move also eliminates even the target's ability to challenge the government's action, because he or she will not be told about it (a practice the Supreme Court has upheld against Fourth, Fifth, Sixth, and Fourteenth Amendment challenges).[12] The supposed advantage of a warrant over this type of subpoena is that it will produce more or better records because the third party may not have the information the government wants. But that advantage is illusory in today's world. Most aspects of our personal life that have been reduced to writing or digitized are stored with some third party. Volumes of data about us can be found in "public" records maintained by the government, and even more data are deposited with hospitals, banks, schools, stores, and ISPs. Under current law, all this information is just a subpoena (or less) away. Thus it is not surprising that law enforcement rarely resorts to a warrant to obtain documents and records.[13]

The following discussion explains how this regulatory regime developed. It begins with the constitutional law governing first-party subpoenas and then examines the law of third-party subpoenas.

Subpoenas Directed at the Target

The origin of the subpoena for documents can be traced back at least to the reign of King Charles II in the late seventeenth century.[14] But it appears that these subpoenas were common only in civil litigation; even at their inception, courts hesitated to allow their use in criminal cases. In 1748, the King's Bench cited cases from 1703 and 1744 in emphasizing that a court may not "make a man produce evidence against himself, in a criminal prosecution."[15] A number of other eighteenth-century English courts straightforwardly held that the government could never demand a person's books and papers in criminal cases.[16] By the time the American Constitution was drafted, the matter was well settled. As Richard Nagareda has noted, "All sources to address the point concur that common law at the time of the Fifth Amendment barred the compelled production of self-incriminatory documents."[17]

American judicial decisions in the nineteenth century appeared to follow English common law, although a few scattered courts did allow compelled production in criminal and quasi-criminal cases.[18] The issue probably did not arise that often in the United States, just as it was seldom litigated in England.[19] Documents sometimes could be obtained from a source other than the suspect, which occasioned no Fifth Amendment issue, and might also be obtained through a search based on a warrant. In any event, street crime usually did not generate documentary evidence, and state regulation of business crimes—much more likely to trigger demands for documents via subpoena—was in its infancy until late in the nineteenth century.[20]

It was a regulatory case, involving nonpayment of taxes, that provided the peak of constitutional protection for papers in the United States. The case was *Boyd v. United States,*[21] handed down by the U.S. Supreme Court in 1886. Consistent with the early English common law, *Boyd* held that using a subpoena to force an individual to produce private documents violated the Fifth Amendment's prohibition against compelled testimony. But Justice Joseph P. Bradley's opinion for the Court added a new twist to the analysis, holding that such subpoenas also violated the Fourth Amendment's prescription against unreasonable searches and seizures. The Court came to this conclusion even though the defendant company was subject only to civil sanctions (which undermines an argument based on the Fifth Amendment's prohibition of compelling testimony in criminal cases) and even though the documents at issue in *Boyd* were not personal papers but merely invoices used to prove fraudulent importation of goods (which are hardly the types of intimate papers most closely associated with the privacy interests the Fourth Amendment protects). Justice Bradley accorded these objections little weight:[22]

> The "unreasonable searches and seizures" condemned in the Fourth Amendment are almost always made for the purpose of compelling a man to give evidence against himself, which in criminal cases is condemned in the Fifth Amendment; and compelling a man "in a criminal case to be a witness against himself," which is condemned in the Fifth Amendment, throws light on the question as to what is an "unreasonable search and seizure" within the meaning of the Fourth Amendment. And we have been unable to perceive that the seizure of a man's private books and papers to be used in evidence against him is substantially different from compelling him to be a witness against himself.[23]

This strong affirmation by the highest court in the land of what had previously been, in the United States at least, an ambiguous constitutional protection for papers had potentially major repercussions. As William Stuntz has noted, *Boyd*'s holding, if allowed to stand, would have seriously undermined the modern regulatory state, which at that time was just building up steam.[24] Without the ability readily to obtain the records of corporations, partnerships, and other entities, government agencies would be frustrated in their efforts to ensure that corporate tax laws, bank laws, securities laws, and a host of other regulatory statutes were enforced.

For precisely that reason, within twenty years the Court reversed itself. In the 1906 case of *Hale v. Henkel*,[25] the defendant corporation, suspected of antitrust violations, relied on *Boyd* in arguing that a grand jury subpoena for its documents violated both the Fifth and Fourth Amendments. In finding for the government, the Court rejected the interpretation of the Fifth Amendment that it had adopted in *Boyd* and limited the Fourth Amendment's relevance in subpoena cases to a prohibition of overbroad requests. Acceptance of the corporation's Fifth Amendment claim, the Court stated, "would practically nullify the whole act of Congress [that outlawed monopolies]. Of what use would it be for the legislature to declare these combinations unlawful if the judicial power may close the door of access to every available source of information upon the subject?"[26] For similar reasons, the Court held that the Fourth Amendment did not prevent use of a subpoena *duces tecum* to compel the production of documentary evidence. Quoting an English decision, the Court stated that "it would be 'utterly impossible to carry on the administration of justice' without this writ."[27] At most, the Court indicated, the Fourth Amendment prohibits a "general subpoena" that is "too sweeping," a holding meant merely to address the now largely moot concern that production of most or all of a company's papers would "completely put a stop to the business of that company."[28]

The move toward the current regime of virtually unlimited subpoena power was not immediate, however. In *FTC v. American Tobacco Co.,* decided in 1924, a unanimous Court held that federal antitrust law required the Federal Trade Commission to provide "some evidence of the materiality of the papers demanded" by an administrative subpoena.[29] Although the holding was based on an interpretation of a statute, the Court, per Justice Oliver Wendell Holmes, also stated that "anyone who respects the spirit as well as the letter of the Fourth Amendment would be loath to believe that Congress intended to authorize one of its subordinate agencies to sweep all our traditions into the fire and to direct fishing expeditions into private papers."[30] Other Supreme Court and lower court cases exhibited similar resistance to blind sanctioning of subpoenas administered by agencies.[31]

By the mid-1940s, however, the Court had carried through to its logical conclusion *Hale*'s assertion that significant restrictions on the government's subpoena power would unduly hamper regulatory investigative efforts. In 1946, in *Oklahoma Press Co. v. Walling*, the Court canvassed the relevant authorities and concluded that

> the Fifth Amendment affords no protection by virtue of the self-incrimination provision, whether for the corporation or for its officers; and the Fourth, if applicable, at the most guards against abuse only by way of too much indefiniteness or breadth in the things required to be "particularly described," if also the inquiry is one the demanding agency is authorized by law to make and the materials specified are relevant.[32]

Oklahoma Press even insinuated that a subpoena is not an "actual search" meriting Fourth Amendment protection.[33] Although this dictum was glossed over four years later in *United States v. Morton Salt Co.,* there the Court adhered to the notion that "it is sufficient if the inquiry is within the authority of the agency, the demand is not too indefinite and the information sought is reasonably relevant."[34] Indeed, "even if one were to regard the request for information in this case as caused by nothing more than official curiosity, nevertheless law enforcing agencies have a legitimate right to satisfy themselves that corporate behavior is consistent with the law and the public interest."[35] In *United States v. Powell,* decided in 1964, the Court reiterated that a government agency subpoena for records is valid if the records are "relevant" to an investigation conducted for a "legitimate purpose" (meaning one authorized by statute).[36] As applied, the *Powell* relevance standard is extremely easy to meet.[37]

What has seldom been noted, however, is that all these cases involved government attempts to obtain corporate or other business documents. Throughout the first half of the twentieth century, the Court had intimated that subpoenas for private records might have to meet a higher standard. For instance, in *Hale* the Court stated that "there is a clear distinction between an individual and a corporation" in cases involving demands for production of books and papers.[38] Because a corporation "is a creature of the State," it "is presumed to be incorporated for the benefit of the public," and it "receives certain special privileges and franchises, and holds them subject to the laws of the State and the limitations of its charter." But an individual "owes no such duty to the State, since he receives nothing therefrom, beyond the protection of his life and property." Thus, in contrast to the corporation, an individual retains the right to refuse "to incriminate himself, and the immunity of himself and his property from arrest or seizure except under a warrant of the law."[39]

In the years following *Hale*, Supreme Court and lower court cases frequently reiterated, albeit usually in dictum, that only corporate documents could be obtained pursuant to subpoena; private documents continued to be immune from compulsory process.[40] Four decades later the Court was still echoing these sentiments when, in *Oklahoma Press*, it characterized its earlier cases authorizing production of documents pursuant to a subpoena as applying "merely to the production of corporate records and papers."[41] Shortly thereafter, in *Morton Salt*, the Court simply stated that "corporations can claim no equality with individuals in the enjoyment of a right to privacy."[42]

In short, in the words of the Court's majority opinion in *Griswold v. Connecticut,* the Fifth Amendment created a "zone of privacy" around personal papers.[43] From our perspective in the twenty-first century, the Fourth Amendment seems a more appropriate source of law for establishing privacy zones. But *Hale* had emasculated the Fourth Amendment, at least in the subpoena context.[44] Thus, it was the Fifth Amendment or nothing.

Eventually, it turned out to be nothing, at least for the last quarter of the twentieth century. A signal of things to come was the perplexing and seldom discussed opinion in *Ryan v. United States.*[45] Decided in 1964 on the same day as *Powell* and a year before *Griswold*'s zone-of-privacy dictum, *Ryan* blithely announced that the minimal *Powell* requirements for administrative subpoenas aimed at corporations governed subpoenas for individual tax records as well. The Court provided virtually no explanation for this abrupt change in direction, merely stating that it had reached its conclusion "for the reasons given in [*Powell*],"[46] without any further discussion. And *Powell*'s holding that probable cause need not be demonstrated to obtain corporate tax records rested solely on an interpretation of the relevant statutory language.[47] The *Powell* opinion (and therefore *Ryan*) did not mention the Fifth Amendment. Nor did it refer to the Fourth Amendment, the ostensible basis of the petitioner's claim in *Ryan*.[48] Thus, with one perfunctory statement that did not purport to address constitutional concerns, the Court seemed to obliterate the sixty-year-old distinction between corporate and personal records in connection with the subpoena process.

Because of its opaqueness, however, *Ryan* left some doubt as to the application of the Constitution to subpoenas. Indeed, in *United States v. Dionisio,*[49] decided nine years later, the Court seemed to have forgotten all about *Ryan*. There, in the course of holding that voice exemplars are not "testimony" under the Fifth Amendment, the Court continued to assert, in apparent contrast with *Ryan*, that papers *are* testimony and that the grand jury "cannot require the production by a person of private books and records that would incriminate him," citing *Boyd*.[50] Although *Dionisio* involved a grand jury subpoena whereas *Ryan* dealt with an administrative summons, the demands for production in these cases were both pursuant to law enforcement investigations and thus were functionally identical.

In the face of *Dionisio*'s reaffirmation of *Boyd* (albeit in dictum), *Ryan* might have been limited to production of personal tax records by analogizing such records to corporate documents and invoking *Hale*'s necessity rationale. Indeed, the Court's decision in *Couch v. United States,*[51] decided the same year as *Dionisio*, suggested as much. Noting that federal law requires disclosure of much of the information in tax records, the Court in *Couch* stated that in a "situation where obligations of disclosure exist and under a system largely dependent upon honest self-reporting even to survive . . . [a person] cannot reasonably claim, either for Fourth or Fifth Amendment purposes, an expectation of protected privacy or confidentiality."[52] Perhaps this reasoning could have differentiated government attempts to obtain tax records from its efforts to obtain other types of private financial records, as well as medical, educational, and similar personal information held in record form.

But that is not the route the Court chose to take. Rather, in *Fisher v. United States,*[53] decided in 1976, it discarded all the language, from *Boyd* through *Dionisio*, regarding the distinction between personal and business papers. Like *Ryan*, *Fisher* involved a tax summons for personal records, but, unlike *Ryan*, *Fisher* directly repudiated the Fifth Amendment *Boyd* claim in a way that appeared to apply to all documents, not just tax records. More specifically, *Fisher* suggested that subpoenas virtually never implicate the Fifth Amendment's prohibition of compelled self-incrimination, either because they do not compel information or because, if they do, the information they compel is not self-incriminating. First, the Court noted, a subpoena does not force the creation of the sought-after documents, and thus the disclosure of document content demanded by a subpoena does not implicate the Fifth Amendment's prohibition of compelled self-incrimination.[54] Second, *Fisher* held that while a subpoena does compel the *production* of documents, that act does not provide the government with any useful incriminating information, at least when the act of production is not an important element of the prosecution's proof or the government can prove the source in some other way (which is often the case).[55]

The most important aspect of *Fisher* is that it shifted Fifth Amendment analysis from the zone-of-privacy paradigm to a focus on coercion. As the Court said, "We cannot cut the Fifth Amendment completely loose from the moorings of its language, and make it serve as a general protector of privacy, a word not mentioned in its text."[56] Because the content of nonbusiness documents is no more compelled than the content of business documents, *Fisher* appeared to repudiate the impersonal-corporate versus personal-individual distinction that earlier cases had emphasized. Indeed, eight years after *Fisher*, Justice O'Connor felt confident enough about this point to assert that "the Fifth Amendment provides absolutely no protection for the contents of private papers of any kind."[57]

That is not the end of the story, however. Subsequent cases indicate that the act of producing papers may be more likely to reveal incriminating information than *Fisher* suggested. For instance, in *Braswell v. United*

States,[58] decided twelve years after *Fisher*, the Court held that while the custodian of records generally may not resist a subpoena on the grounds that production might incriminate him personally, he should be able to prevent the government from mentioning that he was the custodian. The Court also stated that the custodian might even be able to avoid handing over the records in the first place if he could show, for instance, "that he is the sole employee and officer of the corporation [and] that the jury would [thereby] conclude that he produced the records."[59] And, in *United States v. Hubbell,*[60] decided in 2000, the Court held that where the location and identity of the documents demanded by a subpoena are not known by the government beforehand, then compelling their production from the target of the investigation may implicate the Fifth Amendment. In that situation, the respondent is forced to take "the mental and physical steps necessary to provide the prosecutor with an accurate inventory of the many sources of potentially incriminating evidence sought by the subpoena."[61]

Perhaps *Hubbell* moves Fifth Amendment analysis partially back toward *Boyd*. Some commentators have gone so far as to say that *Hubbell* requires probable cause in order to obtain a valid subpoena for documents sought from the target.[62] That is probably an exaggeration of that decision's impact, especially where only a few documents are sought and the target need not guess what the government is after.[63] But even if *Hubbell* does reintegrate the Fourth and Fifth Amendments, it does not affect the lion's share of subpoenas that seek personal papers, because most of these are directed at third parties, not at those who are the subject of the records.

Third-Party Subpoenas

While early twentieth-century cases adhered to the idea that the Fifth Amendment prohibited access to personal papers held by the target, they just as clearly stated that the Fifth Amendment does not prohibit compelling third parties to produce documents that are later used against the target. A 1913 decision by the Supreme Court put the matter quite pithily: "A party is privileged from producing evidence but not from its production."[64] The exception to this rule, recognized at least as far back as the eighteenth century,[65] was that records given to an attorney were protected to the same extent as they would be if retained by their owner. *Fisher* continued to recognize this exception as a means of honoring the attorney-client privilege.[66] But once *Fisher* reduced the scope of the Fifth Amendment privilege for targets, the extent to which attorneys could rely on the Fifth Amendment to resist a subpoena aimed at client records was correspondingly limited.

That treatment of the Fifth Amendment left the Fourth Amendment as the only feasible protector of personal records held by third parties.[67] Although *Hale* had made clear that the Fourth Amendment places few restrictions even on document subpoenas directed at the target of an investigation, in 1967 the Supreme Court decided *Katz*. As already noted in several places in this book, *Katz* appeared to liberalize Fourth Amendment doctrine by rejecting a property-based, formalistic reading of the Fourth Amendment and establishing that its guarantees were meant to protect expectations of privacy that "society is prepared to recognize as 'reasonable.' " Given the private information potentially obtained via a subpoena, *Katz* opened up the possibility that the Court might require probable cause for a subpoena for personal information sought from third parties, or at least impose on third-party subpoenas restrictions roughly equivalent to that imposed on first-party subpoenas by the act-of-production doctrine.

But within ten years of the *Katz* decision the Court had squelched any movement toward converting third-party subpoenas into warrants. The first intimation of its unwillingness to apply *Katz* to subpoenas came in *Couch*, which involved seizure of records from the petitioner's tax accountant. There the Court asserted that "there can be little expectation of privacy where records are handed to an accountant, knowing that mandatory disclosure of much of the information therein is required in an income tax return."[68] At least that language left open a ruling that records not subject to mandatory disclosure would be afforded more Fourth Amendment protection. However, in *United States v. Miller,*[69] handed down the same day as *Fisher*, the Court appeared to eliminate even that possibility. In *Miller*, the Court decided that the Fourth Amendment imposes no restrictions on any type of third-party subpoena, other than those that protect the third party.

The defendant in *Miller* argued that a subpoena *duces tecum* that required his bank to produce various records describing his financial dealings violated his Fourth Amendment rights. But the Court concluded, in effect, that Miller did not have standing to make this argument. Referring to Warren Court cases involving defendants who made incriminating disclosures to undercover agents,[70] the Court noted that it had "held repeatedly that the Fourth Amendment does not prohibit the obtaining of information revealed to a third party and conveyed by him to Government authorities." Just as a person who reveals intimacies to an acquaintance assumes the risk the acquaintance will be or turn into an informant, a bank depositor "takes the risk, in revealing his affairs to another, that the information will be conveyed by that person to the government."[71] The Court concluded, therefore, that Miller possessed no cognizable expectation of privacy in the financial information kept by his bank.

Miller left no doubt that the Court would reject a narrow interpretation of *Couch*. The records at issue in *Miller* were not subject to mandatory disclosure under the tax laws. Further, they described all of Miller's financial activities with the bank and included three monthly statements.[72] Yet these differences with *Couch* did not give the Court pause, as indicated by its declaration that the Fourth Amendment does not protect information in third-party records "even if the information is revealed on the assumption that it will be used only for a limited purpose and the confidence placed in the third party will not be betrayed."[73] This language and the result in *Miller* would also seem to undercut any distinction based on the precise nature of the financial information in question.[74]

In any event, the Supreme Court has applied *Miller*'s rationale to phone company records (in *Smith v. Maryland*)[75] and loan applications (in *United States v. Payner*),[76] and lower courts have used it to uphold subpoenas for personal records from medical institutions,[77] auditors and accountants,[78] trustees in bankruptcy,[79] and government institutions.[80] *Miller* also has been the basis for cases upholding federal statutes that permit government access to the records of ISPs and to stored e-mail.[81] Except in cases where a third party objects on overbreadth grounds, the Fourth Amendment as construed in *Miller* appears to offer no protection for personal records held by third parties, regardless of how much information in those records is provided by the subject of the records or the contractual arrangements between the parties.

This position has assumed ever greater significance as innovations in computerization have made personal information both more likely to be communicated to third-party recordholders and more accessible. When *Hale* was decided, government recordkeeping was minimal and business recordkeeping was sparse.[82] Even in 1976, when *Miller* was handed down, the Information Age had not begun in earnest.[83] Today, as already noted, government agencies keep detailed databases on many aspects of our lives, banks and credit card companies maintain voluminous statements on our financial purchases, phone and Internet companies record our communications, hospitals develop computerized descriptions of our health problems, and digital records exist about our video rentals, library borrowing, and travel destinations. To obtain access to all this information, *Miller* requires, at most, a showing of relevance.

Summary: From Complete to Virtually Nonexistent Protection

At the end of the nineteenth century, *Boyd* affirmed the common law ban on government efforts to obtain incriminating papers from their owners. Although that ban was soon lifted for business papers, only in the last quarter of the twentieth century did the Court relax constitutional strictures on subpoenas for self-incriminating personal papers. In contrast, constitutional restrictions on subpoenas for papers in the possession of third parties have always been lax. In the latter setting the historical change has not been in the law but in the extent to which personal information is now housed with third parties.

The result of these developments is that, as a constitutional matter, the minimal relevance standard once used primarily in connection with business subpoenas now authorizes access to vast amounts of personal information, to wit, any personal information that is in record form, with the possible exception of information found in records possessed by the target that the government is not sure exist. On the surface, at least, that regime seems to conflict with the Fourth Amendment's injunction that searches and seizures of papers, as well as of houses, persons, and effects, be declared unreasonable unless authorized by a warrant based on probable cause. To determine whether the current system is justifiable, a closer look at its rationales is necessary.

II. Rationales for Deregulating Subpoenas

The case law recited above relies, directly or indirectly, on a number of justifications for continuing to leave subpoenas largely unregulated. The discussion below separates these justifications into six rationales. The first four can be characterized as arguments that subpoenas do not involve a search for Fourth Amendment purposes because they do not infringe on reasonable expectations of privacy, while the last two focus on the strength of the government's interest in keeping subpoenas unregulated. The first and last rationales apply to all subpoenas, whereas the rest focus on third-party subpoenas. The conclusion I reach is that a few of these rationales do support relaxed strictures on subpoenas where business and other entity crime is concerned, but that none justify permitting government to obtain personal records merely on a showing of relevance.

Subpoenas Are Not Intrusive

In his concurring opinion in *Hale*, Justice Joseph McKenna took the majority to task for even suggesting that the Fourth Amendment applied to subpoenas. In contrast to the traditional search, he argued, the subpoena does not involve "trespass or force" and "cannot be finally enforced except after challenge."[84] Forty years later, in *Oklahoma Press*, a majority of the Court echoed these sentiments, stating that subpoenas do not trigger "actual searches" because they do not require a physical intrusion; rather, they are, at most, "constructive" searches carried out by the target himself or herself.[85] Thus, several Supreme Court justices have suggested that document subpoenas are not Fourth Amendment searches for the following reasons: (1) they rely on the recordholder, not the government, to produce the documents; (2) the target can challenge them before surrendering any items; and (3) they do not involve physical trespass or intrusion.

If the scope of the Fourth Amendment is to be determined with reference to reasonable expectations of privacy, all three of these rationales for the minimal restrictions on subpoenas are specious. The fact that it is the target (or a third party) rather than the police who locates the documents obviously does not change the nature of the revelations they contain, which can include information about medical treatment, finances, education, the identity of one's communicants, and even the contents of one's communications. The target's ability to challenge a subpoena, while it may inhibit some fishing expeditions, at most will only delay government access to the records, unless something beyond the current relevance standard is applicable; recall also that for many types of third-party subpoenas the target has no right of challenge. And if the notion that searches occur only when the government engages in physical invasion of private space were correct, then communications surveillance and physical surveillance of the home would not be a search, since neither usually requires a trespass or use of force. Yet, as noted in earlier chapters, the Supreme Court has firmly declared that both of the latter government actions are governed by the Fourth Amendment and require warrants based on probable cause.

While the technological surveillance example demonstrates why physical intrusiveness should not be dispositive on the search issue, it does not necessarily dictate that all document subpoenas be based on probable cause. First, not all records are easily categorized as sufficiently private to warrant the degree of constitutional protection provided to communications and activities that take place inside the home. In particular, business records—the type of records involved in all the Supreme Court's early subpoena cases—might be considered much less personal than individual medical, financial, and e-mail records; as the history described above makes clear, the Court has routinely recognized as much in a number of cases.

Second, even when the records sought are personal in nature, the rules governing surveillance in cases like *Berger* and *Kyllo* do not appear to apply when the records are held by *third parties*, because generally only those subjected to surveillance may challenge it.[86] This limitation derives from well-established doctrine that the Fourth Amendment's protections can be asserted only by those whose own private enclave is infringed by the government's action. That doctrine is, of course, the putative basis of the Court's opinion in *United States v. Miller*.

Third-Party Subpoenas Do Not Infringe on the Target's Privacy

Miller held that we cannot challenge government access to our personal information when it is possessed by a third-party recordholder because we have surrendered it "voluntarily" and thus "assume the risk" that the third party will provide it to the government. But *Miller*'s version of Fourth Amendment standing is easily challenged. There are two significant problems with the Court's reasoning in that case.

The first problem, as many have pointed out,[87] is that the Court simply defies reality when it says that one voluntarily surrenders information to doctors, banks, schools, and phone and Internet providers. It is impossible to get treatment, engage in financial transactions, obtain an education, or communicate with others without providing personal information to the relevant facilitating entities or allowing those entities to collect it. To choose to forgo these activities would mean an isolated, unproductive, and possibly much foreshortened existence. The undercover agent cases, on which *Miller* relied, involve an entirely different dynamic, where refusing to interact with a particular individual is a realistic option. *Miller* transforms all recordkeeping institutions into undercover agents, which all but hermits are powerless to avoid.

Even if the choice to reveal personal information to a third party or to allow a third party to collect it could somehow be characterized as voluntary, the *Miller* Court's second key assertion—that one thereby assumes the risk that the third party will convey it to the government—is pure judicial fiat. As I noted in chapter 3, we assume only those risks of unregulated government intrusion that the courts tell us we have to assume. Perhaps more to the point, even though *Miller* has been the law for more than three decades, most people probably would be surprised to learn that banks hand over financial information to the government virtually any time the government wants it. In the Slobogin and Schumacher study described in chapter 2, "perusing bank records" was viewed as more intrusive than "searching [a] footlocker in a car" and a number of other government actions that require probable cause or reasonable suspicion, a finding replicated in a new study reported in chapter 7.[88] Also noteworthy is the fact that a number of state courts have rejected, on state law grounds, *Miller*'s precise holding regarding bank records,[89] and many others have declared that the decision does not apply to medical records.[90]

To say *Miller* is wrong is not to say that third-party subpoenas always require probable cause, however. Again, certain types of records (for example, some forms of public documents) may not be entitled to as much protection as others (for example, those containing medical and financial information), distinctions that chapter 7 develops in more detail. The important point for present purposes is that the government should not have practically unrestricted access to records simply because they contain information that has been surrendered to the recordholder.

Third-Party Records Belong to the Third Party

One also might try to justify *Miller*'s holding by focusing on the recordholder's, rather than the subject's, interest in the information. After all, the third party ostensibly "owns" the records, not only because it physically possesses them but because it (usually) creates them. Arguably, this property interest confers on the recordholder the right to assign the information and eliminates the subject's control over it.[91] A variant of this argument asserts that permitting the subject to limit the third party's use of personal data unduly restricts the third party's interests in commercial freedom and freedom of speech.[92]

This property rationale has both descriptive and normative flaws. The descriptive problem is that although the physical documents maintained by third-party recordholders may be the third party's property alone, their content generally is not wholly within their control. Indeed, federal law recognizes that individuals retain an interest even in information maintained in public records; under the Privacy Act we have a right to participate in the use, review, and disposal of our files,[93] and the Freedom of Information Act circumscribes outsider access to a wide range of personal information in government file cabinets and computers.[94] Jerry Mashaw has gone so far as to say that these two statutes "gave all citizens 'property rights' in the information held by government bureaus."[95] If that is true of public records, it should surely be the case with privately held records such as those maintained by hospitals, banks, and schools, because their contents are even more likely created under laws that give the subject some degree of control over them.[96]

The normative flaw in the property rationale is identical to the flaw in *Miller*. Third-party recordholders possess the personal information they do because people *must* give it to them in order to function in society; in property terms, the subjects are often involuntary or inadvertent bailors of the information, and recordholders are their bailees. Recognition of this point does not mean that the individual can prevent the third party from using the information for the purpose for which it was obtained. But it should mean that the third party does not have total discretion to do whatever it wants with the information simply because it "owns" it, a principle that a number of jurisdictions—domestic and foreign—explicitly recognize.[97] In other words, the subjects of records should have standing to contest their disclosure to law enforcement unless the records were constructed for that purpose.

But suppose the third party has a privacy policy that specifically notifies the subject that information surrendered to it may be transmitted to other entities, including the government? Then hasn't one contracted away any property interest in the information? In theory, of course, a person should be able to consent to disclosure of personal facts. But as Daniel Solove has persuasively argued, contract- and market-based models do not work well in this context.[98] We rarely have any real "relationship" with the third-party entities that acquire our information, possess virtually no bargaining power over them, are often ignorant of or confused about the third party's privacy "offer," and in any event frequently have no way to opt out of or fine-tune the "contract." As Solove says, there is "a problem in the nature of the market itself that prevents fair and voluntary information transactions."[99] That, of course, is the same sort of reason *Miller* is flawed.

Subpoenas Duces Tecum = Subpoenas *Ad Testificandum*

The next rationale for minimally restricting governmental requisition of records rests on an analogy to the law governing demands for testimony from a third party. Many witnesses subject to subpoena are not the targets of the investigation and thus will not be able to (or want to) assert the Fifth Amendment. Because the government can compel these third-party witnesses to reveal information about a person without demonstrating any suspicion regarding that person, this argument posits, it should be able to obtain records from a third party under the same circumstances.[100]

Looked at more closely, however, this analogy between subpoenas *ad testificandum* and subpoenas *duces tecum* does not work. Neither of the two reasons a witness should be able to testify over a target's objection applies to a third-party recordholder. The first reason, having to do with the witness's prerogatives, is discussed here. The second, which has to do with the government's interest in hearing the witness, is discussed in the next section.

It may seem incontestable that, outside of those situations where the attorney-client, spousal, or other privileges apply, no person should be able to prevent another from providing information to the government. But explicating why that is the case for the typical third-party witness makes clear why third-party *institutions* should be treated differently. As Mary Coombs has argued, people in possession of information about others, even information that is "private" and obtained through an intimate relationship, have "an autonomy-based right to choose to cooperate with the authorities."[101] According to Coombs, "To deny even the possibility of such a decision [to cooperate] is to turn a freely chosen relationship into a status, denying one person's full personhood to protect another's interests."[102] In other words, the autonomy interest of a putative witness trumps the privacy interest of a putative target when a witness decides to reveal information about the target. Thus, the target should not be able to control the witness's testimony.

But that analysis makes sense only when the third party is a person. Most records are held by institutions, not people. And as *Hale* suggested a century ago when it denied corporations the privilege against self-incrimination,[103] institutions do not have autonomy interests. A bank, hospital, or ISP is not denied its "personhood" when its ability to turn information over to the government is restricted. Accordingly, the analogy between third-party witnesses and third-party recordholders fails. Targets should be able to expect that information will remain with the institution unless the government demonstrates a substantial need for it.

This view of the Fourth Amendment's intersection with third-party autonomy interests helps to explain why the undercover agent cases do not support *Miller*'s reasoning. Many commentators have argued that both sets of decisions are wrong—that we should be able to expect that the government will not turn either our social or our business relationships into investigative tools without some justification.[104] But even if, relying on Coombs's analysis, one accepts the "social undercover agent" cases as valid law, they are distinguishable from the "institutional undercover agent" cases like *Miller* because social agents have an autonomy interest that institutional agents lack. In cases involving the latter scenario, there is no third-party interest to trump the target's interest in privacy, which should therefore be accorded greater respect than it is under current subpoena jurisprudence.

Third Parties Are Obligated to Provide the Government with Investigative Leads

The second reason that might be given for allowing a witness to testify over a target's objection focuses on government rather than witness interests. The Supreme Court frequently has spoken of the obligation to give testimony to grand juries.[105] Certainly citizens should feel they have a duty to help government apprehend law violators. Thus, the argument here is that third-party recordholders have a duty to hand over documents that might tend to incriminate others, even over strenuous objections by those incriminated.

Again, there are descriptive and normative problems with this argument. Although the Court talks about an obligation to provide evidence against others, in fact most jurisdictions no longer criminalize misprision, and, at least when their interlocutor is a police officer, individuals are not legally required to respond to inquiries even when the potential for self-incrimination is nonexistent.[106] What the Court probably intends to say when it speaks of evidentiary duties is that the individual has an obligation, enforced by the contempt power, to respond to a valid subpoena.

So the real issue is, when is a subpoena valid? My answer to that question should be apparent by now. While a relevance showing may be sufficient to support a subpoena for business documents or testimony from a third-party witness, that low standard ought to be presumptively inadequate when personal information is sought from the subject (in which case a warrant should be required or immunity granted) or from a third-party recordholder such as a bank, hospital, or ISP. In the latter situation, one can counterpose against the recordholder's "duty to give evidence" a fiduciary "duty of allegiance," which obligates the recordholder to use information for the purpose for which it is acquired.[107] As discussed above, empirical evidence suggests that this fiduciary duty is consistent with current societal understandings.

Although the few courts that have addressed the issue have been reluctant to endorse a duty of allegiance, their hesitation has come in cases where the "personal" information disclosed by the third party was not particularly private.[108] Whatever the appropriate result is in such cases, the duty should be much stronger where its breach involves an individual's medical, financial, and similar personal information. Recognition of such a duty may also benefit the third party, which otherwise risks the enmity of many of its customers, as evidenced by recent criticism of the telecom companies that purportedly handed over phone record data to the government.[109] This duty would not, of course, *prohibit* the government from obtaining personal information from third parties. But it would require that the government demonstrate a need for the information beyond mere relevance. Absent such a showing, the obligations of the third party should run to the subject of the records, not the state.

Regulating Subpoenas Would Destroy Investigative Effectiveness

The most common objection to the position just described is the one advanced originally in *Hale:* a higher standard would make government regulation impossible. This rationale frequently appears in cases justifying administrative subpoenas issued by government agencies. In the mid-twentieth-century case of *United States v. White,* for instance, the Supreme Court stated, "The scope and nature of the economic activities of incorporated and unincorporated organizations and their representatives demand that the constitutional power of the federal and state governments to regulate those activities be correspondingly effective," and went on to uphold a subpoena against a labor union.[110] A modern pronouncement of this claim can be found in Judge Bruce M. Selya's dissent in *Parks v. FDIC,*[111] a First Circuit case that briefly recognized enhanced protection for private papers before being withdrawn:

> Administrative investigations differ significantly from criminal investigations: government agencies typically investigate in order to enforce compliance with

> complicated structures of economic regulation. The ability to obtain information from regulated parties and those persons in privity with them typically is vital to the success of the regulatory scheme [citing *Morton Salt Co.* and *Oklahoma Press*] . . . . And it is a fact of life that agencies charged with regulating economic activity often cannot articulate probable cause or even reasonable suspicion that a violation has transpired without first examining documents reflecting a party's economic activity. . . . This incipient problem—the need to hitch the horse in front of the cart—is frequently exacerbated because the subpoena power has great significance for most administrative agencies in the conduct of important public business.[112]

These sentiments about the need to ease restrictions on agency investigations are oft-repeated. But note that both statements refer to cases involving organizational targets. *White*'s call for "effective" regulation is based on a perceived need to probe the "economic activities of incorporated and unincorporated organizations," and Judge Selya specifically distinguishes "administrative investigations" from "criminal investigations." In short, these decisions use the impossibility rationale only in the same subset of cases that previous discussion associated with diminished privacy concerns.

The same sort of distinction can be seen in grand jury cases, although it is less conspicuous. A constant refrain in decisions about grand jury subpoenas since at least 1919 is the notion that "the public has a right to every man's evidence"—the flip side of the idea that citizens have a duty to help the government.[113] That language suggests that the Court believes there is a strong government need for the information that such subpoenas provide. Yet, consistent with the grand jury's historical focus on organizational and, in particular, governmental corruption rather than individual crimes,[114] these cases also routinely note that the grand jury inquiry is limited by the Fifth Amendment's prohibition on compelling a person to incriminate himself or herself.[115] A relatively recent case illustrating this impersonal-personal dichotomy is *Dionisio*. There, in line with previous case law, the Supreme Court baldly stated that the grand jury's right to evidence from every citizen is "necessary to the administration of justice."[116] But recall that *Dionisio* also carefully exempted "private books and records" from its purview.

Of course, once *Fisher* limited the reach of the Fifth Amendment, this exemption was vulnerable. As a result, the impossibility rationale has found its way outside the corrupt-entity investigation context. For instance, one lower court relied on the rationale in permitting a blood test on relevance grounds. Given that grand jurors must have probable cause to indict, the court stated, "it would be peculiar to require them to demonstrate the same degree of probable cause to believe that a target of their investigation committed a crime before the grand jury could properly obtain evidence in aid of their investigation."[117] If applied to document subpoenas, this type of reasoning would make no distinction between organizational documents and personal ones.

That would be a mistake. First, of course, the impossibility rationale is a dangerous one regardless of the context, for the government can always make pleas that the Fourth Amendment and other constitutional rights make its law enforcement job difficult. Even accepting the impossibility rationale on its face, however, it at most justifies minimal restrictions on subpoenas for business records and—at a stretch—for private financial records of individuals that must be maintained for tax purposes (assuming *Couch* is right that otherwise the tax system would not survive).[118] It does not explain why subpoenas as currently conceptualized should authorize compulsory production of personal records in connection with ordinary "criminal investigations," to use Judge Selya's language.

Perhaps judges are not attuned to this problem because they believe that subpoenas are seldom used for such purposes. That assumption, while probably true during much of the twentieth century, is no longer accurate. Since the attacks of September 11, 2001, government subpoenas directed at personal records held by ISPs, banks, and other institutions have been particularly prolific.[119] Even outside the national security context, personal record subpoenas are common. For instance, the Department of Justice uses subpoenas not only to investigate antitrust violations, government fraud, and other organizational crimes but also to obtain records in connection with sexual exploitation and abuse of children, false claims and bribery, racketeering, and possession or sale of controlled substances.[120] And the Justice Department is not shy about taking advantage of its subpoena authority. In 2001, for instance, it issued almost 1,900 subpoenas seeking Internet records concerning child exploitation and abuse.[121]

Whatever might be the case with respect to complex economic wrongdoing, there is no truth to the claim that street crimes are impossible to investigate without the power to subpoena all types of personal records. In most such cases, the content of documents is secondary to other evidence obtained through interviews and interrogations, physical observation, traditional searches, and other nondocumentary investigative techniques.[122]

Even with respect to individual crimes that depend on transactional proof, such as fraud, tax evasion, and computer hacking, development of individualized suspicion is generally easier than in regulatory cases, where the chain of command hides responsibility, proof can involve technical and very complex evidence, and nondocumentary evidence of crime may not exist.[123] The impossibility rationale, as applied to personal papers, is not based on reason but on tradition, a tradition created in cases concerned about the efficacy of the administrative state rather than everyday law enforcement.

III. Separating the Personal from the Impersonal

The foregoing critique of current subpoena law suggests that the distinction between personal and impersonal records is a crucial one because it defines the threshold at which the relevance standard should no longer apply. Thus far not much has been said about the nature of that threshold. As it turns out, Supreme Court case law is very helpful in defining it. This assistance comes not, as one might think, from the Court's Fourth Amendment cases but rather from its Fifth Amendment jurisprudence, which, in its early incarnation, tried to delineate a zone of privacy.

Boyd, the Supreme Court's initial foray into the constitutionality of subpoena law, held that even business papers fell within the privacy zone.[124] But *Hale* soon created the distinction that permeates this chapter. As indicated previously, *Hale* denied the Fifth Amendment right to corporations on the ground that a corporation is "a creature of the state," in contrast to the individual citizen, who "owes no duty to the state . . . to divulge his business."[125] *Hale* was the first in a series of cases that laid out the so-called collective entity exception to the scope of the Fifth Amendment privilege.[126] In effect, the Court used this exception to delineate the difference between personal and impersonal papers.

By the time of *Fisher*, which changed the focus of the Fifth Amendment from privacy to coercion and thus marginalized the exception, the Court had expanded the collective entity doctrine to encompass far more than corporations (the entity prosecuted in *Hale*). For instance, five years after *Hale*, in *Wilson v. United States*, the Court found that a corporate officer's refusal to produce subpoenaed corporate records was not protected by the privilege even when their production might also incriminate him personally, because the records were not "personal"; rather they were "subject to examination by the demanding authority" and their custodian thereby had "accepted the incident obligation to permit inspection."[127] Some three decades after *Wilson,* the Court held in *White* that labor unions were also "collective entities," because a union has "a character so impersonal in the scope of its membership and activities that it cannot be said to embody or represent the purely private or personal interests of its constituents, but rather to embody their common or group interests only."[128]

Thirty years later, and two years before *Fisher,* the Court narrowed the zone of privacy even further by refusing, in *Bellis v. United States,*[129] to permit a small law firm to assert the privilege. Although the firm was a partnership that "embodied little more than the personal legal practice of the individual partners," it was a "formal institutional arrangement organized for the continuing conduct of the firm's legal practice" and thus was "an independent entity apart from its individual members."[130] *United States v. Doe,*[131] decided after *Fisher*, continued in the spirit of *Bellis* by holding that even a sole proprietor's records are not protected by the Fifth Amendment (unless, per *Fisher*, the act of production provides the government with proof of its case), thus dealing the final blow to the *Boyd* doctrine as applied to businesses.[132] Lower courts have also recognized an analogous "government records exception" that governs subpoenas for records describing the operations of a government agency.[133]

During the same period it was developing the collective entity doctrine, the Court was sketching out the contours of a "required records" exception to the Fifth Amendment, in connection with subpoenas for records of individuals. In *Shapiro v. United States,* decided in 1948, the Court held that the Fifth Amendment did not bar a subpoena directing an individual to produce commodity sales records that the Emergency Price Control Act required him to maintain.[134] Although the Court recognized that the government should not be able to vitiate the privilege simply by requiring that an individual keep and surrender written records, it concluded that in this case there was "a sufficient relation between the activity sought to be regulated and the public concern."[135]

More persuasively, in the later case of *Grosso v. United States,* the Court stated that the required records exception applied when the government's purpose was "essentially regulatory," the information sought was of the type "customarily kept" by the individual, and the records "have assumed 'public aspects' which render them at least analogous to public documents."[136] These criteria, it has been said, validate any subpoena for "essentially public documents such as routine income tax forms" and for documents held by "persons engaged in highly regulated industries [that] are required to be maintained as a part of a regulatory scheme."[137] In other words, documents of individuals are subject to subpoena under the required records doctrine when, as in the collective entity cases, their attributes of privacy are minimal.

The collective entity and required records exceptions come from cases construing the Fifth Amendment. But they resonate with Fourth Amendment concerns. Indeed, the required records exception's emphasis on pervasive regulation parallels the Supreme Court's administrative search jurisprudence, which allows searches of pervasively regulated businesses on less than probable cause.[138] Thus, to the extent they adhere to the parameters described above, the collective entity and required records doctrines may provide a satisfactory benchmark for determining when subpoenas may be based solely on relevance and when they should be based on something more.

One might also try to construct the type of distinction described here by relying on the First Amendment's differentiation between political and commercial speech.[139] Traditionally, commercial speech has been entitled to much less protection from government regulation than political speech,[140] and organizational records might similarly be accorded less protection than individual records. But ambiguities in the political-commercial distinction,[141] as well as the fact that business records can contain political information and individual records often contain nothing remotely political,[142] make the First Amendment paradigm far less certain and much harder to administer than the rejuvenated Fourth/Fifth Amendment approach to determining the extent to which government ought to have access to records. At most, the First Amendment supplements the Fourth Amendment's privacy protection in a narrow subset of cases.[143]

Conclusion

Document subpoenas are a standard criminal investigative tool today. But until relatively recently these subpoenas could not be used to obtain records from a person who could show that they would incriminate him or her personally, unless the government could show they were entity documents or "essentially" public documents required to be kept for regulatory purposes. Although said to be mandated by the Fifth Amendment's prohibition of compelled testimony, the latter showings depended on the extent to which the records were personal and private. At the same time, the Fourth Amendment, ostensibly the linchpin of constitutional privacy protection, was pushed into the background and thus provided minimal protection against document subpoenas, whether addressed to third parties or to the target of an investigation, and whether aimed at organizational or personal records. It is entirely possible that the early twentieth-century Court allowed Fourth Amendment limitations on subpoenas to wither because it assumed that personal records would always be well protected by the Fifth Amendment.

Today, however, the Fifth Amendment's restrictions on document subpoenas are substantially reduced, while Fourth Amendment restrictions remain trivial. I have argued that this minimalist regulatory regime is unjustifiable from a privacy perspective. At least where personal (as opposed to organizational) documents are involved, the privacy concerns evinced in earlier Fifth Amendment jurisprudence should be rejuvenated under the aegis of the Fourth Amendment, not—as was initially true under the Fifth Amendment—as an absolute bar to every document subpoena in criminal cases, but rather as a protection against demands based merely on official curiosity. Further, this stronger suspicion requirement for obtaining personal data should apply to third-party as well as first-party subpoenas; the privacy interest in personal information that increasingly *must* be transferred to third parties in order to function in today's world is not diminished simply by the fact of transfer or by the government's avowed need for the information. In short, the Fourth Amendment should be interpreted to demand that all "papers" within the zone of privacy—whether held by the subject or by a third-party institution—be afforded protection similar to that extended to the individual's house, person, and effects.

CHAPTER SEVEN

Regulating Transaction Surveillance by the Government

The previous chapter made the general case for enhanced regulation of transaction surveillance. This chapter fleshes out the argument. Section 1 describes the current law regulating transaction surveillance. Not only is this regulation minimal, it is confusing and contradictory; beyond the traditional subpoena, challengeable by the target of the investigation, current law recognizes a number of subpoena mutations that seem to have little rhyme or reason. If it contributes nothing else, this chapter should at least clarify the nature of today's regulatory framework.

Section 2 criticizes this framework and outlines a more promising approach. The proposed reform recognizes, as does the current regime, that different sorts of records merit different levels of protection. But in contrast to prevailing law, the proposal would significantly increase the degree of protection in several situations: probable cause would be required for private records obtained through target-driven surveillance, and reasonable suspicion would be required for private records obtained through event-driven surveillance and for quasi-private records obtained through target-driven surveillance. The relevance standard that is currently so popular would be reserved primarily for efforts to obtain organizational records and records of public activities.

Section 3 concludes the chapter by examining two alternatives to the proposal (and to the current regime) that sit at opposite ends of the regulatory spectrum: a requirement of probable cause for *all* records searches and a regime permitting *random* records searches on condition that anything discovered be subject to strict limitations on disclosure. In section 3, I suggest why both of these approaches are unsatisfactory. I also express concerns about any regulatory scheme—whatever its precise content—that relies on the legislature, rather than the courts and the Fourth Amendment, to establish fundamental regulatory requirements.

The sum of these arguments is simply stated. Not all recorded information warrants maximum protection from government intrusion. But much of it deserves far better protection than it receives today.

I. Current Legal Regulation of Transaction Surveillance

Transaction surveillance has become a particularly powerful and increasingly popular law-enforcement tool. Even if we focus solely on domestic transaction surveillance—that is, surveillance aimed at American citizens, not at foreigners—the proliferation of record-search programs is astounding. In January 2007 alone, the following newspaper stories appeared:

- The *Washington Post* described a Defense Department program, known as TALON (for Threat and Local Observation Notice), that has collected information on thousands of American citizens who protested the war in Iraq and other government policies and then made the data accessible to 28 government organizations and more than 3,500 government officials.[1]
- The *New York Times* reported that the Pentagon, in its search for spies, has accumulated files on hundreds of Americans from their banks, credit card companies, and other financial institutions, all of which it plans to keep indefinitely, even though apparently no arrests have resulted.[2]
- The *Los Angeles Times* disclosed that the Internal Revenue Service and the Social Security Administration made more than 12,000 "emergency disclosures" of personal data to federal intelligence and law enforcement agencies in 2002 and thousands more such disclosures each year since then, often via a program called REVEAL that combines 16 government databases with databases maintained by commercial data brokers.[3]
- Other news reports revealed that the Department of Homeland Security, already operating an Automated Targeting System designed to assess the security risk of millions of American and foreigners traveling overseas based on their travel histories,[4] is now testing a second program, known as ADVISE (for Analysis, Dissemination, Visualization, Insight and Semantic Enhancement), designed "to troll a vast sea of information, including audio and visual, and extract suspicious people, places and other elements based on their links and behavioral patterns."[5]

More revelations about transaction surveillance by the government came in March 2007. First, it was reported that the Bush administration attempted to persuade ISPs to keep records, for at least two years, of everyone who uploads photographs or videos onto a Web site, to facilitate tracking down people once particular content is determined to be illegal or suggestive of criminal activity.[6] A week later, the Justice Department's inspector general revealed that the FBI had obtained telephone logs, banking records, and other personal information regarding thousands of Americans not only in connection with counterterrorism efforts but also in furtherance of ordinary law enforcement.[7]

As detailed later in this chapter, these programs are just the tip of the iceberg. The government obviously believes that transaction surveillance is a useful law enforcement tool. Given its potential for creating personality mosaics and linking people to crime, this type of surveillance may now be perceived as even more important than visual tracking of a person's activities and eavesdropping on or hacking into a person's communications. But the real beauty of transaction surveillance for the government is that, compared to physical surveillance of activities inside the home and communications surveillance, it is so lightly regulated.

Transaction surveillance *never* requires probable cause or reasonable suspicion, even when its primary purpose is criminal investigation. At most, government agents seeking transactional information need a subpoena, which is valid so long as the information it seeks is "relevant" to a legitimate (statutorily authorized) investigation. Furthermore, as we shall see, the law does not require even a traditional subpoena for most types of transaction surveillance. Instead, the government, particularly Congress, has either invented new forms of authorization that are even easier to obtain or has simply permitted unfettered law enforcement access to transactional information.

The following account of this weak regulatory regime starts with the law governing real-time interception of so-called envelope information connected with communications such as phone calls and e-mail messages. Although technically this type of surveillance does not involve accessing extant records, neither does it involve interception of the *content* of communications. Because of its hybrid nature and because the current legal regime does not treat this type of surveillance in the same fashion as communications surveillance, it is included here. The section goes on to describe the law governing access to the content of public records and the content of records held by private entities.

Real-Time Interception of Transaction Information

The government may intercept the content of communications (commonly via wiretapping) only when authorized by a warrant based on probable cause. But the government may intercept the identifying features of the communication—the names of the communicators, their phone numbers or e-mail addresses, and the addresses of Web sites visited—on a much lesser showing. The Fourth Amendment does not apply at all to this type of transaction surveillance, and statutory law places virtually no restrictions on it.

The key Supreme Court case involving interception of envelope information is *Smith v. Maryland*.[8] There the Court held that any expectation of privacy we may have in the phone numbers we dial is unreasonable because we know or should know that phone companies keep a record of these numbers and thus we assume the risk that the phone company will disclose this information to the government.[9] Because it is also generally known that ISPs monitor, if only temporarily, our e-mails and Internet surfing, the Court would probably also say that we assume the risk these providers will become government informants. Although a uniform resource locator (URL) can be more informative than a mere phone number, both because it is an address and because it allows access to the Web site and thus permits the government to ascertain what the user has viewed, the lower courts applying *Smith* appear not to distinguish the two types of routing information.[10] Accordingly, the government can point to precedent establishing that it may ignore the Fourth Amendment both when intercepting phone numbers and when acquiring Internet addresses in real time.

Congress has imposed statutory restraints on this type of surveillance, but nothing approaching the usual Fourth Amendment protections. The relevant rules are found in the Electronic Communications Privacy Act of 1986 (ECPA), a statute that will figure prominently in much of the following discussion on transaction surveillance law. With respect to the real-time interception of envelope information in particular, ECPA creates a highly streamlined authorization process, one that can be initiated by either a federal government attorney or a state law enforcement officer. In order to use either a pen register (technology that intercepts outgoing data) or a trap and trace device (technology that intercepts incoming data), ECPA merely requires the government agent to certify to a court facts that show the information sought is "relevant to an ongoing investigation" and is "likely to be obtained by [the surveillance]."[11] If that certification is made, the court *must* issue the order.[12]

The original version of ECPA dealt solely with phone numbers. The USA Patriot Act of 2001 expanded the definition of pen registers and trap and trace devices to include all mechanisms that obtain "dialing, routing, addressing, or signaling information utilized in the processing and transmitting of wire or electronic communications."[13] Thus, to use snoopware or other means of ascertaining a person's e-mail correspondents and favorite Web sites, the government need only certify the relevance of this information to a current investigation. Again, if this certification is made, the court must issue an order.

Research has shown that magistrates sometimes rubber-stamp warrant applications, and thus fail to remain "neutral and detached" as demanded by the Fourth Amendment.[14] But the Supreme Court has always assumed that judicial independence is possible, and it has struck down several procedures that undermine that independence.[15] Here, in contrast, Congress has legislatively invented *mandatory* rubber-stamping. It is tempting to call this type of authorization a "rubber-stamp order," but I will instead use the more measured term *certification order*. Whatever one calls the authorization process, it amounts to minimal limitation on interception of transaction information.

Access to Publicly Held Records

Government efforts to access *already-existing* records—true transaction surveillance—is best divided into attempts to obtain records from private institutions and attempts to access public information, the latter of which is covered here. Commercial data brokers such as ChoicePoint have made records held by public entities much more accessible as a technological matter. Nor are there any significant *legal* obstacles to obtaining these types of records. Under current law, law enforcement officials do not need even a certification order to use ChoicePoint or similar computerized vehicles for perusing public documents. In fact, law enforcement officials need not consult any other entity (certainly not a court, and not even a prosecutor) before obtaining such information.

Again, the Fourth Amendment's ban on unreasonable searches and seizures might appear to apply here, because looking for and through records is a search in the usual meaning of the word. But *Smith* and *Miller* made clear that one cannot reasonably expect privacy in connection with information voluntarily given to third parties. Remember the key declaration in *Miller:* "[T]he Fourth Amendment does not prohibit the obtaining of information revealed to a third party and conveyed by him to Government authorities, *even if the information is revealed on the assumption that it will be used only for a limited purpose and the confidence placed in the third party will not be betrayed*" (emphasis added).

The Privacy Act of 1974 does bar or limit access to public records when they are sought by private individuals, and even when most government officials want them.[16] But when *law enforcement* officials are after the records, the Act requires merely a letter from the head of the agency that is seeking the information, detailing the law enforcement reasons a particular person's information is needed.[17] No court is involved, and neither individualized suspicion nor even a relevance showing is required, just the say-so of the law enforcement department. I will call this kind of authorization an *extrajudicial certification*.

Not even this level of authorization is necessary for government access to most public records, however. The Privacy Act applies only to federal documents. Unless there is similar legislation at the state level, law enforcement access to state public records is unrestricted.[18] Furthermore, the federal government takes the position that when it obtains information from companies such as ChoicePoint, the Privacy Act does not apply at all, because the Act's extrajudicial certification requirement is triggered only by government efforts to get records from other government agencies and from private companies that are administering a system of records for the government, and neither description fits commercial data brokers.[19] Under this interpretation, the only obstacle to complete government access to all the data maintained by such companies is the price of the information.[20]

Access to Privately Held Records

Compared to the meager limitations on intercepting envelope information and accessing public records, the restrictions on government access to the contents of records held by nominally private entities, such as hospitals, banks, phone companies, and ISPs, have more teeth, but the teeth are blunt. Again, the Fourth Amendment is pretty much irrelevant here. The notion that one assumes the risk that third parties will turn government informants applies to private entities as well as public agencies. The Supreme Court has specifically so held with respect to phone companies (in *Smith*) and banks (in *Miller*). It has wavered in its willingness to declare private entities untrustworthy confidants only in the medical context, where it has stated, in dictum, that the Fourth Amendment or the Due Process Clause *might* place constitutional limitations on law enforcement access.[21] Although there are also statutory constraints on government's ability to access privately held records, they are, for the most part, extremely weak.

Medical records receive the most protection under statutory law. Even here, however, neither probable cause nor reasonable suspicion is required. Rather, pursuant to rules promulgated under the Health Insurance Portability and Accountability Act of 1996 (HIPAA), the government can obtain medical records from HMOs and hospitals with a subpoena. A subpoena, it will be recalled, requires merely a finding that the information sought is relevant to a law enforcement investigation, although the target is entitled to notice and thus has the opportunity to challenge the government's action on relevance or privilege grounds.[22] Given the limited scope of the Privacy Act described above, even that obstacle is removed if, as is true in some states with respect to certain types of medical data, the information is maintained as a "public record" and the government receives it through a commercial data broker.

Financial records receive similarly minimal protection. To get detailed information from credit agencies, a regular subpoena is required under the Fair Credit Reporting Act.[23] However, analogous to the situation with medical records, no law constrains government requests for such information from database companies and other entities.[24] As a result, government routinely gets the financial information it wants directly from a commercial data broker, without bothering with a subpoena.[25] Bank records are also easily accessible. The Right to Financial Privacy Act generally requires only a traditional subpoena to obtain financial records from a bank. It also recognizes a significant variation to the traditional subpoena process: notification of the seizure may be delayed for up to 90 days if there is concern that service of the subpoena will tip off a suspect, result in loss of evidence, endanger witnesses, or in some other way compromise the government's investigation.[26] In these circumstances, in contrast to the typical subpoena process, the target of a financial investigation will not find out that the government has the information until well *after* it is obtained. I call this type of authorization a *delayed-notice subpoena*.

And this by no means exhausts the government's innovations regarding the subpoena power. Outside of situations covered by the Right to Financial Privacy Act and the Internal Revenue Code, a government agency that is authorized to use administrative subpoenas to obtain financial and business information from third parties need not give *any* notice to the customer whose records are sought.[27] This practice recognizes still another subpoena mutation, which I call an *ex parte subpoena*. This term emphasizes that the customer is outside the process entirely, thus removing, in most cases, the only meaningful inhibition to a fishing expedition via subpoena.

Transaction surveillance of communications-related information is regulated in a similarly weak fashion. Under ECPA, real-time interception of the content of phone and e-mail communications requires a warrant based on probable cause.[28] But if e-mail has sat on a server for longer than 180 days without being opened *or* the recipient of e-mail or voice mail accesses it and stores it on an outside server for any length of time, then a subpoena—delayed if necessary—is all that is needed to obtain the content of the communication.[29] Apparently, the rationale behind permitting easy access to unopened mail that is stored for 180 days is that it is, in effect, abandoned.[30] The rationale for requiring less than probable cause for access to opened e-mail messages and other communications stored by a third party is that they are akin to business records.[31]

ECPA also gives the government virtually unlimited access to business records held by phone companies and ISPs. Under Title II of ECPA, as amended by the Patriot Act of 2001, basic subscriber information—name, address, session times and durations, length and type of service, means and source of payment (including credit card numbers), and the identity of Internet users who use a pseudonym—can be obtained pursuant to an ex parte subpoena, the type of authorization that requires no customer notice.[32] If the government seeks additional transactional information—such as account logs and e-mail addresses of other individuals with whom the accountholder has corresponded—it still need not alert the subscriber, but it must allege "specific and articulable facts showing that there are reasonable grounds to believe that . . . the records or other information sought, are relevant and material to an ongoing criminal investigation."[33]

Apparently, this latter standard, found in Section 2703(d) of ECPA, is meant to be more demanding than the relevance standard normally required for a subpoena. Yet it is not clear that the standard is much different. Although the "specific and articulable" language sounds like it requires reasonable suspicion, note that the specific and articulable facts need only support a finding that the information is "relevant and material" to an ongoing investigation. Even if *material* is meant to augment *relevant*, it does not add much; materiality, in evidence law, means merely that the evidence be logically related to a proposition in the case.[34] Furthermore, whereas *Terry* contemplated that reasonable suspicion exist with respect to the targeted individual, a Section 2703(d) order, like a subpoena, allows access to *any* records that might be relevant to an investigation, not just the target's. Finally, it is not clear that the "relevant and material" language can be meaningfully enforced. The statute seems to say that the only ground on which an order issued pursuant to Section 2703(d) may be challenged is burdensomeness, which eliminates a challenge on relevance grounds.[35]

Post-9/11, government access to some sorts of privately held records is even easier when a significant purpose of the investigation is to nab terrorists or spies. Two separate subpoena-like mechanisms are important here. The first is an order under Section 215 of the Patriot Act. As originally enacted, that provision authorized the FBI to demand the production of "any tangible things (including books, records, papers, documents and other items)" if it followed a two-step process.[36] First, the director or his or her designee had to certify to a court that the items sought were "for an investigation to protect against international terrorism or clandestine intelligence activities," and that the investigation did not focus "solely" on activities protected by the First Amendment. Second, the court had to find that the investigation met these conditions; if so, it was required to issue a Section 215 order authorizing the seizure. In other words, a variant of the certification order discussed in connection with the use of pen registers and trap and trace devices sufficed in this situation.

In March 2006, as part of the USA Patriot Improvement and Reauthorization Act, Congress placed a few more restrictions on this process. First, only high-ranking officials can request a Section 215 order that seeks records regarding library transactions, book sales, and educational and medical matters.[37] Second, a mere certification that the items relate to a national security investigation is no longer sufficient. Rather, the application must include "a statement of facts showing that there are reasonable grounds to believe that the tangible things sought are relevant to an authorized investigation."[38] Third, procedures must be in place to "minimize" dissemination of any information acquired.[39] Fourth, a Section 215 order is subject to judicial review upon request by the recordholder and allows the judge to set aside or modify the order.[40]

Although in theory the amendments have made a Section 215 order more difficult to obtain, the applicable standard is still relevance, and the issuing and reviewing judges apparently are still expected to refrain from inquiring into the basis of the certification and to limit themselves to making sure the relevant statements of fact are provided.[41] Note further that the records that may be obtained in this way are not just those of suspected terrorists but of anyone whose information might "protect against international terrorism or clandestine intelligence activities."[42] Finally, the Section 215 process is ex parte, with a twist: A third party served with a

Section 215 order is *prohibited* from telling the target (or, for that matter, anyone other than a lawyer) about the order.[43] Unlike the delayed-notice subpoena, this gag order operates automatically; no finding that notice might compromise the investigation is required. The 2006 amendments do permit a challenge of this nondisclosure requirement, but only after one year has passed since issuance of the order.[44]

Paul Rosenzweig has argued that the provision for judicial modification, together with the requirements that the government "swear" the certification is correct and that the attorney general report to Congress on the use of Section 215,[45] provides more safeguards than those associated with a subpoena reviewable only after challenge.[46] But if the judge is permitted to modify an order only to accommodate First Amendment concerns (a likely limitation on the judge's prerogatives, given the law regarding national security letters, discussed below), and if Congress is given only general data or trivial bits of information about the surveillance program (which is usually the case),[47] then the typical subpoena process—which allows the *target* to challenge the relevance of the information, either immediately or after delayed notice—is likely to be at least as protective, and is certainly more likely to deter or expose abuses. In any event, neither Section 215 nor the typical subpoena process requires probable cause or even reasonable suspicion, if the latter term requires an articulable suspicion that there is a nontrivial (i.e., 30 percent) chance that the targeted individual's records will provide evidence of crime.

When the FBI seeks a particular subset of "tangible items"—electronic or communication billing records, financial records, or credit records—in connection with a national security investigation, even a Section 215 order is not needed. Rather, all it must do is issue a form of administrative subpoena known as a national security letter (NSL), in which a special agent in charge (in other words, a field agent) certifies that the information sought is relevant to an investigation designed to protect against international terrorism or clandestine intelligence activities.[48] This type of authorization is akin to the extrajudicial certification discussed in connection with law enforcement efforts to seek public documents under the Privacy Act, but with the same gag order that applies to Section 215 orders.[49]

The Patriot Act allowed this extrajudicial process with respect to financial information only when that information was held by banks. However, in December 2003, that power was expanded by the Intelligence Authorization Act of 2003, which was passed by Congress as part of an appropriations bill with no vetting by the Judiciary Committee and no debate on the floor or in the media.[50] The 2003 Act allows the FBI to use extrajudicial certification to obtain statements and records from *any* financial institution "whose cash transactions have a high degree of usefulness in criminal, tax or regulatory matters," including banks, stockbrokers, car dealers, casinos, credit card companies, insurance agencies, jewelers, pawn brokers, travel agents, and airlines.[51]

At one time, all this information could be obtained by the government simply on its say-so. In 2004, however, a federal district court judge declared the NSL scheme unconstitutional to the extent it immunized NSLs from judicial process and prevented third-party recordholders from challenging an order,[52] and in 2005 another court expressed similar concerns.[53] Those decisions, combined with congressional unease about the scope of the program—particularly as it applied to libraries—led to several amendments to the Patriot Act. Libraries are now exempted from its provisions,[54] and third parties are permitted to ask a court to set aside or modify NSLs when they are "unreasonable, oppressive, or otherwise unlawful" as well as challenge any accompanying gag order.[55]

Again, however, the new judicial review power is relatively toothless. In *Doe v. Ashcroft*, the first decision finding the NSL procedure defective, the court indicated that review of an NSL would be limited to whether "the underlying investigation was not duly 'authorized,' was initiated 'solely on the basis of activities protected by the first amendment to the Constitution of the United States,' or did not involve 'international terrorism or clandestine intelligence activities.'"[56] Indeed, the court stated, "the standard of review for administrative subpoenas similar to NSLs is so minimal that most such NSLs would likely be upheld in court."[57] The procedure for reviewing gag orders is similarly illusory, since if the FBI certifies that disclosure would "interfere" with a criminal or national security investigation or endanger someone, the court must abide by that decision.[58] In any event, neither review procedure is triggered unless a third party wants to take the trouble to initiate it. Evidence suggests that virtually no such challenges occur.[59] The pallid nature of these protections was demonstrated in March 2007, when the inspector general of the Department of Justice disclosed that the FBI managed to violate even the Patriot Act's minimal NSL procedural requirements in thousands of cases.[60]

Section 215 is apparently used relatively sparingly, with the Justice Department stating in late 2005 that it had relied on the provision only thirty-five times during the preceding two years, in aid of its efforts to gain access to information about matters such as apartment leases, driver's licenses, and financial dealings.[61] Given the fact that NSLs can authorize the acquisition of much of the same information, this finding is not surprising. Indeed,

NSLs are used quite frequently. The FBI alone issues roughly 30,000 to 50,000 NSLs a year and maintains all the records thereby obtained (even when they are not linked to terrorism).[62]

Summary of Transaction Surveillance Law

Transaction surveillance has spawned a wide array of new regulatory schemes, which are usefully summarized by locating them within the standard Fourth Amendment hierarchy. As the reader well knows by now, the most protective type of authorization is the warrant, based on probable cause. Although interception of the content of communications and physical surveillance of the home both require a warrant, no type of transaction surveillance requires this most demanding form of authorization. The next type of authorization in the hierarchy, at least in theory, is an order based on reasonable suspicion, or what could be called a *Terry* order, after the stop and frisk case that first recognized this degree of justification. Again, none of the statutory provisions described here (or any other regulatory regime for that matter) mandates this type of order; it is included for the sake of comprehensiveness and because it is important to the regulatory scheme proposed below. After a *Terry* order comes the traditional subpoena, issued upon a judicial finding of relevance and challengeable by the target. This is the first type of authorization that plays a role in transaction surveillance; subpoenas are required to access most medical, financial, and stored e-mail records.

Below the traditional subpoena is the delayed-notice subpoena, which temporarily authorizes unobstructed access to financial records and stored e-mail when a traditional subpoena might frustrate the investigation. Next is the ex parte subpoena (unchallengeable by the target), which allows access to many types of customer records held by third parties, including phone and ISP account records. Then comes the certification (judicial rubber-stamp) order, which authorizes use of pen registers, trap and trace devices, and other forms of transaction-oriented snoopware, as well as access to many types of tangible items thought to be relevant to national security investigations.[63] At the bottom of the authorization totem pole is the extrajudicial certification, which permits access to public records, ISP billing records, and many types of financial information relevant to national security investigations. Finally, no authorization is needed to access public records that come from a state with no privacy statute or that are accumulated by a commercial data broker. The chart below shows the eight levels of authorization.

Current Authorization Levels for Transaction Surveillance

Transaction	Authorization Required	Certainty Level
N/A	Warrant	Probable cause
N/A	*Terry* order	Reasonable suspicion
Medical, financial, and tax records; stored e-mail	Subpoena	Relevance, challengeable by target
Financial records and stored e-mail if notification poses risks	Delayed-notice subpoena	Relevance, challengeable by target only after records obtained
Billing records and logs of phone companies and ISPs; most customer records	Ex parte subpoena	Relevance, challengeable only by third-party recordholder
Interception of envelope information re calls and e-mail; tangible items re terrorism	Certification order	Relevance (determined by government), issued by court, challengeable only by third-party recordholder
Federal public records; financial and billing records re terrorism	Extrajudicial certification	Relevance (determined by government), not challengeable except when Section 215 allows third party to do so
State public records not protected by law or that are acquired by a commercial data broker	None	None

One last important aspect of these statutory authorization mechanisms should be emphasized: all of them lack a meaningful remedy. Exclusion is explicitly rejected as a recourse under ECPA and related statutes, administrative sanctions are rare, and a lawsuit will be dismissed unless tangible damage is shown.[64]

II. A Proposal for Regulation of Transaction Surveillance

The differences between the various types of authorization outlined above are sometimes subtle, but one thing is certain: their number goes well beyond (and below) the traditional three-tiered approach of probable cause, reasonable suspicion, and relevance determinations challengeable by the target of the investigation. As a conceptual matter, a system that recognizes more than three authorization levels is not necessarily flawed; indeed, the proportionality framework advanced in chapter 2 contemplates four levels. My quarrel with current law is not with the general approach but with the order and substance of the hierarchy.

The degree to which transaction surveillance is regulated should not depend on whether the information sought is intercepted in real time or is stored, or on whether it may be related to terrorist actions or some other crime. Rather, following the proportionality principle, the key variable should be the intrusiveness of the surveillance. The discussion below pursues this point by providing further theoretical and empirical perspectives on what privacy means in connection with transactional information and then proposing specific rules for protecting it under the Fourth Amendment.

The Case for a Hierarchy of Records

Because the Supreme Court appears to have adopted the position that both corporate records and individual records held by third parties fall outside the zone of privacy, the case law is not much help on the subject of whether and to what extent particular transactional information is private for Fourth Amendment purposes. However, a few lower courts have been willing to resist the broad language in *Miller* and grant Fourth Amendment protection (or protection under the analogous state constitutional provision) to some types of records. Stephen Henderson's survey of the case law identifies more than a dozen factors the courts have considered,[65] principal among them: (1) the extent to which disclosure of the information is necessary to function in society (with one court, for instance, distinguishing between phone numbers maintained by the phone company and information given to a locksmith);[66] (2) the degree to which the information is personal (with one court holding that power consumption records are not personal);[67] and (3) the amount of information obtained (with some courts distinguishing between monthly bank or telephone records and a record of one transaction).[68]

On an abstract level, these are sensible criteria for evaluating Fourth Amendment privacy. But applying them in a judicious manner is another matter. Putting aside the number of variables involved (Henderson himself insists that at least nine of the twelve factors he discusses are relevant to Fourth Amendment analysis),[69] the indeterminacy of the three just described should be apparent. The first, which looks at how important a given service is to modern life, triggers real quandaries: using the case noted above as an example, why are locksmiths any less essential to functioning in today's world than phones, given the need for security and the frequency with which people are locked out of home, office, or car? Also daunting is the task of calibrating the extent to which particular information is "personal"; as chapter 3 noted, the Supreme Court in *Kyllo* explicitly avoided this type of question on the ground it could not be answered coherently, a difficulty brought home by the fact that in the power consumption case noted above, four judges vigorously dissented from the conclusion that electricity usage information is not personal[70] (and in any event, isn't electricity just as crucial to everyday functioning as a phone?). An equally perplexing question, raised by the third factor, is the number of transactions a record must contain before its seizure by the government implicates the Fourth Amendment.

Admittedly, any attempt to assess privacy in a meaningful fashion will run into these types of definitional conundrums (as my proposal below demonstrates). A more fundamental problem is that privacy may not be measurable in the predominately normative terms these courts are applying. Chapter 4 noted Robert Post's conclusion that the scope of privacy, when conceptualized as a form of dignity, is dependent on everyday social practices. In an article about expectations of privacy in the tort context, Lior Strahilevitz agrees that, given the highly contestable nature of the concept, any effort to arrive at an objectively neutral take on privacy is "doomed."[71] Instead Professor Strahilevitz argues that, at least for purposes of defining privacy torts, the law's approach to privacy should derive primarily from empirical investigation of social norms.

The type of empirical work Strahilevitz has in mind for this purpose focuses on how we "network" socially. His reading of the social network literature indicates that unless it is "likely to be regarded as highly interesting, novel, revealing, or entertaining," information that we reveal about ourselves rarely gets past "two degrees of separation"—that is, beyond a friend of a friend.[72] This limited range of disclosure is partly the result of routine inefficiencies in communication. But it would exist even if the Internet were to radically reduce these inefficiencies, because people simply don't care about the private affairs of strangers unless the events are dramatic or are somehow economically useful. Based on these types of insights from social network research, Strahilevitz offers an even more precise definition of privacy:

> Although the studies vary somewhat, it appears that the median adult has met or otherwise interacted with approximately 1,700 people. This does not mean that the average person has 1,700 active ties, but rather that he "knows" roughly this number of people. . . . To determine whether someone has a reasonable expec-

> tation of privacy in information, we therefore might evaluate the possibility that the information will be disseminated to a number of people that exceeds the size of his social network. If there is a low risk of such dissemination (for example, lower than 5 percent), the courts can recognize a reasonable expectation of privacy.[73]

The implications of social network theory for transaction surveillance is straightforward. Unless it is part of a public record designed for consumption by everyone or describes an activity observed by strangers, the transactional information government seeks through such surveillance is rarely known outside our families, much less outside our social network (aside from the third-party institutions to which we provide it). Expectations that such information will remain "private" are reasonable from the social network perspective.

Further empirical support for an enlarged view of privacy in individual records is provided by a study I conducted of lay views (N = 76), similar in structure to the survey of attitudes toward camera surveillance reported in chapter 4 but using scenarios related to transactional information (see table below). For present purposes, the most important result of this study is that the participants considered many types of transaction surveillance to be more intrusive than pat downs (which require reasonable suspicion) and searches of cars (which require probable cause). Consistent with the lower court cases described above, the participants distinguished between the types of information obtained (e.g., credit card records, M = 75.3, as opposed to electricity consumption records, M = 57.4), and surveillance that is isolated as opposed to aggregating (compare scenario 14, obtaining a record of a specific phone call, M = 59.8, with scenario 17, obtaining a person's composite phone records, M = 74.1). Participants also distinguished between event-driven surveillance (indicated in the table by "data mining") and target-driven surveillance of the same types of information (recall from chapter 1 that event-driven surveillance aims at identifying the perpetrator of a past or future event, as distinct from target-driven surveillance, which starts with a suspect). Such distinctions notwithstanding, all these government actions, as well as searches of corporate and public records, were perceived as more intrusive than a roadblock (see scenario 1), which is governed by the Fourth Amendment.

These empirical observations suggest that, contrary to the Supreme Court's insinuation in cases like *Miller* and *Smith*, transferring information to third parties or allowing third parties to accumulate it does not, by

Mean Intrusiveness Ratings of 25 Scenarios

(scenarios not involving transaction surveillance appear in bold)

Scenario	Mean	Confidence Intervals
1. **Roadblock**	30.2	±7.5
2. Airplane passenger lists (data mining)	32.4	8
3. Store patron lists (data mining)	34.1	7.5
4. Criminal/traffic records	36.2	7
5. Anonymous phone, credit card, and travel records (data mining)	38.5	7
6. Corporate records	40.6	7
7. Real estate records	45.5	8
8. **ID check and questioning during brief stop**	49.1	8
9. Club membership records	49.5	8
10. Phone records (data mining)	50.0	8
11. Electricity records	57.5	8
12. High school records	58.3	9
13. Phone, credit card, and travel records (data mining)	59.7	8
14. Record of specific phone call	59.8	7.5
15. List of food purchases	65.3	7.5
16. **Pat down**	71.5	7.5
17. Phone records	74.1	7.5
18. Web sites visited	74.4	8
19. **Search of car**	74.6	7
20. Credit card records	75.3	7.5
21. E-mail addresses sent to and received from	77.1	8
22. Pharmacy records	78.0	7.5
23. Use of snoopware to target subject	79.0	8
24. Bank records	80.3	7.5
25. **Bedroom search**	81.2	6.5

itself, lessen the intrusiveness of government efforts to obtain it. To the members of society queried in this survey, the important variable appears to be the nature of the record, not who or what institution possesses it. Fourth Amendment jurisprudence ought to recognize society's expectation, whether measured directly or through social network research, that this type of information is private.

At the same time, the empirical observations from my study, and to a lesser extent the logic of social network theory, suggest that society does not view all transactional surveillance as equally intrusive. More specifically, the findings summarized in the survey table above suggest three broad categories of intrusiveness, divided by scenario 8 (a police stop demanding identification, which verges on being a seizure)[74] and scenario 16 (a pat down, which requires reasonable suspicion).[75] Into the first category (scenarios 2 though 7) fall government acquisition of corporate records, public records, and many types of data mining. These types of transaction surveillance are all ranked lower than the street identification scenario, although still above a roadblock. At the other end of the spectrum (scenarios 17 through 25) are government efforts to obtain many types of information maintained by private entities, including records of phone and e-mail correspondents, Web sites visited, credit card purchases, and pharmacy and bank records. These types of transaction surveillance are all ranked as more intrusive than a pat down and about as intrusive as either a car search (scenario 19) or a search of a bedroom (scenario 25), both of which require probable cause. Between the identification check and pat-down scenarios are several types of transaction surveillance: acquisition of what might be called "quasi-private" records from clubs, electric companies, high schools, and grocery stores (scenarios 9, 11, 12, and 15); private records depicting a single event (scenario 14); and data mining of private records (scenarios 10 and 13).

Because privacy is as much a positive construct as a normative one, information about societal views such as those depicted in the table above should be taken into account in figuring out how to apply the Fourth Amendment to transaction surveillance. Indeed, the proportionality principle introduced in chapter 2 requires recognition of differences in intrusiveness, which these findings help us deduce. Any general scheme of regulation should also take into account the implications of the exigency principle introduced in chapter 2. Consistent with that principle, ex parte subpoenas, certification orders, and extrajudicial certifications should be insufficient authority to carry out nonconsensual searches and seizures for nonorganizational transaction information unless there is an emergency, and then only if eventually subject to judicial review.

Assuming the types of results summarized in the survey table are replicated, application of these principles might in turn produce the following concrete (and admittedly somewhat complex) rules. In the absence of exigency, the government should have to obtain one of four levels of authorization, depending on the type of surveillance: (1) a traditional subpoena based on relevance, for corporate records; (2) an ex ante court order based on relevance, for public records and event-driven surveillance of public and quasi-private records; (3) a *Terry* order, based on reasonable suspicion, for quasi-private records sought through target-driven surveillance and private records obtained through event-driven surveillance; and (4) a warrant based on probable cause, for private records through target-driven surveillance. The following chart summarizes this proposal.

Proposed Authorization Levels of Transaction Surveillance

Transaction	Authorization Required	Certainty Level
Records re organizations (e.g., corporate records)	Subpoena	Relevance
Public records re individuals (e.g., criminal, real estate records; perhaps tax records sought for tax assessment purposes)	Court order	Relevance
Quasi-private records re individuals (e.g., membership, grocery, travel, utility records)		
Event driven	Court order	Relevance
Target driven	*Terry* order	Reasonable suspicion
Private records re individuals (e.g., communications, financial and medical records)		
Event driven	Court order	Reasonable suspicion
Target driven	*Terry* order	Probable cause

Under this scheme, organizational records are distinguished from individual records, individual records are divided into public, quasi-private, and private categories, and target-driven surveillance is distinguished from event-driven surveillance. When organizational records or public records are sought, only relevance is required. When quasi-private records are sought, relevance is required for event-driven surveillance and reasonable suspicion for target-driven surveillance. When private records are sought, reasonable suspicion is required for event-driven surveillance and probable cause for other target-driven surveillance. Below I flesh out these rules and suggest how to simplify their application for law enforcement officers and the courts.

Organizational versus Individual Records

The important distinctions between organizational and individual records have already been discussed in chapter 6; here they will only be summarized. Many of the justifications for the current relaxed state of transaction surveillance are persuasive in the context in which subpoenas first flourished—government efforts to obtain documentary evidence of crimes committed by or within a business or other regulated organization. As the Supreme Court has recognized on numerous occasions and the results of the survey confirm (see scenario 6 in the survey table), records of businesses and similar entities are associated with a minimal degree of privacy, given their impersonal nature and the high degree of state regulation to which organizations are subject. And, as the Court has also pointed out in several cases, investigation of economic crimes and regulatory violations would be extremely difficult without ready access to documents detailing business activity.

Neither the diminished-privacy rationale nor the heightened-need justification is as easily applied when the records sought involve individuals, however. Both the normative analysis provided earlier and the empirical findings described in this chapter debunk the Supreme Court's assertion in *Miller* that we can't reasonably expect privacy in connection with personal information surrendered to third parties. And the self-serving contention that cause requirements must be relaxed when they are hard to meet should be taken seriously only in extreme cases. While such cases may often exist in connection with organizational crime investigations, where the only evidence may be documentary and even victims may not realize a crime has occurred, they are rare where nonorganizational crime is involved, and thus the heightened-need rationale should be irrelevant in that setting.

If one accepts these arguments, then it is important to separate individual from organizational documents. Fortunately, as chapter 6 explained, the Supreme Court has done much work in this regard, in the course of defining the concept of a "collective" entity and the notion of "required records" for purposes of determining when there is a Fifth Amendment right to resist documentary subpoenas. In essence, in its collective entity cases the Court concluded that the records of any organization that has an identity separate from its individual members lie outside the "zone of privacy." In its required records cases, the Court similarly held that the government may force individuals to keep and disclose documents (such as, perhaps, tax records) that are crucial for regulating their activities and that have "assumed 'public aspects' which render [them] at least analogous to public documents."[76] Consistent with these two lines of cases, records that pertain to a collective entity or that individuals are required to keep (and are sought for the reason the records are required to be kept) ought to be accessible on mere issuance of a subpoena.

Outside of the required records context, however, records about individuals should presumptively receive more protection. The Fourth Amendment specifically speaks of searches of papers, as well as searches of persons, houses, and effects, and it usually requires probable cause for these searches. Accordingly, a search for records about individuals that individuals are not required to keep should require probable cause unless the intrusion associated with the search is less serious than that associated with search of a house, person, or effect. The following sections explore three such situations, based on empirical considerations and normative analysis.

Private versus Public Records

One possible distinction among individual records, suggested by both social network theory and the survey results, focuses on whether they are public in nature, not in the fictionalized sense contemplated by the required records doctrine, but in the sense that they are truly in the public domain. Much of the information held in courthouse records and other government file systems is meant to be available to everyone and can no longer be said to be controlled by either the individual *or* the recordholder. The survey participants seemed to agree, given the low ranking they assigned government accessing of criminal records (scenario 4, M = 36.2) and real estate records (scenario 7, M = 45.5), below even a brief street identification (M = 49.1). In such cases, proportionality reasoning leads to the conclusion that something less than probable cause or reasonable suspicion ought to be sufficient justification for permitting government access in these situations.

That does not mean that these records should be available to officers at their whim, however. The participants ranked all of these public record scenarios above a roadblock. This result probably reflects the intuition that a curious officer should not be permitted to sift through the personal data found in divorce papers, real estate documents, and court proceedings, or pay a commercial data broker for such information, without a specific need to do so. Further, consistent with the exigency principle, that articulation should take place beforehand to a judge or at least, as the Privacy Act provides, to a politically accountable official, rather than, as occurs under current practice, whenever a cop can obtain the data from a broker.

A common complaint about such an approach is that it places more limits on government officials than on members of the public, who can access public records at will and, with the advent of Internet search services and commercial data brokers, can do so more easily than ever before. But most of the time the public seeks public information only when it has a specific need for it (akin to a relevance standard). More important, the government's resources and power are so much more significant, and its hunger for information so much more voracious (especially post-9/11), that its potential for abusing personal information far exceeds anything individuals or even corporations might do. The phrase "Total Information Awareness," the name of the now defunct government data-mining program (discussed further below), describes a goal to which only a government agency could aspire.[77]

Private versus Quasi-Private Records

The paradigmatic examples of private records, whether held by the subject or a third party, are clear from the survey: medical records, bank records, and envelope information (i.e., records describing one's phone and computer communications). In previous work, written without benefit of empirical information about societal attitudes, I proposed that envelope information be accorded minimal Fourth Amendment protection.[78] I have now changed my view on this matter, given the consistently high rating the survey participants give such information (see scenarios 17, 18, 21, and 23) as well as scholarly criticism of my position.[79]

The survey results also suggest, however, that the mere fact that a record is held by a private entity does not automatically mean government attempts to obtain it are perceived as highly intrusive. For instance, the participants viewed transaction surveillance of club membership lists, electricity readings, and grocery store records (scenarios 9, 11, and 15) as less intrusive than a pat down (although more intrusive than a street identification stop). These results can be justified on normative grounds as well. The detail disclosed in a club membership is not much different from what police discover through an ID check, and electricity and food consumption records generally reveal less about one's lifestyle than information found in phone or bank records. In short, membership, utility, and store records might all be called quasi-private, and accordingly, under proportionality reasoning, reasonable suspicion may be all that that is needed to obtain such information.

Just as not all records held by private entities are equally private, not all information held by public agencies should be classified as public.[80] For instance, the survey participants ranked government acquisition of public high school records in the middle tier (see scenario 12, M = 58.3), suggesting that reasonable suspicion should be required here even though such records are held by a public entity. Consider also the treatment of "public" records under the federal Freedom of Information Act (FOIA) and similar state statutes. While these laws establish a presumption in favor of disclosure of records held by government agencies, they do so primarily as a means of increasing government transparency and facilitating social transactions such as real estate deals.[81] Thus, they usually exempt from disclosure a wide array of "personal" records. Under the federal statute, for example, government agencies must resist a FOIA request for "commercial or financial information obtained from a person and privileged or confidential,"[82] "personnel and medical files and similar files the disclosure of which would constitute a clearly unwarranted invasion of personal privacy,"[83] and law enforcement records to the extent they include information that "could reasonably be expected to constitute an unwarranted invasion of personal privacy."[84] State freedom of information statutes or interpretive case law protects various other types of records. For instance, Florida exempts from unrestricted disclosure some types of motor vehicle registration information, identifying information relating to health care provided by the state, credit information held by state agencies, and educational records.[85] In many states some types of licensing information are also exempt from disclosure.[86]

When federal or state law indicates that information found in government records should be withheld despite the strong interest in freedom of information, it probably should be considered nonpublic for Fourth Amendment purposes as well. If so, law enforcement should have to demonstrate more than mere relevance in such cases. Whether reasonable suspicion or probable cause is required would depend on whether the information sought is private (as with medical reports) or quasi-private (as in school records).

A final type of record that might be classified as quasi-private is one that describes only a single event or a few events. Scenario 14 in the survey, which involved seeking a record of a phone call from a particular person to a particular number on a particular day (M = 59.8), was rated as significantly more intrusive than an ID check (M = 49.1) but significantly less intrusive than a pat down (M = 71.5). Thus, in contrast to the lower court rulings holding that no search occurs in this situation, a proportionality approach would require some level of suspicion before such a record could be acquired; at the same time, the empirical results suggest that this level should be no higher than reasonable suspicion.

Here, however, I would favor requiring probable cause, primarily to avoid the aggregation conundrum. While the difference between one call and a month's worth of calls is fairly obvious (particularly if the creation of personality mosaics is the primary concern), the difference between one call and four is not, and the difficulty of drawing a meaningful line anywhere along this spectrum is apparent. There is a normative justification for this unitary approach as well: records such as those memorializing phone communications ought to be treated as private regardless of the amount of information they hold, since any given single event (e.g., a phone call to a lover or a psychiatrist) can be as revealing as multiple events. The same analysis would apply to quasi-private records such as store purchases; although acquisition of data regarding one purchase can be seen as less intrusive than acquisition of records depicting a month's purchases (and thus perhaps permissible on a relevance rather than reasonable suspicion showing), there is no sensible dividing point between the two.

Proportionality reasoning based on empirical results can become complicated. But if the aggregation conundrum is addressed in the manner proposed above, application of the proportionality test is quite manageable. The two ends of the privacy spectrum are relatively easy to discern. Private records reveal information about communications and medical and financial activities. Public records are meant to be available to the public. Quasi-private records are everything else.[87]

Event-Driven Surveillance and Data Mining

The discussion until now has focused on target-based surveillance. Event-driven surveillance, designed to discover the actual or would-be perpetrator of a criminal event rather than to pursue an identified suspect, may raise different concerns. As with target-driven surveillance, proportionality reasoning suggests a nuanced approach.

First consider relatively benign versions of event-driven surveillance. To repeat the hypothetical examples given in chapter 1, this type of surveillance might involve tracking down people who have bought a type of shoe or sweater that has been linked to a sniper incident or individuals who have rented small planes near a shopping mall suspected of being a terrorist target. Another example, this one from an actual rape investigation, involved a computer search of residential records to discover the identities of males who lived in both Philadelphia, Pennsylvania, and Fort Collins, Colorado, at the time several sexual assaults with the same modus operandi occurred in those two cities.[88]

In these examples, the information sought (purchases and residential information) comes from public or quasi-private records. Furthermore, in contrast to many types of transaction surveillance, the government acquires only one or two bits of information about the persons so identified (e.g., that they bought a particular type of shoe, rented a plane on a given day, or lived in a certain city during a certain period). Finally, the information has not been obtained in single-minded pursuit of a particular person but rather in an effort to determine whom to pursue; any given individual's record is merely one of hundreds or thousands and will be discarded or ignored if it does not interest investigators. For all these reasons, this investigative technique is a far cry from the creation of personality mosaics through data aggregation, the scenario that has worried those who criticize large-scale transaction surveillance. Consistent with this intuition, the survey participants rated these types of event-driven surveillance, depicted in scenarios 2 and 3, as less intrusive than an ID check. Both of these scenarios involved quasi-private records (airline passenger lists and store patron lists) that recount actions observed by multiple strangers outside one's social network.

Sometimes, however, event-driven surveillance involves accessing information that is more private in nature. In the past decade, the government has become increasingly interested in acquiring and analyzing vast amounts of personal data using a number of different processes known collectively as data mining. Today the federal government alone probably operates more than 200 data-mining programs, at least 120 of which involve efforts to obtain personal information such as credit reports and credit card transaction records.[89]

Some of these programs are target driven, either in the sense already discussed (as with the TALON and REVEAL programs that seek to acquire financial records of suspects) or in the sense known as data matching, which might involve trying to match a particular person's DNA or fingerprints to a national database or checking the name of a particular person entering the country against watch lists to determine immigration or national security status.[90] Under proportionality reasoning, regulation of the first type of target-driven data mining would depend on the nature of the records being accessed. Regulation of data matching, in contrast, would depend on the nature of the action the government contemplates taking when a match occurs. If, for example, the consequence of being on a no-fly list is arrest, a person should not appear on the list unless probable cause exists to believe the individual is a dangerous criminal. If the consequence is instead a prohibition on boarding, reasonable suspicion might be sufficient.[91]

Event-driven data mining, sometimes called pattern-based data mining, is a somewhat newer development. But as Daniel Steinbock has noted, it has already helped "uncover unreported crimes, identify suspects, [and] aid investigators in tracing irregular financial transactions,"[92] and of course it figures prominently in attempts to detect planned terrorist activity, as evidenced by the new ADVISE program described at the beginning of this chapter.[93] The central issue raised by this type of program is whether Fourth Amendment analysis changes when large-scale event-driven data mining accesses private, as opposed to public and quasi-private, records.

To understand this issue better, consider in more detail a few examples of event-driven data-mining programs. The defunct Terrorism Information Awareness (TIA) program, at one time called Total Information Awareness, consisted of a number of operations designed to gather vast amounts of information useful to targeting terrorist activity. The program had three articulated goals: (1) to increase access to counterterrorism information "by an order of magnitude" (to be accomplished through the Genisys program); (2) to accumulate "patterns that cover at least 90 percent of all known previous foreign terrorists attacks" and "automatically cue analysts based on partial pattern matches" (the objective of the Evidence Extraction and Link Discovery program); and (3) to "support collaboration, analytical reasoning, and information sharing so analysts can hypothesize, test, and propose theories and mitigating strategies about possible futures" (to be implemented through the previous two programs and the Scalable Social Network Analysis algorithms program).[94] Put in plain English, TIA was an attempt to use computers to sift through a large number of databases containing credit card purchases, tax returns, driver's license data, work permits, and travel itineraries to discover or apply patterns predictive of terrorist activity.

Although Congress significantly limited TIA's reach in 2003, the relevant legislation still permits the Defense Department, after "appropriate consultation with Congress," to pursue data mining of records on Americans as well as foreign citizens, for the purpose of gathering information relevant to law enforcement investigations as well as foreign intelligence.[95] The department and related government agencies have taken full advantage of this authority, as evidenced by the disclosure in May 2006 that the National Security Agency has accumulated the phone records of millions of Americans so that it can conduct "link analysis," another term for pattern-based data mining.[96] The NSA, *Time* magazine reported, is trying to "whittle down the hundreds of millions of phone numbers harvested to hundreds of thousands that fit certain profiles it finds interesting; those in turn are cross-checked with other intelligence databases to find, perhaps, a few thousand that warrant more investigation."[97]

Relying on *Miller*, proponents of large-scale data mining have insisted on its legality even when private records are accessed. The survey participants, however, were leery of this type of data mining, ranking it as more intrusive than an ID check, whether aimed at multiple record sets (see scenario 13, involving data mining of phone, credit card, and travel records) or only one (see scenario 10, involving data mining of phone records). Assuming this finding accurately represents society's views, proportionality reasoning would suggest that event-driven surveillance of private records be permitted only if there is at least reasonable suspicion. Given the group nature of the surveillance, that would mean the government's profile should achieve roughly a 30 percent hit rate that useful evidence will be discovered.[98]

Proponents of the NSA program would likely resist this type of restriction by claiming that the program is necessary to stem the threat posed by terrorism. In some cases, that claim is a relevant one; consistent with the danger exception described in chapter 2, the showing usually required under proportionality analysis could be relaxed when the government can demonstrate that the data mining is necessary to detect a significant imminent threat.[99] Outside of the emergency context, however, proportionality reasoning would more strictly regulate data mining of private records than does current law.

While it thus imposes greater restrictions on data mining than presently apply, the upshot of proportionality reasoning is that event-driven surveillance would not be as stringently monitored as target-driven surveillance. Event-driven surveillance of private records would require only reasonable suspicion, and event-driven surveillance of quasi-private and public records could be carried out on a relevance showing. But it should also be noted that even the latter requirement would be difficult to meet in many event-driven data-mining contexts. For instance, as several commentators have pointed out,[100] given the small number of terrorists in the United States, application of a highly accurate profile is likely to produce a very high ratio of false positives (nonterrorists identified as terrorists) to true positives (actual terrorists) if millions of records have to be sifted in the process. Barring an emergency, then, many of the government's antiterrorism data-mining efforts aimed at domestic records might fail to meet the relevant threshold.

The government might be able to finesse this problem by keeping the results of initial data-mining passes anonymous—using pseudonyms or nonhuman (computerized) techniques—until it produces a group for which it has the requisite cause. This latter type of multistage analysis—sometimes called "selective revelation"—is technologically feasible (and was viewed as relatively unintrusive in the survey, as indicated by the ranking of scenario 4 involving anonymous acquisition of personal information). But it is largely untested in most law enforcement contexts.[101] Furthermore, stringent auditing procedures would need to be in place to ensure the government didn't cheat by prematurely linking the files with names or hacking into the computerized investigation.[102]

A separate concern about event-driven data mining is that because it can cast such a wide net, it is easier to manipulate in the service of illegitimate ends. In particular, it might facilitate both harassment of disfavored groups (for instance, when race is an element of a data-mining profile or when government officials choose to interview only the Arab individuals who fit a particular profile) and pretextual searches for evidence of nonprofiled crimes that the government would otherwise have difficulty discovering or proving (known as "mission creep" among data-mining aficionados). When so used, data mining may be unreasonable under the Fourth Amendment or illegal under some other constitutional provision. As argued in chapter 2, profiles should not include race, and as chapter 4 contended in connection with camera surveillance, race-based selection of investigative targets must also be prohibited. And while the Supreme Court has refused to prohibit pretextual searches altogether, it has also indicated a willingness to consider pretext arguments under the Fourth Amendment when searches are grounded on something less than probable cause and thus are more prone to abuse, which would be the case for event-driven surveillance under the proposed regime.[103] Even if that potential limitation ends up being ignored in other contexts, it should apply to transaction surveillance. The temptation to misuse records searches is particularly strong because, unlike physical searches and communications surveillance, they are not conducted in real time and thus are not space- or time-limited.

The potential for racism and pretextual actions should not lead, however, to an absolute prohibition on event-driven data mining. Unfortunately, these improper motivations infect every aspect of criminal justice.

As argued in more detail in chapter 8, the best way to fight them is through direct sanctions, not elimination of useful investigative techniques.

III. Counterproposals

What does this set of proposals mean for Agent Jones, described back in chapter 1? Recall that he was contemplating a target-driven investigation of three different people (a frequent flyer who pays for his tickets with cash, a free spender with no visible means of support, and a young religious Arab man) using various transaction surveillance techniques. Jones would need a court order based on a showing of relevance to access public records about these individuals through ChoicePoint or one of the other commercial data brokers. And he would need a warrant based on probable cause to access the contents of the suspect's financial, medical, and similar personal records as well as to obtain envelope information such as addresses of the person's e-mail correspondents.

If instead the transaction surveillance is event driven, Jones would merely need to show that any profile he uses is relevant to a legitimate investigation (one that is not motivated by racial animus or hidden investigative agendas), unless he seeks private records, in which case he would also need a profile that would produce a roughly 30 percent hit rate. Applying this framework to earlier examples, if the government seeks to ascertain who made certain purchases at a certain store or joined a skydiving club (public activities), it would be on solid ground if this information is likely to increase the probability of identifying the perpetrators. If instead it wanted to obtain a list of who called a particular number or who visited a particular Web site (nonpublic activities), it would need to demonstrate an articulable suspicion why the persons who will be so identified were or will be criminal actors.

Contrary to the Department of Justice's stance, none of these rules should change if government seeks individual information from records acquired by a commercial data broker that has obtained the data from the original recordholders. Otherwise, much of this regulation could be avoided. Information does not become less private simply because it has been shifted from one entity to another. The crucial questions are whether the records sought are about an individual or an organization, whether they are held for private or public purposes, and whether the investigation is target or event driven.

While this set of rules is not uncomplicated, it recognizes fewer types of authorizations than the current regime. Outside of the corporate crime context (the most likely setting in which organizational records will be sought), the officer need merely determine whether the search is target or event driven and whether the records fit in either the private or public category (since any record that is neither is quasi-private). Moreover, since transaction surveillance should generally proceed only pursuant to a court order, confusion on the detective's part can be ameliorated by a judge.

One can imagine numerous alternative methods of regulating transaction surveillance. The Department of Defense's Technical and Privacy Advisory Committee (TAPAC), in its final report issued in 2004, recommended that nonanonymized data mining be preceded by authorization from both the agency head and a court, and also called for minimization and audit procedures, but did not adopt any particular standard to be applied by the decision makers.[104] The recommendations also exempted from these requirements any information "that is routinely available without charge or subscription to the public."[105] While it does not provide as much protection for transactional information as the proportionality approach advanced here, TAPAC did recognize a hierarchy of procedures based on the type of data government is trying to access. If the debate were over those types of issues, it would at least be on the right track.

Other proposals regarding transaction surveillance, however, ignore proportionality reasoning as the means of implementing the Fourth Amendment. Below is an analysis of a few such alternative regimes. While each may seem appealing initially, each suffers from serious flaws.

Jettisoning Privacy

Daniel Solove has advanced a regulatory scheme that is different from both current law and the regime presented here.[106] Rather than attempt to figure out a privacy hierarchy and match authorization requirements to it (the proportionality approach that informs this book), he proposes a uniform regulatory regime for government access to any "system of records."[107] Specifically, Professor Solove proposes that outside of emergency situations, government be prohibited from obtaining information in records—whether it is individual or corporate data, whether it is held by private or public agencies—unless the government can obtain what he calls a "regulated subpoena." To obtain such a subpoena the government would have to demonstrate it has probable cause to believe the person whose records are sought is involved in criminal activity, and that the specific records targeted are of "material importance" to the investigation—a standard he describes as "slightly more permissive" than the probable cause required by a warrant, though more demanding than the relevance required for a subpoena (and, presumably, the reasonable suspicion required for a *Terry* order). As with traditional subpoenas, the regulated subpoena would be challengeable by the target.[108]

Solove asserts that his scheme is superior to a proportionality approach in two respects. First, he points to the difficulty of differentiating between degrees of privacy and intimacy, a difficulty illustrated by my attempts to distinguish individual from organizational records, private from public records, and event- and target-driven surveillance. Second, even if we could resolve these definitional problems, Solove believes that making privacy the linchpin of analysis is conceptually bankrupt. He notes, for instance, that we would never think of requiring the police investigating a rape case to secure a warrant before seeking a description of a suspect's genitals from his sexual partner, yet that information is probably as "private" as anything found in one's medical records. Privacy, Solove argues, is a contextual concept that cannot form the basis for uniform regulation.[109] Rather, in the transaction surveillance setting, the deciding factor should be whether the information is maintained in a system of records.[110] So, to return to his example, the police could interview the sexual partner without restriction, but would need a regulated subpoena to access the medical record of the suspect for the same information.

I agree with the premise of both of Solove's arguments, but am less persuaded that they lead to his conclusion. Solove is right that making the subtle distinctions demanded by a proportionality approach is difficult and can result in over- or underprotection of information at the margins. But requiring probable cause for all record searches, including searches of corporate and public records, goes too far in the other direction. Moreover, the effect of Solove's proposal on law enforcement investigation would be calamitous. Most obviously, regulation of businesses would come to an end if regulated subpoenas were required for *all* records searches. Target-driven searches of public records, which often occur in the initial stages of an investigation, would also be very difficult to conduct. And event-driven surveillance of any sort would be almost impossible. If probable cause were required for such surveillance, for instance, the sniper-killer, mall-bombing, and serial sexual assault investigations described earlier might never get off the ground. Creating a hierarchy of privacy, tricky though it may be, is important as a means of enabling the balancing of government and individual interests that the Supreme Court has sanctioned since the 1960s in *Terry* and related cases.

Similarly, while I agree with Solove that the extent to which we are willing to protect private information is contextual (as his example of the sexual partner interview demonstrates), that conclusion does not mean that privacy should be discarded as the baseline consideration in determining the government's authority to obtain information about its citizens. We should treat witness interviews differently from records requests not because privacy is irrelevant during witness interviews but because the target's interest in privacy is countered by an even stronger interest—the third party's autonomy. As discussed in chapter 6, human information sources, such as the sexual partner, should have a right to decide what to do with the information they possess; in such cases, the subject's privacy interest is outweighed by the source's autonomy interest. When the third party is an impersonal recordholder, on the other hand, concerns about denigrating the third party's "personhood" through limitations on when information may be revealed are nonexistent.[111] It is the absence of a legitimate third-party interest in surrendering the target's private information, not the bare fact that the information happens to reside in a record, that distinguishes the records request scenario from the interview setting.

These considerations lead me to conclude, contrary to Solove, that privacy concerns should be the fundamental consideration in analyzing transaction surveillance. While information generally should be accorded more protection when recorded, the extent of that protection should depend on the degree of privacy associated with the information, not simply on whether it exists in record form. Thus, transactional information found in corporate or truly public records or discovered through event-driven surveillance should be accessible on less than probable cause.

Controlling Dissemination

Another alternative to the proportionality approach advanced here evades the issue of whether it is under- or overprotective of privacy by asserting that it focuses on the wrong sort of privacy invasion. William Stuntz concedes that "secret searches" of our transactional information create risks that "are worth worrying about."[112] But he contends that we would not be particularly bothered by easy government access to such information *if* we never found out about it except in connection with prosecutions for serious crime.[113] In other words, covert access to and stringent control over use of transaction information should permit relaxation of the rules as to how we obtain it.

This ignorance-is-bliss notion is superficially attractive. But limiting information flow, which is essential to Professor Stuntz's scheme, can be very difficult, for reasons alluded to in chapter 4's discussion of this proposal. The assumption that data gathered by law enforcement can be restricted to a small group of government employees is particularly naive in the wake of 9/11, when hundreds of thousands of law enforcement officers are charged with fighting "terrorism"—an amorphous threat, to say the least. Ensuring that the information government officials acquire through covert surveillance is used only for the purpose of prosecuting serious crime could be equally difficult, precisely because the surveillance is covert;[114] in this context, the potential for mission creep is particularly acute.[115] Finally, abandoning all suspicion requirements, as Stuntz would do, virtually guarantees that data would be routinely and randomly gathered about large numbers of innocent people, a practice that would likely increase the chances of government files containing misleading information about its citizens. In contrast, requiring at least a relevance showing for event-driven surveillance and greater suspicion levels for many types of target-driven surveillance, as my proposal does, places meaningful limits on the scope of government efforts to gather transaction evidence.

Even if the information gathered through Stuntz's approach is somehow confined to a limited and discreet group and is not misused or inaccurate in any way, routine suspicionless and covert transaction surveillance can eat away at whatever trust is left between government and its citizenry. Once the public becomes aware that random covert surveillance is pervasive, the panoptic effect of this regime will be greater than occurs with overt surveillance. Although one poll asking for reaction to the NSA phone-sweep program described earlier indicated that 63 percent of those surveyed felt that the program was an "acceptable way to fight terrorism,"[116] 37 percent felt to the contrary, sometimes vigorously so.[117] Furthermore, the latter percentage would undoubtedly climb if covert and unlimited transaction surveillance were known to be routinely conducted not only by the Defense Department but by ordinary police agencies solving ordinary (albeit serious) crimes. Only if the program is able to keep the identity of the phone callers truly anonymous until its algorithm pinpointed those for whom the relevant level of cause exists (akin to the contraband-specific devices discussed in chapter 5) should it be considered constitutional under the Fourth Amendment.[118]

With the power of today's computers, government could monitor the transactions of everybody all the time. A regulatory regime that explicitly *endorsed* that sort of process would destroy any sense of security people might have in today's technological society. Indeed, if government is to be allowed to find out details of our lives whenever it is interested in doing so, we would probably be more comfortable knowing when it is occurring rather than being left in the dark.

Relying on the Legislature

A final means of regulating transaction surveillance is to leave the task up to the legislature, specifically Congress. Orin Kerr has made the most powerful argument for this approach.[119] He correctly points out that congressional statutes have provided more protection against transaction surveillance than the Supreme Court's construal of the Fourth Amendment in cases like *Miller* and that, in theory, legislatures are better equipped than courts to craft clear rules governing transaction surveillance in an era of rapidly changing, complicated technology.[120]

But Kerr's arguments fail to negate two crucial facts about the transaction surveillance rules that Congress has enacted to date: the rules have *not* been particularly clear,[121] and, more important, they do not provide *adequate* protection against government access to our personal records. As evidenced by the passage of legislation in 2006 essentially giving the president carte blanche antiterrorism authority, even with respect to wiretapping,[122] Congress is unlikely to alter its stance on transaction surveillance substantially unless the courts, relying on the Fourth Amendment, nudge it in the right direction.

Will the courts be willing to engage in such nudging? Certainly, *Miller*, *Smith,* and like cases indicate that the Supreme Court is hesitant to do so. But in more recent decisions applying the special needs doctrine, which raises parallel issues, the Court has dropped its nonchalant attitude toward nontraditional searches and seizures and called into question the validity of both the diminished-privacy and heightened-need rationales for eliminating Fourth Amendment restrictions on transaction surveillance. In *Ferguson v. City of Charleston,* the Court declared unconstitutional a policy that authorized hospital drug testing of pregnant patients for the purpose of detecting illegal drug use, over a dissent by Justice Scalia arguing that under *Miller* the patients voluntarily assumed the risk that the results of such tests would be used for investigative purposes.[123] The majority in *Ferguson* ignored Scalia's complaint, concluding that a reasonable patient would assume the test results would be used for diagnostic purposes and that otherwise they would be kept confidential.[124] And in both *Ferguson* and *Indianapolis v. Edmond,* the roadblock case described in chapter 5, the Court emphasized that individualized cause requirements may not be relaxed if the only special need pleaded by the government is a "general interest in law enforcement."[125]

Another recent Supreme Court decision, this one outside the special needs context, registered even stronger qualms about *Miller*'s assumption-of-risk analysis. In *Georgia v. Randolph,*[126] the Court held that when one occupant of a residence consents to entry but another refuses, police must honor the refusal. Justice David Souter stated for the Court that the reasonableness of a search in this situation "is in significant part a function of commonly held understandings about the authority that co-inhabitants may exercise in ways that affect each other's interests," and concluded that an invitee would ordinarily not enter in such a situation.[127] Based on an analysis of property law, he also concluded that "there is no common understanding that one co-tenant generally has a right or authority to prevail over the express wishes of another."[128] What is important about the case for present purposes is the majority's dismissal of Chief Justice John Roberts's assertion in dissent, based on *Miller* and its progeny, that when "an individual shares information, papers, or places with another, he assumes the risk that the other person will in turn share access to that information or those papers or places with the government."[129] Far from agreeing with this statement, the majority chastised the chief justice for his "easy assumption that privacy shared with another individual is privacy waived for all purposes including warrantless searches by police."[130] Roberts averred that with this type of language, *Randolph* "alters a great deal of established Fourth Amendment law."[131] Although Roberts was dismayed by this prospect, I hope he is right.[132]

Ferguson and *Randolph* signal that the Court is reluctant to grant the government an exemption from traditional Fourth Amendment standards simply because information relevant to a criminal investigation has been shared with or given to a third party (thus undermining *Miller*'s diminished-privacy premise). And *Ferguson* and *Edmond* suggest that government claims that relaxation of those standards is necessary to detect criminal activity will not always prevail (thus undermining the heightened-need rationale as a ground for reducing Fourth Amendment protections). These decisions provide a glimmer of hope that, when confronted with cases challenging subpoenas for personal records about medical treatment, personal finances, the contents of e-mail messages, and individual phone logs, the Court will withdraw from its broad pronouncements in *Miller*. If it does so, further, more detailed rule-making along the lines suggested here might best be left to Congress, for the reasons Kerr suggests. The goal should be meaningful protection of personal information, whatever its source.

Conclusion

Analysis of government surveillance has tended to focus on communications and physical surveillance. But transaction surveillance is at least as pervasive as these other types of investigative techniques and can be as inimical to privacy interests. Public and private records contain information regarding virtually every aspect of our lives. In the past few decades, technology has made that information infinitely more easily aggregated and accessible.

Yet neither legislatures nor courts have evidenced much concern about transaction surveillance. Congress appears to think of transaction information as "business records," and thus at most entitled to the protection afforded by subpoenas, while the Supreme Court tells us we must assume the risk that recordholders will betray us. These positions ignore the personal nature of the information in these records. They also fail to acknowledge that disclosure of that information to recordkeepers—disclosure that those of us who live a modern lifestyle cannot avoid—is no different, in expectation of privacy terms, than communicating with others by phone or e-mail or interacting with others inside one's home, both activities clearly protected by the Constitution. As Senator Sam Ervin recognized in 1974, "Government has an insatiable appetite for power, and it will not stop usurping power unless it is restrained by laws they cannot repeal or nullify."[133] When it comes to transaction surveillance, only the Fourth Amendment provides that type of restraint.

CHAPTER EIGHT

Conclusion: A Different Fourth Amendment?

Government surveillance of all types has expanded dramatically since September 11, 2001. The critical tone of this book should not be taken as an unconditional condemnation of that development. Communications surveillance, physical surveillance, and transaction surveillance are essential tools in combating a whole host of ills, including organized crime, drug dealers, corrupt government officials, technologically savvy con artists and, last but not least, terrorists fearless of punishment and even death.

As Benjamin Franklin stated, however, "They that can give up essential liberty to obtain a little temporary safety deserve neither liberty nor safety."[1] Putting this sentiment in Fourth Amendment terms, we must make sure we are "secure" from government overreaching as well as from criminals and our enemies. The Fourth Amendment establishes the method for resolving this tension by prohibiting unreasonable searches and seizures.

One of the two primary theses of this book is that surveillance that is not regulated is unreasonable under the Constitution. Supreme Court case law construing the Fourth Amendment, broadly read, allows government agents to scan our homes with binoculars, continuously track our public movements with cameras and beepers, and access institutional records of all our daily activities, *at their discretion*. It is inconceivable that the drafters of the Constitution meant government to have such uncabined power. If that is the import of its decisions, the Supreme Court has done this country a vast disservice.

This declaration is neither a liberal nor a conservative sentiment. People on both ends of the political spectrum are concerned about the lack of constitutional controls over government authority to intrude on their private lives.[2] At the same time, liberals as well as conservatives are responsible for the current state of affairs. Not just the conservative post-Warren Court, with its decisions in cases like *Dow Chemical*, *Knotts*, *Miller,* and *Smith*, but the liberal Warren Court, whose undercover agent cases laid the groundwork for these decisions, warrant criticism for today's weak constitutional restrictions on surveillance.

Indeed, the liberal agenda may deserve the most blame for the current state of affairs. A good case can be made for the initially counterintuitive position that the most important dogmas of this agenda—specifically, that searches must always be bottomed on individualized probable cause and that unreasonable searches must always result in exclusion of evidence—are responsible for today's constitutional nihilism. When a search *requires* probable cause to be constitutional, courts are naturally more reluctant to denominate every police attempt to find evidence a search. When suspicion must be individualized, they are more likely to gloss over the harms caused by investigations of groups. And when the sole serious sanction for an illegal search is suppression at trial, many judges have less sympathy for viable claims because they cannot stomach dismissal of criminal charges for lack of evidence.

Thus, the second principal thesis of this book, underlying the first, is that Fourth Amendment jurisprudence needs to relinquish its focus on the traditional probable cause/individualized suspicion model, backed by a motion for exclusion, as the primary means of protecting individual interests. Instead, this book argues, Fourth Amendment regulation should flow from the proportionality and exigency principles, and violation of those principles should often occasion more direct, less incendiary sanctions than exclusion. The following three sections revisit the rationale for these views, using physical and transaction surveillance scenarios as illustrations. Along the way, the core proposals advanced in this book are summarized.

I. Probable Cause Forever

Of course, probable cause is not required for every police action that is called a search or seizure. As chapter 2 noted, *Terry v. Ohio,* a Warren Court decision, stands for the proposition that detentions short of arrest and pat downs of outer clothing are permissible on reasonable suspicion. The Court was willing to relax Fourth Amendment strictures with respect to stops and frisks because the government's interest in "effective crime prevention and detection" on the streets justified the "brief, though far from inconsiderable, intrusion upon the sanctity of the person" these actions occasion.[3]

In the seizure context, the post-Warren Court has relied on this balancing approach in approving several types of detentions short of an arrest on less than probable cause.[4] In the search context, however, it has been much less willing to follow this route. Instead, the Court has insisted, in the words of Justice Stewart in *Katz*, that "searches conducted . . . without prior approval by judge of magistrate [and therefore without probable cause], are per se unreasonable under the Fourth Amendment, subject only to a few specifically established and well-delineated exceptions."[5] Almost twenty years later, in *New Jersey v. T.L.O.*, a much more conservative Court similarly stated, "Ordinarily, a search—even one that may permissibly be carried out without a warrant—must be based upon 'probable cause' to believe that a violation has occurred."[6]

T.L.O. then went on to hold that probable cause was *not* required to search a schoolchild's purse for evidence of disciplinary infractions, in the course of creating the one major exception (other than *Terry*'s frisk rule) to the probable-cause-forever dogma. Called the special needs doctrine, after a phrase in Justice Blackmun's concurrence in *T.L.O.*, the exception requires only that government action be reasonable,[7] which in practice has meant that neither a warrant nor probable cause is required. But the special needs exception is usually applicable only when those conducting the government action are pursuing some end other than criminal law enforcement (such as drug testing for administrative purposes; searches of schoolchildren's purses or employees' desks for disciplinary infractions; and inspections of gun shops, coal mines, and other businesses for regulatory, health, and safety violations). Indeed, the classic statement of the special needs paradigm is that it kicks in only when "special needs, beyond the normal need for law enforcement, make the warrant and probable-cause requirement impracticable."[8] The Court has on several occasions called these special needs situations "exceptional" and "limited."[9] In other words, outside of frisks, the usual law enforcement search for evidence of criminal activity requires probable cause.

While that outcome may please many who favor strong Fourth Amendment protection, its ultimate effect has been just the reverse. As chapter 2 documented, the consequences of this probable-cause-forever position have been dramatic: a whole host of intrusive police actions—

flyovers, open field trespasses, undercover activity—are now immunized from Fourth Amendment strictures. This hands-off attitude developed because, like the stop and frisk at issue in *Terry*, these types of investigative techniques are exploratory, based on suspicion rather than probable cause. Without these techniques, probable cause might never be developed. When forced to choose between permitting such actions at police discretion or in effect ending them, even many aggressive civil libertarians might choose the former route.

Thus, it is no surprise that this has also been the response of most members of the Supreme Court, even moderate and liberal ones. For instance, in holding that the Fourth Amendment does not govern use of undercover agents to gain entry to the home, Chief Justice Earl Warren himself stated, "Were we to hold the deceptions of the agent in this case constitutionally prohibited, we would come near to a rule that the use of undercover agents in any manner is virtually unconstitutional per se."[10] The Supreme Court cases most relevant to physical and transaction surveillance are also apt reflections of the dilemma created by the probable-cause-forever position. Had the Court decided for the defendants in *Knotts*, *Miller,* and *Smith*, for example, it might have created precedent for banning public tracking of any individual whom the police couldn't already arrest and for invalidating all exploratory subpoenas for third-party records, even though both practices are crucial first-stage law enforcement techniques. That prospect must have been daunting, for even the "liberal" justices signed on to the unanimous *Knotts* opinion, only William Brennan and Thurgood Marshall wrote dissenting opinions in *Miller*, and only they plus Stewart dissented in *Smith;* moreover, only Marshall was adamant about requiring a warrant in the latter two cases.[11]

The damage done by the probable-cause-forever position in the surveillance context does not end with the specific holdings in these cases. Even more insidious is the assumption-of-risk rationale that it has spawned, first in the Warren Court in its undercover cases and then in *Knotts*, *Miller,* and *Smith*. That rationale not only has given carte blanche to public surveillance and third-party subpoenas but also underlies *Kyllo*'s dictum that police may use technological means to spy on the interior of homes so long as the technology is in general public use. The general public use doctrine stems directly from the notion that we cannot expect privacy from technology we should know ordinary people use on a daily basis.

Given these developments, some have argued that the real problem in these cases is not the probable cause requirement but *Katz*'s adoption of privacy as the linchpin of Fourth Amendment analysis. Various other concepts—among them, government-citizen trust, coercion, and property—have been proposed as substitutes. I argued in chapter 2 that none of these concepts satisfactorily captures the gravamen of the Fourth Amendment. But even assuming one or more of these alternatives is conceptually viable, there is no reason to believe that any of them would have fared better in dealing with the conundrum created by the probable-cause-forever dogma.

Consider property, probably the most commonly touted substitute for privacy as the core Fourth Amendment value. Of course, privacy analysis takes property interests into account; one has more of a privacy interest in a house one owns or rents than in a house that one temporarily occupies as a guest. Commentators such as Morgan Cloud, however, want a Fourth Amendment "*rooted* in property theories."[12] Cloud prefers this approach in large part because, he says, property concepts are less "malleable" than privacy concepts and thus less likely to permit significant encroachments on the Fourth Amendment's scope.[13] But property doctrine is eminently manipulable as well. For instance, back in the heyday of the property-oriented approach to the Fourth Amendment, the Court had no problem permitting suspicionless searches of privately owned open fields.[14] The definition of criminal instrumentalities was also stretched beyond recognition so that government could assert a superior possessory interest over personal property,[15] a ploy that would be vastly facilitated today by the advent of forfeiture statutes giving government an interest in any item with a nexus to criminal activity.[16] Worse yet, under a property-oriented regime surveillance of any kind could easily be said to be untouched by the Fourth Amendment, since it does not involve physical trespass.[17] In other words, even had the Court adhered to a property-based Fourth Amendment, it could have (and probably would have) succumbed to the pressure created by the probable-cause-forever position. And that pressure would have been particularly hard to resist in the physical and transaction surveillance context, given the amorphous property interests people have in their public movements and in records kept by third parties.

The allegiance to a unitary probable cause standard has still one other downside: the minimization of ex ante review as a regulatory option for searches that don't require probable cause. As Justice Scalia stated in *Griffin v. Wisconsin,* "The Constitution prescribes . . . that where the matter is of such a nature as to require a judicial warrant, it is also of such a nature as to require probable cause."[18] Conversely, Scalia implied, if probable cause is not required, neither is ex ante review. Thus, Justice Blackmun's suggestion, offered in his dissent in *Griffin*, that the search of a probationer's home is reasonable only if authorized by a judge was brusquely dismissed by the majority once it found that such searches present a special needs situation outside normal law enforcement.[19] According to the majority, a court order based on less than probable cause is "a combination that neither the text of the Constitution nor any of our prior decisions permits."[20] If that is the law in special needs cases, then the idea that a court could issue an order on mere reasonable suspicion or something less in connection with *normal* law enforcement would likely be even more oxymoronic to the justices who joined this language. Thus, for instance, even if the Court adopted the notion that public tracking is a search and further permitted such searches on reasonable suspicion, it would likely resist requiring, in addition, that police convince a magistrate that the standard was met.

In a variety of ways, then, the probable-cause-forever dogma forces courts grappling with the realities of law enforcement to exempt many varieties of surveillance from the Fourth Amendment's restrictions. That dogma is not required by the Fourth Amendment, however. Again, the Fourth Amendment requires only that searches and seizures be reasonable.

That declaration might conjure up the specter of a Fourth Amendment swallowed entirely by the special needs exception. But there are other ways of conceptualizing reasonableness. The proportionality and exigency principles discussed throughout this book more sensibly implement this mandate because they ameliorate the pressure created by the probable-cause-forever stance without sacrificing the core protection of the Fourth Amendment. The proportionality principle allows courts to modulate the cause needed to carry out physical and transaction surveillance depending on its intrusiveness, and the exigency principle ensures that, whenever there is time to do so, even surveillance authorized on less than probable cause will be subject to ex ante review by someone not involved in the search.

Under this regime, courts would be more willing to say that police attempts to find evidence are searches because the consequences of such a holding would not be as dramatic. For instance, undercover work, even if called a search, might require probable cause only when it involves long-term infiltration.[21] Observation of public activities like the tracking that occurred in *Knotts* could more easily be denominated a Fourth Amendment event because, for reasons outlined in chapters 4 and 5, such a holding would not require probable cause for public surveillance unless it is prolonged. And all subpoenas for records could more comfortably be called searches because only subpoenas for personal records like those sought in *Miller* or the individual phone log such as that obtained in *Smith* would require probable cause; organizational records could be obtained on a much lesser showing.

Nor would this application of the proportionality principle have required different results on the specific facts of *Knotts*, *Miller,* and *Smith*. The government had probable cause to believe that Miller's bank records would prove his involvement in an illegal liquor operation and that Smith's phone records would reveal attempts to harass a former victim, and at least a reasonable suspicion that the purchaser of the beepered can that eventually led to Knotts was up to no good.[22] Under the regime advanced in this book, the only possible challenge in these cases, and then only in *Knotts* and *Smith*, would be that ex ante review was not sought, in possible violation of the exigency principle.

Thus, if the proportionality and exigency principles ruled, courts could more easily avoid the temptation to define the Fourth Amendment threshold in terms of assumptions of risk, and might be more willing to speak of that threshold in the terms *Katz* has always stood for: expectations of privacy *society* recognizes as reasonable. This development would ensure adequate regulation not only of physical surveillance of public movements such as occurred in *Knotts* and transaction surveillance of the type involved in *Miller* and *Smith*, but also of physical surveillance of the home. For as chapter 3 argued, *Kyllo*'s dictum endorsing the general public use and naked eye exceptions could never become formal law if the courts viewed the home in the same way society does (and the Framers did).

Reduction of Fourth Amendment conundrums is not the only reason the proportionality and exigency principles should be adopted, of course. Chapter 2 made additional normative arguments in their favor. But particularly in this age of heightened concern over security, the pragmatic impact of a Fourth Amendment theory on judicial decision-making is far from an irrelevant consideration.

II. The Fixation on Individualized Suspicion

Hand in glove with the Court's probable cause doctrine is the individualized suspicion requirement. As the Court has stated, "A search or seizure is ordinarily unreasonable in the absence of individualized suspicion of wrongdoing."[23] That precept is normally a wise one. But it cannot be honored when large groups of people are subjected to searches or seizures, like those that occur in connection with roadblocks, drug testing, and, most relevant to this book, camera surveillance and data mining. In these situations, an individualized suspicion requirement would stop the government's investigation dead in its tracks.

One response to this quandary is to adhere to the individualized suspicion requirement and simply prohibit group searches. But that solution is as "unreasonable" as the eradication of first-stage investigative techniques that occurs under a probable-cause-forever stance. Group searches are an important means of keeping us safe, a fact even liberal justices recognize.[24]

The Court's approach, in contrast, has been to determine whether the group intrusion is a special needs situation. If ordinary law enforcement is involved, the Court continues to require individualized suspicion.[25] In special needs situations, however, the Court has been satisfied with a bland assertion by the government that the group search or seizure is meant to deal with an unquantified problem, such as illegal immigration, drunken driving, business safety violations, or substance abuse among customs agents and schoolchildren.[26] In other words, just as the probable cause dogma has encouraged a narrow definition of search, the individualized suspicion dogma has left the Court with no tools for dealing with group searches, with the result that it has essentially adopted a hands-off attitude toward them (and vastly increased the potential for arbitrary and pretextual police actions).

The proportionality principle counsels an intermediate approach. It would permit group searches, but only if, as outlined in previous pages, there is reason to believe that the proportion of criminals likely to be so discovered roughly equals the hit rate required by the intrusion involved. For instance, if the government wants to conduct full searches of everyone in a group, it should have to show why there is reason to believe that roughly one out of two of those searches will produce evidence of crime (unless the danger exception discussed in chapter 2 applies).[27] Similarly, event-driven data mining using personal records of identifiable individuals ought to be able to finger viable suspects approximately one-third of the time, given the intrusion involved. Public physical surveillance of large numbers of people is not as invasive, but in open public areas, where the right to anonymity is most robust, cameras and other physical surveillance technology should not be installed unless a demonstrable, concrete threat is present in the monitored area.[28] The "generalized suspicion" notion operating in these examples provides concrete guidelines for the reasonableness inquiry, which otherwise demands only vague assertions of government need, if it is triggered at all (depending on whether the Court ultimately considers investigative techniques like public camera surveillance and data mining to be searches).

The exigency principle also places limitations on group searches. As Scalia's comments in *Griffin* indicate, the Court's special needs jurisprudence not only jettisons a warrant requirement but appears to abandon all pretense of ex ante review. The exigency principle, in contrast, would require such review before *all* nonexigent group searches, special or not, just as is required when a single house, person, paper, or effect is searched. The rationale for the ex ante review requirement in this situation is the same as it is for individual searches and seizures. Justice Robert H. Jackson famously defended warrants as a means of forcing "inferences [to] be drawn by a neutral and detached magistrate instead of being judged by the officer engaged in the often competitive enterprise of ferreting out crime."[29] That rationale doesn't change simply because the government is no longer engaged in ordinary law enforcement.

At the same time, the exigency principle does not pose the obstruction to law enforcement objectives that the probable-cause-forever and individualized suspicion requirements do. Ex ante review would be required only when there is time to obtain it. Furthermore, when the justification requirement is less than probable cause, as is often true with group searches, judges might not need to be involved in the review process. For instance, as chapter 5 suggested, camera installation could be approved by a judge, but it could also be sanctioned by any high-level, politically accountable official who is divorced from front-line law enforcement.

Finally, the Fourth Amendment's reasonableness command dictates rules with respect to execution of group searches and use of their results, two matters legislatures and courts have largely neglected. For instance, with respect to public camera surveillance, citizens are entitled to notice of the surveillance, protections against discriminatory monitoring, and circumscribed dissemination of anything recorded. Destruction of recordings after a reasonable period of time and periodic reports about their efficacy in fighting crime might also be required. Data mining should be treated similarly; minimization techniques should be in place and regular audits and periodic reports required. These procedural aspects of regulation are particularly important in connection with group searches given the number of innocent people they catch in their net.

III. The Obsession with Exclusion

Since 1961, when the Supreme Court decided *Mapp v. Ohio,*[30] exclusion has been the remedy of choice when the Fourth Amendment is violated. The *Mapp* Court was convinced that other remedies were "worthless and futile" and that, in any event, both the Fourth and Fifth Amendments required suppression of illegally obtained evidence.[31] The post-Warren Court has completely eliminated the Fifth Amendment basis for the rule[32] and pretty much done away with its Fourth Amendment foundation as well, insisting that exclusion is merely a judicially created remedy designed to deter police misconduct.[33] Yet it remains the primary sanction for Fourth Amendment violations. In the meantime, administrative and damages remedies have atrophied or been explicitly narrowed by a Supreme Court hostile to lawsuits against law enforcement agents and their employers.[34]

Elsewhere I have discussed at length how the exclusionary rule undermines civil liberties, albeit unintentionally and indirectly (as is true with the probable cause and individualized suspicion mantras).[35] First, the rule is ineffective as a deterrent, in either the specific or general sense, because it seldom comes into play and is only an indirect punishment when it does so. Police know that most questionable searches and seizures never result in arrest or prosecution, and that many of those that do result in formal processing don't trigger a suppression hearing because of the prevalence of plea bargaining. When a hearing does take place, miscreant officers often prevail because of perjury, the hindsight biasing effect of judicial knowledge that criminal evidence was found, and judicial reluctance to exclude evidence. Even when evidence is suppressed, the prosecutor is hurt much more than the officer, whose primary goal is obtaining "collars," not convictions, and whose superiors are likely to be sympathetic to aggressive policework so long as it does not result in egregious abuse.[36] The latter point also helps explain why the rule does not have much of a "systemic" effect, either. Research strongly suggests that training programs (run by the same superiors or supervisors like them) routinely slight constitutional issues and that officers are not well versed in Fourth Amendment law.[37]

It is the damage to that law, however, that is the exclusionary rule's most insidious effect. The exclusionary remedy, designed to suppress evidence of crime, ensures that the only Fourth Amendment claims most judges see are brought by guilty people seeking to elude conviction. Thus, most decision makers responsible for interpreting the Fourth Amendment are rarely confronted by a breach of privacy claim from an innocent individual. To the contrary, in the typical case they know that vindication of the claim will diminish or end any possibility of punishing an obvious criminal. That is hardly a prescription for a fair, open-minded assessment of Fourth Amendment issues.

The best argument for retaining the rule despite its flaws is that current alternatives to it are worse. Police are not good at policing themselves, criminal prosecution against misbehaving officers will usually be overkill, and suits for damages are seldom brought and seldom won because of plaintiffs' ignorance of their rights, the expense of civil litigation, the inchoate nature of the injury (which deters lawyers as well as potential plaintiffs from bringing suit), the biases of juries, and, as with the suppression remedy, the efficacy of police perjury. Furthermore, even if a misbehaving officer is sued and loses, he or she is usually indemnified or judgment proof or both, minimizing the impact of the verdict on the officer.[38]

A damages action need not be so toothless, however. I have proposed a different damages regime consisting of several core components: (1) a liquidated damages/penalty for all unconstitutional actions, preferably based on the average officer's salary; (2) personal, unindemnifiable liability, at the liquidated damages sum, of officers who knowingly or recklessly violate the Fourth Amendment; (3) entity liability, at the liquidated damages sum, for all other violations; (4) state-paid legal assistance for those with Fourth Amendment claims; and (5) a judicial decision-maker.[39] With these components in place, innocent people as well as criminals will have an incentive to bring Fourth Amendment claims; officers who knowingly or recklessly violate the Fourth Amendment will receive direct, unalloyed punishment; and departments will have a financial incentive to ensure that their employees know the law. Just as important, judges will be more likely to acknowledge the true base rate of unconstitutional actions, because they will see in their courtrooms numerous people who were searched and found to have *no* evidence of crime in their pockets, homes, or records. Under these conditions, judges will be more likely to evaluate accurately the overall societal impact of progovernment findings (as well as much less likely to condone perjury). In short, in a damages regime of the type described here, judges will be forced to internalize the purpose of the Fourth Amendment—protecting the privacy and autonomy interests of *all* citizens.

In addition, as chapter 5 pointed out, a damages regime is a much better remedial fit for certain types of Fourth Amendment violations. When the violation is inappropriate installation of cameras, failure to give notice of their presence, or incompetent and malicious dissemination of personal information obtained through physical or transaction surveillance, compensatory or injunctive relief is the only meaningful response; exclusion either makes no sense or is disproportionately harsh. Most important, exclusion provides no remedy for the *innocent* victims of police abuse of camera surveillance, technological tracking, and record collection and data mining.

I am not arguing for replacement of the exclusionary rule with a damages regime, although a persuasive argument to that effect can be made. Rather, I am saying that the dominance of the exclusionary rule has been one of many reasons regulation of physical and transaction surveillance has been stymied. And I am saying that without a meaningful damages regime, the Fourth Amendment law that we do have in this area is not likely to make much of a practical difference.

Conclusion

As it has in every other part of life, technology has wrought dramatic changes in government surveillance techniques. What was once unthinkable or at least highly uneconomical is now possible with the flick of a mouse or the push of a button. Technology has reduced or eliminated the practical and fiscal barriers that used to keep law enforcement officials from peering into our homes, watching us on the streets, and accessing our personal records. So today we must depend on the law to keep those barriers intact.

The Fourth Amendment must be the primary source of that law. Legislation can flesh out the details, and government agencies can elaborate even further through administrative rule-making, but the basis of regulation must be constitutional. Given the immense power technological surveillance gives the government and the potent incentives to use it in this post-9/11 era, only the fundamental law of the land can provide a sufficient bulwark against inquisitive agents of the government.

The cornerstone of this bulwark should be the expectation-of-privacy concept. *Katz*'s interpretation of the Fourth Amendment has been declared incoherent, overly susceptible to manipulation, and insufficiently descriptive of the values underlying the amendment. But as this book demonstrates, expectations of privacy and autonomy can be meaningfully gauged and thus need not be the product of judicial whimsy. The book also makes clear that for physical and transaction surveillance, at least, no other Fourth Amendment model provides a useful basis for regulation.

What is in need of repair is not the definition of the Fourth Amendment's threshold but the Supreme Court's implementation of *Katz* and its characterization of the types of justifications and remedies the Fourth Amendment demands. The Court's assumption-of-risk analysis is tautological, its insistence on an individualized probable cause standard for ordinary searches misguided, and its adherence to the exclusionary rule as the principal Fourth Amendment remedy short-sighted. None of these precepts is required by the Fourth Amendment, and all should be abandoned or supplemented where appropriate. At the least, they should not control regulation of physical and transaction surveillance. Instead, the proportionality and exigency principles should govern and a realistic damages regime should be instituted.

These are not ivory tower prescriptions. Chief Justice Warren Burger himself proposed a legislative damages scheme similar to the one outlined here.[40] Despite its rejection in cases like *Griffin*, the exigency principle embraces a commonsense notion routinely espoused in a number of other Court opinions.[41] And as chapter 2 explained, the proportionality principle derives directly from *Terry v. Ohio.* Nor have the Court's subsequent decisions, despite their antiregulatory bent, foreclosed implementation of the latter principle in surveillance cases. *Kyllo*'s general public use and naked eye exceptions are dictum. *Knotts* signaled that prolonged public surveillance could be a search. The pen register in *Smith* was used only to ascertain whether Smith contacted one specific number, so the Court has yet to deal with a case involving the constitutionality of suspicionless target-driven aggregation.[42] And the recent decisions in *Ferguson* and *Randolph*, discussed in chapter 7, hint that the Court no longer endorses the broad language in *Miller* exempting from Fourth Amendment protection all information shared with a third party; if *Miller* were construed narrowly to cover only the most impersonal records, it would not be a major obstacle to the approach advocated here. In short, even if it remains good precedent, the Court's case law governing surveillance would not prevent the continued development of Fourth Amendment jurisprudence in a manner consistent with the proportionality principle.

If that were to happen, physical and transaction surveillance would no longer be constitutionally invisible. At the same time, both types of investigative techniques would be available to the government whenever the government really needed them. It is possible to achieve security in our houses, persons, papers, and effects from both overweening government officials and those who wish to do us harm.

Notes

Chapter One

1. Omnibus Crime Control and Safe Streets Act of 1968, Pub. L. No. 90-351, 82 Stat. 197, codified at 18 U.S.C. §§ 2510–2520.

2. Pub. L. No. 99-508, amending 18 U.S.C. §§ 2510 et seq.

3. Communications surveillance in the national security context was at one time thought to be governed by the Foreign Intelligence Security Act, 50 U.S.C. § 1801, which requires judicial authorization for interception of nondomestic communications but on a lesser showing than that demanded by Title III for domestic surveillance. In 2005–2006, however, the Bush Administration asserted that FISA did not apply in certain surveillance situations, after controversy erupted over the National Security Agency's apparently extensive warrantless communications surveillance of domestic and foreign individuals allegedly connected with terrorist organizations. See James Risen & Eric Lichtblau, Spying Program Snared US Calls, *New York Times*, Dec. 21, 2005, at A1. As of this writing, litigation and debate about the constitutionality of the NSA's program is ongoing. See, e.g., ACLU v. NSA, 438 F. Supp. 2d 754 (E.D. Mich. 2006) (declaring NSA program unconstitutional); Hepting v. AT&T, 439 F. Supp. 2d 974 (N.D. Cal. 2006) (refusing to dismiss suit challenging the NSA program); Dan Eggen, Surveillance Bill Meets Resistance in Senate, *Washington Post*, July 21, 2006. For a critique of the program, see David Cole, NSA Spying Myths, *The Nation*, Feb. 20, 2006.

4. American Bar Association, Standards for Criminal Justice, *Electronic Surveillance, Section B: Technologically-Assisted Physical Surveillance* (1999), available at http://www.abanet.org/crimjust/standards/taps_toc.html. I was the Reporter for these standards and describe in detail the process of drafting them in Christopher Slobogin, Technologically-Assisted Physical Surveillance: The American Bar Association's Tentative Draft Standards, 10 *Harvard Journal of Law & Technology* 383 (1997).

5. See, e.g., James Barron, Designer/Surveillance Consultant Sells Pricey Spy

Ties, *San Antonio Express-News*, Sept. 22, 1996, available at 1996 WL 11498094 (describing various items, including ties and teddy bears, into which video cameras can be installed); Kim Christensen, Snoopy Sales/Spies: Don't Look Now, but Big Brother Might Just Be Your Big Brother, *Orange County Register*, Aug. 2, 1996, available at 1996 WL 7041469 (explaining the use of pinhole-lens video cameras in briefcases and wall clocks).

6. See Note, Tracking *Katz:* Beepers, Privacy and the Fourth Amendment, 86 *Yale Law Journal* 1461, 1463–64 (1977) (explaining that beepers emit "periodic signals which can be picked up on radio frequency [to] establish the approximate location of the object" and that beepers "have been used . . . to trace the movement of subjects on private property, along public thoroughfares, or in public airways . . . [and] have [been] attached . . . to contraband drugs discovered during border searches, to motor vehicles used by suspects, to packages or drums of chemicals, to airplanes, and to an item of personal property").

7. John Ganz, It's Already Public: Why Federal Officers Should Not Need Warrants to Use GPS Tracking Devices, 95 *Journal of Criminal Law & Criminology* 1325, 1328–29 (2005) (GPS is "a network of at least twenty-four satellites" which can be used to triangulate the position and time of receivers on earth and establish "a track, or chronological record, of travel . . . accurate up to fifteen feet and two miles per hour of speed," although "tracks can be adjusted to record position more frequently, giving a more detailed representation of the target's path.").

8. Cell phones can be triangulated to within about three hundred yards of their position. Kristina Dell, The Spy in Your Pocket, *Time*, March 27, 2006.

9. U.S. Government Accountability Office, *Radio Frequency Identification Technology in the Federal Government* (May 2005), available at http://www.gao.gov/new.items/d05551.pdf.

10. Dorothy Glancy, Privacy on the Open Road, 30 *Ohio Northern University Law Review* 295, 296 (2004) ("Some of these ITS systems . . . , such as automatic vehicle identification (AVI), can . . . pinpoint where a person is [and] connect that location with other records, such as where that person has been in the past. . . . In part because of funding by the federal government, [these systems] are almost everywhere.").

11. See, e.g., United States v. Lace, 669 F.2d 46, 53 (2d Cir. 1982), where police use the Javelin night scope, capable of magnifying existing light 50,000 times, and infrared night goggles to facilitate their movement in the dark.

12. Krysten C. Kelly, Warrantless Satellite Surveillance: Will Our Fourth Amendment Privacy Rights Be Lost in Space? 13 *John Marshall Journal of Computer & Information Law* 729, 737 (1995) (describing the ability "to generate and sell images derived from satellites capable of detecting objects as small as one square yard").

13. Melvin Gutterman, A Formulation of the Value and Means Models of the Fourth Amendment in the Age of Technologically-Enhanced Surveillance, 39 *Syracuse Law Review* 647, 678 n.162 (1988) ("Star-[T]ron 606 manufactured by Smith &

Wesson is a high-performance nightvision device designed primarily for long-range military surveillance.").

14. See Richard S. Julie, High-Tech Surveillance Tools and the Fourth Amendment: Reasonable Expectations of Privacy in the Technological Age, 37 *American Criminal Law Review* 127, 139–40 (2000) (describing concealed-weapon detectors' capability generally and Millivision's capabilities specifically).

15. See David A. Harris, Superman's X-Ray Vision and the Fourth Amendment: The New Gun Detection Technology, 69 *Temple Law Review* 1, 7–8 n.38 (1996).

16. Id.

17. The "zNose" purports be able to use "chemical vapor analysis technology" that can "analyze the chemistry of any aroma, fragrance, odor, or vapor in just 10 seconds." According to its developer, Electronic Technology Sensor, zNose can detect "odors and chemical vapors produced by explosives, chemical and biological weapons, contraband of all kinds, hazardous industrial materials, improvised explosives, and flammable materials." See http://www.znose.com/homeland.htm.

18. Such thermal-imaging devices are sometimes called FLIRs (Forward-Looking Infrareds). See generally Scott J. Smith, Thermal Surveillance and the Extraordinary Device Exception: Redefining the Scope of the *Katz* Analysis, 30 *Valparaiso University Law Review* 1071 (1996).

19. The Web site for one of these companies can be found at http://digdirt.com.

20. http://www.accurint.com (accessed May 15, 2006). Accurint has since changed its Web site content.

21. Id., section titled "How We Do It."

22. Robert Ellis Smith, Here's Why People Are Mad, 29 *Privacy Journal* 7, 7 (Jan. 2003) (citing Stephen Grimes, administrator of the Judicial Records Center in Rhode Island), available at http://www.privacyjournal.net/.

23. See Duane Stanford & Joey Ledford, Matrix Links Up Private Data, *Atlanta Journal-Constitution*, Oct. 3, 2003, at A1.

24. Chris Jay Hoofnagle, Big Brother's Little Helpers: How ChoicePoint and Other Commercial Data Brokers Collect and Package Your Data for Law Enforcement, 29 *North Carolina Journal of International & Commercial Regulation*, 595, 617–18 (2004) (describing the FBI's "secret, classified contract" with ChoicePoint).

25. Id. at 601–2. Note also that once a social security number and other bits of identifying information are obtained, other personal information might become much more easily accessible. See Lynn M. LoPucki, Human Identification Theory and the Identity Theft Problem, 80 *Texas Law Review* 89, 108–14 (2001) (pointing out that schools, financial institutions, and other entities make personal information accessible by anyone with the right social security number, address, and mother's maiden name).

26. Hoofnagle, Big Brother's Little Helpers, 4–6. In 2001, the Immigration and Naturalization Service conducted approximately 23,000 such searches a month. Id. at 11.

27. Janet Dean Gertz, The Purloined Personality: Consumer Profiling in Financial Services, 39 *San Diego Law Review* 943, 944–45, 951 (2002).

28. See also Gavin Skok, Establishing a Legitimate Expectation of Privacy in Clickstream Data, 6 *Michigan Journal of Telecommunications & Technology Law Review* 61, 68–69 (2000) (detailing the type of information government can obtain through clickstream data).

29. Interview with Peter P. Swire, C. William O'Neill Professor in Law and Judicial Administration, Michael E. Moritz College of Law, Ohio State University, Sept. 20, 2004.

30. See Cade Metz, Spyware: It's Lurking on Your Machine, *PC Magazine*, April 22, 2003, 85, 88.

31. Jeremy C. Smith, The USA Patriot Act: Violating Reasonable Expectations of Privacy Protected by the Fourth Amendment without Advancing National Security, 82 *North Carolina Law Review* 412, 448–49 (2003). In 2005, the FBI announced that it would no longer use DCS-1000 but would instead rely on unspecified commercial software to eavesdrop on computer traffic. FBI Ditches Carnivore Surveillance System, Jan. 18, 2005, available at http://www.foxnews.com/story/0,2933,144809,00.html.

32. Metz, Spyware, 85. Some snoopware, using keystroke-logging (or "keylogger") technology, can even tell the user the content of your computer screen. Id. DCS-1000 can also be programmed to access content as well as identifying information. Joseph F. Kampherstein, Internet Privacy Legislation and the Carnivore System, 19 *Temple Environmental Law & Technology Journal* 155, 167 (2001). Both functions are forms of communications surveillance that are beyond the scope of this book.

33. Anthony Paul Miller, Teleinformatics, Transborder Data Flows and the Emerging Struggle for Information: An Introduction to the Arrival of the New Information Age, 20 *Columbia Journal of Law & Social Problems* 89, 111 (1986).

34. This scenario is borrowed from Task Force on National Security in an Information Age, *Creating a Trusted Network for Homeland Security*, app. D (vignette 4) (2003) (commonly known as the "Markle Report," after the foundation that funded the task force).

35. For a general description of data mining and its prevalence, see Andrew J. McClurg, A Thousand Words Are Worth a Picture: A Private Tort Response to Consumer Data Profiling, 98 *Northwestern University Law Review* 63, 71–88 (2003).

36. Id. at 64.

37. 389 U.S. 347 (1967).

38. Silverman v. United States, 365 U.S. 505, 510 (1961) (noting that the crux of the Court's search cases up to that time was whether the police investigation was "accomplished by means of an unauthorized physical encroachment within a constitutionally protected area").

39. 389 U.S. at 351.

40. Id. at 352.

41. Id. at 361.

42. Id.

43. Id. at 351.

44. 388 U.S. 41 (1967).

45. Id. at 52 ("Statements in [Olmstead v. United States, 277 U.S. 438 (1928)] that a conversation passing over a telephone wire cannot be said to come within the Fourth Amendment's enumeration of 'persons, houses, papers, and effects' have been negated by our subsequent cases as hereinafter noted.").

46. 18 U.S.C. § 2518(c).

47. 392 U.S. 364 (1968).

48. Id. at 369.

49. 394 U.S. 165, 1799 n.11 (1969).

50. California v. Greenwood, 486 U.S. 35 (1988).

51. Illinois v. Andreas, 463 U.S. 765 (1983).

52. Oliver v. United States, 466 U.S. 170 (1984).

53. 533 U.S. 27 (2001).

54. United States v. Knotts, 460 U.S. 276 (1983).

55. California v. Ciraolo, 476 U.S. 207 (1986); Florida v. Riley, 488 U.S. 445 (1989).

56. Dow Chemical v. United States, 476 U.S. 227 (1986).

57. United States v. Place, 462 U.S. 696 (1983).

58. Texas v. Brown, 460 U.S. 730 (1983); United States v. Dunn, 480 U.S. 294 (1987).

59. United States v. Miller, 425 U.S. 435 (1976).

60. 442 U.S. 735 (1979).

Chapter Two

1. 392 U.S. 1 (1968).

2. Id. at 21 (quoting Camara v. Municipal Court, 387 U.S. 523, 536–37 (1967), parentheticals added by *Terry* Court).

3. The phrase "reasonable suspicion" was never actually used in the opinion. But for all practical purposes the sentence in the text encapsulates the standard wisdom regarding *Terry*. See Charles H. Whitebread & Christopher Slobogin, *Criminal Procedure: An Analysis of Cases and Concepts* ch. 11 (4th ed. 2000).

4. See Akhil Amar, Fourth Amendment First Principles, 107 *Harvard Law Review* 757, 759 (1994).

5. See William J. Mertens, The Fourth Amendment and the Control of Police Discretion, 17 *University of Michigan Journal of Law Reform* 551, 614–25 (1984) (criticizing *Terry* for severing the probable cause requirement from the reasonableness inquiry); Carol S. Steiker, Second Thoughts about First Principles, 107

Harvard Law Review 820, 855 (1994) (stating that "the dangers that [the balancing/reasonableness] approach poses to the security that the Fourth Amendment is meant to ensure cannot be overstated and should not be overlooked"); Scott E. Sundby, A Return to Fourth Amendment Basics: Undoing the Mischief of *Camara* and *Terry*, 72 *Minnesota Law Review* 383, 401–4, 418–20 (1988) (criticizing the "balancing" approach).

6. See 392 U.S. at 27.

7. The *Terry* Court stated that a frisk "must be limited to that which is necessary for the discovery of weapons which might be used to harm the officer or others nearby, and may realistically be characterized as something less than a 'full' search, even though it remains a serious intrusion. . . ." Id. at 26.

8. See, e.g., Burdeau v. McDowell, 256 U.S. 465, 475 (1921) (asserting that the Fourth Amendment is meant "to secure the citizen in the right of unmolested occupation of his dwelling and the possession of his property"); Henry v. United States, 361 U.S. 98, 103 (1959) (stating that the Fourth Amendment is implicated when officers "restrict[ ] liberty of movement").

9. See Telford Taylor, *Two Studies of Constitutional Interpretation* 24–41 (1969).

10. *Merriam-Webster's Eleventh New Collegiate Dictionary* 1120 (2003).

11. Id. at 1125.

12. See generally Daniel Solove, Conceptualizing Privacy, 90 *California Law Review* 1087 (2002).

13. 389 U.S. at 350–51.

14. Id. See also id. at 353 ("the reach of [the Fourth] Amendment cannot turn upon the presence or absence of a physical intrusion into any given enclosure").

15. Scott E. Sundby, "Everyman' "s Fourth Amendment: Privacy or Mutual Trust between Government and Citizen? 94 *Columbia Law Review* 1751, 1758–63 (1994).

16. Id. at 1765.

17. Id. at 1765–71.

18. See id. at 1777 ("I would characterize the jeopardized constitutional value underlying the Fourth Amendment as that of 'trust' between the government and the citizenry.").

19. William Stuntz, Privacy's Problem and the Law of Criminal Procedure, 93 *Michigan Law Review* 1016, 1033 (1995).

20. See id. at 1068, 1077 (calling signs that "police coercion is displacing privacy as a focus of attention in the law of criminal investigation . . . a good thing" while branding as "backward" the fact that "we have a large and detailed body of law to tell police when they may open paper bags or the trunks of cars" and very little law on "the level of force that may be used in making an arrest or conducting a search").

21. Stuntz makes much of the fact that business and other types of records are fairly private yet can be obtained through a subpoena issued on a mere showing of

relevance. But as chapter 6 develops in more detail, most business records do not contain private information, only corporate data.

22. 392 U.S. at 29–30.

23. Id. at 23.

24. United States v. Robinson, 414 U.S. 218 (1973).

25. New York v. Belton, 453 U.S. 454 (1981).

26. See Maryland v. Buie, 494 U.S. 325, 334 (1990).

27. See Maryland v. Wilson, 519 U.S. 408 (1997).

28. See generally Christopher Slobogin, A Jurisprudence of Dangerousness, 98 *Northwestern University Law Review* 1, 53–58 (2003).

29. See 392 U.S. at 38 (Douglas, J., dissenting) ("The infringement on personal liberty of any 'seizure' of a person can only be 'reasonable' under the Fourth Amendment if we require the police to possess 'probable cause' before they seize him.").

30. See Morgan Cloud, The Fourth Amendment during the *Lochner* Era: Privacy, Property, and Liberty in Constitutional Theory, 48 *Stanford Law Review* 555, 623–24 (1996) (concluding that "the core rule requires a warrant for every search or seizure" except in circumstances in which "law enforcers cannot obtain warrants before they must act"); Gerald S. Reamey, When "Special Needs" Meet Probable Cause: Denying the Devil Benefit of Law, 19 *Hastings Constitutional Law Quarterly* 295, 340 (1992) ("If the constitutional scheme requires probable cause and a warrant for searches designed to produce criminal evidence, it is hard to imagine what further societal need would be so significant that its presence should reduce the standard of suspicion and judicial review.").

31. The majority opinion in *Terry* stated that "there is some suggestion in the use of such terms as 'stop' and 'frisk' that such police conduct is outside the purview of the Fourth Amendment because neither action rises to the level of a 'search' or 'seizure' within the meaning of the Constitution." See 392 U.S. at 16. In support, the Court cited, among other material, the Ohio Court of Appeals decision in *Terry*, which the Ohio Supreme Court affirmed on the ground that no substantial constitutional question was involved. See State v. Terry, 214 N.E.2d 114, 120 (Ohio Ct. App. 1966), aff'd, Terry v. Ohio, 392 U.S. 1 (1968).

32. See 392 U.S. at 15 ("[A] rigid and unthinking application of the exclusionary rule, in futile protest against practices which it can never be used effectively to control, may exact a high toll in human injury and frustration of efforts to prevent crime.").

33. See Amar, Fourth Amendment First Principles, 782–85.

34. See generally Alice Ristroph, Proportionality as Principle of Limited Government, 55 *Duke Law Journal* 263, 263 (2005) ("Principles of proportionality put the limits into any theory of limited government.").

35. See Addington v. Texas, 441 U.S. 418, 428–29 (1979) (justifying the clear and convincing standard on three grounds: (1) the nonpunitive nature of civil commit-

ment; (2) the fact that "it cannot be said . . . that it is much better for a mentally ill person to 'go free' than for a mentally normal person to be committed," and (3) the difficulty of proving dangerousness).

36. See generally John E. Nowak & Ronald D. Rotunda, *Constitutional Law* 601 (5th ed. 1995).

37. See Mathews v. Eldridge, 424 U.S. 319, 340–41 (1976) (finding there is no need for the evidentiary hearing required by Goldberg v. Kelly, 397 U.S. 254 (1970), when the state terminates disability benefits rather than welfare benefits, since the former are not based on need and an erroneous determination will not work as much hardship).

38. See Dan B. Dobbs, *The Law of Torts* 1069 (2000). I suppose the best counterexample is that we apply the same reasonable doubt standard of proof at any criminal trial, whether it is adjudicating capital murder charges or a misdemeanor. See *In re* Winship, 397 U.S. 358 (1970) (applying the reasonable doubt standard to a juvenile delinquency proceeding). In practice, however, the procedures in the former instance (ranging from jury and counsel rights to the nature of the sentencing proceeding) are much more protective. See Argersinger v. Hamlin, 407 U.S. 25 (1972) (holding that there is no right to counsel if defendant does not face jail term); Baldwin v. New York, 399 U.S. 66 (1970) (declaring there is no right to jury trial for petty crimes).

39. See Winston v. Lee, 470 U.S. 753, 766 (1985) (requiring that before conducting surgery on a defendant for the purpose of obtaining evidence, the state must show that the procedure does not unduly threaten the defendant's health or safety, or his or her dignitary interest, and that it is necessary to effect the government's interest); Berger v. New York, 388 U.S. 41, 59–60 (1967) (requiring for electronic surveillance a warrant plus a showing of "exigent circumstances," by which the Court appeared to mean a particular need for the surveillance).

40. See Florida v. Bostick, 501 U.S. 429, 437 (1991) (remanding to Florida Supreme Court for ultimate disposition on seizure issue); California v. Hodari D., 499 U.S. 621, 629 (1991) (fleeing youths); Immigration Serv. v. Delgado, 466 U.S. 621, 629 (1991) (questioning at the workplace); United States v. Mendenhall, 446 U.S. 544, 555 (1980) (plurality opinion holding no seizure on these facts).

41. See Berkemer v. McCarty, 468 U.S. 420, 439 (1984) (stating that a person subject to a *Terry* stop "is not obliged to respond" to questions).

42. See *Bostick,* 501 U.S. at 437.

43. See Tracey Maclin, The Decline of the Right of Locomotion: The Fourth Amendment on the Streets, 75 *Cornell Law Review* 1258, 1306 (1990) (stating that "very few persons will have the moxie to assert their Fourth Amendment rights in the face of police authority").

44. The Court came closest to saying as much in United States v. Dionisio, 410 U.S. 1, 9–13 (1973), in which it held that grand jury subpoenas are not seizures because the "minimal intrusion" associated with such a subpoena is justified by the investigative tradition of the grand jury.

45. 466 U.S. 170, 173 (1984).

46. *Ciraolo*, 476 U.S. 207, 209 (1986) (stating that police had an anonymous tip); *Greenwood*, 486 U.S. 35, 37 (1988) (noting that police "received information").

47. 499 U.S. 621, 629 (1991).

48. See Daniel B. Yeager, Search, Seizure and the Positive Law: Expectations of Privacy outside the Fourth Amendment, 84 *Journal of Criminal Law & Criminology* 249 (1993).

49. See Christopher Slobogin & Joseph E. Schumacher, Reasonable Expectations of Privacy and Autonomy in Fourth Amendment Cases: An Empirical Look at "Understandings Recognized and Permitted by Society," 42 *Duke Law Journal* 727 (1993).

50. See Michigan Dep't of State Police v. Sitz, 496 U.S. 444, 451 (1990); United States v. Martinez-Fuerte, 428 U.S. 543, 557–60 (1976).

51. See United States v. Chadwick, 433 U.S. 1, 12–13 (1977) (listing reasons why cars are associated with a "diminished expectation of privacy" vis-à-vis houses and luggage).

52. See *Terry*, 392 U.S. at 27.

53. See Vernonia Sch. Dist. 47J v. Acton, 515 U.S. 646, 658 (1995) (concluding that collecting urine samples from fully clothed students while they are monitored from behind involves "negligible" privacy intrusion); National Treasury Employees Union v. Von Raab, 489 U.S. 656, 671 (1989) (asserting that "the 'operational realities of the workplace' may render entirely reasonable certain work-related intrusions by supervisors and co-workers that might be viewed as unreasonable in other contexts").

54. See O'Connor v. Ortega, 480 U.S. 709, 717 (1987) ("Public employees' expectations of privacy in their offices, desks, and file cabinets . . . may be reduced by virtue of actual office practices and procedures, or by legitimate regulation."). Although in New Jersey v. T.L.O., 469 U.S. 325, 337–38 (1985), the Court insisted that a search of a child's purse, "no less than a similar search carried out on an adult, is undoubtedly a severe violation of subjective expectations of privacy," it noted that privacy expectations might change if the search focused on a locker, desk, or other school property. Id. at 337 n.5. Further, its subsequent decision in *Vernonia* suggests that even its stance with respect to purses might have shifted somewhat. 515 U.S. at 658.

55. See United States v. Biswell, 406 U.S. 311, 316 (1972) (declaring that "when a dealer chooses to engage in this pervasively regulated business [sale of guns] and to accept a federal license, he does so with the knowledge that his business records, firearms, and ammunition will be subject to effective inspection"); Colonnade Catering Corp. v. United States, 397 U.S. 72, 77 (1970) (holding suspicionless, warrantless searches of liquor stores permissible).

56. Out of 50 scenarios assessed by our sample on a scale of 0 (for not intrusive) to 100 (for very intrusive), a pat down was ranked (hereafter designated as "R") nineteenth and had a mean score (hereafter designated as "M") of 54.76, while the

use of an undercover agent posing as a chauffeur (R = 31; M = 67.56) or secretary (R = 34; M = 69.98) was viewed as more intrusive. See Slobogin & Schumacher, Reasonable Expectations of Privacy and Autonomy, 738–39 tbl. 1.

57. Flying four hundred yards above the backyard in a helicopter was ranked tenth (M = 40.32) and going through garbage was ranked thirteenth (M = 44.95), compared to a pat down (R = 19; M = 54.76). See id.

58. Using a magnetometer at an airport was ranked second (M = 13.47) and inspecting the exterior of a car was ranked fourth (M = 19.46). See id.

59. 46 U.S. 325 (1985).

60. 536 U.S. 822 (2002).

61. 489 U.S. 656 (1989).

62. For instance, in *Vernonia,* 515 U.S. at 665, the Court justified random drug testing of student athletes in part because the testing "was undertaken in furtherance of the government's responsibilities, under a public school system, as guardian and tutor of children entrusted to its care." In *T.L.O.,* 469 U.S. at 337 n.5, the Court deferred deciding whether the reduced protection it endorsed for schoolchildren would apply if the search had been carried out by police looking for evidence of crime rather than schoolteachers investigating disciplinary infractions. Cf. *Camara,* 387 U.S. at 537 (discussing "public acceptance" of residential health and safety inspections).

63. See Slobogin & Schumacher, Reasonable Expectations of Privacy and Autonomy, 768–69 (discussing empirical support for an "implied consent" theory when the government's object is to prevent imminent harm (as in airport frisks) or to facilitate and aid (as in fire, safety, and health inspections)).

64. Id. at 737–38 tbl. 1.

65. Compare the following findings to a pat down (R = 19; M = 54.76): using a secretary as an undercover agent (R = 34; M = 68.98), accompanying subject of drug test to a urinal at work and listening for sounds of urination (R = 39; M = 72.49), and searching a high school student's purse (R = 41; M = 75.14). See id. at 738–39 tbl. 1.

66. See Amar, Fourth Amendment First Principles, 804–11.

67. Tracey Maclin, "Black and Blue Encounters"—Some Preliminary Thoughts about Fourth Amendment Seizures: Should Race Matter? 26 *Valparaiso University Law Review* 243 (1991).

68. See id. at 250–62.

69. See Christopher Slobogin, The World without a Fourth Amendment, 39 *UCLA Law Review* 1, 85–86 (1991). See also Akhil Reed Amar, *Terry* and Fourth Amendment First Principles, 72 *St. John's Law Review* 1097 (1998) ("Attention to issues of race and sex and possible discrimination yields a surprising thought: sometimes equality values may counsel a broader search or seizure, and perhaps this broader search—though more threatening to privacy values—may be more constitutionally reasonable because less susceptible to discrimination and discretion.").

70. Slobogin & Schumacher, Reasonable Expectations of Privacy and Autonomy, 759–60 ("[T]his study provides clear support for the proposition that searches and seizures tend to be viewed as more intrusive when . . . their objective is not clear rather than specified.").

71. See, e.g., Rhode Island v. Innis, 441 U.S. 261 (1980) ("since the police surely cannot be held accountable for the unforeseeable results of their words or actions, the definition of interrogation can extend only to words or actions on the part of police officers that they should have known were reasonably likely to elicit an incriminating response.").

72. See Maclin, "Black and Blue Encounters," 267–78.

73. See id. at 257; see also id. at 251–52 (describing six cases, none of which involved reasonable suspicion).

74. Id. at 259.

75. See 392 U.S. at 14–15 ("The wholesale harassment by certain elements of the police community, of which minority groups, particularly Negroes, frequently complain, will not be stopped by the exclusion of any evidence from any criminal trial.").

76. See Christopher Slobogin, *Regulation of Police Investigation* 552–65 (3d ed. 2003) (detailing problems with these alternative sanctions).

77. See Randall Kennedy, The State, Criminal Law, and Racial Discrimination: A Comment, 107 *Harvard Law Review* 1255, 1259 (1994) ("Although the administration of criminal justice has, at times, been used as an instrument of racial oppression, the principal problem facing African-Americans in the context of criminal justice today is not over-enforcement but under-enforcement of the laws.").

78. The special needs rubric first surfaced in Justice Blackmun's concurring opinion in *T.L.O.*, 469 U.S. at 351 (Blackmun, J., concurring) (permitting searches of students' possessions in public schools on reasonable suspicion that a disciplinary infraction has occurred). But it has since become the label applied to a host of situations in which "ordinary law enforcement" is not involved. See, e.g., *O'Connor,* 480 U.S. at 724 (reasonable suspicion sufficient to authorize investigation of workplace infractions); Skinner v. Railway Labor Executives' Ass'n, 489 U.S. 602, 620 (1989) (permitting suspicionless drug testing); Griffin v. Wisconsin, 483 U.S. 868, 873–74 (1987) (permitting searches of probationer's possessions on relevance grounds).

79. See Winston v. Lee, 470 U.S. 753 (1985) (requiring probable cause for surgery, plus a showing that the procedure does not seriously threaten the individual's safety and is necessary to obtain evidence crucial to the state's case).

80. See generally Wayne R. LaFave, Jerold H. Israel & Nancy J. King, *Criminal Procedure* 144–45 (4th ed. 2004); C. M. A. McCauliff, Burdens of Proof: Degrees of Belief, Quanta of Evidence, or Constitutional Guarantees? 35 *Vanderbilt Law Review* 1293, 1325 (1982) (summarizing a survey of federal judges).

81. See McCauliff, Burdens of Proof, 1327–28 (summarizing a survey of federal judges).

82. This is a combination of the "brief stop" standard adopted by the New York

courts in cases such as People v. de Bour, 352 N.E.2d 562, 571–72 (N.Y. 1976) (requiring "some objective credible reason" for the "minimal intrusion of approaching [an individual] to request information"), and the standard adopted by the ABA to govern technologically assisted physical surveillance of public places. See American Bar Association, Standards for Criminal Justice, *Electronic Surveillance, Section B: Technologically-Assisted Physical Surveillance,* 2–9.2(d) cmt. (1999).

83. Chandler v. Miller, 520 U.S. 305, 313 (1997) ("To be reasonable under the Fourth Amendment, a search ordinarily must be based on individualized suspicion of wrongdoing").

84. 392 U.S. at 27.

85. The U.S. Supreme Court has avoided deciding whether the use of profiles is permissible. See, e.g., United States v. Sokolow, 490 U.S. 1 (1989); Florida v. Rodriguez, 469 U.S. 1 (1984). Most lower courts hold that profiles either cannot establish reasonable suspicion or can do so only when supplemented with other facts. See Morgan Cloud, Search and Seizure by the Numbers: The Drug Courier Profile and Judicial Review of Investigative Formulas, 65 *Boston University Law Review* 843, 851 nn.37, 38 (1985).

86. See Cloud, Search and Seizure by the Numbers, 853; see also United States v. Berry, 670 F.2d 583, 600 (5th Cir. 1982) ("A profile does not focus on the particular circumstances at issue."). Critics have also pointed out that many profiles appear to be ad hoc in nature and not really worthy of the name. See *Sokolow,* 490 U.S. at 13–14 (Marshall, J., dissenting). This criticism of profiles is well taken, but it is aimed at the implementation of profiles rather than their underlying premise.

87. I take this example from John Monahan & Larry Walker, *Social Science in Law: Cases and Materials* 226–27 (1985).

88. However, search-by-profile might need to be circumscribed when the contemplated search is particularly invasive yet is meant to obtain only evidence of petty crime. Justice Jackson called it "a shocking proposition that private homes, even quarters in a tenement, may be indiscriminately invaded at the discretion of any suspicious police officer engaged in following up offenses that involve no violence or threats of it." McDonald v. United States, 355 U.S. 451, 458 (1948) (Jackson, J., concurring). See also Welsh v. Wisconsin, 466 U.S. 740 (1984) (prohibiting warrantless searches of homes for evidence of minor crime).

89. See *Martinez-Fuerte,* 428 U.S. 543 (illegal immigrant checkpoint); *Sitz,* 496 U.S. 444 (sobriety checkpoint); National Treasury Employees Union v. Von Raab, 489 U.S. 656 (1989) (drug testing of customs agents); *Vernonia,* 515 U.S. 646 (drug testing of students); *Camara,* 387 U.S. 523 (health and safety inspections of residences); New York v. Burger, 482 U.S. 691 (1987) (junkyards); *Biswell,* 406 U.S. 311 (gun stores).

90. See, e.g., *Sitz,* 496 U.S. at 453–54 (noting the magnitude of the drunken-driving problem and thus that "the choice among . . . reasonable alternatives remains with . . . governmental officials"); Donovan v. Dewey, 452 U.S. 594, 602

(1981) (stating that the pervasively regulated business exception to the warrant requirement is met if the government has a "substantial" interest in the business activity being regulated); *Martinez-Fuerte,* 428 U.S. at 557–58 (asserting that the illegal-immigration problem is "substantial" and that roadblocks will apprehend many such immigrants).

91. See Stuntz, Privacy's Problem, 1033 (describing the Court's special needs and regulatory cases as "reasonableness review of ordinary regulatory legislation").

92. See *Vernonia,* 515 U.S. at 661 (concluding that the government's interest in deterring drug use among physiologically vulnerable children is "compelling" and that drug infractions at the school in question had increased in recent years). But see *Chandler,* 520 U.S. at 321–22 (holding that the state interest of ensuring that illegal drug use neither impairs the ability of elected officials to carry out public functions nor undermines public confidence and trust in elected officials is insufficient to justify suspicionless testing).

93. See 489 U.S. at 607.

94. 489 U.S. 656, 681 (1989) (Scalia, J., dissenting).

95. Id. at 681–82.

96. Id. at 683–84.

97. Office of National Drug Control Policy, Drug Use Trends, Oct. 2002, available at http://www.whitehousedrugpolicy.gov/publications/factsht/druguse/index.html (table 1, showing that in 2001, 7.1 percent of a national sample had used illicit drugs in the past thirty days and 18.8 percent of those between 18 and 25 had done so).

98. If the government, despite diligent efforts, cannot generate the necessary data to permit informed speculation about the problem, it might be entitled to conduct the proposed search in an effort to get the relevant justifying information.

99. See Richard Worf, The Case for Rational Basis Review of General Suspicionless Searches and Seizures, 23 *Touro Law Review* 93 (2007).

100. *Chandler,* 520 U.S. 305 (striking down a statute that required drug testing of political candidates). Interestingly, under political process theory, this case should have come out the other way.

101. Worf, The Case for Rational Basis Review, 138–58.

102. 198 U.S. 45 (1905).

103. 304 U.S. 144 (1938).

104. See Amar, Fourth Amendment First Principles, 811.

105. See generally Louis Michael Seidman, The Problems with Privacy's Problem, 93 *Michigan Law Review* 1079 (1995).

106. Id. at 1096.

107. Id. at 1100.

108. See William J. Stuntz, Warrants and Fourth Amendment Remedies, 77 *Virginia Law Review* 881, 912–15 (1991).

109. Duizend, Sutton & Carter, *The Search Warrant Process,* 148–49.

110. 387 U.S. 523 (1967).

111. See id. at 536.

112. Amar argues that "the watering down of 'probable cause' necessarily authorizes ex parte warrants on loose terms that would have shocked the Founders . . . [In allowing such warrants,] history has been turned on its head." Amar, Fourth Amendment First Principles, 785. But see Joseph Grano, Probable Cause and Common Sense: A Reply to the Critics of *Illinois v. Gates,* 17 *University of Michigan Journal of Law Reform* 465, 478–95 (1984) (in England and in America until the 1940s, probable cause was not equated with a more-likely-than-not standard but rather with a much looser "suspicion" standard).

113. 470 U.S. 811, 817 (1985).

114. 468 U.S. 705, 718 n.5 (1984).

115. See, e.g., Fed. R. Crim. P. 41(c)(2).

116. Anthony G. Amsterdam, Perspectives on the Fourth Amendment, 58 *Minnesota Law Review* 349, 393 (1974). Elsewhere Professor Amsterdam has even choicer words for the proportionality approach. Id. at 415 (calling the approach "splendid in its flexibility, awful in its unintelligibility, unadministrability, unenforcibility and general ooziness").

117. Id.

118. Id.

119. See Minnesota v. Dickerson, 508 U.S. 366, 378 (1993) (holding that "squeezing, sliding and otherwise manipulating the contents of the defendant's pocket" went beyond the scope of a frisk); Arizona v. Hicks, 480 U.S. 321, 324–25 (1987) (holding that moving a stereo set to see serial numbers is a search requiring probable cause).

120. A number of other Supreme Court cases permit seizures based on something short of probable cause. See, e.g., Michigan v. Summers, 452 U.S. 692 (1981) (holding that an occupant of a house may be detained for the duration of the search of the house pursuant to a warrant); Pennsylvania v. Mimms, 434 U.S. 106 (1977) (per curiam) (holding that requesting the driver of a stopped car to exit does not require suspicion); *Martinez-Fuerte,* 428 U.S. 543 (holding that a checkpoint stop for illegal immigrants does not require probable cause or reasonable suspicion).

121. See 18 U.S.C. § 1518(4) (requiring a finding that "normal investigative procedures have been tried and failed or reasonably appear to be unlikely to succeed if tried or to be too dangerous" before electronic surveillance is permitted); Winston v. Lee, 470 U.S. 753 (1985) (requiring a finding that evidence is important to state's case before surgery to obtain it may proceed).

Chapter Three

1. 533 U.S. 27 (2001).

2. Wayne LaFave states that prior to *Kyllo*, the "overwhelming majority of appellate decisions" found that use of a thermal imager to detect items in a home

was not a search. 1 Wayne R. LaFave, *Search and Seizure: A Treatise on the Fourth Amendment* 495 (4th ed. 2004); see, e.g., United States v. Myers, 46 F.3d 668, 670 (7th Cir. 1995) (noting that a thermal imager "does not intrude in any way into the privacy and sanctity of a home" and detects only "waste products intentionally or inevitably exposed to the public"); United States v. Pinson, 24 F.3d 1056, 1059 (8th Cir. 1994) ("Detection of the heat waste was not an intrusion into the home; no intimate details of the home were observed, and there was no intrusion upon the privacy of the individuals within.").

3. 533 U.S. at 40 (emphasis added).

4. Id. at 47 (Stevens, J., dissenting).

5. Id. at 39 n.6.

6. Id. at 47 n.5; see also United States v. Ishmael, 48 F.3d 850, 856 n.6 (5th Cir. 1995) ("The [thermal imaging] technology is 'off the shelf,' having been in general use for fifteen years."). Such imagers, however, can be expensive: a cheap version, the "Thermal-Eye Imager," costs more than $8,000, and higher resolution devices can cost over $13,000. See http://www.nightvis.com/thermal/. High-end versions used in helicopters cost more than $100,000. Telephone interview with Azar Louh, salesperson, FLIR Systems, Jan. 8, 2002.

7. 533 U.S. at 39 n.6.

8. 476 U.S. 207 (1986).

9. Id. at 213–14 ("any member of the public flying in this airspace who glanced down could have seen everything that these officers observed").

10. 476 U.S. 227 (1986).

11. Id. at 238.

12. 468 U.S. 705 (1984).

13. 476 U.S. at 213–14 (citations omitted).

14. 488 U.S. 445 (1989).

15. 476 U.S. at 215.

16. 533 U.S. at 39 n.6.

17. 476 U.S. at 238.

18. 428 N.W.2d 272, 275 (S.D. 1988).

19. 909 P.2d 280, 286 (Wash. 1996).

20. See, e.g., United States v. Van Damme, 48 F.3d 461, 463 (9th Cir. 1995) ("A 35 mm camera with a 600 mm lens is a kind of vision enhancer commonly available to the public and used typically for telephoto landscape photography."); United States v. Allen, 675 F.2d 1373, 1380 (9th Cir. 1980) (use of a special lens is not a search because "such equipment is widely available commercially"); State v. Lange, 463 N.W.2d 390, 395 (Wis. Ct. App. 1990) ("We specifically limit our holding here to approval of the use of standard binoculars and cameras equipped with generally available standard and zoom lenses.").

21. Baldi v. Amadon, No. Civ. 02-313-M, 2004 WL 725618, at *3 (D.N.H. Apr. 5, 2004); People v. Katz, No. 224477, 2001 WL 1012114, at *2 n.4 (Mich. App. Sept. 4, 2001) (per curiam), appeal denied, 465 Mich. 961, 640 N.W.2d 877 (2002). Cameras

and dogs have also been found to fit the *Kyllo* exception for purposes of determining what is in a house. Dean v. Duckworth, 99 Fed. Appx. 760 (8th Cir. 2004) (camera); Fitzgerald v. State, 837 A.2d 989, 1036 (Md. App. 2003) (noting that *Kyllo* dealt with use of technology, not animals). Contra United States v. Jackson, 2004 WL 1784756 (S.D. Ind. 2004).

22. See, e.g., People v. Ferguson, 365 N.E.2d 77, 79 (Ill. App. Ct. 1977) (use of binoculars to look through the windows of a second-floor apartment from sixty feet away); People v. Hicks, 364 N.E.2d 440, 442 (Ill. App. Ct. 1977) (use of night binoculars to look in a hotel room window at 1:00 a.m.); State v. Littleton, 407 So. 2d 1208, 1210 (La. 1981) (use of binoculars to look into a hangar with a thirty- to forty-foot-wide opening); People v. Ward, 308 N.W.2d 664, 667 (Mich. Ct. App. 1981) (observation through a telephoto lens to look in a home); State v. Thompson, 241 N.W.2d 511, 512 (Neb. 1976) (use of binoculars to look into house windows); State v. Louis, 672 P.2d 708, 709 (Or. 1983) (use of a telephoto lens to observe a person repeatedly positioning self at window); Commonwealth v. Williams, 396 A.2d 1286, 1289–90 (Pa. Super. Ct. 1979) (use of binoculars and Star-Tron to look in a home); Commonwealth v. Hernley, 263 A.2d 904, 905 (Pa. Super. Ct. 1971) (use of binoculars to look into printing shop); State v. Manly, 530 P.2d 306, 307 (Wash. 1975) (use of binoculars to look into a home). The Supreme Court has made statements consistent with these holdings, albeit in cases involving targets outside the home. See Texas v. Brown, 460 U.S. 730, 740 (1983) (stating that "the use of artificial means to illuminate a darkened area simply does not constitute a search" in the context of a car search); On Lee v. United States, 343 U.S. 747, 754 (1952) (stating that "the use of bifocals, field glasses or the telescope to magnify the object of a witness' vision is not a forbidden search or seizure, even if they focus without his knowledge or consent upon what one supposes to be private indiscretions" in the context of shining a searchlight on a boat). But see United States v. Taborda, 635 F.2d 131, 139 (2d Cir. 1980) (use of binoculars to look in a home deemed a search); United States v. Kim, 415 F. Supp. 1252, 1257–58 (D. Haw. 1976) (same); People v. Arno, 153 Cal. Rptr. 624, 626 (Ct. App. 1979) (same).

23. See, e.g., People v. Oynes, 920 P.2d 880, 883 (Colo. Ct. App. 1996) ("Absent evidence in the record indicating that the deputy's binoculars were extraordinarily powerful, we conclude that the observation [of a house] was not a 'search' for constitutional purposes."); Bernstiel v. State, 416 So. 2d 827, 828 (Fla. Dist. Ct. App. 1982) (stating that the use of binoculars to look in a greenhouse is not a search because "the emphasis appears to be on the danger imposed by more sophisticated devices such as telescopes"); State v. Stachler, 570 P.2d 1323, 1328 (Haw. 1977) (stating that the use of binoculars to look in a backyard is not a search but "if the lower court had found . . . that highly sophisticated viewing devices had been employed, we might well decide differently").

24. In his survey of the case law, Professor LaFave lists "the level of sophistication of the equipment utilized by the police" as one of "two primary considerations"

relevant to "assessing in a particular case whether [an] expectation [of privacy in the home] was in fact justified." 1 LaFave, *Search and Seizure*, 473–74. The other consideration is "the extent to which the incriminating objects or actions were out of the line of normal sight from contiguous areas where passersby or others might be." Id.

25. 468 U.S. 705 (1984).

26. *Merriam-Webster's Collegiate Dictionary* 520 (11th ed. 2003).

27. Id.

28. Id. at 84.

29. The prices reported here came from a visit to http://www.walmart.com in May 2006.

30. 476 U.S. at 238.

31. The dissent asserted that according to the majority, "it is the FAA regulations rather than any empirical inquiry that is determinative," a characterization that seems accurate. 488 U.S. at 461 n.5 (Brennan, J., dissenting).

32. Id. at 457.

33. Id. at 455 (O'Connor, J., concurring).

34. Justice Brennan's dissent, joined by Justices Marshall and Stevens, stated that "the question before us must be not whether the police were where they had a right to be, but whether public observation of Riley's curtilage was so commonplace that Riley's expectation of privacy in his backyard could not be considered reasonable." Id. at 460, 465 (Brennan, J., dissenting). Justice Blackmun, who wrote a separate dissent, similarly stated that "answering [the search] question depends upon whether Riley has a 'reasonable expectation of privacy' that no such surveillance would occur, and does not depend upon the fact that the helicopter was flying at a lawful altitude under FAA regulations." Id. at 467, 468 (Blackmun, J., dissenting).

35. Christopher Slobogin, Technologically-Assisted Physical Surveillance: The American Bar Association's Tentative Draft Standards, 10 *Harvard Journal of Law & Technology* 383, 389–98 (1997).

36. *Ciraolo*, 476 U.S. at 213 (referring to the home and curtilage as the area "where privacy expectations are most heightened"); *Riley*, 488 U.S. at 452 (noting that "no intimate details connected with the use of the home or curtilage were observed"); *Dow Chemical*, 476 U.S. at 237 n.4 ("We find it important that this is not an area immediately adjacent to a private home, where privacy expectations are most heightened."). It is interesting to note, however, that none of these cases made a distinction between the home and the curtilage in terms of privacy protection.

37. 476 U.S. at 211 ("Yet a 10-foot fence might not shield these plants from the eyes of a citizen or a policeman perched on the top of a truck or a two-level bus.").

38. *Dow Chemical*, 476 U.S. at 237 n.4 ("Simply keeping track of the identification numbers of any planes flying overhead, with a later follow-up to see if photographs were taken, does not constitute a 'procedure designed to protect the facility from aerial photography.' ").

39. *Ciraolo*, 476 U.S. at 213 (noting that the observations by the police "took place . . . in a physically nonintrusive manner"); *Riley*, 488 U.S. at 452 ("Neither is there any intimation here that the helicopter interfered with respondent's normal use of the greenhouse or of other parts of the curtilage."); *Dow Chemical*, 476 U.S. at 237 ("Any actual physical entry by EPA into any enclosed area would raise significantly different questions").

40. *Riley*, 488 U.S. at 452 (noting that "no intimate details connected with the use of the home or curtilage were observed"); *Dow Chemical*, 476 U.S. at 238 (noting that "the photographs here are not so revealing of intimate details as to raise constitutional concerns").

41. 476 U.S. at 239 ("An electronic device to penetrate walls or windows so as to hear and record confidential discussions of chemical formulae or other trade secrets would raise very different and far more serious questions"). The Court also distinguished the photography in *Dow Chemical* from satellite photography. Id. at 238.

42. 488 U.S. at 452.

43. 533 U.S. at 33, 40.

44. Id. at 27, 34, 39.

45. Id. at 45 (Stevens, J., dissenting).

46. Id. at 44–46 (Stevens, J., dissenting) (noting that the imager did not "penetrate" the walls and that "what was involved in this case was nothing more than drawing inferences from off-the-wall surveillance, rather than any 'through-the-wall' surveillance").

47. Id. at 35.

48. Id. at 37, 44 (Stevens, J., dissenting).

49. Id. at 37.

50. Id. at 43 (Stevens, J., dissenting) (suggesting that a passerby could have noticed rainwater evaporating or snow melting at different rates from different parts of the house).

51. Id. at 35 n.2.

52. Id.

53. Id. at 40 (emphasis added).

54. Id. at 34 (quoting Silverman v. United States, 365 U.S. 505, 512 (1961)) (emphasis added).

55. A caveat to this conclusion is that *Kyllo* rejected the four factors discussed above only in connection with home searches that do not use generally available technology. Thus, when police looking into a home rely on technology in general public use, the Court might still call the action a Fourth Amendment search if what is viewed is "intimate," the technology replicates more than could be seen through unenhanced viewing, or one of the other factors is implicated.

56. Today, thermal imaging devices are used fairly routinely by a large number of groups, including firefighters, doctors, and those engaged in maritime navigation,

maintenance of electrical apparatus, product development, and industrial production quality assurance. See http://www.flir.com.

57. *Van Damme*, 48 F.3d at 463; United States v. Allen, 675 F.2d 1373, 1380 (9th Cir. 1980).

58. Keith Wilson, *Photography* 10 (1994).

59. See, e.g., Invention of the Flashlight, at http://inventors.about.com/library/inventors/blflashlight.htm (noting that the flashlight was invented in 1898 and was being heavily advertised the next year).

60. Sometimes enhancement devices might be used not because they avoid detection but because they cost less than naked eye observation (e.g., naked eye observation that would have required an elaborate deception, such as officers posing as telephone line repairpeople). If so, the Catch-22 is avoided, but the second problem with the naked eye exception, discussed further in the text, is not—how is a court to assess whether this more costly operation would have occurred and what it would have allowed the police to see? Enhancement devices might also be used to "confirm" naked eye observation. See, e.g., State v. Holbron, 648 P.2d 194, 197 (Haw. 1982) (finding no search where binoculars are used only to confirm unaided observations). In this type of case, however, the enhanced observation sees more detail than the naked eye; otherwise, "confirmation" wouldn't be necessary. See Robert C. Power, Technology and the Fourth Amendment: A Proposed Formulation for Visual Searches, 80 *Journal of Criminal Law & Criminology* 1, 49–50 (1989) (objecting that in cases like *Holbron* "objects that officials can see but not fully identify without enhancement are treated as if they were in full public view").

61. See 1 LaFave, *Search and Seizure,* 572 (observing that "the prevailing rule" is that using the senses to investigate the interior of a residence from a lawful vantage point is not a search).

62. Compare, e.g., State v. Taylor, 401 N.E.2d 459, 462 (Ohio Ct. App. 1978) (looking into an apartment from the "semi-public walkway" leading to the building is not a search), and Borum v. United States, 318 A.2d 590, 592 (D.C. 1974) (looking through a crack or hole in an apartment door is not a search) with State v. Carter, 569 N.W.2d 169, 178 (Minn. 1997) (looking into an apartment window from the common area just outside the apartment window where bushes had to be walked around is a search). Compare State v. Morrow, 291 N.W.2d 298, 299 (Wis. Ct. App. 1980) (looking under a door is a search), with Moody v. State, 295 So. 2d 272, 273–74 (Ala. Crim. App. 1974) (looking through partially open blinds is not a search), and State v. Jordan, 631 P.2d 989, 990, 992 (Wash. Ct. App. 1981) (looking through a space between drape and window frame is a search). Compare Commonwealth v. Hernley, 263 A.2d 904, 905–6 (Pa. Super. Ct. 1970) (peering into a window using a four-foot ladder is not a search), with State v. Kender, 588 P.2d 447, 449, 451 (Haw. 1978) (climbing three-quarters of the way up a fence and bracing oneself on a fellow officer's shoulder to see into a backyard is a search). The last two cases involved use of enhancement devices.

63. 385 U.S. 206 (1966).

64. 274 U.S. 559 (1927).

65. 385 U.S. at 211 ("When, as here, the home is converted into a commercial center to which outsiders are invited for purposes of transacting unlawful business, that business is entitled to no greater sanctity than if it were carried on in a store, a garage, a car, or on the street.").

66. 274 U.S. at 563.

67. See, e.g., Maryland v. Macon, 472 U.S. 463, 465 (1985) (information displayed in public store); Smith v. Maryland, 442 U.S. 735, 737 (1979) (to phone company); United States v. Miller, 425 U.S. 435, 442–43 (1976) (to bank); Hoffa v. United States, 385 U.S. 293, 296 (1966) (to friend); *On Lee*, 343 U.S. at 749 (information voluntarily revealed to undercover agent).

68. *Ciraolo*, *Dow Chemical*, and *Riley* all involved flyovers of the curtilage, as noted earlier. See also California v. Greenwood, 486 U.S. 35, 37 (1988) (garbage at curbside); United States v. Dunn, 480 U.S. 294, 304 (1987) (open fields); Oliver v. United States, 466 U.S. 170, 173 (1984) (open fields).

69. 442 U.S. 735 (1979).

70. Id. at 744.

71. 533 U.S. at 34.

72. Id.

73. Id.

74. 19 How. St. Tr. 1029, 1066, 95 Eng. Rep. 807 (K.B. 1765) (Note: early English law reporters sometimes offer different accounts of the same proceedings. The English Reports version is provided for easy retrieval of the case; however, the quotation is from Howell's State Trials version.).

75. The Court actually quoted Boyd v. United States, 116 U.S. 616, 628 (1886), which in turn quoted at length from *Entick*.

76. 335 U.S. 451 (1948).

77. Id. at 454.

78. 1 *Legal Papers of John Adams* 137 (L. Kinvin Wroth & Hiller B. Zobel eds., 1965) (quoting Adams's notes of his argument in the 1774 case *King v. Stewart*).

79. Thomas Y. Davies, Recovering the Original Fourth Amendment, 98 *Michigan Law Review* 547, 643 (1999).

80. Id. at 643 n.261 (quoting 4 William Blackstone, *Commentaries on the Laws of England* 226 (facsimile ed., University of Chicago Press 1979) (1769)); see also Curtis v. Hubbard, 1 Hill 336, 338 (N.Y. 1841) (holding that "lifting a latch is, in law, just as much a breaking, as the forcing of a door bolted with iron").

81. After describing prosecutions for eavesdropping, David Flaherty recounts two early cases alleging voyeurism:

> Peeping Toms were similarly held up to ignominy at law [in colonial times]. A New Haven man won a slander and defamation suit against a fellow citizen who had

> accused him of coming "in the night to peep in at his window." John Severns of Salisbury entered a complaint against two young men in 1680, "for hovering about his house, peeping in at the window."

David H. Flaherty, *Privacy in Colonial New England* 89 (1972).

82. See, e.g., State v. Williams, 2 Tenn. (2 Overt.) 108 (1808). Blackstone's description of the laws of England in the eighteenth century included within the "common nuisance" category "eavesdroppers, or such as listen under walls or windows or the eaves of a house, to harken after discourse, and thereupon to frame slanderous and mischievous tales." 4 *Blackstone's Commentaries on the Laws of England* 132 (Wayne Morrison ed., 2001).

83. Commonwealth v. Lovett, 6 Clark's Pa. L.J. Reps. 226, 226–27 (1831).

84. City of Grand Rapids v. Williams, 70 N.W. 547, 548 (Mich. 1897) (affirming a conviction for disorderly conduct for peering into a window near midnight); Moore v. N.Y. Elevated R.R., 29 N.E. 997, 997–98 (N.Y. 1892) (granting damages for an apartment dweller's loss of privacy due to exposure to an elevated train platform).

85. *Williams*, 70 N.W. at 548.

86. As of 2006, the following statutes were on the books (other states may have similar statutes): Ala. Code § 13A-11-32; Ariz. Rev. Stat. Ann. § 13-1504; Ark. Code Ann. § 5-71-213(a)(8); Cal. Penal Code § 647(k); Del. Code Ann. tit. 11, § 820; Fla. Stat. Ann. § 810.14; Ga. Code Ann. § 16-11-61; Haw. Rev. Stat. § 711-1111; Idaho Code Ann. § 18-7006; 720 Ill. Comp. Stat. Ann. 5/26-1(5); Ind. Code Ann. § 35-45-4-5; La. Rev. Stat. Ann. § 14:284; Minn. Stat. § 609.746; Miss. Code Ann. § 97-29-61; N.J. Stat. Ann. § 2C:18-3; N.C. Gen. Stat. § 14-202; Ohio Rev. Code Ann. § 2907.08; Okla. Stat. Ann. tit. 21, § 1171; R.I. Gen. Laws § 11-45-1(6); S.C. Code Ann. § 16-17-470; S.D. Codified Laws § 22-21-3; Tenn. Code Ann. § 39-13-607; Va. Code Ann. § 18.2-130. In addition, Massachusetts, Oregon, and the District of Columbia have affirmed convictions for voyeurism under disorderly conduct statutes. See Commonwealth v. Lepore, 666 N.E.2d 152, 156 (Mass. App. Ct. 1996) (construing the Massachusetts disorderly conduct statute to include voyeurism); Carey v. District of Columbia, 102 A.2d 314, 315 (D.C. Cir. 1954) (construing a disorderly conduct statute to permit conviction for voyeurism); DeLashmitt v. Journal Publ'g Co., 114 P.2d 1018, 1019 (Or. 1941) (describing imposition of a fine for "looking in the windows of another's home"). Since most states have disorderly conduct statutes, in theory peeping toms could be prosecuted in those states as well.

87. See, e.g., People v. Horton, 2005 WL 3445572 (Cal. Ct. App. Dec. 15, 2005); Glasper v. State, 914 So. 2d 708 (Miss. 2005); Howard v. State, 596 S.E.2d 627 (Ga. App. 2004); J.F.C. v. City of Daphne, 2001 WL 564263, at *3–4 (Ala. Crim. App. May 25, 2001); Copeland v. Commonwealth, 525 S.E.2d 9, 11 (Va. Ct. App. 2000).

88. See, e.g., Wolfson v. Lewis, 924 F. Supp. 1413, 1432 (E.D. Pa. 1996) (finding "a reasonable likelihood of success on the merits of [plaintiff's] claim for invasion of privacy based on intrusion upon seclusion" when a media crew used a shotgun

mike, binoculars, and zoom cameras to monitor activity inside a home); Gonzales v. Southwestern Bell Tel. Co., 555 S.W.2d 219, 221 (Tex. Civ. App. 1977) ("An intrusion upon a plaintiff's seclusion or solitude amounting to an invasion of privacy includes eavesdropping upon private conversations by wiretapping, microphones or spying into windows of a home."); *Prosser and Keeton on the Law of Torts* 855 (W. Page Keeton ed., 5th ed. 1984) (citing cases holding that the tort of intrusion "is to be applied to peering into the windows of a home"). The Restatement states that "one who intentionally intrudes, physically or otherwise, upon the solitude or seclusion of another or his private affairs or concerns, is subject to liability to the other for invasion of his privacy, if the intrusion would be highly offensive to a reasonable person." *Restatement (Second) of Torts* § 652B (1977).

89. Several also limit conviction to those who have a "lewd" intent or some other sexual motivation. See, e.g., Fla. Stat. Ann. § 810.14(1) (requiring "lewd, lascivious, or indecent intent"); Miss. Code Ann. § 97-29-61 ("lewd, licentious and indecent purpose"); Ohio Rev. Code Ann. § 2907.08 ("for the purpose of sexually arousing or gratifying the person's self"); R.I. Gen. Laws § 11-45-1(a)(6) ("lascivious purpose"); Tenn. Code Ann. § 39-13-607(a)(2) (similar language). Two also exclude from their purview officers involved in "lawful criminal investigation." Va. Code Ann. § 18.2-130; see also Minn. Stat. § 609.746(f).

90. La. Rev. Stat. Ann. 14:284 (emphasis added).

91. Id.; see also Souder v. Pendleton Detectives, Inc., 88 So. 2d 716, 718 (La. Ct. App. 1956).

92. Ark. Code Ann. § 5-71-213(8) ("on or about the premises of another"); Ga. Code Ann. § 16-11-61(a) ("on or about the premises of another"); Ind. Code Ann. § 35-45-4-5 (penalizing "a person who peeps into an occupied dwelling of another"); Okla. Stat. Ann. tit. 21, § 1171A ("Every person who hides, waits or otherwise loiters in the vicinity of any private dwelling house, apartment building or any other place of residence . . . with the unlawful and willful intent to watch, gaze, or look upon any person in a clandestine manner" is guilty of a misdemeanor); S.C. Code Ann. § 16-17-470 ("on or about the premises of another"); see also N.J. Stat. Ann. § 2C:18-3 (penalizing a person who, "knowing that he is not licensed or privileged to do so, . . . peers into a window or other opening of a dwelling"); N.C. Gen. Stat. § 14-202 ("Any person who shall peep secretly into any room occupied by a female person shall be guilty of a Class 1 misdemeanor.").

93. See, e.g., Carey v. District of Columbia, 102 A.2d 314, 315 (D.C. 1954) (affirming the voyeurism conviction of a defendant who stood on "the lawn outside the window" but emphasizing the act of looking, stating, "what action could be more disturbing, offensive, or insulting than to have a total stranger peeping into the window of one's lighted apartment, especially at 1:30 in the morning?"); People v. Miller, 415 N.E.2d 538 (Ill. App. Ct. 1980) (finding valid the arrest for disorderly conduct of an individual found in a walkway next to a women's dormitory at 9 p.m.); Commonwealth v. LePore, 666 N.E.2d 152, 155–56 (Mass. App. Ct. 1996) (affirming a conviction for disorderly conduct when defendant looked in a window from an

alleyway); Government v. Stagger, 13 V.I. 233 (1977) (conviction for "disturbing the peace" upheld where the defendant stood on the ledge of an adjacent building and looked into a lighted room).

94. See, e.g., *Daphne*, 2001 WL 564263, at *2 (stating that "even if an individual is generally licensed and privileged to use the common areas of the property on which the apartment building is situated, [he would violate the criminal surveillance provision by] using the common areas in a manner so as to invade the privacy of the residents of other apartments located on the property"); State v. Serrano, 702 P.2d 1343 (Ariz. Ct. App. 1985) (affirming a conviction for criminal trespass of the individual who looked into a lighted dorm window from bushes lining the side of the dorm).

95. See, e.g., Lorenzana v. Superior Court, 511 P.2d 33, 35 (Cal. 1973) (en banc) ("A sidewalk, pathway, common entrance or similar passageway offers an implied permission to the public to enter which necessarily negates any reasonable expectancy of privacy in regard to observations made there.").

96. See Minnesota v. Carter, 525 U.S. 83, 103–4 (1998) (Breyer, J., concurring) (arguing that there was no Fourth Amendment violation when "the apartment in question was a garden apartment that was partly below ground level; . . . families frequently used the grassy area just outside the apartment's window for walking or for playing; . . . members of the public also used the area just outside the apartment's window to store bicycles; . . . [and the officer] walked to a position about 1 to 1½ feet in front of the window [and] stood there for about 15 minutes looking down through a set of venetian blinds").

97. Compare Cal. Penal Code § 647(i) (prohibiting "peeking in the door or window of any inhabited building or structure while loitering, prowling, or wandering upon the private property of another") with § 647(k) (prohibiting "looking through a hole or opening into, or otherwise viewing, by means of any instrumentality, including, but not limited to, a periscope, telescope, binoculars, camera, motion picture camera, or camcorder, the interior of a bathroom, changing room . . . or the interior of any other area in which the occupant has a reasonable expectation of privacy, with the intent to invade the privacy of a person or persons inside"). See also Derek L. Kinnen, 8 Hilliard Men Charged in Case, *Florida Times-Union*, Sept. 15, 2001, at P-2 (stating that a man was charged with voyeurism after he was found walking on the beach near midnight using binoculars to look in people's windows).

98. Christopher Slobogin & Joseph Schumacher, Reasonable Expectations of Privacy and Autonomy in Fourth Amendment Cases: An Empirical Look at "Understandings Recognized and Permitted by Society," 42 *Duke Law Journal* 727, 737–39 tbl. 1 (1993).

99. See, e.g., Michigan Dep't of State Police v. Sitz, 496 U.S. 444, 450 (1990).

100. See, e.g., United States v. Ross, 456 U.S. 798 (1982) (requiring probable cause for a search of a car); Taylor v. United States, 286 U.S. 1 (1932) (requiring probable cause for the search of a garage).

101. 533 U.S. at 32 n.1 ("One might think that . . . examining the portion of a house that is in plain public view . . . is a 'search' . . . . When the Fourth Amendment was adopted, as now, to 'search' meant 'to look over or through for the purpose of finding something; to explore; to examine by inspection; as, to search the house for a book; to search the wood for a thief.' ") (quoting Noah Webster, *An American Dictionary of the English Language* 66 (1828) (reprint of facsimile ed., 6th ed. 1989)).

102. Laura Loh, Specialists in Surveillance Get Their Man, *Los Angeles Times*, Dec. 26, 2001, at B3.

103. 449 F.2d 1355 (D.C. Cir. 1971).

104. Id. at 1368 (Wright, J., dissenting) (quoting James v. United States, 418 F.2d 1150, 1151 n.1 (D.C. Cir. 1969)).

105. 468 U.S. 705 (1984).

106. See also United States v. Place, 462 U.S. 696, 723 (Blackmun, J., concurring in the judgment) ("[A] dog sniff may be a search, but a minimally intrusive one that could be justified in this situation under *Terry* upon mere reasonable suspicion.").

107. 449 F.2d at 1357–60 (discussing a "closer look at a challenging situation" and "plain view" as alternative justifications, with the former assuming a search occurred, albeit perhaps in the absence of probable cause).

108. See State v. Christensen, 953 P.2d 583, 588 (Idaho 1998) (holding that entry onto property marked with a No Trespassing sign was a search, but could be permissible without a warrant if justified by something more serious than inquiries about nearby residents); State v. Torres, 645 A.2d 529, 534–35 (Conn. 1994) (assuming a dog sniff of a car was a search, but lawful because it was on "reasonable and articulable suspicion"); State v. Cloutier, 544 A.2d 1277, 1280 (Me. 1988) (concluding that entry onto private property was permissible based on recent burglary reports in the area and the fact that the basement was the only illuminated room in the house, even though these facts did not constitute either probable cause or reasonable suspicion; to enter property "a police officer must be on some police business," which may be action based on a suspicion that turns out to be without substantial basis, provided the suspicion is held in good faith rather than as a pretext for an arbitrary search"); United States v. Bassford, 601 F. Supp. 1324, 1331 (D. Me. 1985) ("The brief surveillance involved in the present case . . . was undertaken in response to the receipt of specific information concerning the cultivation of marijuana on the Bassford property.").

109. It is worth noting that the *Kyllo* majority never firmly adopted the general public use doctrine. In a footnote, it stated that general public use "may" be a factor in the search analysis, and it intimated that it might "reexamine" this factor in the future. 533 U.S. at 39 n.6. The naked eye doctrine was also unnecessary to the Court's decision, as the thermal imager obviously detected more than the naked eye could see from a public vantage point.

110. Id. at 30 (noting that the police also relied on tips from informants and on utility bills).

111. Id. at 38.

112. See Steven Penney, Reasonable Expectations of Privacy and Novel Search Technologies: An Economic Approach (June 2006), available at http://ssrn.com/abstract=906874.

113. See, e.g., Terry v. Ohio, 392 U.S. 1 (1968) (requiring probable cause for search of a person that goes beyond a frisk); United States v. Chadwick, 433 U.S. 1 (1977) (requiring a warrant for search of a footlocker that is not in a car).

114. 462 U.S. 696, 707 (1983) ("The sniff discloses only the presence or absence of narcotics, a contraband item.").

115. 466 U.S. 109, 123 (1984).

116. See 18 U.S.C. §§ 2510–2520. This federal statute preempts state law on electronic surveillance. See 18 U.S.C. § 2516(2); cf. United States v. Tortorello, 480 F.2d 764 (2d Cir. 1973).

117. 18 U.S.C. § 2510(2).

118. 18 U.S.C. § 2510(4).

119. 18 U.S.C. § 2511(2). There are a few other exceptions to the prohibition, but they are not pertinent here. See generally 18 U.S.C. § 2511.

120. 18 U.S.C. § 2511(4), (5) (respectively criminal penalties and civil suits).

121. 18 U.S.C. § 2512(1).

122. See United States v. Biro, 143 F.3d 1421, 1427 (11th Cir. 1998) (holding that § 2512 encompasses "pens, wall plugs, and calculators containing concealed transmitters"); United States v. Pritchard, 745 F.2d 1112, 1123 (7th Cir. 1984) (finding that a "briefcase containing a tape recorder, an amplifier, a voice activation unit, a power source, and [various] patch cords" was "sufficient basis" for a conviction under § 2512); United States v. Wynn, 633 F. Supp. 595 (C.D. Ill. 1986) (holding that a drop-in telephone microphone was clearly covered by § 2512).

123. Note that several courts have, in effect, already extended Title III in this fashion to the regulation of video surveillance of homes and like places. See, e.g., United States v. Falls, 34 F.3d 674, 679–80 (8th Cir. 1994); United States v. Koyomejian, 970 F.2d 536, 538–39 (9th Cir. 1992); United States v. Torres, 751 F.2d 875, 884–85 (7th Cir. 1984).

124. See 18 U.S.C. § 2512(2) (permitting possession of surreptitious listening devices only by providers of communication services or "an officer, agent, or employee of, or a person under contract with, such a provider, in the normal course of the business of providing that wire or electronic communication service," and by government agents and those under contract with the government).

125. S. Rep. No. 99-541, at 12 (1986), *reprinted in* 1986 U.S.C.C.A.N. 3555, 3566; accord Dorsey v. State, 402 So. 2d 1178 (Fla. 1981); State v. Howard, 679 P.2d 197 (Kan. 1984) (accord).

126. Pub. L. No. 103-414, § 202, 108 Stat. 4279, 4281 (1994) (codified at 18 U.S.C. § 2510(a)).

127. Walker v. Darby, 911 F.2d 1573, 1579 (11th Cir. 1990).

128. See S. Rep. No. 99-541, at 23 (1986), *reprinted in* 1986 U.S.C.C.A.N. 3555,

3577 (explaining that after "discussions with the Department of Justice," it was decided not to require exclusion when the rules governing interception of electronic communications were violated).

129. One possible obstacle to such a statute is the Supreme Court's recent willingness to strike down laws that are not clearly based on congressional powers authorized by the Constitution. See, e.g., United States v. Lopez, 514 U.S. 549 (1995) (holding that the Gun-Free School Zones Act, which makes it a federal offense for any individual to knowingly possess a firearm in a place that the individual believes or has reasonable cause to believe is a school zone, exceeded Congress's Commerce Clause authority). While a statute regulating technology that is sold across state lines meets this test, a statute that regulates naked eye viewing may not.

Chapter Four

1. 460 U.S. 276 (1983).
2. Id. at 281.
3. Id. at 282.
4. Id. at 283.
5. The government had installed the beeper in a chloroform container, which an accomplice of Knotts purchased. The accomplice placed the container in his car, which police followed. The container was soon transferred to the car of another accomplice, which police also followed. But the driver used evasive maneuvers, and the police had to resort to the beeper signal to discover the whereabouts of the container, which was located in a cabin in which Knotts and others had constructed a drug laboratory. Id. at 278–79.
6. Id. at 284.
7. See Christopher S. Milligan, Facial Recognition Technology, Video Surveillance, and Privacy, 9 *Southern California Interdisciplinary Law Journal* 295, 303–8 (1999) (describing digital and biometric technology).
8. Spencer S. Hsu, D.C. Forms Network of Surveillance, *Washington Post*, Feb. 17, 2002, at C1.
9. Id.
10. Jess Bravin, Washington Police to Play "I Spy," *Wall St. Journal*, Feb. 13, 2002, at B1, B6 (quoting Stephen J. Gaffigan, former Justice Department Director of Community Policing and head of the Washington Metropolitan Police Department camera installation project, as stating, "The next logical extension is into communities to aid our crime-fighting efforts.").
11. Id. at B6.
12. Eric M. Weiss, D.C. Considering More Police Cameras, *Washington Post*, July 14, 2005, at B1 (mayor asking for more federal funds for and greater use of cameras).

13. Fran Spielman, Feds Give City $48 Million in Anti-terrorism Funds, *Chicago Sun-Times*, Dec. 4, 2004, at 10; Fran Spielman, City Surveillance Cameras Go Undercover, *Chicago Sun-Times*, Oct. 3, 2006, at 8.

14. Doug Donovan, 24-Hour Camera Surveillance in City Is Part of Bigger Plan, *Baltimore Sun*, June 10, 2004, at A1.

15. Marcus Nieto, Public Video Surveillance: Is It an Effective Crime Prevention Tool? CRB-97-005 (California Research Bureau, California State Library, June 1997), 14–18, available at http://www.library.ca.gov/CRB/97/05/.

16. Lane DeGregory, Click. BEEP! Face Captured, *St. Petersburg Times*, July 19, 2001, at 1D. See also Richard Willing, Airport Anti-terror Systems Flub Tests, *USA Today*, Sept. 2, 2003, at 3A (Boston's Logan Airport discontinued facial recognition technology). Researchers are not giving up on the technology, however. The head of biometric research in the United Kingdom concluded that "it seems unlikely that the accuracy of automated facial-recognition technology will ever match that of fingerprints," but that it could still have "a vital role to play within the investigative process." Steve Ranger, U.K. Cops Look in Face-Recognition Tech, Jan. 17, 2006, available at http://news.zdnet.com/2100-1009_22-6027631.html.

17. Matt Baron, Cameras to Keep Eye on Cicero, *Chicago Tribune*, Feb. 10, 2005; Richard Salit, Newport Nets Aid for Bridge Cameras, *Providence Journal*, Jan. 7, 2005, Mark F. Bonner, Parish Gets Money for Street Camera, *New Orleans Times-Picayune*, July 24, 2004, at 1.

18. International Association of Chiefs of Police, The Use of CCTV/Video Cameras in Law Enforcement, Executive Summary, Mar. 2001, 4, available at http://www.theiacp.org/documents/pdfs/Publications/UseofCCTV%2Epdf.

19. Id.

20. David A. Fahrenthold, Federal Grants Bring Surveillance Cameras to Small Towns, *Washington Post*, Jan. 19, 2006, at A01.

21. M. J. Zuckerman, Chances Are, Somebody's Watching You, *USA Today*, Nov. 30, 2000, at 1A (describing $40 million surveillance center, controlling 110 remote control cameras in the suburbs of Washington, that can "peer inside a vehicle" and "easily see into the homes and offices along the interstates").

22. In Anchorage, for instance, volunteer video patrols funded by the business community and state grants train cameras on residential and commercial sections of the city. In Hollywood, cameras are monitored by local residents and Los Angeles Guardian Angels. Nieto, Public Video Surveillance, 20–21.

23. Karen Hallberg, Nationwide Survey of Companies with Security Expenses, September 1996.

24. Nieto, Public Video Surveillance, 7–8. Lilian Edwards, Switching Off the Surveillance Society? Legal Regulation of CCTV in the United Kingdom, in *Reasonable Expectations of Privacy? Eleven Country Reports on Camera Surveillance and Workplace Privacy* 91 (Sjaak Nouwt, Berend R. de Vries & Corien Prins eds., 2005) (as of 2004, "over 4 million cameras were being used in the UK, 20 percent

of all the CCTV cameras in use in the world, and the average Briton was caught on camera 300 times a day.").

25. Simon G. Davies, Re-engineering the Right to Privacy: How Privacy Has Been Transformed from a Right to a Commodity, in *Technology and Privacy: The New Landscape* 150 (Phillip E. Agre & Marc Rotenberg eds., 1997) (estimating that 200,000 cameras cover public spaces and indicating that this figure would grow at 20 to 30 percent annually).

26. Id.

27. Clive Norris, From Personal to Digital: CCTV, the Panopticon and the Technological Mediation of Suspicion and Social Control, in *Surveillance and Social Sorting: Privacy Risk and Automated Discrimination* 11 (David Lyon ed., 2002).

28. Nieto, Public Video Surveillance, 8.

29. Id. at 9–10 (describing CCTV programs in Canada, France, Ireland, Spain, Monaco, Russia, Italy, China, Iran, and Iraq). See generally Nouwt, de Vries & Prins eds., *Reasonable Expectations of Privacy?*

30. Clive Norris & Gary Armstrong, *The Maximum Surveillance Society: The Rise of CCTV* 212–14 (1999) (describing "intelligent scene monitoring").

31. Id. at 214–16 (describing "automatic license plate identification"); Mary Jordan, Electronic Eye Grows Wider in Britain, *Washington Post*, Jan. 6, 2006, at A1 (Britain "will soon be able to automatically track the movements of millions of cars on most of its major roads").

32. Norris & Armstrong, *The Maximum Surveillance Society*, 216–19; Stewart Tendler & Lucy Bannerman, Aiming to Catch Criminal Red-Footed, *London Times*, July 10, 2006, at 11 (describing development of a system that can identify individuals through their gait).

33. Lee, Big Brother, 7 (reporting British Home Office figures showing a 63 percent decline in crime rates in areas where cameras have been installed); Nick Taylor, Closed Circuit Television: The British Experience, 1999 *Stanford Technology Law Review* ¶ 12 (reporting British police claims that car thefts in King's Lynn were reduced by 91 percent, and general crime in Bedford and Swansea was reduced by 55 percent and 51 percent, respectively); Emelyn Cruz, Video Cameras Shooting Down Some Crime Rates, *The Seattle Times*, July 28, 1996, at B-1 (in Tacoma after cameras were installed, crimes such as assaults, trespassing, prostitution, and vandalism dropped from 244 reported incidents in 1993 to 87 in 1994 and 125 in 1995).

34. The success of CCTV in stores, transportation centers, and the like is better documented. For instance, London's Gatwick Airport saw a 78 percent drop in crime in its parking lots after cameras were installed, and Chesterfield railway station saw a drop in vehicle crime of 96 percent. Stephen Wright, Police Release CCTV Images of BBC Presenter, *Daily Mail (London)*, May 3, 1999, 2. But even here the effectiveness of CCTV is not proven beyond doubt. See Emma Short & Jason Ditton, Does CCTV Affect Crime? *CCTV Today*, Mar. 1995, at 11 (the

results of independent and competently conducted evaluations of CCTV systems installed in parking lots, buses, subdivisions, football stadiums, and subway systems are "fairly contradictory regarding the effectiveness of CCTV as a crime prevention method," with some showing no effect, others showing high levels of displacement rather than overall reduction, and others showing clear reductions).

35. Ray Pawson & Nick Tilley, What Works in Evaluation Research? 34 *British Journal of Criminology* 291, 294 (1994); see also Taylor, Closed Circuit Television, ¶ 13 (stating that "the vast number of evaluation schemes that have been carried out to date have been undertaken by those with an interest in promoting the cameras and have been technically inadequate").

36. Clive Norris, Remarks at a Conference of Experts—Video Surveillance: A Crime Prevention Instrument in European Comparison 32 (Feb. 22–24, 2001) (manuscript available at Georg-August University, Göttingen, Germany).

37. Brandon C. Welsh & David P. Farrington, Crime Prevention Effects of Closed Circuit Television: A Systematic Review 41 (Aug. 2002) (Home Office Research Study 252). This study also noted that all five North American CCTV studies showed no evidence of a desirable effect on crime. Id. at 42.

38. Helene A. Wells, Troy Allen & Paul Wilson, *Crime and CCTV in Australia: Understanding the Relationship* 96 (Dec. 2006), available at http://epublications.bond.edu.au/hss_pubs/70.

39. See Jason Ditton, The Effect of Closed Circuit Television Cameras on Recorded Crime Rates and Public Concern about Crime in Glasgow, Scottish Centre for Criminology, 1999, available at http://www.scotcrim.u-net.com/researchc.htm.

40. Jason Ditton, Glasgow City's Cameras—Hype or Help? Scottish Centre for Criminology, available at http://www.scotcrim.u-net.com/news1.htm.

41. UPI, "Spy" Cameras vs. Villains in Britain (Mar. 8, 2002), available at http://www.upi.com/archive/view.php?archive=1&StoryID=08032002-020813-4448r. This article also notes that in London's Newham district, with three hundred cameras, street crime in 2001 increased by 20 percent over the previous year, and car thefts increased by 3.6 percent.

42. Bruce Andrews, Here's Looking at You, *Sydney Morning Herald*, Dec. 26, 2001, at 16, available at 2001 WL 31626512.

43. Quentin Burrows, Scowl Because You're on Candid Camera: Privacy and Video Surveillance, 31 *Valparaiso University Law Review* 1079, 1103 (1997).

44. Id. See also Maureen O'Donnell, Cameras around Every Corner, *Chicago Sun-Times,* Feb. 18, 1996, at 2, available at 1996 WL 6732224.

45. Surveillance Cameras in the District of Columbia, *Privacy vs. Security: Electronic Surveillance in the Nation's Capital: Hearing before the Subcomm. on the District of Columbia of the Comm. on Government Reform,* 107th Cong. 3 (2002) (statement of Johnny Barnes, Executive Director, ACLU of National Capital Area) (quoting Report of Joseph Samuels Jr., Chief of Police, Oakland Police Department,

to Oakland City Council), statement available at http://www.aclu.org/natsec/emerg powers/14361leg20020322.html.

46. Fahrenthold, Surveillance Cameras, A-1.

47. Stephen Janis, Blue Light Special: Life in a City under Surveillance, *Baltimore City Paper*, Aug. 17, 2005, available at http://www.citypaper.com/news/story.asp?id=10405.

48. Liz Kay, Camera Becomes New Weapon in War on Graffiti Vandalism: Officials Say the Motor Sensing Device Deters Taggers, but Critics Say It Just Pushes the Problem to New Location, *Los Angeles Times*, Dec. 24, 2001, at B4, available at 2001 WL 28939163.

49. See UPI, "Spy" Cameras.

50. Remarks of Thomas Coty (Manager of the National Institute of Justice Video Sensor and Processing Program), Meeting of the Security Industry Association and International Association of Chiefs of Police 39 (Apr. 17, 2002) (on file with author) [hereafter SIA and IACP Meeting] ("One of the problems we see in CCTV is that if it's being operator maintained or monitored, after about twenty minutes the eyes start to glaze and it's difficult to keep monitoring the monitor."). According to Norris and Armstrong, "It is not possible for one or even two operatives to continuously monitor the output of a twenty-camera system and, of course, as soon as they selectively focus on one incident, other screens are going unmonitored. This is exacerbated by the inherent boredom of watching dozens of screens and the inattentiveness that results. But even the most attentive of operators are swamped by the volume of information. For instance . . . a medium-sized 24-hour city centre system with twenty cameras generates a quite staggering 43 million 'pictures' per day." Norris & Armstrong, *The Maximum Surveillance Society*, 211.

51. Norris, From Personal to Digital, 19.

52. See Taylor, Closed Circuit Television, ¶ 32 (noting that soon after cameras were introduced in Bingley, Yorkshire, the number of officers based in town was reduced from twenty-four to three).

53. Norris & Armstrong, *The Maximum Surveillance Society*, 166 (concluding that the reason many suspects reported by a field agent to the camera operator were never located by the operator was that "location is often imprecise and descriptions are too vague to significantly differentiate a suspect from the crowd").

54. Id. at 188–96 (describing implications of fact that "the practice of street policing, which traditionally enjoyed low visibility from managerial scrutiny is now potentially subject to a far more intrusive supervisory gaze").

55. Tampa abruptly suspended its face recognition program after less than two months, apparently because the system failed to identify correctly a single face in its database of suspects and thus did not result in any arrests. The Failure of Facial Recognition Technology in Tampa, Florida (ACLU Special Report), Jan. 3, 2002, at 1. This report also describes several studies indicating that the technology to date has not been very effective. Id. at 3.

56. See generally Remarks of Stephen McMahon (Central District Commander for Baltimore City), SIA and IACP Meeting, 39 (noting that tapes are destroyed after ninety-six hours and that tapes of a few "non-crime-related" incidents were therefore lost).

57. Kay, Camera Becomes New Weapon, 4 (stating that Los Angeles "officials have not made any arrests based on photos taken by the camera at any location because pictures are seldom clear enough to identify the person responsible for the graffiti."); Zuckerman, Chances Are, Somebody's Watching You, 1A (noting that tape at ATM machine had been used so many times that image of person using a murder victim's card was too obscured for identification purposes).

58. Although the tape clearly showed officers beating King, it did not capture the high-speed chase and King's aggressive actions prior to the beating. See George P. Fletcher, *With Justice for Some* 38–41 (1996) (recounting the behavior of King and the officers prior to the videotaping); see also Rodney King Police Brutality Case and the 1991 Los Angeles Riots, at http://www.crimsonbird.com/history/rodneyking.htm (discussing police chase and subsequent beating).

59. Zoë Henderson, Vicki Bruce & A. Mike Burton, Matching the Faces of Robbers Captured on Video, 15 *Applied Cognitive Psychology* 445 (2001).

60. Norris, Remarks at a Conference of Experts—Video Surveillance, 17 (recounting one case that involved four thousand man-hours of video analysis) & 35 (noting that multiplexing cameras, a common efficiency procedure that takes only a few frames per second from each of many cameras, produces a loss of information that can make incident spotting difficult); cf. State v. Bonnell, 856 P.2d 1265, 1271 (Haw. 1993) (describing accumulation of fifty videotapes with twelve hundred hours of footage, containing just one minute of conduct that might have reflected gambling activity).

61. Jason Ditton & Emma Short, Evaluating Scotland's First Town Centre CCTV Scheme, in *Surveillance, Closed Circuit Television, and Social Control* (Clive Norris, Jade Moran & Gary Armstrong eds., 1998) (after a year of cameras in Glasgow's town center, "only between a quarter and a third of the ambulatory population were even aware of their existence"); John Naughton, Video Eyes Are Everywhere: "Big Brother" in Britain, *The Observer (U.K.)*, Nov. 13, 1994, at 13 (noting that most people in Britain are unaware of the extent to which camera surveillance occurs).

62. Chris Arnot, We've All Been Framed: It's Not Big Brother Who's Watching Over Us—It's All His Young Siblings, Monitoring Our Every Move in Public (and Many Private) Places, *The Guardian (UK)*, Dec. 13, 1999 (stating "when young men have had between five and 10 pints of lager and their honour is challenged, the presence of a camera makes no difference.").

63. See also Emma Short & Jason Ditton, Seen and Now Heard: Talking to the Targets of Open Street CCTV, 38 *British Journal of Criminology* 404, 418–20 (1998) (noting that eight of thirty criminals interviewed claimed CCTV cameras had no effect on their pattern of offending, with others saying they committed offenses

outside of camera range, and a "small minority" saying they gave up offending altogether).

64. See Nieto, Public Video Surveillance, 11 (discussing the results of a study undertaken by Rosemary Erickson of the Athena Research Corp.).

65. Stephen Graham, Towards the Fifth Utility? On the Extension and Normalisation of Public CCTV, in *Surveillance, Closed Circuit Television, and Social Control*, 89, 106 ("Anecdotal evidence has already emerged that the Newcastle West End scheme has significantly cut phone calls to the police, because local residents assume that the CCTV system will have spotted any event, anywhere, and at any time.").

66. For instance, Tacoma, Washington, one of the few American cities that has kept crime statistics and reported significant reductions as a result of CCTV, added street lights, removed graffiti, and cleaned up vacant lots at the same time it installed cameras. Burrows, Scowl Because You're on Candid Camera, 1124 n.361. In Washington, D.C., a crime cleanup on Rhode Island Avenue was "jump-started by the camera but it then was followed up with a lot of other action." John Thompson (Lieutenant Colonel in United States Army), SIA and IACP Meeting, 12; see also Ben Brown, CCTV in Town Centres: Three Case Studies, Police Research Group, Crime Detection and Prevention Series Paper 68, at 37 (1995) (stating that in Birmingham efforts were made at "pedestrianisation" of key areas of the city center at the same time cameras were installed), available at http://www.popcenter.org/Responses/Supplemental_Material/video_surveillance/Brown_1995_Full.pdf); Norris, Video Surveillance, 16 ("the rapid growth of the number of CCTV systems [in the United Kingdom] (between 1993 and 1997) occurred at precisely the same time as the only sustained fall in recorded crime since the 1950s"). Norris's paper recounts a number of other reasons reported crime reductions may not be accurate or not attributable to CCTV.

67. See David Skinns, Crime Reduction, Diffusion and Displacement: Evaluating the Effectiveness of CCTV, in *Surveillance, Closed Circuit Television, and Social Control*, 185 (noting that although the town center experienced a 16 percent reduction in crime after camera installation, crime in the surrounding townships jumped by 31 percent, so that overall reduction was only 6 percent); Brown, CCTV in Town Centres, 35 ("Since the installation of cameras, the incidence of [street robbery, theft from the person, and theft from a motor vehicle] in areas surrounding zone A has increased sharply, and by the end of the study period, the number of offences per month is over three times as high as when the cameras were installed."); Chris Sarno, The Impact of Closed Circuit Television on Crime in Sutton Town Centre, in *Towards a Safer Sutton? CCTV One Year On* (Marjorie Bulos & Doug Grant eds., 1996) (reporting that after camera installation street thefts declined by 7 percent, but thefts inside commercial premises increased by 30 percent).

68. Steve Stecklow, Jason Singer & Aaron O. Patrick, Watch on the Thames, *Wall St. Journal*, July 8, 2005, at B1.

69. International Association of Chiefs of Police, The Use of CCTV/Video Cameras in Law Enforcement, 5 (96 percent of the U.S. agencies surveyed by the IACP "do not incorporate measurement systems of any kind" to determine the effect of CCTV on crime rates).

70. Emma Short & Jason Ditton, Does Closed Circuit Television Prevent Crime? An Evaluation of the Use of CCTV Surveillance Cameras in Airdrie Town Center, The Scottish Office Central Research Unit, Crime and Criminal Justice Research Findings No. 8 (1995), available at http://www.scotland.gov.uk/cru/resfinds/crf08-00.htm.

71. See Brown, CCTV in Town Centres, 17. Brown also notes, however, that the decline in vehicle thefts in the CCTV area "appears to fade after 8 months and the number of thefts of vehicles rises sharply." Id. at 20.

72. Rachel Armitage, Graham Smyth & Ken Pease, Burnley CCTV Evaluation, in *Surveillance of Public Space: CCTV, Street Lighting and Crime Prevention* (Kate Painter & Nick Tilley eds., 1999).

73. Arnot, We've All Been Framed (noting that law enforcement claimed a 74 percent crime drop in Airdrie).

74. See Brandon C. Welsh & David P. Farrington, CCTV and Street Lighting: Comparative Effects of Crime, in *Reducing Crime: The Effectiveness of Criminal Justice Interventions* 97, 104 (Amanda E. Perry, Cynthia McDougall & David P. Farrington eds., 2006) (tables indicating an average 13 percent decrease in crime in city centers across the nine studies with the most positive results, although only a trivial amount of this reduction was in violent crime).

75. G. Wade, Funding CCTV: The Story So Far, *CCTV Today,* Mar. 1998, at 28 (stating that several local townships are "dealing with operating budgets in excess of £500,000 per year").

76. Remarks of Joseph Dunne, SIA and IACP Meeting, 22.

77. Welsh and Farrington note that only three of the thirty-two studies concerning the impact of CCTV and street lighting that they examined carried out a cost-benefit analysis. They state that in each of these three studies "benefits from reduced crime substantially outweighed programme costs" but do not specify which, if any, of these studies evaluated CCTV as opposed to street lighting. Welsh & Farrington, CCTV and Street Lighting, 109.

78. Norris, Video Surveillance, 23 (describing a study by A. Beck & A. Willis, Crime and Security: Managing the Risk to Safe Shopping (1995)).

79. Norris, Video Surveillance, 23.

80. See Davies, Re-engineering the Right to Privacy, 150 (quoting a Home Office spokesman who, in commenting on the potential of CCTV, stated that "if this all saves just one life, it's worth it.").

81. Vaseekaran Sivarajasingam & Jonathan P. Shepherd, Effect of Closed Circuit TV on Urban Violence, 16 *Journal of Accident and Emergency Medicine* 255 (1999) (finding in a study of three Welsh cities "an overall reduction in town/city

centre violence . . . of 1% in the 2 years after closed-circuit TV installation," which the authors concluded meant that CCTV "had no obvious influence on levels of assaults," a finding they said was consistent with the British Crime Survey finding of "no overall change" in rates of urban violence following the installation of public surveillance devices); Norris & Armstrong, *The Maximum Surveillance Society*, 166–67 (finding that although 38 percent of the 45 deployments they witnessed were for violent action, most of them were fist fights and none involved death or required an ambulance).

82. Welsh & Farrington, Crime Prevention Effects of Closed Circuit Television; Rachel Armitage, Nat'l Ass'n for the Criminal Rehab. of Offenders, *To CCTV or Not to CCTV? A Review of Current Research into the Effectiveness of CCTV Systems in Reducing Crime* (2002), available at http://www.epic.org/privacy/surveillance/spotlight/0505/nacro02.pdf.

83. Burrows, Scowl Because You're on Candid Camera, 1106 (quoting a property owner who was a catalyst in implementing a CCTV system in Los Angeles as stating, "you can't commit crimes if you know Big Brother is watching you.").

84. Davies's comments about government attitudes in the United Kingdom are instructive:

> The government has placed video surveillance at the center of its law-and-order policy. . . . CCTV is quickly becoming an integral part of crime-control policy, social control theory, and "community consciousness." It is widely viewed as a primary solution for urban dysfunction. It is no exaggeration to conclude that the technology has had more of an impact on the evolution of law enforcement policy than just about any other technology initiative in the past two decades.

Davies, Re-engineering the Right to Privacy, 151.

85. Lisa Guernsey, Living under an Electronic Eye, *New York Times*, Sept. 27, 2001, at G1, col. 5 (describing poll conducted after September 11, 2001, that showed increased public support for giving up "some personal freedoms in order to make the country safe from terrorist attacks" and that showed increased support for governmental monitoring of e-mail and phone conversations on a regular basis).

86. Davies, Re-engineering the Right to Privacy, 152; see also Edwards, Switching Off the Surveillance Society? 112 (neither statutory law nor rules of evidence normally sanction use of public camera surveillance results).

87. See, e.g., Guidelines for Using Video Surveillance Cameras in Public Places (2001), available at http://www.ipc.on.ca/images/Resources/video-e.pdf. These guidelines were promulgated by the Information and Privacy Commissioner, Ontario, Canada. They provide for "regular audits" to "address the institution's compliance with the operational policies and procedures." But there are no provisions regarding sanctions if the audit reveals misconduct. In one interesting case, the Privacy Commissioner for Canada attempted to limit the use of public cameras set up by the Royal Canadian Mounted Police in British Columbia on the ground

that monitoring and recording activities of law-abiding citizens violates their right to privacy. The Canadian Supreme Court vindicated this decision, but the commissioner's subsequent attempt to enforce the decision in British Columbia failed when the British Columbia Supreme Court held that the commissioner did not have authority to bring court actions to enforce privacy rights. Colin J. Bennett & Robin M. Bayley, Video Surveillance and Privacy Protection Law in Canada, in *Reasonable Expectations of Privacy?* 74–76.

88. Remarks of John Firman (Director of Research for the International Association of Chiefs of Police), SIA and IACP Meeting, 32 ("the massive amount of policies, procedures and guidelines in place with eighteen thousand law enforcement agencies all over the country are voluntary").

89. See Guidelines for Closed Circuit Television (CCTV) for Pub. Safety and Community Policing (Proposed Official Draft No. 9, 2000), in Overview on [*sic*] Guidelines for Closed Circuit Television (CCTV) for Pub. Safety and Community Policing 10–17, available at http://www.siaonline.org/research/privacy_guidelines_overview.pdf (calling for an internal "system of review or audit," id. at 15); Remarks of Lessing Gold (Moderator), SIA and IACP Meeting, 19 (describing framework for developing IACP guidelines on CCTV).

90. The IACP survey indicated that 53 percent of the respondents had no formal written guidelines or policies governing use of CCTV. International Association of Chiefs of Police, The Use of CCTV/Video Cameras in Law Enforcement, 9.

91. Ariz. Rev. Stat. Ann. § 13-3019. A number of states have similar laws, but "overwhelmingly, . . . this protection does not extend to the public space." Lance E. Rothenberg, Re-thinking Privacy: Peeping Toms, Video Voyeurs, and the Failure of Criminal Law to Recognize a Reasonable Expectation of Privacy in the Public Space, 48 *American University Law Review* 1127, 1145 (2000).

92. See Robert Gellman, A General Survey of Video Surveillance Law in the United States, in *Reasonable Expectations of Privacy?* 7, 27.

93. Remarks of Thomas Lambert (Attorney), SIA and IACP Meeting, 50 ("there really isn't currently any statute that expressly deals with CCTV use"). An interesting California statute prevents use of particular funds for video surveillance "of the general population" unless "there is an articulable suspicion that the persons who are the target of the surveillance or monitoring are engaging or have engaged in illegal conduct." Cal. Gov't Code § 30071. In the District of Columbia, video surveillance "from places open to the public or otherwise legally made available" is permissible if "authorized" by the police department. D.C. Code § 5-333.07.

94. See, e.g., United States v. Vega, 309 F. Supp. 2d 609 (S.D.N.Y. 2004) (detailing warrant requirements for video surveillance of home); United States v. Mesa-Rincon, 911 F.2d 1433, 1437 (10th Cir. 1990) (holding "the general fourth amendment requirements are still applicable to video surveillance" of the home).

95. See, e.g., Kowalski v. Scott, 126 Fed. Appx. 558, 559–60 (3d Cir. 2005) (covert surveillance during vacation on beach and other public places); United States v.

Jackson, 213 F.3d 1269, 1281 (10th Cir. 2000) (covert video cameras on a telephone pole overlooking outside of defendants' residences); United States v. Reed, No. 99-16439, 2000 U.S. App. LEXIS 22684, at *8 (9th Cir. 2000) (covert video of shared hallway of an apartment complex); United States v. McIver, 186 F.3d 1119 (9th Cir. 1999) (unmanned video in national forest); United States v. West, 312 F. Supp. 2d 605, 616 (D. Del. 2004) (covert surveillance outside store); Rodriguez v. United States, 878 F. Supp. 20, 24 (S.D.N.Y. 1995) (covert video surveillance of activities on public street); State v. Augafa, 992 P.2d 723, 732–33 (Haw. Ct. App. 1999) (video of defendant on public sidewalk taken from camera on a pole nearby); McCray v. State, 581 A.2d 45, 47–48 (Md. Ct. Spec. App. 1990) (covert video of defendant crossing the street); State v. Costin, 720 A.2d 866, 867 (Vt. 1998) (covert video of private but unposted fields 150 yards from defendant's house). See also Vega-Rodriguez v. Puerto Rico Tel. Co., 110 F.3d 174, 181 (1st Cir. 1997) (covert video of workers in an "open and undifferentiated work area"); United States v. Taketa, 923 F.2d 665, 677 (9th Cir. 1991) ("the defendant had no objectively reasonable expectation of privacy that would preclude video surveillance of activities already visible to the public"); State v. Bailey, 2001 WL 1739445, at *2–3 (Del. Super. Ct. 2001) (surveillance of commercial storage facility); Michigan v. Lynch, 179 Mich. App. 63, 445 N.W.2d 803 (1989) (covert video of common area of restroom); Sponick v. City of Detroit Police Dep't, 49 Mich. App. 162, 211 N.W.2d 674 (1973) (covert video of defendant talking in public bar); Young v. State, 849 P.2d 336, 340–42 (Nev. 1993) (covert video of doorless bathroom stall). Even video surveillance of the curtilage may not implicate the Fourth Amendment. See United States v. Clarke, 2005 WL 2645003 (D. Conn. 2005) (eight-month surveillance of defendant outside the home); United States v. McMillon, 350 F. Supp. 593 (D.D.C. 1972) (video of backyard not a search); People v. Wemette, 728 N.Y.S.2d 805, 805 (App. Div. 2001) (videotaping defendant on his open front porch exposed to plain view of public did not infringe any reasonable expectation of privacy); State v. Holden, 964 P.2d 318, 320–22 (Utah Ct. App. 1998) (videotape of front yard from neighbor's window not a search). But see United States v. Cuevas-Sanchez, 821 F.2d 248 (5th Cir. 1986) (prolonged video surveillance of backyard is a search).

96. See, e.g., *Costin*, 720 A.2d at 870 ("this is not a case where video surveillance is aimed indiscriminately at public places and captures lawful activities of many citizens in the hope that it will deter crime or capture what crime might occur"); *Augafa*, 992 P.2d at 737 n.14 (after noting that the camera's zoom capacity probably did not play a major role in defendant's arrest, the court stated that "there may be circumstances under which video camera surveillance, even in a public place, may constitute an unconstitutional intrusion violative of our state constitution's guarantee against unreasonable searches, seizures, and invasions of privacy.").

97. See, e.g., United States v. Torres, 751 F.2d 875 (7th Cir. 1984).

98. William H. Rehnquist, Is An Expanded Right of Privacy Consistent with Fair and Effective Law Enforcement? Or: Privacy, You've Come a Long Way, Baby, 23 *Kansas Law Review* 1, 9 (1974).

99. Id. at 14. Rehnquist also states, "I think almost all of us would regard this as simply not the kind of governmental interest that ought to rate high in a free society." Id. at 11.

100. Id. at 9.

101. Webster's New Collegiate Dictionary 47 (1977) (defining anonymous as "having or giving no name").

102. Allan F. Westin, *Privacy and Freedom* 31 (1967).

103. Id.

104. See 4 *The Works of Jeremy Bentham* 37–172 (John Bowring ed., Russell & Russell 1962) (1838–43).

105. Id. at 60–64.

106. See generally Michel Foucault, *Discipline and Punish* 195–229 (Alan Sheridan trans., Vintage Books 2d ed. 1995) (1977).

107. Id. at 202–3. See also id. at 187 ("It is the fact of being constantly seen, of being able always to be seen, that maintains the disciplined individual in his subjection.").

108. Id. at 201.

109. See id. at 170–76 (discussing how "the exercise of discipline presupposes a mechanism that coerces by means of observation" in military camps, hospitals, schools, workshops, and factories); id. at 205 ("The Panopticon . . . must be understood as a generalizable model of functioning; a way of defining power relations in terms of the everyday life of men.").

110. Id. at 209; see also id. at 202 (in a panoptic regime, "it is not necessary to use force to constrain the convict to good behaviour, the madman to calm, the worker to work, the schoolboy to application, the patient to the observation of the regulations.").

111. Id. at 202.

112. 405 U.S. 156, 164 (1972).

113. Id. at 164 (noting Whitman's "Song of the Open Road," Vachel Lindsay's "I Want to Go Wandering," and an excerpt from Henry David Thoreau's "Walking" about the "successful saunterer").

114. Foucault, *Discipline and Punish*, 218.

115. Id. at 219.

116. Id.

117. Shoshana Zuboff, *In the Age of the Smart Machine: The Future of Work and Power* 344–45 (1988).

118. Jeffrey H. Reiman, Driving to the Panopticon: A Philosophical Exploration of the Risks to Privacy Posed by the Highway Technology of the Future, 11 *Santa Clara Computer & High Technology Law Journal* 27, 38 (1995).

119. As Roger Clarke states, "[L]eaders of demonstrations in the future should expect . . . their locations to be transparent to the police." Roger Clarke, While You Were Sleeping . . . Surveillance Technologies Arrived, 73 *Australian Quarterly* 1 (2001), available at http://www.anu.edu.au/people/Roger.Clarke/DV/AQ2001.html.

120. These latter kinds of activities are apparently routinely spied upon by camera operators. See DeGregory, Click. BEEP! Face Captured, 1D (quoting camera operator as saying, "I've seen it all. Some things are really funny, like the way people dance when they think no one's looking. Others, you wouldn't want to watch."); Norris & Armstrong, *The Maximum Surveillance Society*, 129 ("10 percent of all targeted surveillances on women, and 15 percent of operator-initiated surveillance were for apparently voyeuristic reasons, outnumbering protective surveillance by five to one."), 130 ("The 'appreciation' of such public displays [of sex in cars] was a regular feature of the night shift in one of our suites and not just confined to those with access to the monitors. Many such encounters could be found on the 'shaggers alley greatest hits tape' which was compiled and replayed for the benefit of those who missed the 'entertainment.' ").

121. Richard Wasserstrom, Privacy: Some Arguments and Assumptions, in *Philosophical Dimensions of Privacy* 325–26 (Ferdinand David Schoeman ed., 1984); cf. United States v. White, 401 U.S. 745, 788 (1971) (Harlan, J., dissenting) ("Authority is hardly required to support the proposition that words would be measured a good deal more carefully and communication inhibited if one suspected his conversations were being transmitted and transcribed. Were third-party bugging a prevalent practice, it might well smother that spontaneity—reflected in frivolous, impetuous, sacrilegious, and defiant discourse—that liberates daily life.").

122. See Daniel J. Solove, Conceptualizing Privacy, 90 *California Law Review* 1087, 1154 (2002).

123. Nicholas C. Burbules, Privacy, Surveillance, and Classroom Communication on the Internet (1997), available at http://faculty.ed.uiuc.edu/burbules/articles.html.

124. See, e.g., Anita Allen, *Uneasy Access: Privacy for Women in a Free Society* 124 (1988) (stating that public "anonymity is wrongfully disturbed if uninvited attention is paid or drawn to another person without justification," because that disturbance "impedes individual tasks and purposes"); Stanley I. Benn, Privacy, Freedom, and Respect for Persons, in *Nomos XIII: Privacy* 26 (J. Ronald Pennock & J. W. Chapman eds., 1971) (the observed "becomes aware of himself as an object, knowable, having a determinate character and is fixed as something—with limited probabilities rather than infinite, indeterminate possibilities."); cf. Lawrence Lessig, *Code and Other Laws of Cyberspace* 152–53 (1999) ("Privacy, or the ability to control data about yourself . . . disables the power of one dominant community to norm others into oblivion").

125. Richard H. McAdams, Tying Privacy in *Knotts*: Beeper Monitoring and Collective Fourth Amendment Rights, 71 *Virginia Law Review* 297, 322 (1985).

126. Disa Sim, The Right to Solitude in the United States and Singapore: A Call for a Fundamental Reordering, 22 *Loyola of Los Angeles Entertainment Law Review* 443, 468 (2002) (noting that "in a crowded society, we are often driven to find peace and solace in public parks, pubs, and other public places," and asserting that this practice would be inhibited by wide-open public photography).

127. Jeffrey Rosen, *The Unwanted Gaze: The Violation of Our Privacy* 16 (2000) (citing Erving Goffman, *Behavior in Public Places: Notes on the Social Organization of Gatherings* 84–85, 116 (1963)).

128. Rosen, *The Unwanted Gaze,* 16.

129. The best research in this regard comes from Carl Botan. In one study, based on the responses of 465 workers in the communications industry, he found that "employees who are surveilled . . . experience several panoptic effects, including a reduced sense of privacy, increased uncertainty [as to job security], and reduced communication." Carl Botan, Communication Work and Electronic Surveillance: A Model for Predicting Panoptic Effects, 63 *Communications Monographs* 293, 308–9 (1996). A second study based on the same survey results, conducted with Mihaela Vorvoreanu, noted other deleterious effects:

> The overwhelming meta-message that surveillance seems to send to employees is that they are distrusted. . . . In a closely related interpretation, many employees see surveillance as setting someone, possibly themselves, up for dismissal or discipline. . . . Many subjects also perceive surveillance as implying that management feels they deserve to be treated as children, . . . and heavily surveilled employees reported reduced motivation to do more quantity of work . . . and reduced motivation to do higher quality work . . . . Finally, heavily surveilled subjects reported reduced loyalty to the organization, increased stress at work, and reduced enthusiasm about even going to work, all of which are supported by qualitative comments. . . .

Carl Botan & Mihaela Vorvoreanu, "What Are You Really Saying to Me?" Electronic Surveillance in the Workplace (June 2000) (unpublished manuscript, on file with author).

130. As reported in section 3 of this chapter, surveys asking what people think of CCTV routinely produce overwhelmingly positive results. But no survey, outside of the one that I conduced for this chapter, has focused on CCTV's panoptic effects (and even the study reported here does so only indirectly).

131. Roger Clarke, Information Technology and Dataveillance, 31 *Communication of the ACM* 498 (May 1988), available at http://www.anu.edu.au/people/Roger.Clarke/DV/CACM88.html.

132. Quoted in News, *CCTV Today*, May 1995, at 4.

133. Simon Davies, Welcome Home Big Brother, *Wired*, May 1995, at 58–62, cited in Graham, Towards the Fifth Utility? 101.

134. Michael McCahill, The Surveillance Web: The Rise and Extent of Visual Surveillance in a Northern City (unpublished Ph.D. dissertation, Hull University), cited in Norris, From Personal to Digital, 28 (using this term); see also Alice Wakefield, Situational Crime Prevention in Mass Private Property, in *Ethical and Social Perspectives on Situational Crime Prevention* 125, 133 (Andrew von Hirsch, David Garland & Alison Wakefield eds., 2000) (reporting 578 persons excluded from

shopping and arts centers during a five-week period as a result of CCTV-based security system).

135. See Alan Reeve, The Panopticisation of Shopping: CCTV and Leisure Consumption, in *Surveillance, Closed Circuit Television, and Social Control*, 78 (reporting that town center managers wanted to use CCTV primarily to discourage "anti-consumer" people and activities from entering the center, and that a quarter wanted to exclude political gatherings, youth who want to "hang out," and beggars); Roy Coleman & Joe Sim, "You'll Never Walk Alone": CCTV Surveillance, Order and Neo-liberal Rule in Liverpool City Centre, 51 *British Journal of Sociology* 623 (2000) (reporting a study leading the authors to conclude that "the activities targeted [and] the gathering of intelligence and its dissemination [focus] on recurring categories: youth, 'known and potential' shoplifters, the homeless and licensed and unlicensed street traders.").

136. Jeffrey Rosen, A Watchful State, *New York Times Magazine*, Oct. 7, 2001, at 38.

137. Id. See also Taylor, Closed Circuit Television, ¶ 31 (reporting that soon after installation of cameras in Newcastle, local residents attacked the community center in the belief that it housed the camera-monitoring room).

138. See generally Dorothy E. Roberts, Foreword: Race, Vagueness, and the Social Meaning of Order-Maintenance Policy, 89 *Journal of Criminal Law & Criminology* 775 (1999) (exploring how order maintenance policies reinforce and are reinforced by preconceived notions of African American criminality).

139. Taylor, Closed Circuit Television, ¶ 23 ("Shopping malls and city centres are becoming increasingly purified and privatised to the extent that the limits of acceptable behaviour are being driven by the forces of consumerism. Public spaces are becoming increasingly less public."); Jon Bannister et al., Closed Circuit Television and the City, in *Surveillance, Closed Circuit Television, and Social Control*, 24–32.

140. These incidents are described in Electronic Privacy Information Center, Spotlight on Surveillance: D.C.'s Camera System Should Focus on Emergencies, Not Daily Life, Dec. 2005, available at http://www.epic.org/privacy/surveilance/spotlight/1205/.

141. Michalis Lianos & Mary Douglas, Dangerization and the End of Deviance: The Institutional Environment, 40 *British Journal of Criminology* 261, 266 (2000) ("It is the first time in history that we have the opportunity to experience forms of control that do not take into account any category of social division. . . . Automated environments . . . cannot discriminate among users on other grounds than their quality as users.").

142. Amy Herdy, They Made Me Feel like a Criminal, *St. Petersburg Times*, Aug. 8, 2001, at 1B (recounting story of police confronting a man erroneously identified by Tampa's facial recognition system as someone wanted for child abuse).

143. Norris, From Personal to Digital, 40–41.

144. See, e.g., Orwell, *1984*, 6–7 (the telescreen "could be dimmed, but there was no way of shutting it off completely. . . . It received and transmitted simultaneously. . . . You had to live—did live, from habit that became instinct—in the assumption that every sound you made was overheard, and, except in darkness, every movement scrutinized.").

145. See, e.g., Orwell, *1984*, 19–20.

146. Foucault's writings predict this result. See Burbules, Privacy, Surveillance (noting that, consistent with Foucault's thesis, "few people even notice any longer how frequently they are monitored through partially hidden video cameras," despite the fact that this surveillance inhibits "all sorts of activities—and not only illegal activities").

147. Kevin D. Haggerty & Richard V. Ericson, The Surveillant Assemblage, 51 *British Journal of Sociology* 605, 619 (2000).

148. Laurence H. Tribe, Seven Deadly Sins of Straining the Constitution through a Pseudo-Scientific Sieve, 36 *Hastings Law Journal* 155, 165 (1984).

149. Id.

150. 490 U.S. 19, 25 (1989).

151. Id. at 25 ("[W]e do not think the Constitution recognizes a generalized right of 'social association' that includes chance encounters in dance halls. . . . [Griswold v. Connecticut, 381 U.S. 479 (1965)] recognizes nothing more than that the right of expressive association extends to groups organized to engage in speech that does not pertain directly to politics.").

152. 408 U.S. 1 (1972).

153. Id. at 10.

154. Id. at 13–14 ("Allegations of a subjective 'chill' are not an adequate substitute for a claim of specific present objective harm or a threat of specific future harm").

155. Meese v. Keene, 481 U.S. 465, 478 (1987) (finding standing to argue that government labeling of a film as propaganda chilled the showing of the films, but ultimately finding no First Amendment violation because the labeling "neither prohibits nor censors the dissemination of advocacy materials").

156. 408 U.S. at 6.

157. Id. at 9 (Respondents "freely admit that they complain of no specific action of the Army against them. . . . So far as is yet shown, the information gathered is nothing more than a good newspaper reporter would be able to gather by attendance at public meetings and the clipping of articles from publications available on any newsstand.").

158. Id. at 13–14 n.7 ("Respondents . . . have also cast considerable doubt on whether they themselves are in fact suffering from any . . . chill. . . . If respondents themselves are not chilled, . . . respondents clearly lack that 'personal stake in the outcome of the controversy' essential to standing.").

159. For instance, in Lamont v. Postmaster General, 381 U.S. 301 (1965), the

Court unanimously struck down a government regulation requiring individuals to make a special written request to the post office for delivery of mail containing communist literature:

> [U]nder such a regulation, any addressee is likely to feel some inhibition in sending for literature which federal officials have condemned as "communist political propaganda." The regime of this Act is at war with the "uninhibited, robust, and wide-open" debate and discussion that are contemplated by the First Amendment.

Id. at 307; see also Bantam Books, Inc. v. Sullivan, 372 U.S. 58 (1963) (finding the First Amendment violated when the city government sent letters that identified certain books as "objectionable," stated it would turn its list of distributors of those books over to police, and sometimes sent police officers to see whether distributors took any action with respect to the books). In both *Lamont* and *Bantam Books* the First Amendment violation was the government's suggestion that the speech activity was inappropriate.

160. See, e.g., Donohoe v. Duling, 465 F.2d 196 (4th Cir. 1972) (finding no justiciable controversy where police conducted surveillance of demonstrations and public vigils and photographed demonstrators); Philadelphia Yearly Meeting of the Religious Society of Friends v. Tate, 519 F.2d 1335, 1337–38 (3d Cir. 1975) (no justiciable controversy where police photographed public meetings and disseminated information to other law enforcement agencies).

161. See Presbyterian Church (U.S.A.) v. United States, 870 F.2d 518 (9th Cir. 1989) (distinguishing *Tatum* because church suffered diminished membership as a result of surveillance); Olagues v. Russoniello, 797 F.2d 1511 (9th Cir. 1986) (distinguishing *Tatum* because plaintiffs here were targets of surveillance); cf. United States v. Montemarano, 1987 WL 13729, at *1 (S.D.N.Y. 1987), where the court drew attention to the lack of police intimidation:

> It should be noted that the intrusion upon the spiritual and psychological milieu preceding or following the services was minimized by the lack of a discernible law enforcement presence, the photographs having been taken from a concealed location. This is not a situation where uniformed government personnel impliedly, or expressly, menaced churchgoers.

162. *Tate*, 519 F.2d at 1338.

163. 310 N.L.R.B. 1197 (1993).

164. Id. at *1.

165. Id. See also National Steel v. N.L.R.B., 156 F.3d 1268 (D.C. Cir. 1998); Road Sprinkler Fitters Local Union No. 669 v. N.L.R.B., 681 F.2d 11, 19 (D.C. Cir. 1982) (citing cases); Waco, Inc., 273 N.L.R.B. 746, 747 (1984).

166. Talley v. California, 362 U.S. 60, 64 (1960) (striking down a ban on anonymous handbills, noting that "persecuted groups and sects from time to time through-

out history have been able to criticize oppressive practices and laws either anonymously or not at all.").

167. Buckley v. American Constitutional Law Found., 525 U.S. 182, 200 (1999) (holding that Colorado's requirement that petition solicitors wear an identification badge "discourages participation in the petition circulation process by forcing name identification without sufficient cause.").

168. NAACP v. Alabama ex rel. Patterson, 357 U.S. 449, 462 (1958) ("It is hardly a novel perception that compelled disclosure of affiliation with groups engaged in advocacy may constitute an effective . . . restraint on freedom of association."); see also Shelton v. Tucker, 364 U.S. 479, 490 (1960) (prohibiting a requirement that teachers disclose group memberships).

169. 514 U.S. 334, 341–42 (1995).

170. McAdams, Tying Privacy in *Knotts*, 322.

171. Reporters Comm. for Freedom of the Press v. AT&T, 593 F.2d 1030 (D.C. Cir. 1978) ("Physical surveillance consistent with Fourth Amendment protections and *in connection with a bona fide law enforcement investigation* does not violate First Amendment rights, even though it may be directed at communicative or associational activities, and even though it may inhibit those activities.") (emphasis added); see also Grayned v. City of Rockford, 408 U.S. 104, 115 (1972) ("the right to use a public place for expressive activity may be restricted only for weighty reasons"); Alliance to End Repression v. City of Chicago, 627 F. Supp. 1044, 1056 (N.D. Ill. 1985) ("Without any reasonable suspicion of criminal conduct, the court cannot conceive of any remotely compelling interest the City has in recording which political activities an individual chooses to involve herself in").

172. Williams v. Fears, 179 U.S. 270, 274 (1909).

173. 357 U.S. 116 (1958).

174. Id. at 126 (quoting Zechariah Chafee Jr., *Three Human Rights in the Constitution of 1787*, at 197 (1956)); see also Shapiro v. Thompson, 394 U.S. 618, 629 (1969) ("[O]ur constitutional concepts of personal liberty unite to require that all citizens be free to travel throughout the length and breadth of our land uninhibited by statutes, rules, or regulations which unreasonably burden or restrict this movement.").

175. 357 U.S. at 126.

176. Saenz v. Roe, 526 U.S. 489, 502–3 (1999).

177. 527 U.S. 41, 53–54 (1999).

178. Id. at 64; Kolender v. Lawson, 461 U.S. 32 (1983); Papachristou v. Jacksonville, 405 U.S. 156 (1972); Coates v. Cincinnati, 402 U.S. 611 (1971).

179. Roe v. Wade, 410 U.S. 179, 213 (1973) (Douglas, J., concurring).

180. 714 So. 2d 1149, 1150 (Fla. Dist. Ct. App. 1998).

181. No. 92-3198, 1995 WL 78289, at *2 (Wis. Ct. App. 1995); see also Pro-Choice Network of W. N.Y., 799 F. Supp. 1417, 1437–39 (W.D.N.Y. 1992) (cautioning that if defendants continue to use cameras to intimidate women entering abortion clinics,

the court would not hesitate to restrict defendants' use of cameras); Planned Parenthood v. Aakhus, 17 Cal. Rptr. 2d 510, 515 (Ct. App. 1993) (photographing and videotaping clients of abortion clinics violated the right to privacy under the California Constitution); Chico Feminist Women's Health Ctr. v. Scully, 256 Cal. Rptr. 194, 196–97 (Ct. App. 1989) (upholding an injunction against abortion protesters who were photographing license plates and people entering or leaving an abortion clinic). Although these decisions were based on varying considerations, including, as in *Aakhus*, informational privacy, the immediate harm was the unjustifiable inhibition of the plaintiffs' ability to go about their business.

182. 924 F. Supp. 1413, 1420 (E.D. Pa. 1996); see also Galella v. Onassis, 533 F. Supp. 1076 (S.D.N.Y. 1982) ("under certain circumstances, surveillance may be so 'overzealous' as to render it actionable. It does not strain credulity or imagination to conceive of the systematic 'public' surveillance of another as being the implementation of a plan to intrude on the privacy of another") (citing Nader v. General Motors Corp., 255 N.E.2d 765, 771, 772 (N.Y. 1970)).

183. 924 F. Supp. at 1432–33.

184. *Goosen*, 714 So. 2d at 1150 ("While the First Amendment confers on each citizen a powerful right to express oneself, it gives the citizen no boon to jeopardize the health, safety, and rights of others"); *Baumann*, 1995 WL 78289, at *7 ("no matter how public the setting or the subject, there is no First Amendment right to use a camera as a tool of intimidation"); *Wolfson*, 924 F. Supp. at 1433 ("A reasonable jury would likely conclude that it is difficult to understand how hounding, harassing, and ambushing the Wolfsons would advance the newsworthy goal of exposing the high salaries paid to U.S. Healthcare executives or how such conduct would advance the fundamental policies underlying the First Amendment which include providing information to 'enable members of society to cope with the exigencies of their period.' ").

185. Aptheker v. Secretary of State, 378 U.S. 500, 507–8 (1964) (quoting NAACP v. Alabama ex rel. Flowers, 377 U.S. 288, 307 (1964)). *Aptheker* went on to find unconstitutional the State Department's revocation of passports held by members of the Communist Party because "the prohibition against travel is supported only by a tenuous relationship between the bare fact of organizational membership and the activity Congress sought to proscribe." Id. at 514.

186. See Erwin Chemerinsky, *Constitutional Law: Principles and Policies* 785, 790 (2d ed. 2002) (noting these differing bases for the privacy right).

187. *Roe*, 410 U.S. at 153.

188. Loving v. Virginia, 388 U.S. 1, 12 (1967).

189. Eisenstadt v. Baird, 405 U.S. 438, 453 (1972); Griswold v. Connecticut, 381 U.S. 479, 485 (1965).

190. Jed Rubenfeld, The Right of Privacy, 102 *Harvard Law Review* 737, 752–54 (1989).

191. Id. at 783–87 & 794.

192. Andrew E. Taslitz, The Fourth Amendment in the Twenty-First Century:

Technology, Privacy, and Human Emotions, 65 *Law & Contemporary Problems* 125, 152 (2002).

193. Id. at 169 (quoting Michael Reisman, *Law in Brief Encounters* 31 (1999)).

194. Taslitz, The Fourth Amendment in the Twenty-First Century, 171.

195. Id. at 171–72.

196. Roberts v. United States Jaycees, 468 U.S. 609, 619 (1984).

197. Rubenfeld, The Right of Privacy, 784.

198. Id. at 784–92.

199. Id. at 775.

200. Davies, Re-engineering the Right to Privacy, 144 & n.1.

201. See in particular Smith v. Maryland, 442 U.S. 735, 744 (1979).

202. See, e.g., Bond v. United States, 529 U.S. 334, 337 (2000) (in holding that feeling soft luggage was a search, the Court stated that "physically invasive inspection is simply more intrusive than purely visual inspection"); Dow Chem. Co. v. United States, 476 U.S. 227, 237 (1986) (in holding that EPA photography of a chemical plant's curtilage from a plane was not a search, the Court stated that "actual physical entry by EPA into any enclosed area would raise significantly different questions"); California v. Ciraolo, 476 U.S. 207, 213 (1986) (in holding that looking into a backyard from an airplane is not a search, the Court stated that "the observations took place within public navigable airspace . . . in a physically nonintrusive manner").

203. Terry v. Ohio, 392 U.S. 1, 20 n.16 (1968).

204. Michigan v. Chesternut, 486 U.S. 567, 569 (1988).

205. See id. at 574 (holding police car driving alongside defendant not a seizure); California v. Hodari D., 499 U.S. 621, 629 (1991) (police chase of defendant not a seizure).

206. Sim, The Right to Solitude, 470–71; see also Andrew J. McClurg, Bringing Privacy Law out of the Closet: A Tort Theory of Liability for Intrusions in Public Places, 73 *North Carolina Law Review* 989, 1041–44 (1995).

207. 343 U.S. 747, 753 (1952) (the defendant "was talking confidentially and indiscreetly with one he trusted, and he was overheard . . . . due to aid from a transmitter and receiver, to be sure, but with the same effect on his privacy as if agent Lee had been eavesdropping outside an open window.").

208. United States v. Caceres, 440 U.S. 741 (1979).

209. See also Sheldon Halpern, The Traffic in Souls: Privacy Interests and the Intelligent Vehicle-Highway Systems, 11 *Santa Clara Computer & High Technology Law Journal* 45, 59–60 (1995) (noting that "to the limited extent that . . . observation per se, absent publication . . . has been deemed actionable, it has been surreptitious and offensively intrusive").

210. See also Daniel J. Solove, Privacy and Power: Computer Databases and Metaphors for Information Privacy, 53 *Stanford Law Review* 1393, 1440–44 (2001) (describing the legislation and its flaws).

211. A Harris poll conducted in the United States in October 2002 did indicate

that 63 percent of those surveyed were in favor of "increased video surveillance" of public places such as airports. Ken Kaye, High Tech Security Gets Tests at Airports, *Ft. Lauderdale Sun-Sentinel*, Jan. 20, 2002, at A1.

212. See Taylor, Closed Circuit Television, ¶ 16 (reporting polling results that found between 69 percent and 95 percent in favor of the cameras). Note, however, that the way survey questions about CCTV have been framed apparently distorts the results obtained. See Jason Ditton, Public Support for Town Centre CCTV Schemes: Myth or Reality? in *Surveillance, Closed Circuit Television, and Social Control*, 227 (finding that positive framing of questions increased CCTV's acceptance by 20 percent, and that if that proportion were subtracted from the 69 percent positive response in previous professional surveys, "we have a minority—albeit a very large minority—but only a minority finding open street city centre CCTV acceptable.").

213. Davies, Re-engineering the Right to Privacy, 152 (describing a British Home Office survey conducted in 1992).

214. Id.

215. The survey actually contained twenty-five scenarios, but the results pertaining to several of them (involving, e.g., searches of personal diaries and car trunks) do not add appreciably to the discussion and are not reported here.

216. See, e.g., Florida v. Bostick, 501 U.S. 429, 438 (1991).

217. The confidence intervals are larger for the camera surveillance scenarios because, given the desire to test variations of those scenarios, there were fewer surveys completed for each.

218. Chimel v. California, 395 U.S. 752, 768 (1969) (nonexigent search of bedroom requires warrant); Katz v. United States, 389 U.S. 347, 361 (1967) (bugging requires warrant); Blackford v. United States, 247 F.2d 745, 753 (9th Cir. 1957) (body cavity search at border permissible upon "precise knowledge of what, and how much was where"—if conducted reasonably).

219. *Terry*, 392 U.S. at 27 (holding that a pat down requires reasonable suspicion). The legality of electronic frisks has yet to be taken up directly, but because they reveal items underneath one's clothing, they presumably would require at least reasonable suspicion.

220. Donovan v. Dewey, 452 U.S. 594, 603 (1981) (requiring that inspection programs for coal mines provide "a constitutionally adequate substitute for a warrant"); Marshall v. Barlow's, Inc. 436 U.S. 307, 324 (1978) (requiring administrative warrant for nonconsensual factory inspections); United States v. Martinez-Fuerte, 428 U.S. 543, 556 (1976) ("It is agreed that checkpoint stops are 'seizures' within the meaning of the Fourth Amendment."); New York v. Burger, 482 U.S. 691 (1987) (applying *Dewey* to inspections of junkyards for stolen auto parts).

221. Florida v. Riley, 488 U.S. 445 (1989) (helicopter four hundred feet above backyard); *Chesternut*, 486 U.S. 567; California v. Greenwood, 486 U.S. 35 (1988) (searching garbage separated from other garbage).

222. Christopher Slobogin & Joseph E. Schumacher, Reasonable Expectations of Privacy and Autonomy in Fourth Amendment Cases: An Empirical Look at "Understandings Recognized and Permitted by Society," 42 *Duke Law Journal* 727, 743–51 (1993).

223. Id. at 744.

224. Anonymous Account of the Boston Massacre, at http://www.let.rug.nl/usa/D/1751-1775/bostonmassacre/anon.htm (stating that "the challenging of the inhabitants by sentinels posted in all parts of town . . . occasioned many quarrels and uneasiness"); see also Westin, *Privacy and Freedom*, 57–58 (noting that "the whole network of American constitutional rights . . . was established to curtail the ancient surveillance claims of governmental authorities."); Don B. Kates, The Second Amendment and the Ideology of Self-Protection, 9 *Constitutional Commentary* 87, 103 (1992) (stating that, for the Founders, "the very idea of empowering government to place an armed force in constant watch over the populace was vehemently rejected as a paradigm of abhorrent French despotism," and noting that organized police forces were resisted in colonial times). In correspondence with the author, Davies, who has closely studied the Fourth Amendment's history, emphasized the last fact, noting that, other than "snooping" by British informers (which occasioned hostility among the colonists), there was no one available to conduct surveillance: "the constable had better things to do (trying to make a living) than stand around looking for hints of crime." E-mail from Thomas Davies, Professor of Law, University of Tennessee School of Law, to Christopher Slobogin, July 8, 2002, 2:16 PM CST. Davies also noted the lack of surveillance technology in colonial times and pointed out that "surveillers would have had more difficulty blending into the smaller, closer social settings of that time." Id.

225. See generally David Sklansky, The Fourth Amendment and the Common Law, 100 *Columbia Law Review* 1739, 1739 (2000):

> Anchoring the Fourth Amendment in common law will do little to make it more principled or predictable, in part because common-law limits on searches and seizures were thinner, vaguer, and far more varied than the Court seems to suppose. What the common law has of value to offer Fourth Amendment law is what it has to offer constitutional law more generally: not its rules but its method.

226. Miller v. California, 413 U.S. 15, 24 (1973) (whether a work appeals to the "prurient interest" is to be defined by "community standards").

227. See, e.g., Miranda v. Arizona, 384 U.S. 436 (1966).

228. See, e.g., Tinker v. Des Moines Indep. Cmty. Sch. Dist., 393 U.S. 503 (1969).

229. See, e.g., Illinois v. Gates, 462 U.S. 213 (1983).

230. Cf. West Virginia State Bd. of Educ. v. Barnette, 319 U.S. 624, 638 (1943).

231. Robert C. Post, Three Concepts of Privacy, 89 *Georgetown Law Journal* 2087 (2001).

232. Id. at 2087, 2087–92, 2096–98.

233. Id. at 2092, 2094.

234. Id. at 2094.

235. Slobogin & Schumacher, Reasonable Expectations of Privacy and Autonomy, 753 (relying on David L. Faigman, "Normative Constitutional Fact-Finding": Exploring the Empirical Component of Constitutional Interpretation, 139 *University of Pennsylvania Law Review* 541, 581–88 (1991)).

236. Slobogin & Schumacher, Reasonable Expectations of Privacy and Autonomy, 753.

237. Note, however, one difference between a right to anonymity and the other rights. Each of the other rights could be said to be inhibited by crime at least as much as by cameras (consider in particular the right to movement and repose). Thus, one could argue that those rights are infringed if government does not install CCTV, at least in high crime areas. The right to anonymity is more clearly independent of the fear of crime; it is always implicated by CCTV.

238. Albright v. Oliver, 510 U.S. 266, 273 (1994) ("Where a particular amendment provides an explicit textual source of constitutional protection against a particular sort of government behavior, 'that Amendment, not the more generalized notion of "substantive due process," must be the guide for analyzing these claims' " (quoting Graham v. Connor, 490 U.S. 386, 395 (1989)).

239. See generally Chemerinsky, *Constitutional Law*, 764–768.

Chapter Five

1. Erik Luna, Constitutional Roadmaps, 90 *Journal of Criminal Law & Criminology* 1125, 1193 (2000).

2. Id. at 1185–87.

3. Id. at 1193.

4. Id. at 1200–1206.

5. American Bar Association, Standards for Criminal Justice, *Electronic Surveillance, Section B: Technologically-Assisted Physical Surveillance* (1999), available at http://www.abanet.org/crimjust/standards/taps_toc.html [hereafter ABA Standards].

6. Given the intrusiveness ratings of the coal mine and factory inspection scenarios reported in chapter 4, another source of precedent would be the closely regulated industry cases. See Charles H. Whitebread & Christopher Slobogin, *Criminal Procedure: An Analysis of Cases and Concepts* 295–300 (4th ed. 2000) (describing the cases). These cases require the government to show a "substantial" interest in the activity being regulated and also require limitations on when and how searches can be carried out that amount to "a constitutionally adequate substitute for a warrant." Dewey v. Donovan, 452 U.S. 594, 602–3 (1981). Note, however, that these decisions deal with specific industries, not the public at large, so roadblocks provide a closer analog to CCTV.

7. 428 U.S. 543, 566–67 (1976).
8. 496 U.S. 444, 455 (1990).
9. 440 U.S. 648, 657, 663 (1979).
10. 540 U.S. 419 (2004).
11. 531 U.S. 32, 41 (2000).
12. Id. at 38–43.
13. 540 U.S. at 424–25.
14. Id. at 44 n.1.
15. Id. at 44.
16. Id. at 42.
17. 496 U.S. at 455.
18. *Martinez-Fuerte*, 428 U.S. at 546 ("The 'point' agent standing between the two lanes of traffic visually screens all northbound vehicles, which the checkpoint brings to a virtual, if not a complete, halt. Most motorists are allowed to resume their progress without any oral inquiry or close visual examination.").
19. 440 U.S. at 659–60.
20. Cf. Erik Luna, Transparent Policing, 85 *Iowa Law Review* 1107, 1173 (2000) ("Criminologists have offered geographic theories of target hunting, fugitive migration, crime trips, escape routes, and repeat location victimization, as well as theories of aggregate behavior based on market distribution, crime displacement, and police-crackdown effects.").
21. 531 U.S. at 44 ("the Fourth Amendment would almost certainly permit an appropriately tailored roadblock set up to thwart an imminent terrorist attack or to catch a dangerous criminal who is likely to flee by way of a particular route").
22. 496 U.S. at 453.
23. Id. at 453–54.
24. ABA Standard 2–9.3(b) cmt. at 69.
25. William J. Stuntz, Implicit Bargains, Government Power, and the Fourth Amendment, 44 *Stanford Law Review* 553 (1992).
26. Id. at 588.
27. Should the public be able to force the installation of cameras when they are not warranted under the foregoing analysis? Tracey Meares and Dan Kahan argue that when "the community has internalized the burden that a particular law imposes on individual freedom," courts "should presume that the law does not violate individual rights." Tracey L. Meares & Dan M. Kahan, The Wages of Antiquated Procedural Thinking: A Critique of *Chicago v. Morales,* 1998 *University of Chicago Legal Forum* 197, 209. But the "community" is hard to gauge. Compare Remarks of Joseph Dunne, Meeting of the Security Industry Association and International Association of Chiefs of Police 21 (Apr. 17, 2002) (on file with author) [hereafter SIA and IACP Meeting] ("Virtually every housing development in New York City has requested a CCTV monitoring program") with Burrows, Privacy and Video Surveillance, 1082 (describing how cameras were installed when long-term, largely elderly residents became concerned about crime as black and Hispanic individuals

moved in nearby). And while chapter 4 argues that community views are crucial to the privacy issue, it is clear that Fourth Amendment reasonableness is ultimately a judicial matter. Nonetheless, if a well-informed community clearly favors cameras, a (rebuttable) presumption in their favor may be a workable approach.

28. See, e.g., Remarks of Lessing Gold, SIA and IACP Meeting, 19 ("we must form a coalition or partnership with law enforcement, city council, citizens groups and private sector"); Jerry Semper (Maryland Police Trainer), SIA and IACP Meeting, 55 ("community inclusion is the most important aspect of what we've got going on here").

29. ABA Standard 2-9.3(b)(i).

30. ABA Standard 2-9.2(d).

31. ABA Standard 2-9.3(b)(ii).

32. See Current Projects: Respectful Cameras, available at http://www.cs.berkeley.edu/~jschiff/RespectfulCameras/.

33. Clive Norris & Gary Armstrong, *The Maximum Surveillance Society* 150 (1999).

34. 496 U.S. at 451.

35. 428 U.S. at 564 n.17.

36. Id. at 547.

37. ABA Standard 2-9.1(c)(ii)(E) & (F).

38. 460 U.S. at 278.

39. See, e.g., Richard McAdams, Tying Privacy in *Knotts*: Beeper Monitoring and Collective Fourth Amendment Rights, 71 *Virginia Law Review* 297, 332–35 (1985).

40. 428 U.S. at 559.

41. Id.

42. 489 U.S. 656, 672 n.2 (1989) (citing Delaware v. Prouse, 440 U.S. 648, 657 (1979)).

43. 400 U.S. 309, 320–21 (1971).

44. See, e.g., United States v. Knights, 534 U.S. 112, 119 (2001) ("The probation order [allowing suspicionless searches of probationers] clearly expressed the search condition and Knights was unambiguously informed of it"); United States v. Biswell, 406 U.S. 311, 316 (1972) (holding that warrantless, suspicionless searches of gun dealers are permissible, stating, "[W]hen a dealer chooses to engage in this pervasively regulated business and to accept a federal license, he does so with the knowledge that his business records, firearms, and ammunition will be subject to effective inspection.").

45. Norris & Armstrong, *The Maximum Surveillance Society*, 150.

46. Id. They also reported that 30 percent of targeted surveillances on black people, but only 13 percent of targeted surveillances on whites, lasted nine minutes or more, id., and that blacks, teens, and males were much more likely to be targeted for "no obvious reason" compared to other groups. Id. at 113–16 tbls. 6.5, 6.7, 6.9 (68

percent of blacks, compared to 35 percent of whites; 65 percent of teens, compared to 38 percent of those age 20–29, and 21 percent of those age 30–39; 47 percent of males, compared to 16 percent of females).

47. 517 U.S. 806, 813 (1996) ("We of course agree with petitioners that the Constitution prohibits selective enforcement of the law based on considerations such as race.").

48. ABA Standard 2-9.1(d)(i).

49. 428 U.S. at 546–47.

50. 496 U.S. at 444.

51. 470 U.S. 675, 686 (1985). Although *Sharpe* firmly rejected a bright-line twenty-minute limitation on *Terry* stops as "clearly and fundamentally at odds with our approach in this area," it went on to justify the twenty-minute stop in *Sharpe* on the grounds that the defendant's evasions were partly responsible for the delay and that the officer made diligent efforts to expedite the detention. Id. at 686–87 ("Except for Savage's maneuvers, only a short and certainly permissible pre-arrest detention would likely have taken place.").

52. ABA Standard 2-9.1(d)(ii).

53. Later I suggest that regulatory rules be disseminated to the public as a way of limiting panoptic effects. One objection to this rule is that once it is made known to the citizenry, it will be manipulated by perpetrators who will simply wait five minutes before engaging in any suspicious activity. However, the five-minute period need not start when the subject enters the camera area (and in fact shouldn't start at all unless something suspicious occurs), which can be made clear in the rule disseminated to the public. Such a rule could simply read this way: "Camera operators will not focus on individuals unless they engage in activity indicative of criminal intent or are in need of aid, and will not continue surveillance unless criminal intent or harm is confirmed."

54. Norris and Armstrong found that somewhere around 12–15 percent of all targeted surveillances lasted more than nine minutes (that percentage increased to 25 percent for blacks), and that close to 40 percent lasted between two and six minutes. Norris & Armstrong, *The Maximum Surveillance Society*, 150. Deployment resulted in only 5 percent of targeted surveillances, and arrest occurred in only 24 percent of deployments. Id. at 168.

55. See Blackmail Concern as CCTV Video Sex Footage Goes on Sale, *The Herald (Glasgow)*, Nov. 27, 1995, at 5 (recounting sale of CCTV clips and public release of tapes showing a prostitute providing oral sex to a businessman and a man in a Santa hat stripping and then masturbating); William G. Staples, *Everyday Surveillance: Vigilance and Visibility in Postmodern Life* 61–62 (2000) (describing the "potential market for tapes" and noting the high sales of the "Caught on Tape" and "Really Caught on Tape" videos).

56. 526 U.S. 603 (1999).

57. Id. at 614.

58. 429 U.S. 589 (1977).

59. Id. at 601 ("There is no support in the record, or in the experience of the two States that New York has emulated, for an assumption that the security provisions of the statute will be administered improperly."). The Court also noted that it did not need to address the constitutionality of "the unwarranted disclosure of accumulated private data whether intentional or unintentional or by a system that did not contain comparable security provisions." Id. at 605–6.

60. Id. at 605.

61. 532 U.S. 67, 78 & n.14 (2001).

62. 489 U.S. 749, 770 (1989).

63. Id. at 774.

64. See Remarks of Stephen McMahon, SIA and IACP Meeting, 6.

65. ABA Standard 2-9.1(d)(vi) cmt. See Harold J. Krent, Of Diaries and Data Banks: Use Restrictions under the Fourth Amendment, 74 *Texas Law Review* 49, 85–92 (1995) (giving reasons for requiring that disclosure rules be promulgated by deliberative bodies).

66. William J. Stuntz, Local Policing after the Terror, 111 *Yale Law Journal* 2137, 2183–84 (2002) ("The law could allow a given search tactic whenever the police want to engage in it, but forbid public disclosure of anything uncovered save in a criminal trial.").

67. Id. at 2184–85.

68. See UPI, "Spy" Cameras vs. Villains in Britain (Mar. 8, 2002), available at http://www.upi.com/archive/view.php?archive=1&StoryID=08032002-020813-4448r.

69. Specifically, the scenario read as follows: "Police at a central control center monitoring hidden video cameras positioned at 300-yard intervals that can zoom in on the face and body of a person."

70. George Orwell, *1984,* 3 (1949).

71. See William J. Stuntz, Warrants and Fourth Amendment Remedies, 77 *Virginia Law Review* 881, 913–15 (1991) (discussing the ease with which police can commit perjury at suppression hearings because of their ability to reconstruct what happened based on knowledge of what was found, the tendency to believe police rather than criminal defendants, and the hindsight bias created by arrest).

72. ABA Standard 2-9.1(f)(i) (emphasis added).

73. The Supreme Court has indicated that the failure to maintain accurate records of a search is not a violation of the Fourth Amendment when the underlying search is valid. Cady v. Dombrowski, 413 U.S. 433, 449 (1973). But it has yet to address this issue when the validity of the search is questionable or indeterminable because of police failure to provide adequate information. Furthermore, it has held that the Fourth Amendment is violated when police intentionally hide or mischaracterize information relevant to a search. Franks v. Delaware, 438 U.S. 154, 155–56 (1978) ("where the defendant makes a substantial preliminary showing that a false

statement knowingly and intentionally, or with reckless disregard for the truth, was included by the affiant in the warrant affidavit, and if the allegedly false statement is necessary to the finding of probable cause, the Fourth Amendment requires that a hearing be held at the defendant's request").

74. David Brin, *The Transparent Society* 334 (1998).

75. See generally Christopher Slobogin, *Criminal Procedure: Regulation of Police Investigation* 561–63 (3d ed. 2003) (describing ineffectiveness of administrative sanctions); Jerome Skolnick, *Justice without Trial* 224 (1975) (asserting that so long as a search or seizure is "in conformity with administrative norms of police organization," superiors will be sympathetic).

76. Mapp v. Ohio, 367 U.S. 63 (1961).

77. See Norris & Armstrong, *The Maximum Surveillance Society*, 168.

78. See Arizona v. Evans, 514 U.S. 1 (1995) (holding that exclusion is not required where arresting officer relies on computer records maintained by civilian court personnel).

79. Cf. United States v. Ceccolini, 435 U.S. 268, 278 (1978) (holding that since witnesses will often come forward of their own accord, and "since the cost of excluding live-witness testimony often will be greater [than excluding tangible evidence], a closer, more direct link between the illegality and that kind of testimony is required" before witness testimony will be excluded).

80. See Whitebread & Slobogin, *Criminal Procedure*, 61–62 (describing obstacles to criminal prosecutions for Fourth Amendment violations).

81. Suits under 42 U.S.C. § 1983, the main avenue for constitutional damage actions, would not be worth the effort for many people who are illegally surveilled because actual injury in such cases would be negligible and "symbolic" injury is not compensable. Memphis Sch. Dist. v. Stachura, 477 U.S. 299 (1986). Further, unless the violation is somehow ratified by a superior, the government would usually have a "policy or custom" defense. Pembaur v. Cincinnati, 475 U.S. 469 (1986).

82. Hague v. C.I.O., 307 U.S. 496 (1939) (holding that a state official may be enjoined under 42 U.S.C. § 1983). Because the issue concerns whether a planned CCTV system may be installed, it is justiciable; the Court's rigid barriers to injunctive relief against discretionary decisions, see, e.g., Los Angeles v. Lyons, 461 U.S. 95 (1983), would be avoided.

83. A constitutional damages suit against the government might be stalled by a policy and custom defense, see *Pembaur*, and the party that receives the tape may be immune. See Bartnicki v. Vopper, 532 U.S. 514 (2001). But the individuals who release the tape are still liable. Of course, a state law tort action, based on public disclosure of private facts, may also be available. See *Restatement (Second) of Torts* § 652C (1977); *Restatement (Third) of the Law of Unfair Competition* § 46 (1993) (nonconsensual appropriation of name of likeness for commercial purposes is actionable).

84. ABA Standard 2-9.1(f)(iv).

85. ABA Standard 2-9.1(f)(v).

86. 18 U.S.C. § 2529(3) (requiring periodic reports of number of surveillance warrants and warrant extensions, types of crimes investigated with surveillance, number of people overheard, arrests generated by surveillance, and so on).

87. See McAdams, Tying Privacy in *Knotts*, 318–19:

> The amendment guarantees the people a right to be "secure," a word that means "free from fear, care, or anxiety: easy in mind . . . having no doubt." Manifestly concerned with the repose of the people, the framers of the Fourth Amendment did not merely create a right of individuals to be free from unreasonable searches or seizures, but a societal right to be free from the fear such practices create.

88. See Quentin Burrows, Scowl Because You're on Candid Camera: Privacy and Video Surveillance, 31 *Valparaiso University Law Review* 1079, 1114–22 (1997) (discussing state constitutional provisions on which regulation of CCTV might be based).

Chapter Six

1. See Eric Lichtblau & Mark Mazzetti, Pentagon, CIA Step Up Spying on Americans, *New York Times*, Jan. 14, 2007, at A1; Leslie Cauley, NSA Has Massive Database of Americans' Phone Calls: 3 Telecoms Help Government Collect Billions of Domestic Records, *USA Today,* May 11, 2006, at 1A; Eric Lictblau & James Risen, Bank Data Sifted in Secret by U.S. to Block Terror, *New York Times*, June 23, 2006, at A1 (describing government attempts to use the databases compiled by the Society for Worldwide Interbank Financial Telecommunications (SWIFT), which routes approximately $6 trillion daily among banks, brokerages, and other institutions); Josh Meyer & Greg Miller, U.S. Secretly Tracks Global Bank Data, *Los Angeles Times*, June 23, 2006, at 1 (noting that the SWIFT data could have been combined with resources from other companies to obtain information about domestic transactions).

2. Although as a formal matter the grand jury normally issues the subpoena, in only a small number of states does the grand jury actually control the subpoena power; in most it is exercised by the prosecutor. 1 Sara Sun Beale et al., *Grand Jury Law and Practice* § 6:2 (2d ed. 2004).

3. See generally 3 Jacob A. Stein, Glenn A. Mitchell & Basil J. Mezines, *Administrative Law* § 21.02 (1977 & Supp. 2002).

4. See 1 Beale et al., *Grand Jury Law and Practice*, § 6:21; 3 Stein, Mitchell & Mezines, *Administrative Law*, 21-4 to 21-6.

5. Wayne R. LaFave, Jerold H. Israel & Nancy J. King, *Criminal Procedure* 437–38 (4th ed. 2004).

6. United States v. R. Enters., Inc., 498 U.S. 292, 301 (1991) (emphasis added). See also LaFave, Israel & King, *Criminal Procedure*, 437 (noting that "courts generally give grand juries considerable leeway in judging relevancy"); id. at 435–36 (describing Supreme Court and lower court case law suggesting that irrelevance, independent of overbreadth, is not a ground for finding a subpoena invalid under the Fourth Amendment).

7. United States v. Morton Salt Co., 338 U.S. 632, 652 (1950).

8. See United States v. Hunton & Williams, 952 F. Supp. 843, 854 (D.D.C. 1995). See also 3 Stein, Mitchell & Mezines, *Administrative Law*, 20-59 (stating that lower courts have held "that subpoenas will be enforced as to any documents that 'are not plainly immaterial or irrelevant to the investigation' " (citing Donovan v. Shaw, 668 F.2d 985, 989 (5th Cir. 1982))).

9. In section 2 of this chapter I provide some details. See also Samuel A. Alito Jr., Documents and the Privilege against Self-Incrimination, 48 *University of Pittsburgh Law Review* 27, 30 (1986) (stating that "subpoenas and summonses for documents have become a staple of investigations regarding every variety of sophisticated criminal activity, from violations of regulatory provisions to political corruption and large-scale drug dealing").

10. Well over a century ago the Supreme Court made clear that police must have a warrant before searching papers seized from an individual without a valid subpoena. Ex parte Jackson, 96 U.S. 727, 732 (1877).

11. See 1 Beale et al., *Grand Jury Law and Practice*, 6-6 to 6-7 ("While . . . suspects may be tempted to destroy evidence when it is called for by a subpoena, there is at least a somewhat greater chance that the evidence will be produced, since the failure to produce the evidence may be punishable by contempt and the destruction of the evidence may constitute obstruction of justice.").

12. SEC v. Jerry T. O'Brien, Inc., 467 U.S. 735, 742–43 (1984). See also Ellen S. Podgor & Jerry H. Israel, *White Collar Crime in a Nutshell* 252, 269 (2004) (noting that generally the target of a subpoena has no standing to contest either grand jury or administrative subpoenas directed at third parties, although also noting that Congress has authorized such standing with respect to subpoenas of bank records, stored electronic communications, and tax records).

13. Lance Cole, The Fifth Amendment and Compelled Production of Personal Documents after *United States v. Hubbell*—New Protection for Private Papers? 29 *American Journal of Criminal Law* 123, 128 (2002) ("Subpoenas are used much more frequently than search warrants").

14. Wertheim v. Continental Ry. & Trust Co., 15 F. 716, 722 (C.C.S.D.N.Y. 1883) ("No trace of the use of this writ [subpoenas *duces tecum*] by the common-law courts of England is to be found in the books earlier than the time of Charles II").

15. King v. Purnell, 96 Eng. Rep. 20 (K.B. 1748) (citing Queen v. Mead, 92 Eng. Rep. 119 (K.B. 1703)); King v. Cornelius, 93 Eng. Rep. 1133 (K.B. 1744)).

16. Chetwind v. Mernell, Exr., 1 Bos. & P. 271 (1798); Rex v. Dixon, 3 Burrow

1687 (1765); Rex v. Cornelius, 2 Strange 1210 (1728); Rex v. Worsenham, 91 Eng. Rep. 1370 (K.B. 1701).

17. Richard A. Nagareda, Compulsion "to Be a Witness" and the Resurrection of *Boyd*, 74 *New York University Law Review* 1575, 1619 n.172 (1999). See also United States v. Three Tons of Coal, 28 F. Cas. 149, 151–52 (D. Wis. 1875) (noting that the English decisions cited in the text "accomplished the permanent overthrow in England, of the right at common law to search for and seize the private papers of the citizen, for the purpose of convictions for crime, or for the purpose of recovery in civil causes, where the evidence when produced would convict of a felony.").

18. United States v. Reyburn, 31 U.S. 352, 363 (1832) ("The privilege of refusing to [produce a document] is one, personal to [the target] himself, of which he may avail himself or not at his pleasure."); Mitchell's Case, 12 Abb. Pr. 249 (N.Y. Sup. Ct. 1861) (holding that neither parties nor their attorneys "could be required to produce documents to be used in evidence, if the production of the paper might materially affect the rights or prejudice the interests of the witness or person to whom it belonged"); Ex parte Maulsby, 13 Md. 625, 639 (1859) (quoting 1 Thomas Starkie, *Practical Treatise on the Law of Evidence,* 86 to the effect that while a person may be compelled to answer questions orally, he is not "compellable" to produce documents "when the production might prejudice his civil rights"); Bull v. Loveland, 27 Mass. 9, 14 (1830) (stating "a witness may be called and examined in a matter pertinent to the issue, where his answers will not expose him to criminal prosecution, or tend to subject him to a penalty or forfeiture," and equating compulsion of a witness to compulsion under a subpoena *duces tecum*); Anonymous, 8 Mass. 370 (1811) (holding that counsel had no duty to deliver his client's papers to the grand jury). See generally McKnight v. United States, 115 F. 972, 980 (6th Cir. 1902) (summarizing nineteenth-century law as holding that "it would be beyond the power of the court to require the accused to criminate himself by the production of the paper as evidence against himself" and reversing a conviction in which the defendant was required to produce a document at trial). However, a number of nineteenth-century federal cases upheld subpoenas for documents relating to taxes and fees. See, e.g., United States v. Hutton, 26 F. Cas. 454 (S.D.N.Y. 1879); United States v. Hughes, 26 F. Cas. 417 (C.C.N.Y. 1875) (No. 15417). See also United States v. Tilden, 28 F. Cas. 174, 177 (S.D.N.Y. 1879) (stating, in a tax case, that "while the law jealously protects private books and papers from unreasonable searches and seizures . . . yet the principle is equally strongly held that parties litigant have the right to have private writings which are competent for proof in their causes produced in evidence," and permitting such production upon "preliminary proof of the necessity").

19. Indeed, the Supreme Court asserted in 1886 that a congressional act passed in 1863 was

> the first act in this country, and, we might say, either in this country or in England, so far as we have been able to ascertain, which authorized the search and seizure of

a man's private papers, or the compulsory production of them, for the purpose of using them in evidence against him in a criminal case.

Boyd v. United States, 116 U.S. 616, 622–23 (1886).

20. See Harry First, *Business Crime* 2 (1990) ("the initial era of federal regulation began with the Interstate Commerce Act of 1887").

21. 116 U.S. 616 (1886).

22. Specifically, Justice Bradley held for the Court that although a suit for a civil penalty was not within the "literal terms" of either amendment, it was "quasi-criminal [in] nature" and thus within their spirit. Id. at 633, 634.

23. Id. at 633.

24. William J. Stuntz, The Substantive Origins of Criminal Procedure, 105 *Yale Law Journal* 393, 428 (1995).

25. 201 U.S. 43 (1906).

26. Id. at 70.

27. Id. at 73 (quoting Summers v. Moseley, 2 Cr. & M. 477, 489 (1834)).

28. Id. at 77, 76.

29. 264 U.S. 298, 306 (1924).

30. Id. at 305–6.

31. See, e.g., Jones v. SEC, 298 U.S. 1, 27 (1936) ("An investigation not based upon specified grounds is quite as objectionable as a search warrant not based upon specific statements of fact."). See also FTC v. Smith, 34 F.2d 323, 324–25 (S.D.N.Y. 1929) (requiring probable cause before a subpoena could be enforced); FTC v. P. Lorillard Co., 283 F. 999, 1006 (S.D.N.Y. 1922), aff'd on other grounds sub nom. FTC v. American Tobacco Co., 264 U.S. 298 (1924).

32. 327 U.S. 186, 208 (1946).

33. Id. at 195 (stating that "the records in these cases present no question of actual search and seizure, but raise only the question whether orders of court for the production of specified records have been validly made").

34. 338 U.S. 632, 652 (1950).

35. Id.

36. 379 U.S. 48, 57–58 (1964).

37. See, e.g., United States v. Hunton & Williams, 952 F. Supp. 843, 854 n.28 (D.D.C. 1997) (noting that the *Powell* inquiry is more deferential than the "arbitrary and capricious" standard of review for agency action under the Administrative Procedure Act). See also United States v. LaSalle Nat'l Bank, 437 U.S. 298, 316 (1978) (holding that bad faith on the part of an individual bureaucrat is insufficient to invalidate an administrative subpoena under *Powell*). *LaSalle* also held that an administrative summons may not be used as a criminal discovery device in tax cases. 437 U.S. at 318. This holding is now codified at 26 U.S.C. § 7602(d). Of course, at that point the grand jury continues the investigation, so the standard for issuing a subpoena does not change substantially.

A very small minority of federal courts have purported to require a greater evidentiary showing before issuing a subpoena, but, if that is so, the showing is only minimally different. The case most frequently cited for this proposition is In re Grand Jury Proceedings (Schofield), 486 F.2d 85 (3d Cir. 1973), which required the government to make "some preliminary showing by affidavit that each item requested [is] at least relevant to an investigation being conducted by the grand jury and properly within its jurisdiction and not sought primarily for another purpose." 486 F.2d at 93.

38. 201 U.S. at 43.

39. Id. at 74.

40. See, e.g., Wheeler v. United States, 226 U.S. 478, 490 (1913) ("It was the character of the books and papers as corporate records and documents which justified the court in ordering their production."); Wilson v. United States, 221 U.S. 361, 377 (1911) ("Undoubtedly [the privilege against self-incrimination] also protected him against the compulsory production of his private books and papers."); Linn v. United States, 251 F. 476, 480 (2d Cir. 1918) ("While a person is privileged from producing his books in a prosecution against himself, a corporation is not privileged from producing its papers and books, even though they incriminate the officer who produces them."); Flagg v. United States, 233 F. 481, 484 (2d Cir. 1916) (holding invalid a subpoena for personal books and papers); Hillman v. United States, 192 F. 264, 266 (9th Cir. 1911) ("It will be observed that in the plea there is no distinct averment that any of the books or papers so taken upon the subpoena *duces tecum* were the private books or papers of the plaintiff in error."); United States v. Hart, 214 F. 655, 661 (N.D.N.Y. 1914) ("Hart could not have been compelled to produce these [private] papers and documents by subpoena *duces tecum* without gaining immunity for himself.").

41. 327 U.S. at 208. See also United States v. Bausch & Lomb Optical Co., 321 U.S. 707, 726 (1944) ("The Fifth Amendment does not protect a corporation against self-incrimination through compulsory production of its papers, although it does protect an individual.").

42. 338 U.S. at 652.

43. 381 U.S. 479, 484 (1965) ("The Fifth Amendment in its Self-Incrimination Clause enables the citizen to create a zone of privacy which government may not force him to surrender to his detriment.").

44. In the search warrant context, by contrast, the Court for a time relied on a combination of the Fourth and Fifth Amendments to prohibit seizure of private papers, under the so-called mere evidence doctrine. Gouled v. United States, 255 U.S. 298, 309 (1921) (citing *Boyd,* 116 U.S. 616, in holding that search warrants "may not be used as a means of gaining access to a man's house or office and papers solely for the purpose of making search to secure evidence to be used against him in a criminal or penal proceeding"). This doctrine is tangential to the subject of this book, which focuses on subpoenas, and in any event has also since been

emasculated. See, e.g., Zurcher v. Stanford Daily, 436 U.S. 547, 558 (1978) ("Once it is established that probable cause exists to believe a federal crime has been committed a warrant may issue for the search of any property which the magistrate has probable cause to believe may be the place of concealment of evidence of the crime."); Warden v. Hayden, 387 U.S. 294, 301 (1967) ("Nothing in the language of the Fourth Amendment supports the distinction between 'mere evidence' and instrumentalities, fruits of crime, or contraband."). It is also worth emphasizing that the doctrine was based more on the Fifth Amendment than the Fourth. See *Gouled*, 255 U.S. at 306 (stating that whether private papers are seized from a person via a warrant or a subpoena, "in either case he is the unwilling source of the evidence, and the Fifth Amendment forbids that he shall be compelled to be a witness against himself in a criminal case").

45. 379 U.S. 61 (1964).

46. Id. at 62.

47. 379 U.S. at 52–56.

48. The petitioner argued, among other things, that the IRS needed probable cause to obtain his records. 379 U.S. at 62. However, the petitioner did not make an explicit Fourth Amendment argument, relying instead on statutory language.

49. 410 U.S. 1 (1973).

50. Id. at 11.

51. 409 U.S. 322 (1973).

52. Id. at 335–36.

53. 425 U.S. 391 (1976).

54. Id. at 409–10. *Fisher* involved compulsion of documents from the defendant's accountant, but *Fisher*'s reasoning clearly applied to compulsion of documents from the defendant himself, as the Court later made clear in United States v. Doe, 465 U.S. 605 (1984).

55. For example, in most tax cases "the existence and location of the papers are a foregone conclusion and the taxpayer adds little or nothing to the sum total of the Government's information by conceding that he in fact has the papers." *Fisher*, 425 U.S. at 411.

56. Id. at 401.

57. *Doe*, 465 U.S. at 618 (O'Connor, J., concurring).

58. 487 U.S. 99 (1988).

59. Id. at 118 n.11.

60. 530 U.S. 27 (2000).

61. Id. at 42.

62. William J. Stuntz, O. J. Simpson, Bill Clinton, and the Transsubstantive Fourth Amendment, 114 *Harvard Law Review* 842, 865 (2001).

63. See LaFave, Israel & King, *Criminal Procedure*, 39 (4th ed. Supp. 2005) (noting that many subpoenas provide enough information about the documents sought that the target need not use the "contents" of his mind to identify them, and

stating that "there is nothing in *Hubbell*'s discussion of the foregone conclusion doctrine that mandates . . . a conclusive showing on the temporal components of existence and possession").

64. Johnson v. United States, 228 U.S. 457, 458 (1913).

65. Rex v. Dixon, 97 Eng. Rep. 1047 (K.B. 1765) (holding that an attorney need not turn over a client's papers in connection with a forgery prosecution).

66. 425 U.S. at 405 (stating that "the papers, if unobtainable by summons from the client, are unobtainable by summons directed to the attorney by reason of the attorney-client privilege").

67. Later in this chapter I discuss and for the most part dismiss the argument that the First Amendment might provide meaningful protection for most papers.

68. 409 U.S. at 335.

69. 425 U.S. 435 (1976).

70. The Court cited Hoffa v. United States, 385 U.S. 293 (1966) (holding that government use of an acquaintance as an informant is not a search), and Lopez v. United States, 373 U.S. 427 (1963) (holding that the use of a body bug on an informant is not a search). It also could have cited United States v. White, 401 U.S. 745 (1971) (holding, post-*Katz*, that the use of a body bug on an informant is not a search); Lewis v. United States, 385 U.S. 206 (1966) (holding that an undercover agent invited into a house is not conducting a search).

71. 425 U.S. at 443.

72. Id. at 438 (describing the information obtained as including "all checks, deposit slips, two financial statements, and three monthly statements").

73. Id. at 443.

74. Cf. California Bankers Ass'n v. Shultz, 416 U.S. 21 (1974) (holding that the Fourth Amendment does not protect negotiable instruments held by banks, which are exposed to numerous individuals and thus are arguably less private than the type of monthly statements involved in *Miller*).

75. 442 U.S. 735 (1979).

76. 447 U.S. 727 (1980).

77. Webb v. Goldstein, 117 F. Supp. 2d 289 (E.D.N.Y. 2000); State v. Guido, 698 A.2d 729 (R.I. 1997); Corpus v. State, 931 S.W.2d 30 (Tex. App. 1996). See 1 Wayne R. LaFave, *Search and Seizure: A Treatise on the Fourth Amendment* 754–57 (4th ed. 2004) (citing various cases).

78. Wang v. United States, 947 F.2d 1400, 1403 (9th Cir. 1991); Kinney v. United States, No. 96-550, 1995 WL 813170 (M.D. Fla. Feb. 1, 1996).

79. In re Lufkin, 255 B.R. 204, 211 (Bankr. E.D. Tenn. 2000).

80. Doe v. DiGenova, 642 F. Supp. 624 (D.D.C. 1986) (V.A. records); People v. Carpenter, 998 P.2d 531 (Cal. 1999) (prison and parole records).

81. Guest v. Leis, 255 F.3d 325, 336 (6th Cir. 2001) (holding that "plaintiffs . . . lack a Fourth Amendment privacy interest in their subscriber information because they communicated it to the systems operators"); United States v. Kennedy, 81 F.

Supp. 2d 1103, 1110 (D. Kan. 2000) (holding that defendant could not "claim to have a Fourth Amendment privacy interest in his subscriber information" because "when defendant entered into an agreement with Road Runner for Internet service, he knowingly revealed" the information to his ISP).

82. Daniel J. Solove, Access and Aggregation: Public Records, Privacy and the Constitution, 86 *Minnesota Law Review* 1137, 1142 (2002) ("Public record-keeping is largely a product of the twentieth century.").

83. Thomas A. Stewart & Jane Furth, The Information Age in Charts, *Fortune*, Apr. 4, 1994, at 75 (asserting that 1991 signified the definitive end of the Industrial Age and the beginning of the Information Age, because in that year business expenditures on computers and communications for the first time exceeded the amount spent on industrial, agricultural, and construction machinery).

84. 201 U.S. at 80 (McKenna, J., concurring).

85. 327 U.S. at 202.

86. The exception to this rule arises when the challenger, although not a party to the intercepted conversation, owns the house in which the conversation takes place. See Alderman v. United States, 394 U.S. 165, 176 (1969).

87. United States v. Miller, 425 U.S. 435, 451 (1976) (Brennan, J., dissenting) (stating that "the disclosure by individuals or business firms of their financial affairs to a bank is not entirely volitional, since it is impossible to participate in the economic life of contemporary society without maintaining a bank account"); LaFave, Israel & King, *Criminal Procedure*, 139.

88. Christopher Slobogin & Joseph E. Schumacher, Reasonable Expectations of Privacy and Autonomy in Fourth Amendment Cases: An Empirical Look at "Understandings Recognized and Permitted by Society," 42 *Duke Law Journal* 727, 738 (1993).

89. Burrows v. Superior Court, 529 P.2d 590 (Cal. 1974); Charnes v. DiGiacomo, 612 P.2d 1117 (Colo. 1980); Commonwealth v. DeJohn, 403 A.2d 1283, 1291 (Pa. 1979).

90. King v. State, 535 S.E.2d 432, 495 (Ga. 2000); Thurman v. State, 861 S.W.2d 96, 98 (Tex. Ct. App. 1993). See also Doe v. Broderick, 225 F.3d 440, 450–51 (4th Cir. 2000) (finding *Miller* inapplicable to medical records). See generally Stephen E. Henderson, Learning from All Fifty States: How to Apply the Fourth Amendment and Its State Analogs to Protect Third Party Information from Unreasonable Search, 55 *Catholic University Law Review* 373, 413 (2006) ("eleven states reject the federal third-party doctrine and ten others have given some reason to believe they might reject it, for a total of twenty-one states.").

91. See, e.g., David Lazarus, Personal Information Isn't That Confidential: Experts Weigh in on AT&T's Assertion That It Owns Your Data, *San Francisco Chronicle*, June 23, 2006, at D1 (describing an AT&T policy that states, "While your account information may be personal to you these records constitute business records that are owned by AT&T."). It should also be noted that in Perlman v.

United States, 247 U.S. 7, 15 (1918), the Court held that even continued ownership of property does not confer a constitutional interest in property that has been surrendered to a third party.

92. Eugene Volokh, Freedom of Speech and Information Privacy: The Troubling Implications of a Right to Stop People from Speaking about You, 52 *Stanford Law Review* 1049, 1080–84 (2000). See also U.S. West, Inc. v. FCC, 182 F.3d 1224 (10th Cir. 1999) (overturning, on First Amendment grounds, Federal Communications Commission regulations requiring customer approval of use of personal information for marketing).

93. 5 U.S.C. § 552a(d) (entitling an individual to a copy of his or her record and "any information pertaining to him which is contained in the system," and providing a procedure in contested cases, ultimately involving judicial review, for amending the record).

94. 5 U.S.C. § 552(b)(6) (prohibiting disclosure of "personnel and medical files, and similar files the disclosure of which would constitute a clearly unwarranted invasion of personal privacy"); 5 U.S.C. § 552(b)(7) (prohibiting disclosure of law enforcement records that "could reasonably be expected to constitute an unwarranted invasion of personal privacy").

95. Jerry L. Mashaw, "Rights" in the Federal Administrative State, 92 *Yale Law Journal* 1129, 1137 (1983) ("The Freedom of Information Act and the Privacy Act gave all citizens 'property rights' in the information held by government bureaus."). See also Julie E. Cohen, Examined Lives: Informational Privacy and the Subject as Object, 52 *Stanford Law Review* 1373, 1436 (2000) ("Personally-identified data is neither unambiguously data processors' property nor simply their speech").

96. See, e.g., 45 C.F.R. § 164.524 (providing individuals a right to copy and inspect their otherwise private health information under the Health Insurance Portability and Accountability Act of 1996); Fair Credit Reporting Act, 15 U.S.C. §§ 1681g–i (providing individuals a right to access their credit reports and insist upon corrections); Family Educational Rights and Privacy Act, 20 U.S.C. § 1232q(a)(b) (requiring schools to provide parental access to student records and permitting parents to challenge the records if they are misleading, inaccurate, or violate the student's privacy). No analogous statute for bank records exists, presumably because the customer either generates the records (e.g., through checks) or receives a detailed periodic statement describing the information possessed by the bank, the latter of which can be corrected by the customer.

97. See *King*, 535 S.E.2d at 495 ("Even if the medical provider is the technical 'owner' of the actual records, the patient nevertheless has a reasonable expectation of privacy in the information contained therein, since that data reflects the physical state of his or her body."). An even stronger statement of this idea (perhaps too strong) is found in international laws and the laws of other countries. Consider, for instance, the United Nations Guidelines for the Regulation of Computerized Personal Files, G.A. Res. 45/95, U.N. GAOR, adopted Dec. 14, 1990, as General

Assembly Resolution 45/95. Under "Principle of the Purpose-Specification," the Guidelines state:

> The purpose which a file is to serve and its utilization in terms of that purpose should be specified, legitimate and, when it is established, receive a certain amount of publicity or be brought to the attention of the person concerned, in order to make it possible subsequently to ensure that: . . . (b) None of the said personal data is used or disclosed, except with the consent of the person concerned, for purposes incompatible with those specified.

See Marc Rotenberg, *The Privacy Law Sourcebook 2003: United States Law, International Law, and Recent Developments* 368 (2003).

98. Daniel J. Solove, *The Digital Person: Technology and Privacy in the Information Age* 81–91 (2004).

99. Id. at 91. See also John Schwartz, Privacy Policy Notices Are Called Too Common and Too Confusing, *New York Times*, May 17, 2000, at B1.

100. Cf. State ex rel. Pollard v. Criminal Court, 329 N.E.2d 573, 585 (1975) ("[A] witness, subpoenaed to produce his records to a grand jury . . . may not assert his fourth amendment expectation of privacy in such records"; like a witness subpoenaed to testify, he has "no right to privacy . . . and may not decline to answer on the grounds that his responses might prove embarrassing or result in an unwelcome disclosure of his personal affairs.") (quoting United States v. Calandra, 414 U.S. 338, 353 (1974)).

101. Mary Irene Coombs, Shared Privacy and the Fourth Amendment, or The Rights of Relationships, 75 *California Law Review* 1593, 1643 (1987).

102. Id. at 1644.

103. *Hale*, 201 U.S. at 70 ("The amendment is limited to a person who shall be compelled in any criminal case to be a witness against himself, and if he cannot set up the privilege of a third person, he certainly cannot set up the privilege of a corporation.").

104. See, e.g., James J. Tomkovicz, Beyond Secrecy for Secrecy's Sake: Toward an Expanded Vision of the Fourth Amendment Privacy Province, 36 *Hastings Law Journal* 645, 728 (1985) (describing the logic of the "false friend" cases as "fundamentally defective and exceedingly dangerous to liberty"). I have made similar arguments, at least when the false friend is a person who has been importuned by the government to be an informant rather than, as discussed in the text, one who makes contact with the police after the legally relevant event occurs. See Christopher Slobogin, The World without a Fourth Amendment, 39 *UCLA Law Review* 1, 103–6 (1991).

105. *Dionisio,* 410 U.S. at 9–10. See also Blackmer v. United States, 284 U.S. 421, 438 (1932) ("One of the duties which the citizen owes to his government is to support the administration of justice by . . . giving his testimony whenever he is properly summoned."); Blair v. United States, 250 U.S. 273, 281 (1919) ("The

personal sacrifice [associated with giving testimony to a grand jury] is a part of the necessary contribution of the individual to the welfare of the public.").

106. LaFave, Israel & King, *Criminal Procedure*, 431.

107. See Solove, *The Digital Person*, 103 ("The law should hold that companies collecting and using our personal information stand in a fiduciary relationship with us.").

108. Compare Shibley v. Time, Inc., 341 N.E.2d 337 (Ohio Ct. App. 1975) (dismissing the claim that Time's distribution of names and addresses to a direct marketing company violated its readers' privacy), with Weld v. CVS Pharmacy, No. Civ. A 98-0897F, 1999 WL 494114, at 5 (Mass. Super. Ct. June 29, 1999) (denying summary judgment for CVS against claims that its use of prescription information to support a direct mail campaign violated statutory right to privacy, unfair practices law, confidentiality and fiduciary duties, and the tort of misappropriation of private personal information). Falling between these two cases is Dwyer v. American Express Co., 652 N.E.2d 1351 (Ill. App. Ct. 1995) (dismissing the claim that American Express's rental of customer spending histories stated an intrusion into privacy claim but holding that American Express did violate a deceptive practice law).

109. Tom Zeller Jr., Qwest Goes from the Goat to the Hero, *New York Times*, May 15, 2006, at C5 (compared to AT&T, Verizon and BellSouth, which allegedly gave NSA phone records, Qwest, which refused to do so, is seen favorably by customers). See also Jessica Litman, Information Privacy/Information Property, 52 *Stanford Law Review* 1283, 1305–7 (2000) (detailing examples of businesses bowing to pressure to stop using personal data for marketing purposes and noting that "[n]one of the businesses caught misusing customer data responded by suggesting that nobody really expected her data to be private in today's world").

110. 322 U.S. 694, 700 (1944).

111. 65 F.3d 207 (1st Cir. 1995). The opinion was later withdrawn from the Federal Reporter after a rehearing en banc was granted. See 49 *Administrative Law Review* 519, 547 n.266 (citing In re Gimbel, 77 F.3d 593 (2d Cir. 1996)).

112. Parks v. FDIC, No. 94-2262, 1995 WL 529629, at *11 (1st Cir. Sept. 13, 1995) (Selya, J., dissenting).

113. Branzburg v. Hayes, 408 U.S. 665, 688 (1972) (citing United States v. Bryan, 339 U.S. 323, 331 (1950)); *Blackmer*, 284 U.S. at 438 (1932); *Blair*, 250 U.S. at 281.

114. See LaFave, Israel & King, *Criminal Procedure,* 409 (describing the "public watchdog" function of the grand jury during the eighteenth and nineteenth centuries).

115. See, e.g., *Branzburg*, 408 U.S. at 689–90.

116. 410 U.S. at 10.

117. In the Matter of a Grand Jury Investigation, 692 N.E.2d 56, 59 (Mass. 1998).

118. I think survival would be likely. Before *Ryan,* the Supreme Court case that rejected a probable cause requirement in the tax context, some courts had required probable cause in order to obtain tax records. See, e.g., Lash v. Nighosian,

273 F.2d 185 (1st Cir. 1959). In *Ryan* itself, the IRS likely had probable cause ("The complaint alleged that on the basis of estimated net worth calculations the agent strongly suspected fraud"). The IRS usually selects tax return audits based on "mathematical formulas developed from intensive examination of returns selected at random to identify those with a high probability of error." Boris I. Bittker, Martin J. McMahon Jr. & Lawrence A. Zelenak, *Federal Income Taxation of Individuals* 47–3 (3d ed. 2002). Audits are also triggered by identification of items that do not appear allowable, complaints by former employees, former spouses and acquaintances, and conspicuous tax protests. Id. But assuming I am wrong about this, I would carve out a narrow exception for tax records under the "required records" doctrine described in section 3 of this chapter.

119. Chris Jay Hoofnagle, Big Brother's Little Helpers: How ChoicePoint and Other Commercial Data Brokers Collect and Package Your Data for Law Enforcement, 29 *North Carolina Journal of International Law & Commercial Regulation* 595, 621 (2004) (quoting one ISP official to the effect that government requests for information have "increased fivefold" since September 11, 2001).

120. 15 U.S.C. §§ 1311–1314 (antitrust); 5 U.S.C. App. §§ 3, 6(a)(4) (fraud); 18 U.S.C. § 3486(a)(1)(A)(i)(II), (a)(1)(C) (limiting access to e-mail subscriber information connected with sexual exploitation and abuse of children); 31 U.S.C. § 3733 (false claims and bribery); 21 U.S.C. § 876(a) (possession of controlled substances).

121. U.S. Dep't of Justice, Report to Congress on the Use of Administrative Subpoena Authorities by Executive Branch Agencies and Entities 37 (2002). Information about the number of DOJ subpoenas issued in connection with false claims, bribery, racketeering, and controlled substance investigations is not available.

122. See 1 Beale et al., *Grand Jury Law and Practice*, 6-3 (noting that "ordinarily, investigations of so-called 'street crime' such as murder, rape, robbery, and assault can be conducted effectively without resort to the subpoena power"). Even in business investigations, this is often the case. See, e.g., United States v. Goldfine, 538 F.2d 815, 818–19 (9th Cir. 1976) (noting that an agency carrying out an administrative inspection had developed probable cause to believe that pharmacists were violating the Comprehensive Drug Prevention and Control Act, based on reports of large shipments of controlled substances to the pharmacy, tracing of certain shipments, surveillance of the pharmacy, and the arrest of some of the pharmacy's customers). If, as I argue in chapter 7, the government need merely meet the relevance standard in order to obtain truly public records and engage in most types of data mining (for instance, to determine who traveled to the residence of a murder victim on the day of the murder), there is even less reason to relax the standard applicable to more intrusive transaction surveillance.

123. On the difficulty of proving corporate crime, see Stacey Neumann Vu, Corporate Criminal Liability: Patchwork Verdicts and the Problem of Locating a Guilty Agent, 104 *Columbia Law Review* 459, 467–68 (2004) (noting that corporate crime is difficult to solve because victims "are typically unaware of their injury" and it "is

challenging to identify within an organization a particular guilty actor."); Francis Cullen, William J. Maakestad & Gray Cavender, *Corporate Crime under Attack* 350 (1987) ("the labyrinthian structure of many modern corporations often makes it extremely difficult to pinpoint individual responsibility for specific decisions").

124. 116 U.S. at 631–32 (stating that "any compulsory discovery by extorting the party's oath, or compelling the production of his private books and papers, to convict him of crime, or to forfeit his property, is contrary to the principles of a free government").

125. 201 U.S. at 74–75.

126. See Charles H. Whitebread & Christopher Slobogin, *Criminal Procedure: An Analysis of Cases and Concepts* 392 (4th ed. 2000) (discussing the collective entity doctrine).

127. 221 U.S. 361, 378, 382 (1911).

128. 322 U.S. 694, 702 (1944).

129. 417 U.S. 85 (1974).

130. Id. at 95, 94, 92.

131. 465 U.S. 605 (1984).

132. Currently, the most heavily litigated issue in this context is whether an employee's personal writings, such as pocket calendars, are corporate records. See, e.g., United States v. Stone, 976 F.2d 909 (4th Cir. 1992).

133. In re Sealed Case, 950 F.2d 736 (D.C. Cir. 1991).

134. 335 U.S. 1 (1948).

135. Id. at 32.

136. 390 U.S. 62, 67–68 (1968).

137. 1 Beale et al., *Grand Jury Law and Practice*, 6-112. Even medical records might be "required" when they are sought for the purpose of monitoring medical practice. See, e.g., In re Kenney, 715 F.2d 51, 53 (2d Cir. 1983) (involving patients' x-rays and medical records).

138. See, e.g., United States v. Biswell, 406 U.S. 311, 316 (1972) ("When a dealer chooses to engage in this pervasively regulated business and to accept a federal license, he does so with the knowledge that his business records, firearms, and ammunition will be subject to effective inspection.").

139. See Daniel Solove, The First Amendment as Criminal Procedure, 82 *New York University Law Review* 112, 116 (2007) ("I contend that there are doctrinal, historical, and normative foundations for the First Amendment to play a significant role in regulating government information gathering").

140. Central Hudson Gas & Elec. Corp. v. Public Serv. Comm'n of N.Y., 447 U.S. 557, 566 (1980).

141. See Robert Post, The Constitutional Status of Commercial Speech, 48 *UCLA Law Review* 1, 34–53 (2000).

142. See, e.g., Nike v. Kasky, 539 U.S. 654 (2003), where Nike argued that the First Amendment prevented sanctions for making false statements about its overseas

labor policies because the statements contributed to the ongoing debate about international labor practices.

143. Note, The Rights of Criminal Defendants and the Subpoena *Duces Tecum:* the Aftermath of *Fisher v. United States*, 95 *Harvard Law Review* 683, 702 (1982) (arguing that "the First Amendment can prevent the government from probing into a defendant's most personal papers"); Anne Wells Branscomb, Anonymity, Autonomy, and Accountability: Challenges to the First Amendment in Cyberspaces, 104 *Yale Law Journal* 1639 (1995) (noting that the First Amendment might provide protection for records necessary to carry out speech, such as records identifying e-mail users who use pseudonyms).

Chapter Seven

1. Walter Pincus, Protesters Found in Database, *Washington Post*, Jan. 27, 2007, at A8. In April 2007, the Pentagon stated it was contemplating terminating TALON, mostly because the program had proven ineffective, but also because, as a Pentagon spokesperson put it, because of "its image in Congress and the media." William Fisher, Pentagon Backtracks as Advocacy Groups Blast Ethnic Profiling, April 28, 2007, available at http://www.truthout.org./docs_2006/042807A.shtml.

2. Eric Lichtblau & Mark Mazzetti, Military Expands Intelligence Role in U.S., *New York Times*, Jan. 14, 2007, at 1.

3. Dalia Naamani-Goldman, Anti-terrorism Program Mines IRS' Records, *Los Angeles Times*, Jan. 15, 2007, at C1.

4. Michael J. Sniffen, Terror Ratings Are Applied to Travelers, *Associated Press*, Dec. 7, 2006, available at http://findarticles.com/p/articles/mi_qn4188/is_20061201/ai_n16908886.

5. Ellen Nakashima & Alec Klein, U.S. Tests Data Sweep in Bid to Net Terrorists, *Washington Post*, Mar. 1, 2007, at B1.

6. Declan McCullagh, Justice Department Takes Aim at Image-Sharing Sites, *CNET News*, Mar. 2, 2007, available at http://news.com.com/2102-1028_3-6163679.html?tag=st.util.print.

7. David Johnston & Eric Lipton, U.S. Report to Fault FBI on Subpoenas, *New York Times*, Mar. 9, 2007, at 1.

8. 442 U.S. 735 (1979).

9. Id. at 744 ("petitioner voluntarily conveyed numerical information to the telephone company and 'exposed' that information to its equipment in the ordinary course of business [thereby] assum[ing] the risk that the company would reveal to police the numbers he dialed").

10. Cf. Thygeson v. U.S. Bancroft, 2004 WL 2066746, at *22 (D. Or. Sept. 15, 2004) ("when the information defendants collected was only the website addresses, rather than the actual content of the websites Thygeson visited, [the] surveillance. . . .

is analogous to a pen registry search, where in the Fourth Amendment context, courts have held that defendants have no reasonable expectation of privacy in the telephone numbers they dial because the numbers are conveyed to the telephone company."); United States v. Kennedy, 81 F. Supp. 2d 1103, 1110 (D. Kan. 2000) ("When defendant entered into an agreement with Road Runner for Internet service, he knowingly revealed all information connected to the IP address"). Billing records of ISPs may also be unprotected by the Fourth Amendment. United States v. Hambrick, 225 F.3d 656 (4th Cir. 2000) (unpublished opinion) (holding that a person does not have a reasonable expectation of privacy "in the account information given to the ISP in order to establish the e-mail account," because it is "non-content information" disclosure of which "to a third party destroys the privacy expectation that might have existed previously."); Freedman v. America Online, Inc., 412 F. Supp. 2d 174 (D. Conn. 2005) (accord); State v. Kaufman, 130 Wash. App. 1009, 2005 WL 2746676 (Oct. 25, 2005) (accord). Indeed, some courts have held that the *content* of e-mails, once they are opened, deserve no Fourth Amendment protection because one assumes the risk the recipient will reveal it to others. United States v. Charbonneau, 979 F. Supp. 1177, 1184 (S.D. Ohio 1997); Smyth v. Pillsbury, 914 F. Supp. 97, 101 (E.D. Pa. 1996); United States v. Maxwell, 45 M.J. 406, 417–18 (C.A.A.F. 1996). But see Warshak v. United States, 2007 WL 1730094 (6th Cir. June 18, 2007).

11. 18 U.S.C. § 3123(a)(1).

12. United States v. Fregoso, 60 F.3d 1314, 1320 (8th Cir. 1995) (the "judicial role in approving use of trap and trace devices is ministerial in nature.").

13. 18 U.S.C. § 3121(c).

14. See Richard Van Duizend, L. Paul Sutton & Charlotte A. Carter, *The Search Warrant Process: Preconceptions, Perceptions and Practices* 47–48 (1985) (describing study of warrant process indicating varying degrees of judicial rubber-stamping across jurisdictions).

15. See, e.g., Connally v. Georgia, 429 U.S. 245 (1977) (state may not pay magistrate based on number of warrants issued); Coolidge v. New Hampshire, 403 U.S. 443 (1971) (prosecutor may not issue warrant); Lo-Ji Sales, Inc. v. New York, 442 U.S. 319 (1979) (magistrate who accompanies police to site of search insufficiently neutral).

16. See 5 U.S.C. § 552a(b) (stating that "[n]o agency shall disclose any record which is contained in a system of records," but going on to list twelve exceptions under which disclosure is permitted).

17. 5 U.S.C. § 552a(b)(7) (permitting disclosure "to another agency or to an instrumentality of any governmental jurisdiction within or under the control of the United States for a civil or criminal law enforcement activity if the activity is authorized by law, and if the head of the agency or instrumentality has made a written request to the agency which maintains the record specifying the particular portion desired and the law enforcement activity for which the record is sought").

18. See Paul M. Schwartz, Privacy and Participation: Personal Information and Public Sector Regulation in the United States, 80 *Iowa Law Review* 553, 595–97

(1995) (most states lack "omnibus data protection laws" and instead have "scattered laws [that] provide only limited protections for personal information in the public sector.").

19. 5 U.S.C. § 552a(m).

20. See Chris Jay Hoofnagle, Big Brother's Little Helpers: How ChoicePoint and Other Commercial Data Brokers Collect and Package Your Data for Law Enforcement, 29 *North Carolina Journal of International & Commercial Regulation* 595, 623 (2004) ("a database of information that originates at a CDB would not trigger the requirements of the Privacy Act [and thus would allow CDBs] to amass huge databases that the government is legally prohibited from creating.").

21. Cf. Ferguson v. City of Charleston, 532 U.S. 67, 78 (2001) ("The reasonable expectation of privacy enjoyed by the typical patient undergoing diagnostic tests in a hospital is that the results of those tests will not be shared with nonmedical personnel without her consent."); Whalen v. Roe, 429 U.S. 589, 605 (1977) (recognizing, in a case involving disclosure of medical information, that a "statutory or regulatory duty to avoid unwarranted disclosures . . . in some circumstances . . . arguably has its roots in the Constitution").

22. 45 C.F.R. § 164.512(f)(1)(ii)(B) (disclosure of medical records under HIPAA is permissible without permission of the subject if information is sought for law enforcement purposes through a grand jury subpoena). Some courts have required a greater showing to obtain medical records. See, e.g., Doe v. Broderick, 225 F.3d 440, 450–51 (4th Cir. 2000) (finding *Miller* inapplicable to medical records); Hawaii Psychiatric Soc'y v. Ariyoshi, 481 F. Supp. 1028 (D. Haw. 1979); King v. State, 535 S.E.2d 432, 495 (Ga. 2000); Thurman v. State, 861 S.W.2d 96, 98 (Tex. App. 1993).

23. 15 U.S.C. § 1681b(a)(1). Name, addresses, and places of employment can be obtained upon request. 15 U.S.C. § 1681f.

24. Daniel J. Solove, Digital Dossiers and the Dissipation of Fourth Amendment Privacy, 75 *Southern California Law Review* 1083, 1146 (2002).

25. Chris Hoofnagle has made the argument that this ability to obtain information through a private agency circumvents the Privacy Act, which prohibits government from collecting such information unless there is a specific need for it. Hoofnagle, Big Brother's Little Helpers, 18.

26. 12 U.S.C. § 3409. Furthermore, when subpoena power is not available, the government need only submit a formal written request for the information (in other words, "extrajudicial certification" is sufficient). 12 U.S.C. § 3408. Indeed, apparently banks still occasionally hand over information upon request. See David F. Linowes, *Privacy in America: Is Your Private Life in the Public Eye?* 106–8 (1989) (describing a number of cases in which banks surrendered account information to law enforcement officers upon request and describing a survey finding that 74 percent of banks did not inform customers of their routine disclosures to law enforcement).

27. Ellen S. Podgor & Jerold H. Israel, *White Collar Crime in a Nutshell* 269 (2004).

28. 18 U.S.C. § 2518(3).

29. 18 U.S.C. § 2703(a), (b)(1)(B). Further, a subpoena is required only when the information is sought from a "remote computing service" (e.g., a service available to the general public, like AOL). If the information is stored with a private service (e.g., one run by an employer), then ECPA does not apply *at all* and government may obtain the stored information (content or identifying) upon request. See 18 U.S.C. § 2703(a) and (b). See also 18 U.S.C. § 2711(2) (defining remote computing service); U.S. Dep't of Justice, *Searching and Seizing Computers and Obtaining Electronic Evidence in Criminal Investigations* 89 (July 2002). But see *Warshak*, 2007 WL 1730094 at *13 (requiring a warrant for stored e-mail).

30. See Patricia L. Bellia, Surveillance Law through Cyberlaw's Lens, 72 *George Washington Law Review* 1375, 1421 (2004).

31. See Clifford S. Fishman & Anne T. McKenna, *Wiretapping and Eavesdropping* § 26:9 (2d ed. 1995) (in the view of Congress, when an e-mail message stays on a server longer than 180 days, the service provider is less like a post office and more like a storage facility).

32. 18 U.S.C. § 2703(c)(1)(E) (describing information that can be obtained); 18 U.S.C. § 2703(c)(3) ("A governmental entity receiving records or information under this subsection is not required to provide notice to a subscriber or customer.").

33. 18 U.S.C. § 2703(c)(d) (describing requirements for a court order to obtain "records concerning electronic communication service or remote computing service"). Note that most courts have held that companies that acquire clickstream data about where a Internet user goes on the Internet do not violate ECPA because the Web sites visited by the user have authorized the companies to access this information. See In re DoubleClick, Inc. Privacy Litig., 154 F. Supp. 2d 497, 526 (S.D.N.Y. 2001); Chance v. Ave. A, Inc., 165 F. Supp. 2d 1153, 1163 (W.D. Wash. 2001); In re Toys R Us, Inc., Privacy Litig., 2001 U.S. Dist. LEXIS 16947, at *28 (N.D. Cal. Oct. 9, 2001). An argument could be made, analogous to the government's argument with respect to records obtained from commercial data brokers, that government should be able to obtain this information simply by asking for it. But ECPA probably requires a subpoena. See, e.g., United States v. Steiger, 318 F.3d 1039, 1050 (11th Cir. 2003).

34. Charles Tilford McCormick, *McCormick on Evidence* 541–42 (3d ed. 1984) ("Materiality looks to the relation between the propositions for which the evidence is offered and the issues in the case. . . . A fact that is 'of consequence' is material. . . . It is enough if the item could reasonably show that a fact is slightly more probable than it would appear without that evidence.").

35. 18 U.S.C. § 2703(d) (providing court may quash or modify order if the request is "unusually voluminous in nature or compliance with such order otherwise would cause an undue burden on such provider.").

36. 50 U.S.C. § 1861.

37. 50 U.S.C. § 1861(a)(3) (2006).

38. 50 U.S.C. § 1861(b)(2)(A).

39. 50 U.S.C. § 1861(g).

40. 50 U.S.C. § 1861(f)(2)(B).

41. Id. (a judge may grant a petition challenging the order "only if the judge finds that such order does not meet the requirements of this section or is otherwise unlawful").

42. 50 U.S.C. § 1861(a)(1). See generally Peter Swire, The System of Foreign Intelligence Surveillance Law, 72 *George Washington Law Review* 1, 80–81 (2004). See also 18 U.S.C. § 2709(b) (wire or electronic service providers); 20 U.S.C. § 1232g(j)(A) (school records).

43. 50 U.S.C. § 1861(d)(1).

44. 50 U.S.C. § 1861(f)(2)(A)(i). Abiding by a gag order is no fun. See Luke O'Brien, Librarians Describe Life under an FBI Gag Order, *Wired*, June 25, 2007.

45. The amendments require the Department of Justice to provide Congress, on an annual basis, information about "the total number of applications made for [215] orders approving requests for the production of tangible things; and the total number of such orders that were granted, modified, or denied."

46. Paul Rosenzweig, Civil Liberty and the Response to Terrorism, 42 *Duquesne Law Review* 663, 694–95 (2004).

47. Philip B. Heymann, *Terrorism, Freedom, and Security: Winning without War* 154–56 (2003) (describing complaints from congressional intelligence committees about the difficulty of obtaining information from the FBI and the CIA).

48. 12 U.S.C. § 3414(a)(5)(A) ("financial records"); 18 U.S.C. § 2709(b) ("name, address, length of service and local and long distance toll billing records"). Again, the recordholder is prohibited from informing the target of the request. 12 U.S.C. § 3414(a)(5)(D).

49. 12 U.S.C. § 3414(a)(5)(D); 18 U.S.C. § 2709(c).

50. Kyle O'Dowd, Congress Hands FBI "Patriot II" Snooping Power, 28 *Champion* 18 (Feb. 2004).

51. 31 U.S.C. § 5312.

52. Doe v. Ashcroft, 334 F. Supp. 2d 471 (S.D.N.Y. 2004).

53. Doe v. Gonzales, 386 F. Supp. 2d 66, 67 (D. Conn. 2005). Both *Gonzales* and *Ashcroft* were vacated as a result of the new legislation, described below. See Doe v. Gonzales, 2006 WL 1409351 (2d Cir. May 23, 2006).

54. See, e.g., 18 U.S.C. § 2709(f).

55. See, e.g., 18 U.S.C. § 3511(a) & (b).

56. 334 F. Supp. 2d at 496.

57. Id. at 502.

58. See, e.g., 18 U.S.C. § 2709(c)(1).

59. Barton Gellman, The FBI's Secret Scrutiny, *Washington Post*, Nov. 6, 2005, at A1 (reporting that only one out of scores of thousands of NSLs had been chal-

lenged by a third party through 2005, although it must be noted that the availability of judicial review during this period was unclear). See also Lichtblau & Mazzetti, Military Expands Intelligence Role in U.S. (reporting that the CIA and Pentagon have been using "noncompulsory" versions of the NSL to obtain information from banks, credit card companies, and other financial institutions, virtually always without resistance).

60. Johnston & Lipton, U.S. Report to Fault FBI on Subpoenas.

61. Eric Lichtblau, Frustration over Limits on an Antiterror Law, *New York Times*, Dec. 11, 2005, at A1.

62. Gellman, The FBI's Secret Scrutiny, A1 (30,000 a year); Anne Broache, House Questions "Overreaching" FBI Spy Powers, *CNET News*, Mar. 20, 2007, available at http://news.com.com/House+questions+overreaching+FBI+spy+powers/2100-1028_3-6168922.html (143,074 requests between 2003 and 2005). The Department of Justice at one time disputed these figures, stating that in 2005, 9,254 NSLs were issued that "related to U.S. persons." See 79 *Criminal Law Reporter* (BNA) 161 (May 10, 2006). However, a recent report by the Justice Department's inspector general suggested that the earlier report vastly underestimated the prevalence of NSLs. Johnston & Lipton, U.S. Report to Fault FBI on Subpoenas.

63. People who have worked at the Department of Justice (Paul Ohm, Orin Kerr) state that in practice, a certification order may be harder to obtain than a subpoena. But I rank the certification order lower in the hierarchy of protection because the judge issuing the order plays such a minimal role; in contrast, when deciding whether to issue a subpoena, the judge is permitted to find a seizure invalid on relevance grounds, although he or she may rarely do so.

64. See Charles H. Whitebread & Christopher Slobogin, *Criminal Procedure: An Analysis of Cases and Concepts* 344–45 (4th ed. 2000) (no exclusionary remedy under ECPA); United States v. Kingston, 801 F.2d 733 (5th Cir. 1986) (no exclusionary remedy under the Right to Financial Privacy Act); Rob Stein, Medical Privacy Law Nets No Fines, *Washington Post*, June 5, 2006, at A01 (in the three years since passage of HIPAA, despite "thousands of complaints" alleging violation of disclosure rules, the government "has not imposed a single civil fine and has prosecuted just two criminal cases"); Doe v. Chao, 306 F.3d 170, 177 (4th Cir. 2002) (holding that, under ECPA, "a person must sustain actual damages to be entitled to the statutory minimum damages award" of $1,000).

65. Stephen E. Henderson, Beyond the (Current) Fourth Amendment: Protecting Third Party Information, Third Parties, and the Rest of Us Too, 34 *Pepperdine Law Review* 975, 985–1018 (2007).

66. People v. Abbott, 162 Cal. App. 3d 635, 640 (1984).

67. In re Maxfield, 945 P.2d 196, 207 (Wash. 1997).

68. People v. Jackson, 452 N.E.2d 85, 89 (Ill. App. 1983) (bank transactions); People v. Sporleder, 666 P.2d 135, 142 (Colo. 1983) (phone numbers).

69. Henderson, Beyond the (Current) Fourth Amendment, 989.

70. *Maxfield,* 945 P.2d at 200–201. See also Deirdre Mulligan & Jack Lerner, Taking the "Long View" on the Fourth Amendment: Stored Records and the Sanctity of the Home, *Stanford Technology Law Review* (forthcoming, 2007) ("Over time, power consumption can reveal personal sleep and work habits, the presence of certain medical equipment and other specialized devices, and of course signal the illegal behavior which today prompts law enforcement to seek [these types of data] in certain drug production cases.")

71. Lior Strahilevitz, A Social Networks Theory of Privacy, 72 *University of Chicago Law Review* 919, 932 (2005).

72. Id. at 967.

73. Id. at 974.

74. Compare Brown v. Texas, 443 U.S. 47, 50 (1979) ("When the officers detained appellant for the purpose of requiring him to identify himself, they performed a seizure subject to the requirements of the Fourth Amendment."), with INS v. Delgado, 466 U.S. 210, 216 (1984) ("[I]nterrogation relating to one's identity or a request for identification by the police does not, by itself, constitute a Fourth Amendment seizure.").

75. Terry v. Ohio, 394 U.S. 1, 27 (1967) (requiring reasonable suspicion for a frisk).

76. See Grosso v. United States, 390 U.S. 62, 67–68 (1968).

77. See also Daniel J. Solove, *The Digital Person: Technology and Privacy in the Information Age* 168–75 (2002) (describing current government efforts to obtain information about millions of citizens and concluding that "we are already closer to Total Information Awareness than we might think"); id. at 175–87 (describing possible abuses of information gathering, including "creeping totalitarianism," inhibition of freedom of association, and J. Edgar Hoover's misuse of surveillance against alleged Communist Party members, civil rights activists, and Vietnam War opponents).

78. See Christopher Slobogin, Transaction Surveillance by the Government, 75 *Mississippi Law Journal* 168–69 (2005) (suggesting that "catalogic information" should receive lesser protection).

79. Henderson, Beyond the (Current) Fourth Amendment, 1019–22.

80. See Solove, *The Digital Person*, 127 (describing "a system where the government extracts personal information from the populace and places it in the public domain").

81. Id. at 140.

82. 5 U.S.C. § 552(b)(4). Many circuits have held that voluntarily submitted information will be deemed "confidential" for the purpose of this exemption if it is of a kind that would customarily not be released to the public by the person from whom it has been obtained. See, e.g., Critical Mass Energy Project v. Nuclear Regulatory Comm'n, 975 F.2d 871, 872 (D.C. Cir.), cert denied, 507 U.S. 984 (1992). See generally What Constitutes "Trade Secrets and Commercial or Financial In-

formation Obtained from Person and Privileged or Confidential" Exempt from Disclosure under Freedom of Information Act (5 U.S.C.A. § 552(b)(4)) (FOIA), 139 A.L.R. Fed. 225 (2004).

83. 5 U.S.C. § 552(b)(6). The Supreme Court has defined "similar files" broadly to include "detailed Government records on an individual which can be identified as applying to that individual," U.S. Dep't of State v. Washington Post Co., 456 U.S. 595, 602 (1982), although it has also made clear that such files cannot be withheld simply because anonymity cannot be guaranteed, and that redaction of identifying names may be sufficient to safeguard privacy. Department of Air Force v. Rose, 425 U.S. 352, 381–82 (1976). See generally When Are Government Records "Similar Files" Exempt from Disclosure under Freedom of Information Act Provision (5 U.S.C. § 552(b)(6)) Exempting Certain Personnel, Medical, and "Similar" Files, 106 A.L.R. Fed. 94 (2004).

84. 5 U.S.C. 552(b)(7)(c). Thus, for instance, even a person's rap sheet may be exempt from disclosure if the result is exposure to the public. See U.S. Dep't of Justice v. Reporters Comm. for Freedom of the Press, 489 U.S. 749, 774 (1989). See generally What Constitutes "Unwarranted Invasion of Personal Privacy" for Purposes of Law Enforcement Investigatory Records Exemption of Freedom of Information Act (5 U.S.C.A. § 552(b)(7)(C)), 52 A.L.R. Fed. 181 (2004).

85. Fla. Stat. §§ 119.07(aa), (bb), (cc), (dd), (hh); 1002.22(d).

86. See, e.g., Mager v. Department of State Police, 595 N.W.2d 142, 143 (Mich. 1999) (holding that "gun ownership is information of a personal nature" requiring exemption from the state freedom of information act). See also Or. Rev. Stat. § 656.702(1) ("[t]he records of the State Accident Insurance Fund Corporation, *excepting employer account records and claimant files*, shall be open to public inspection") (emphasis added).

87. An alternative approach would be to permit any type of transaction surveillance that is rated as less intrusive than a pat down on a relevance showing. That approach would vastly simplify the analysis while still providing a modicum of protection for quasi-private records.

88. Blake Harrison, MATRIX Revolution, *State Legislatures* 13 (May 2004), cited in William J. Krouse, The Multi-state Anti-terrorism Information Exchange (MATRIX) Pilot Project, *Congressional Research Service Report RL32536* 9 (Aug. 18, 2004).

89. U.S. Gen. Accounting Office, *Data Mining: Federal Efforts Cover a Wide Range of Uses* 10 (May 2004). See also James Bamford, Private Lives: The Agency That Could Be Big Brother, *New York Times*, Dec. 25, 2005, sec. 4, at 1.

90. I have called this latter type of data mining "match driven" to distinguish it from data mining that starts with a target; with match-driven data mining, the goal is not to find out more about a suspect but rather to determine whether a particular person is a known suspect. See Christopher Slobogin, Government Data Mining and the Fourth Amendment, *University of Chicago Law Review* (forthcoming). For

other examples of match-driven data mining, see Eric Lichtblau & James Risen, Bank Data Sifted in Secret by U.S. to Block Terror, *New York Times*, June 23, 2006, at A1 (describing CIA's use of the Society for Worldwide Interbank Financial Telecommunications to comb tens of thousands and perhaps hundreds of thousands of bank records); Bart Elias, William Krouse & Ed Rappaport, Homeland Security: Air Passenger Prescreening and Counterterrorism, *Congressional Research Service Report RL32802* (Mar. 4, 2005) (describing federal data-matching programs aimed at discovering national security risks through air passenger lists).

91. See Slobogin, Government Data Mining and the Fourth Amendment.

92. Daniel J. Steinbock, Data Matching, Data Mining, and Due Process, 40 *Georgia Law Review* 1, 10–16 (2005).

93. U.S. Gen. Accounting Office, *Data Mining*, 30 (describing a program called Verity K2 Enterprise, which mines data from the intelligence community and Internet searches in an effort to identify foreign terrorists or U.S. citizens connected to foreign intelligence activities, and a program known as Pathfinder, which provides the ability to rapidly analyze and compare government and private sector databases).

94. See also Defense Advanced Research Projects Agency, U.S. Dep't of Defense, *Report to Congress Regarding the Terrorism Information Awareness Program* 3–9 (May 20, 2003).

95. 10 U.S.C. § 2241(d). Apparently most components of TIA are still alive, under the aegis of the National Security Agency rather than the Pentagon. See Shane Harris, TIA Lives On, *National Journal*, Feb. 23, 2006, available at http://nationaljournal.com/about/njweekly/stories/2006/0223nj1.htm.

96. Eric Lichtblau & Scott Shane, Bush Is Pressed over New Report on Surveillance, *New York Times*, May 12, 2006, at A1.

97. Karen Tumulty, Inside Bush's Secret Spy Net, *Time*, May 22, 2006, at 35.

98. How is the government to meet this burden? Sometimes the government's profile may satisfy the requisite certainty level on its face, as in a fraud investigation where the profile singles out individuals who have bought items they are clearly not authorized to buy. Other types of profiles might be tested through hypothetical computer runs, something the government is apparently doing now. See Defense Advanced Research Projects Agency, *Report to Congress Regarding the Terrorism Information Awareness Program* 17 (describing use of "synthetic data" to test the efficacy of data-mining processes). As a last resort, an actual data-mining program could be carried out on a small sample under secure conditions to determine its efficacy. But in some situations, none of these methods will be feasible. As indicated in chapter 2, if the government can provide a convincing explanation as to why relevant data cannot be obtained, while at the same time suggesting why the relevant hit rate can be met, it might be allowed to proceed.

99. It is worth noting in this regard that Germany, which has had considerable, and often negative, experience with dragnet information-gathering, permits event-

driven surveillance *only* in response to a specifically articulated danger. Francesca Bignami, European versus American Liberty: A Comparative Privacy Analysis of Anti-terrorism Data-Mining, 48 *Boston College Law Review* 609, 653–55 (2007) (describing a German court decision finding unconstitutional a post-9/11 data-mining program aimed at identifying people with certain characteristics—male, age 18–40, student or former student, Islamic faith, citizenship or birthplace in a country with a predominantly Islamic population—because there were no facts demonstrating "an imminent and specific endangerment"). This is the kind of analysis contemplated by the danger exception.

100. According to the *New York Times,* the NSA program generated thousands of tips in the months following 9/11 but not one lead panned out. Lowell Bergman et al., Domestic Surveillance: The Program; Spy Agency Data after Sept. 11 Led F.B.I. to Dead Ends, *New York Times*, Jan. 17, 2006, at A1. See generally Bruce Schneier, *Beyond Fear: Thinking Sensibly about Security in an Uncertain World* 253–54 (2003) (describing why it is very difficult to uncover terrorist plots through data mining); Jeffrey Rosen, *The Naked Crowd* 106 (2004) (a profile that is 99 percent accurate would still misidentify three million people if applied to the entire U.S. population). Others are more optimistic about the potential for law enforcement use of data mining, but only if several relatively onerous conditions are met. David Jensen, Mathew Rattigan & Hannah Blau, Information Awareness: A Prospective Technical Assessment (2003), available at http://kdl.cs.umass.edu/papers/jensen-et-al-kdd2003.pdf.

101. For a description of how selective revelation might work, see K. A. Taipale, Data Mining and Domestic Security: Connecting the Dots to Make Sense of Data, 5 *Columbia Journal of Law & Technology* 2, 79–80 (2003). But the technology has yet to reach the stage at which true anonymity can be preserved. See Palo Alto Research Company Web site, Privacy Appliance, http://www.parc.com/research/projects/privacyappliance/ (describing yet-to-be-developed protocols that ensure "inference control," that is, protection against the identification of an individual through combining different pieces of information).

102. Even if the government knows only a person's sex, zip code, and year of birth, it can identify up to 87 percent of the U.S. population. This "inference channel" must be disguised if true anonymity is to be preserved. See Palo Alto Research Center Web site, Privacy Appliance.

103. Whren v. United States, 517 U.S. 806, 811–12 (1996).

104. Technical and Privacy Advisory Comm., U.S. Dep't of Defense, *Safeguarding Privacy in the Fight against Terrorism* 48–60 (Mar. 2004).

105. Id. at 46–48.

106. Solove, Digital Dossiers, 1083.

107. Id. at 1152–59.

108. Id. at 1164–65.

109. Id. at 1152–54. Solove develops this point in much more detail in Daniel J. Solove, Conceptualizing Privacy, 90 *California Law Review* 1087, 1088–99 (2002).

110. Solove, Digital Dossiers, 1157 ("Focusing on 'systems of records' targets the type of information flow that raises concern. Because the problem of modern government information-gathering is caused by the increasing dossiers maintained in private sector record systems, the architecture targets those third parties that store data in record systems.").

111. Of course, the employees of the recordholder might want to reveal private information. See, e.g., Susan Freiwald, Uncertain Privacy: Communication Attributes after the Digital Telephony Act, 69 *Southern California Law Review* 949, 1013 (1996) ("As the president of the United States Telephone Association put it in explaining that telephone companies are interested in acceding to law enforcement requests for assistance, the companies want to be 'good local citizen[s].' "). But limiting that ability is not denying the employee's "personhood," because the information is maintained by the institution, not the person.

112. William J. Stuntz, *Local Policing after the Terror*, 111 *Yale Law Journal* 2137, 2181 (2002).

113. Id. at 2184–85.

114. Peter Swire observes that "the history of previous cycles shows the temptation of surveillance systems to justify an ever-increasing scope of activity, in the hopes that just a little bit more surveillance will catch the terrorists or prevent an attack" and points to "a long-run concern that secret . . . orders [allowing] access to entire databases of records . . . will be used expansively to intrude into a wide array of domestic matters." Swire, The System of Foreign Intelligence Surveillance Law, 1366, 1371.

115. See Matthew R. Hall, Constitutional Regulation of National Security Investigation: Minimizing the Use of Unrelated Evidence, 41 *Wake Forest Law Review* 61 (2006) (discussing the likelihood of mission creep in the national security context and judicial mechanisms for combating it).

116. Tumulty, Inside Bush's Secret Spy Net, 33.

117. Three comments about the NSA program from letters to the editor of the *Portland Oregonian*: "This is a violation of the Fourth Amendment, an assault on Americans' most fundamental privacy rights, and the latest outrage in the growing list compiled by president-turned-dictator George W. Bush." (Paul Chasman, Waldport); "Whether the next president is a Republican or Democrat, there is nothing to prevent him from using this Executive Branch database for his own political purposes. That is a real threat to America. This database needs to be immediately and completely destroyed." (Michael E. Stabeno, Beaverton) "This is an egregious overreach into the conduct of private citizens' lives." (Peter Baker, Boring). *Portland Oregonian*, May 16, 2006, at B09, available at 2006 WLNR 8457654. It is also worth noting that each of the phone companies that allegedly cooperated with the NSA has come under heavy fire. Peter Grier, For Telecoms, a Storm of Lawsuits Awaits, *Christian Science Monitor*, May 24, 2006, at A1.

118. An example of such a "digital dog sniff" is use of a hash value to determine whether two files (e.g., a known pornographic file and a file contained in

a person's computer) are identical. See Orin S. Kerr, Searches and Seizures in a Digital World, 119 *Harvard Law Review* 531, 546 (2005). Even here, however, the government should have to demonstrate to a judge that the model file (in this case the pornographic one) is contraband before it can be digitally compared to other files.

119. Orin S. Kerr, The Fourth Amendment and the New Technologies: Constitutional Myths and the Case for Caution, 102 *Michigan Law Review* 801 (2004). See also Orin S. Kerr, Congress, the Courts, and New Technologies: A Response to Professor Solove, 74 *Fordham Law Review* 779 (2005).

120. Kerr, The Fourth Amendment, 856–87.

121. Kerr himself has noted that much of the legislation governing transaction surveillance is complicated. See, e.g., Orin S. Kerr, A User's Guide to the Stored Communications Act, and a Legislator's Guide to Amending It, 72 *George Washington Law Review* 1208, 1208 (2004) ("courts, legislators, and even legal scholars have had a very hard time making sense of the [Stored Communications Act of ECPA]"; Orin S. Kerr, Lifting the "Fog" of Internet Surveillance: How a Suppression Remedy Would Change Computer Crime Law, 54 *Hastings Law Journal* 805, 820 (2003) (the "law of electronic surveillance is famously complex, if not entirely impenetrable").

122. Richard B. Schmitt, House OKs Expanded Wiretap Program, *Los Angeles Times*, Sept. 29, 2006, pt. A, at 18. Although the White House subsequently agreed to allow the Foreign Intelligence Surveillance court to oversee its national security eavesdropping program, it is still not clear "whether the administration will be required to seek a warrant for each person it wants to monitor or whether the FISA court has issued a broader set of orders covering a multitude of cases." Dan Eggen, Bush Team Reverses Course on Warrantless Taps, *Washington Post*, Jan. 18, 2007, at A1. Congress has also expressed concern about the abuse of NSLs but to date has not reined in the practice beyond its 2006 amendments to the Patriot Act. See Dan Eggen & John Solomon, Lawmakers Demand Limits on Anti-terrorism Laws, *Washington Post*, Mar. 10, 2007, at A1; Declan McCullagh, Senators Won't Take Away FBI Surveillance Power, *CNET News*, Mar. 21, 2007, available at http://news.com.com/2100-1028_3-6169459.html.

123. 532 U.S. 67, 94–95 (2001) (Scalia, J., dissenting) ("Until today, we have *never* held—or even suggested—that material which a person voluntarily entrusts to someone else cannot be given by that person to the police, and used for whatever evidence it may contain.") (emphasis in original).

124. Id. at 78 ("The use of an adverse test result to disqualify one from eligibility for a particular benefit, such as a promotion or an opportunity to participate in an extracurricular activity, involves a less serious intrusion on privacy than the unauthorized dissemination of such results to third parties. The reasonable expectation of privacy enjoyed by the typical patient undergoing diagnostic tests in a hospital is that the results of those tests will not be shared with nonmedical personnel without her consent.").

125. Id. at 79; *Edmond*, 531 U.S. at 47.

126. 547 U.S. 103 (2006).

127. Id. at 111, 114.

128. Id. at 114.

129. Id. at 128 (Roberts, C.J., dissenting) (emphasis omitted).

130. Id. at 115 n.4.

131. Id. at 141.

132. I am more sympathetic to *Randolph*'s rejection of the assumption-of-risk rationale than its actual holding, however. I would have decided *Randolph* differently because, for reasons recounted earlier, I think the consenting co-occupant's autonomy is denigrated by automatically honoring the refusal. In cases of competing desires expressed by autonomous actors, the government ought to be able to choose which decision to honor (which will normally be that of the consentor). In the transaction surveillance context, however, there is no countervailing autonomy interest on the part of the consenting recordholder.

133. Introductory Remarks of Senator Sam J. Ervin on S. 3418, H.R. Rep. No. 93-1416 (1974), reprinted in U.S. Congress, *Legislative History of the Privacy Act of 1974*, 3–8 (1975).

Chapter Eight

1. Benjamin Franklin, Pennsylvania Assembly: Reply to the Governor (Nov. 11, 1755), reprinted in 6 *The Papers of Benjamin Franklin* 238, 242 (Leonard W. Labaree ed., 1963).

2. One of the more conspicuous examples is Bruce Fein, deputy attorney general to Ronald Reagan and well-known conservative commentator, who testified in support of Senate Resolution 398 censuring President Bush for, as Fein put it, "seeking to cripple the Constitution's checks and balances and political accountability by secretly authorizing the National Security Agency to spy on American citizens in the United States in contravention of the Foreign Intelligence Surveillance Act and misleading the public about the secret surveillance program." Testimony, Senate Judiciary Committee, March 31, 2006.

3. Terry v. Ohio, 392 U.S. 1, 26 (1968).

4. See, e.g., United States v. Martinez-Fuerte, 428 U.S. 543 (1976) (checkpoints); Pennsylvania v. Mimms, 434 U.S. 106 (1977) (seizure of car occupants); Ohio v. Robinette, 519 U.S. 33 (1996) (detention after issuance of citation); Michigan v. Summers, 452 U.S. 692 (1981) (detention of occupant during search of house).

5. 389 U.S. 347, 357 (1967).

6. 469 U.S. 325, 340 (1985).

7. See Charles H. Whitebread & Christopher Slobogin, *Criminal Procedure: An Analysis of Cases and Concepts*, ch. 13 (4th ed. 2000).

8. *T.L.O.*, 469 U.S. at 351 (Blackmun, J., concurring).

9. Id. ("exceptional"); Ferguson v. City of Charleston, 532 U.S. 67, 74–75 (2001) (same); Skinner v. Railway Labor Executives' Ass'n, 489 U.S. 602, 624 (1989) ("limited").

10. Lewis v. United States, 385 U.S. 206, 210 (1966).

11. Brennan and Marshall clearly called for a probable cause requirement in *Smith.* 442 U.S. 735, 751 (1979). However, Stewart's opinion in that case merely stated that phone numbers fall "within the constitutional protection recognized in *Katz*," without indicating whether a warrant was required to obtain them. Id. at 747. In *Miller*, Brennan simply spoke of requiring "appropriate legal process," without specifying what that might mean. 425 U.S. 435, 450 (1976). Only Marshall explicitly stated he would require a warrant based on probable cause on *Miller*'s facts. 425 U.S. at 456.

12. Morgan Cloud, A Liberal House Divided: How the Warren Court Dismantled the Fourth Amendment, 3 *Ohio State Journal of Criminal Law* 33, 72 (2005) (emphasis added).

13. Id. Cloud also argues that this approach, taking its cue from *Boyd*, would provide almost absolute protection for particularly private papers, communications and the like, but of course a privacy-based Fourth Amendment can accomplish the same goal.

14. Hester v. United States, 265 U.S. 57 (1924).

15. See Warden v. Hayden, 387 U.S. 294, 302 (1967) ("[D]epending on the circumstances, the same 'papers and effects' may be 'mere evidence' in one case and 'instrumentality' in another.").

16. See Eric Blumenson & Eva Nilsen, Policing for Profit: The Drug War's Hidden Economic Agenda, 65 *University of Chicago Law Review* 35, 42–56 (1998) (detailing the breadth of today's forfeiture statutes).

17. This was the gist of Justice Black's dissent in *Katz*, where he argued the words "search" and "seizure" "connote the ideal of tangible things with size, form and weight, things capable of being searched, seized, or both." 389 U.S. at 365 (Black, J., dissenting).

18. 483 U.S. 868, 877 (1987).

19. Id. at 877–78.

20. Id. at 877.

21. For further discussion of this approach, see Christopher Slobogin, Deceit, Pretext and Trickery: Investigative Lies by the Police, 76 *Oregon Law Review* 775, 805–8 (1997).

22. *Miller*, 425 U.S. at 437 (before seeking records, agents discovered distillery equipment in truck driven by Miller's colleagues and found a distillery in Miller's warehouse after a fire broke out there); *Smith*, 442 U.S. at 737 (agents who installed pen register on Smith's phone knew the victim of robbery had received threatening and obscene calls from person claiming to be the robber and had discovered that Smith owned a car that was seen at scene of robbery and was also seen by the victim

after receiving a phone call asking her to step outside her house); *Knotts*, 460 U.S. at 278 (agents who installed beeper in can of chemicals purchased by Armstrong and later traced to Knotts knew that chemicals used to make illegal drugs had previously been stolen and purchased by Armstrong).

23. City of Indianapolis v. Edmond, 531 U.S. 32, 37 (2000).

24. Id. at 44 (language regarding roadblock to thwart terrorist attack joined by Ginsburg, Breyer, and Stevens, as well as the rest of the Court).

25. Id.

26. See chapter 2, section 2.

27. Christopher Slobogin & Joseph Schumacher, Reasonable Expectations of Privacy and Autonomy in Fourth Amendment Cases: An Empirical Look at "Understandings Recognized and Permitted by Society," 42 *Duke Law Journal* 727, 768–69 (1993) (discussing implied consent theory).

28. One formulation of this idea was developed (but ultimately discarded) by the ABA Task Force on Law Enforcement and Technology:

> An action by a law enforcement officer is "reasonably likely to achieve a legitimate law enforcement objective" if there are articulable reasons for concluding that the action will:
> (i) discover the commission of a particular offense or type of offense;
> (ii) further an ongoing investigation of a particular offense or type of offense;
> (iii) deter or prevent a particular offense;
> (iv) deter a significant number of offenses in a given area; or
> (v) prevent one or more persons from suffering serious physical harm.

Christopher Slobogin, Technologically-Assisted Physical Surveillance: The American Bar Association's Tentative Draft Standards, 10 *Harvard Journal of Law & Technology* 383, 429 n.239 (1997).

29. Johnson v. United States, 333 U.S. 10, 14 (1948).

30. 367 U.S. 643 (1961).

31. Id. at 652, 648–49.

32. See Andresen v. Maryland, 427 U.S. 463 (1976) (holding that the Fifth Amendment is never violated when police seize voluntarily created papers).

33. United States v. Calandra, 414 U.S. 338, 348 (1973) ("In sum, the rule is a judicially created remedy designed to safeguard Fourth Amendment rights generally through its deterrent effect, rather than a personal constitutional right of the party aggrieved.").

34. See generally Whitebread & Slobogin, *Criminal Procedure*, 48–59 (discussing the good faith, policy and custom, and concrete damages limitations on damages actions under 42 U.S.C. § 1983).

35. Christopher Slobogin, Why Liberals Should Chuck the Exclusionary Rule, 1999 *Illinois Law Review* 363.

36. Id. at 374–79.

37. Id. at 393–94 (describing nonchalance toward constitutional issues in both academy and field training and several studies showing that police perform barely better than chance on questions concerning Fourth Amendment law).

38. Id. at 384–86.

39. Id. at 442.

40. Bivens v. Six Named Unknown Agents of the Federal Bureau of Narcotics, 403 U.S. 388, 422–23 (1971) (Burger, C.J., dissenting).

41. See Whitebread & Slobogin, *Criminal Procedure*, 139, 141 (summarizing exceptions to warrant requirement).

42. 442 U.S. at 737 ("The register revealed that on March 17 a call was placed from petitioner's home to McDonough's phone.").

Index